CANADIAN DEMOCRACY

CANADIAN DEMOCRACY

AN INTRODUCTION

SECOND EDITION

STEPHEN BROOKS

OXFORD UNIVERSITY PRESS
TORONTO   NEW YORK   OXFORD
1996

Oxford University Press
70 Wynford Drive, Don Mills, Ontario M3C 1J9

Oxford New York
Athens   Auckland   Bangkok   Bombay
Calcutta   Cape Town   Dar es Salaam   Delhi
Florence   Hong Kong   Istanbul   Karachi
Kuala Lumpur   Madras   Madrid   Melbourne
Mexico City   Nairobi   Paris   Singapore
Taipei   Tokyo   Toronto

and associated companies in
Berlin Ibadan

Oxford is a trade mark of Oxford University Press

Canadian Cataloguing in Publication Data

Brooks, Stephen, 1956–
   Canadian democracy: an introduction

2nd ed.
Includes bibliographical references and index.
ISBN 0-19-541205-2

1. Canada—Politics and government.   I. Title.

JL65 1993.B76 1996   320.971   C96-931189-3

Cover design: Max Izod
Text design: Brett Miller
Formatting: Linda Mackey

1 2 3 4 — 99 98 97 96

This book is printed on permanent (acid-free) paper ∞.

Printed in Canada

Contents

List of Figures

List of Tables

■ Preface

hirty years ago, one's choice of a textbook for introductory Canadian politics and government was quite simple: Dawson's *The Government of Canada* or nothing! This is no longer the case. As one of the reviewers for this book reminded me, the shelves today are groaning under the weight of Canadian politics texts, so any addition to their number needs some justification.

Canadian Democracy has two goals. Like any textbook, it attempts to cover all the basic elements of Canadian politics and government, providing the reader with the information and concepts needed for more specialized study of the subject. With this goal in mind, I have included chapters on the nuts-and-bolts structures of Canadian government (the constitution, federalism, the machinery of government) and others on key features of the political process (interest groups, the media, political parties). As well, the first two chapters are devoted to fundamental concepts in the study of politics and to the role of ideas in Canada's political system.

The second goal of this book is to convey to the reader the complexities and controversies associated with democracy. Chapter 1 examines the contested meaning of the term 'democracy', focusing on its two key themes, equality and freedom. These themes resurface in subsequent chapters, particularly in the chapters on rights and freedoms, language, and gender. Other chapters examine controversies about access, influence, and, most fundamentally, who wins and who loses from the institutions and processes of Canadian politics.

This text does not attempt to be all things to all readers. It rejects the encyclopedic approach in favour of a leaner treatment of some standard textbook topics—e.g., the constitution, the machinery of government—and a more elaborate treatment of other subjects that are especially useful for understanding the nature and shortcomings of Canadian democracy. I assume, however, that this book will not be the only reading used in the introductory courses for which it is written. Canadian Democracy is intended to be the core text for such courses, but it does not attempt to replicate the A-to-Z format favoured by some authors.

This book is divided into five parts. The introduction (Part I) examines some basic concepts in the study of politics and government, including the key concept of democracy. Part

II, chapters 2 and 3, focuses on the broad societal context of Canadian politics. Chapter 2 looks at the ideological roots of contemporary politics and governing institutions, while Chapter 3 surveys some of the chief social and economic characteristics of Canadian society. Part III, chapters 4, 5, and 6, turns to the structures of governance. Here we examine the constitution (Chapter 4), federalism (Chapter 5), and the machinery of government (Chapter 6). Part IV considers the main vehicles for individual and group participation in politics: Chapter 7 discusses the origins and contemporary character of Canada's political parties, their role in politics, and the nature and consequences of our electoral system; Chapter 8 looks at the characteristics and influence of interest groups; Chapter 9 examines the crucial place occupied by the mass media in modern democracies and the particular features of the media's role in Canadian politics. Part V, chapters 10, 11, and 12, focuses on three important issues in modern Canadian politics—rights and freedoms, language, and gender inequality—that illustrate well the complex interplay of values in democratic politics. Other issues are equally deserving of attention, and instructors may wish to supplement this material with an issue-oriented reader such as Christopher Dunn's *Canadian Political Debates*.

Writing a book may sometimes be a solo flight. It has never been so for me. I am indebted to a number of people who have contributed to whatever merit this book may have. My first debt is to Michael Harrison, formerly of McClelland & Stewart, who originally set me thinking about this book and provided valuable encouragement and advice over the life of the first edition. McClelland & Stewart's college division, and Penelope Grows, director of the college division, helped pilot the second edition to what I hope will be judged a successful landing.

The two anonymous reviewers provided some of the most thoughtful and helpful comments that it has ever been my pleasure to receive. Their efforts saved me from several errors of omission and commission. Richard Tallman's meticulous editing and suggestions on numerous points of style and substance worked much of the flabbiness out of the original manuscript. These people are, of course, blameless for my stubborn failure to follow all of their advice.

The entire manuscript was typed, entered onto computer, and revised on too many occasions to count by Barbara Faria of Windsor's Political Science Department and by Lucie Brown, Patricia Jolie, and Dianne Dupuis, who make the Word Processing Centre a model of efficiency and good nature, *sans pareil*. Photographs for several of the chapters were kindly provided by Greg Vickers. The diligence and resourcefulness of my research assistant, Paul Mageau, made it possible for me to finish the first edition of this book while abroad. Jacqueline Wilson helped update material and track down information for this second edition.

Finally, I would like to thank my family, without whose support this book would not have been written.

Stephen Brooks
Rotselaar, Belgium, and
Windsor, Canada

PART ONE

Introduction

Competitive elections are one of the cornerstones of democracy. (Greg Vickers)

To understand politics and government, one requires a toolkit consisting of the fundamental concepts and terms that are useful in analysing political life. This chapter aims to equip the reader with these tools by examining the following topics:

❖ What is politics?
❖ Power.
❖ State and government.
❖ Democracy.
❖ Political identities.
❖ Continuity and change in politics.

CHAPTER ONE

An Introduction to Political Life

olitics, we all agree, is a fact of life. Some people rejoice in this, seeing in political participation and government the possibility of building a better society, or at least of fulfilling some of their personal goals. Others lament the fact, viewing politics as a corrupt and debasing activity that is largely devoid of principle and more likely to be harmful and meddlesome than socially beneficial. Then there are those who neither rejoice in nor lament the pervasiveness and character of politics, but who simply do not care one way or another. If they think about politics at all it is probably to reflect on how little difference they could make to what gets done, or how incomprehensible the whole affair seems. Retreat into indifference or ignorance, or both, is their way of 'dealing' with political life.

These three stances—the enthusiast, the cynic, and the apathetic—are obviously caricatures. Most people combine elements of each in their own political attitudes and behaviour: following politics much as they would sports (though probably less avidly); occasionally talking about the parties, their leaders, or some 'hot' issue with friends or family; voting in most elections; but maintaining a measure of cynicism about politicians and their craft. Relatively few people are passionately involved in politics, to the point where it serves as the focus of their lives. The vast majority observe the political spectacle at some distance. But even the least 'politicized' among us must concede the modern fact of government whose tendrils wrap themselves around every important aspect of our existence. The old adage about the state being present from cradle to grave does not go far enough when technology compels governments to legislate on when life begins and on when and how it may end.

Platitudes about 'big government' do not, however, take us very far toward an understanding of politics and government. In fact, they may obscure matters by giving the impression that politics suffuses and encompasses everything. The boundaries of the political disappear, leaving the would-be student of politics with little to grasp hold of except the idea that government is somehow at the centre of it all. But politics does have boundaries, and an identification of these is an important first step toward understanding the political process.

What Is Politics?

Politics arises from the fact of scarcity. In the real world it is not possible for all people to satisfy all of their desires to the fullest extent. Limits on the stock of those things that people desire—such things as wealth, privacy, clean air and water, and social recognition—ensure that conflicts will take place between rival claimants. These conflicts explain why politics comes about. But politics is about more than the fact of conflict. It is also about how rival claims are settled. What distinguishes politics from the conflicts, struggles, and rivalries that take place in such settings as the family, the workplace, and the economic marketplace and in social organizations like churches and labour unions is the *public nature* of political disputes and the use of public authority—embodied in the state—to deal with them. *Politics, then, is the activity by which rival claims are settled by public authorities.* The boundaries of the political are defined by the scope of the state's authority to intervene in society.

As Box 1.1 shows, this definition does not have the field all to itself. All of these contending definitions agree that politics is about the exercise of power. They disagree, however, about what power relations count as political ones. Dahl, Lasswell, Marx, and Millet define politics in ways that would include the relations between bosses and workers in a cor-

---

Box 1.1 Some Well-known Definitions of Politics

'[A] political system can be designated as those interactions through which values are authoritatively allocated for a society.' David Easton, *A Systems Analysis of Political Life.*

Politics: Who Gets What, When and How, Harold Lasswell.

'Politics, then, can be simply defined as the activity by which differing interests within a given unit of rule are conciliated by giving them a share in power in proportion to their importance to the welfare and the survival of the whole community.' Bernard Crick, *In Defence of Politics.*

'A political system is any persistent pattern of human relationships that involves, to a significant extent, power, rule, or authority.' Robert Dahl, *Modern Political Analysis.*

'Political power, properly so called, is merely the organized power of one class for oppressing another.' Karl Marx and Frederick Engels, *The Communist Manifesto.*

'The term "politics" shall refer to power-structured relationships, arrangements whereby one group of persons is controlled by another.... [E]very avenue of power within [our] society ... is entirely in male hands.' Kate Millet, *Sexual Politics.*

poration, between parents and children in a family, between teacher and students in schools, and between spiritual shepherd and flock in a church. And in a sense they are right. In the words of American political scientist Charles Merriam, 'obviously there is governance everywhere—government in heaven; government in hell; government and law among outlaws; government in prison.'[1] Crick and Easton both offer a more limited definition of politics, one that goes back to Aristotle's conception of the Greek *polis*. They argue that what is distinctive about politics is the association of this activity with a system of settling disputes that is both public and binding on the whole community. At the centre of this system is the state, or government, as those raised in the Anglo-American tradition are more likely to call it.

These definitions disagree in another important way. Both the Marxist and feminist (Millet) definitions associate politics with a pervasive pattern of oppression—between social classes according to Marxists, and between males and females according to feminist theorists. Politics is, for them, fundamentally about how inequalities are generated and reinforced through the power relations that exist between classes/gender groups at all levels of society.

Does it matter, in the end, how we define politics? Or is this mainly a harmless diversion for academic hairsplitters? We would argue that there is a very practical reason for rejecting those definitions of politics that confer on all power relations, wherever they may be located and however limited they may be, the title 'political'. If politics is viewed as being everywhere and in all social interactions we lose the ability to see the boundary that separates the public and private realms. This boundary may not be very distinct, but it is crucial for understanding the politics of any society. Moreover, the existence of such a boundary is necessary in order to protect the freedoms that most of us believe to be important features of a democratic society. Political conflict is largely about where exactly this boundary between public and private should be drawn about what should be considered a proper matter for public life and decisions by the state and what should remain private matters. We can agree that power relations are ubiquitous without going the next step to claim that politics, therefore, has no bounds.

But there is another reason for adopting the more limited definition of politics put forward here. Only those power relations that take place in the public realm can legitimately be associated with the use of force in its most naked, punitive forms. Compulsion, punishment, and violence do of course take place in all sorts of social settings. It is clear, however, that only the public authorities—the state—have the legitimate right to back up their decisions with the full power of society. All other power relations are more limited than this. The reason for this difference is that the state is the only institution that can reasonably claim to speak and act on behalf of the entire community, and its unique function is to ensure the conditions for some degree of social order. This social order is a necessary condition for all other social activities, for without it there is no peaceful basis for reconciling conflicts in society.

Power

Power is the ability to influence what happens. It is found in all sorts of settings, not simply political ones. When IBM introduces a new line of personal computers, other companies that produce PCs react. IBM has power in that product market. When the Vatican issues an official proclamation on birth control or the ordination of women, elements within the Roman Catholic Church respond. The Vatican has power within the community of Roman Catholics. When a person is persuaded to give up his wallet at gunpoint, his attacker has power. Parents who are able to compel their children's obedience through the threat or fact of punishment, or through persuasive arguments, have power. A television network whose programs shape the issues that viewers are thinking about has power. And when a peaceful demonstration of citizens outside the headquarters of a corporation, or in front of the legislature, changes the behaviour of the targeted institution, that, too, is power. In each of these cases one party affects the behaviour of another, although the reasons for compliance differ.

Social scientists like to unpack the concept of power, breaking it down into species that are distinguished from one another according to the reason why the compliant party obeys. Compliance may result from the threat or use of force (*coercion*); from the ability of A to convince B that a particular action is reasonable or otherwise in B's best interests (*influence*); or from the recognition on the part of the compliant party that the person or organization issuing a command has the right to do so and should be obeyed (*authority*). Politics involves all of these faces of power—coercion, influence, and authority—at various times and in different circumstances. Democratic politics relies primarily on the two non-coercive species of power. But coercion is used, and no democracy is without its system of courts, the police, and prisons.

How far coercion and democracy are compatible is, however, an open question. This is illustrated by a famous exchange between former Prime Minister Pierre Trudeau and CBC journalist Tim Ralfe in October, 1970, a few days after the Liberal government had suspended civil liberties by invoking the War Measures Act at the time of the FLQ crisis in Quebec.

RALFE: Sir, what is it with all these men with guns around here?

TRUDEAU: Haven't you noticed?

RALFE: Yes, I've noticed them. I wondered why you people decided to have them.

TRUDEAU: What's your worry?

RALFE: I'm not worried, but you seem to be.

TRUDEAU: If you're not worried, I'm not worried.

RALFE: I'm worried about living in a town that's full of people with guns running around.

TRUDEAU: Why? Have they done anything to you? Have they pushed you around or anything?... [T]here are a lot of bleeding hearts around who just don't like to see people with helmets and guns. All I can say is, go on and bleed, but it is more important to keep law and order in the society than to be worried about weak-kneed people.... I think the society must take every means at its disposal to defend itself against the emergence of a parallel power which defies the elected power in this country, and I think that goes to any distance.

Is Trudeau right? One of the great ironies of democracy is that, unlike other political systems, it requires that dissenting points of view and opposition to those in power be respected. Arresting people suspected of terrorist acts is, most would agree, necessary to protect democratic government. At some point, however, the protection of law and order may exact a high cost in terms of personal freedoms. In a democracy, those in power must justify their use of coercion as being necessary to maintain such values as freedom, equality, justice, and the rule of law. Inevitably, however, people will disagree over the meaning and relative importance of these values, and over how much coercion, in what circumstances, is acceptable.

State and Government

The existence of the state is, we argued earlier, a necessary condition for the existence of politics. But what is the 'state'? To this point we have used the terms 'state' and 'government' as though they meant the same thing. This failure to make a distinction between them is often harmless, but it can lead to serious confusion. For example, to argue that the government is corrupt or wasteful, or that its policies are undesirable, does not necessarily call into question the state. It does, however, challenge the authority of the particular people who control the levers of the governmental system. In an established democracy, political activity is far more likely to be directed at influencing and changing the government than at reforming the state.

Canadian political scientist Leo Panitch provides this definition of the *state*:

> [The state is] a broad concept that includes government as the seat of legitimate authority in a territory but also includes bureaucracy, judiciary, the Armed Forces and internal Police, structures of legislative assemblies and administration, public corporations, regulatory boards, and ideological apparatuses such as the education establishment and publicly owned media. The distinguishing characteristic of the state is its monopoly over the use of force in a given territory.[2]

Defined this way, the state has three main characteristics. First, it involves territorial boundaries. States have borders, beyond which their legal authority is either nil or strictly limited. Second, the state consists of a complex set of institutions that wield public authority. The courts, the police, and the educational system are outposts of the state's authority no less than are the elected legislature and the bureaucracy. Third, the state is defined in terms of power, what Weber (see Box 1.2) called its 'monopoly of the legitimate use of physical force in the enforcement of its order'. For what purposes and in whose interests this power is exercised are questions left unanswered, but they, too, view the state in terms of class conflict.

Some definitions of the state do, however, offer answers to these questions. The Marxist and Leninist definitions in Box 1.2 characterize the state as an instrument of class oppression. Marx argued that the end of class conflict would sound the deathknell for the state. It would 'wither away', no longer having any function to perform. Contemporary Marxists, except for a few diehards, no longer predict the state's demise. Feminists view the state as a patriarchal institution, reinforcing and perpetuating the social superiority of men over

---

Box 1.2 Alternative Definitions of the State

'The state is the product of the *irreconcilability* of class antagonisms. The state arises when, where and to the extent that class antagonism *cannot* be reconciled.' Vladimir Lenin, *State and Revolution.*

'The executive of the modern State is but a committee for managing the common affairs of the whole bourgeoisie.' Marx and Engels, *The Communist Manifesto.'*

'The state is that fiction by which everyone seeks to live at the expense of everyone else.' French economist Frédéric Bastiat, *circa* 1840.

'L'Etat, c'est moi.' [I am the state.] Louis XIV of France.

'[The state is that institution which] successfully upholds a claim to the monopoly of the legitimate use of physical force in the enforcement of its order ... within a given territorial area.' Max Weber, *The Theory of Social and Economic Organization.*

---

women. Many political scientists, and probably most economists, would argue that the state is responsive to any group with enough political clout to persuade policy-makers that it is in their interest to meet the group's demands for public actions on private wants.

An adequate explanation of the state must ask on whose behalf and in whose interests the state's authority is exercised. This is an issue that will be addressed at various points throughout this book. Our immediate concern is to establish the difference between the state and government. *Government* is a term more usefully reserved for those who have been elected to power. It is more personal than the state, being associated with a particular group of people and, usually, with political parties. In democratic political systems governments are chosen and removed through elections. These elections—the rules and procedures by which governments are formed—are part of the state system. And like the rest of the state, they are much less likely to generate political division and to undergo change than is the government and its policies.

Underlying this distinction between state and government is an important practical difference in the basis on which each compels the obedience of citizens, corporations, and associations that fall within their jurisdiction. The willingness of individuals and groups to obey the decisions of government—decisions that they may vigorously disagree with, and a government that they may not have voted for—is based on their view that the state's authority is *legitimate*. By legitimate we mean that the rules and institutions that comprise the state, and which determine how governments are chosen, are accepted by most people as being reasonable. The legitimacy of the state is, therefore, based on the *consent* of those who are governed. It does not depend on an ever-present fear of the penalties that follow from disobeying the law. It rests instead on what is usually an unquestioning acceptance of the rules of the political game. If the state's authority, and ultimately the ability of governments to govern, depended on a sort of constant referendum of the popular will, politics would be a brittle enterprise. In reality, this popular consent is not something that people regularly (if ever!) reflect on or consciously avow (the 'Pledge of Allegiance' recited by American schoolchildren has no Canadian counterpart).

Government may be upheld by consent or by force. In fact it is usually upheld by both. When anti-abortion protesters defy court injunctions against demonstrating near an abortion clinic and are arrested and charged for this act of civil disobedience, they are challenging the authority of the state. When Quebec nationalists demand political independence for their province they are registering their belief that the existing boundaries of the Canadian state, and its authority in Quebec society, are not legitimate. And when striking unions ignore back-to-work legislation, and in doing so run the risk of being fined or of having their leaders imprisoned, this also goes beyond disagreement with government policy to challenge the legitimacy of the state. The state's authority is sometimes questioned by individuals or by organized interests. When this happens the public authorities may resort to force to crush civil disobedience and maintain their ability to govern.

Government that relies primarily on threats and violence to maintain its rule is generally unstable. Even the most repressive political authorities generally come to realize that popular consent is a firmer basis on which to govern. In some societies the popular consent that legitimizes political rule may appear to emerge more or less spontaneously from the unco-ordinated activities of the media, the schools, the family, governments: from the various social institutions that influence the ideological outlook of citizens. In other societies, the state's legitimacy is deliberately and assiduously cultivated through the organs of official propaganda. The calculated fostering of consent is a characteristic feature of totalitarian rule. Totalitarianism is a system of government that suppresses all dissent in the name of some supreme goal. This goal may be tied to the destiny of the 'race', as it was in Nazi Germany, or to class struggle, as it was in the Soviet Union under Stalin. Distinctions between the state, government, and society lose all meaning—indeed, they are considered to be subversive—under totalitarianism.

The active mobilization of society by the state, the deliberate manipulation of public attitudes, and the ruthless suppression of dissent by the public authorities are not features that most of us associate with democracy. The way in which legitimacy is generated in political democracies is more subtle than under totalitarian rule, depending primarily on social institutions that are not part of the state system. This gives legitimacy the appearance of being based on the free choice of individuals, an appearance that some argue is an illusion. Marxist critics use the term *cultural hegemony* to signify the ability of society's dominant class to get its values and beliefs accepted as the conventional wisdom in society at large. American social critic Noam Chomsky takes this position in arguing that the privately owned mass media reinforce and perpetuate inequalities in wealth and power by presenting 'facts', images, and interpretations that either justify or gloss over these inequalities.[3] Feminists take a similar line, arguing that sexist attitudes of male superiority are pervasive in social institutions—from the bedroom to the boardroom—so that the legitimacy of patriarchal power relations is reinforced on a daily basis. For both Marxists and feminists, government by 'popular consent' is a sham that conceals the fundamentally undemocratic character of society and politics.

Democracy

When political systems as different as those of Canada, the People's Republic of China, and Iran all claim to be democracies, we may be excused for asking just what 'democracy' means.

Canadian political philosopher C.B. Macpherson argued that there are in fact *three* different types of democracy in the modern world.[4] Only one of these, *liberal* democracy, is characterized by competition between political parties. What Macpherson calls the *developmental* and *communist* versions of democracy do not have competitive elections, and probably would not be considered democratic by most Canadians. But they both claim to attach greater importance to the social and economic equality of individuals than does liberal democracy, in addition to recognizing the formal political equality of citizens. If democracy is about equality, Macpherson argues, the developmental and communist versions are at least as democratic as the liberal version that we in the capitalist world automatically assume to be the genuine article.

If we accept Macpherson's argument that there are three types of democracy, each with a legitimate claim to the title, the world looks like a very democratic place. Leaving aside personal and military dictatorships, and the odd monarchy like Saudi Arabia and the Kingdom of Swaziland, most of what is left would seem to qualify. While common sense suggests that democracy is not as widespread as this, Macpherson is challenging us to reflect on what makes politics and society democratic or not. Is democracy a system of government? Or does democracy connote a type of society? Was Canada 'democratic' before the female half of the population received the vote? Do the persistence of poverty and the clear evidence of large inequalities in the economic condition and social status of different groups in Canada oblige us to qualify our description of Canadian society as 'democratic'?

About the only thing that everyone can agree on is that democracy is based on equality. Agreement breaks down over how much equality, in what spheres of life, is necessary for a society to qualify as democratic. Majority rule, government by popular consent, one person–one vote, and competitive elections are the political institutions usually associated with democratic government. But it has long been recognized that the operation of democratic political institutions can result in oppressive government. If, for example, a majority of Quebecers agree that legislative restrictions on the language rights of non-Francophones are needed to preserve the French character of Quebec, is this democratic? In order to safeguard the rights and freedoms of individuals and minorities against what Alexis de Tocqueville called 'democratic despotism', constitutional limits on the power of the state over its citizens may be set, or the political status of particular social groups may be entrenched in the formal rules and informal procedures of politics. For example, the Canadian constitution entrenches the co-equal official status of the French and English languages at the national level, and the operation of federalism and the Canadian electoral system reinforce the political power of this country's French-speaking minority, 90 per cent of whom live in Quebec.

Perhaps even more important than constitutional guarantees and political practices are the social and cultural values of a society. Tocqueville argued that the best protection against the tyranny of the majority is the existence of group identities in society. When individuals perceive themselves as being members of particular social groups—whether a religious denomination, an ethnic or language group, a regional community, or whatever the group identity happens to be—in addition to sharing with everyone else a common citizenship, the likelihood of the democratic state being turned to oppressive ends is reduced. After all, everyone has a personal interest in the tolerance of social diversity because the rights and status of one's own group depend on this.

Some twentieth-century writers have argued that cultural values represent the main bulwark against the tyranny of the majority. Democratic government, they argue, depends on popular tolerance of diversity. In *The Civic Culture*, American political scientists Gabriel Almond and Sidney Verba make the argument that democratic government is sustained by cultural attitudes.[5] The determination of how democratic a society is, according to this political culture approach, must be based on an examination of the politically relevant attitudes and beliefs of the population. This, and not the mere fact of apparently democratic political institutions, is argued to be the true test of democracy.

Not everyone would agree. Socialists argue that a society in which a large number of people are preoccupied with the problem of feeding and housing themselves decently cannot be described as democratic. This preoccupation effectively excludes the poor from full participation in political life, and in this way socio-economic inequality is translated into political inequality. The formal equality of citizens that democratic government confers, and even the fact that most people—including society's disadvantaged—may subscribe to democratic values, does not alter the fundamental fact that social inequalities produce inequalities in political power. Marxists would go even further in dismissing the democratic claims of capitalist societies. They argue that inequality results from the simple fact that a very small proportion of the population—the capitalist class—controls the vast majority of the means of economic production and distribution. This inequality in property ownership, Marxists argue, far outweighs the importance of one person–one vote and competitive elections in determining the real political influence of different classes in society.

Inequalities between bosses and workers, between parents and children, between men and women, between ethnic or language communities—the list could go on—are often claimed to undermine the democratic character of societies whose formal political institutions are based on the equality of citizens. Indeed, if we use any of the all-inclusive definitions of politics examined earlier in this chapter it is impossible to resist the logic of this argument. Inequalities confront us wherever we turn, and true democracy seems to be terribly elusive. Even if we define politics more narrowly to include only those activities that focus on the state, it is obvious that a small portion of all citizens actually dominates public life. This is true even in the most egalitarian societies. For most of us, participation in politics takes the form of short bursts of attention and going to the polls at election time. Is it reasonable to speak of democratic government when the levers of state power are in the hands of an élite?

The short answer is, 'It depends on what we expect from democracy.' If we expect that all citizens should have the opportunity to participate in the law-making process, we are bound to be disappointed. With some historical exceptions like the Greek *polis* and the township democracies of seventeenth- and eighteenth-century America, examples of direct government of the citizens by the citizens are scarce. Direct democracy survives in some isolated pockets like the Swiss *Landsgemeinde*, where citizens gather once a year on a mountain pasture in the canton of Appenzell to vote on important public questions. Modern technology has, however, created the possibility of direct democracy from people's living rooms in all advanced industrial societies. An idea of how this brave new world of participatory democracy could work was provided when an interactive soap opera called *The Spot* appeared on the Internet in 1995. Followers of this weekly program—a sort of Internet version of *Beverly Hills 90210*—were given the opportunity to vote on plot development and how characters in this fictional series should behave. There is no physical or technological reason why this method of popular choice could not be adapted to political decision-making. There may, however, be other reasons for rejecting what modern technology makes possible (see Box 1.3).

All modern democracies are *representative democracies*. Government is carried out by elected legislatures that represent the people. Citizens delegate law-making authority to their representatives, holding them responsible for their actions through periodic elections. Representative democracies sometimes include decision-making processes that provide opportunities for greater and more frequent citizen participation than simply voting every few years. *Plebiscites* and *referenda*—direct votes of citizens on important public questions—frequently held elections, choosing judges and some administrative officials through election, and formal procedures for removing an elected official before the end of his or her term, as through voter petitions and 'recall' elections, are democratic institutions that appear to allow for widespread citizen participation in public affairs.

Box 1.3 Democracy by Polls?
A Letter to the Editor

Sir:

I agree with you that American congressmen (and everyone else, for that matter) should pay little attention to public-opinion polls…but for a more fundamental reason. You point out that 'craven poll-following' over-emphasises special interests, which is true, but the real problem lies with the polls themselves, not in the following of them. They are founded on a contradiction: the anonymous collection of public opinions. This is an important issue because, as you say, to ignore public opinion sounds undemocratic, and runs contrary to the commonly held view that 'government by referendum' would be true democracy.

In expressing an opinion in public, an individual takes action of some significance—not only does he risk his reputation, but he also commits himself to defending the opinion in the future. These costs make him think twice before opening his mouth—time to rehearse his words and weigh their impact on those around him. In the process, selfish urges are often subordinated to the 'public good'.

In contrast, the anonymity of a poll frees the individual from personal involvement and removes the obligation to censor himself, nicely matching the conditions of vicarious life in front of the television. An opinion formed under these circumstances costs little, pays scant attention to the interests of others—and most certainly can lay no claim to being publicly declared. Thus a public poll in the age of television amounts to little more than the averaging of everybody's private whim. In attempting to short-cut the democratic process, polls trivialise opinion and degrade society along the way. They richly deserve the disdain you recommend.

Duncan Butlin
Tulsa, Oklahoma
(*The Economist*, 14 December 1991, 8).

This appearance may be deceiving. In countries like the United States and Switzerland, where referenda are a normal part of the political process, voter turnout is usually very low. Partly because of this, and partly because vested interests are quick to spend money on advertising and mobilizing their supporters, referenda may produce outcomes that do not appear to be democratic. Short terms of office and elections for judicial and administrative positions also have a potentially undemocratic side. The possibility that the majority may 'tyrannize' the rights of minorities may be increased in such circumstances. But the protection of individual and group rights must temper the practice of majority rule; otherwise, democracy shades into despotism.

Respect for rights and freedoms is generally considered a distinguishing feature of democratic government. Which rights and freedoms warrant protection, and in what circumstances they may legitimately be limited by government, are matters of dispute. Libertarians, many economists, and conservative philosophers argue that government which levies heavy taxes on citizens is undemocratic. Their reasoning is that individual choice is reduced when government, representing the collectivity, decides how a large share of people's income will be spent. Others argue that the same levels of taxation actually promote freedom by paying for policies that give less advantaged groups opportunities they would not have in a 'free' market. Even a value apparently as uncontroversial as freedom of speech often becomes embroiled in controversies over democracy. For example, some believe that any person or organization should have the right to spend money on advertising a political point of view during an election campaign. Others argue that unlimited freedom of speech in these circumstances is undemocratic because some individuals and groups are better endowed than others and, therefore, the points of view of the affluent will receive the greatest exposure.

Rights and freedoms are believed by most of us to be important in democracies, but everyone except extreme libertarians believes that protecting these rights or freedoms can sometimes produce undemocratic outcomes. No sure-fire test will tell us when democracy is promoted or impaired by protecting a right or freedom. Indeed, this is one of the greatest sources of conflict in modern democracy, sometimes portrayed as a struggle between the competing pulls of individualism (the private realm) and collectivism (the public realm). A private realm that is beyond the legitimate reach of the state is a necessary part of what is sometimes called a free society. Where this realm does not exist—where the individual's right to be protected from the state is obliterated by the state's right to impose its will on the individual—democracy does not exist. In its place one finds Tocqueville's tyranny of the majority that is able to control the levers of public authority. Civil liberties and group rights must enjoy some respect if a society's politics is to be judged democratic.

We will argue throughout this book that formal institutions are only part of what makes a society's politics democratic or not. The activities of the media, interest groups, and political parties are at least as crucial to the quality of democracy. Likewise, the socio-economic and ideological backgrounds to democratic government have important effects on how the formal and informal features of the political system operate. Democracy, then, cannot be reduced to a simple constitutional formula, nor to some particular vision of social equality. Several complex elements come into play, so that defining the term 'democracy' is a perilous task. Someone is bound to disagree, either with what is included in the definition, or with what has been left out. In full recognition of these hazards, we offer the following definition. *Democracy is a political system based on the formal political equality of all citizens, in which there is a realistic possibility that voters can replace the government, and in which certain basic rights and freedoms are protected.*

Political Identities

For a century and a half, race has been a crucial issue in American politics, sometimes simmering just below the surface of public attention and other times bursting onto the public consciousness as it did in the Los Angeles riots of 1992. Race has nowhere near the same significance in Canadian politics. For most of the twentieth century, British politics was best understood in terms of class conflict: between the working class, represented by the Labour Party, and the middle and upper classes, whose support went mainly to the Conservative Party. Class conflict has had a much lower profile in Canadian politics. Ethnic clashes are important in politics throughout the world, often producing violence and civil war. Canada has been spared the bloodshed that has accompanied such ethnic conflicts as those between Serbs and Croats in the former Yugoslavia. But ethnicity—particularly the French-English conflict—has been important in this country's politics.

Journalists, pundits, and professors find Canadian politics a source of endless fascination, but most Canadians have other things on their minds. (Roy Peterson, *Vancouver Sun*)

What identities are politically relevant? When and why do they become relevant? How are group identities organized into the political process, and how may they be 'disorganized', suppressed below the surface of politics? What is the difference between an interest and an identity in politics? These are crucial questions. Without answering them, we cannot hope to understand the politics of any society.

Let us begin with the difference between an interest and an identity. Most of us have no difficulty in recognizing that corporations in the same industry, or consumers, municipal ratepayers, or university students have identifiable interests in common. These interests are related to the conditions that promote or impair the material well-being of the members of these groups. They become political interests when they are organized under a collective association that claims to represent the members of the group and attempts to influence the actions of the state. Organization is expected to provide the group's members with more collective influence in politics than any individual member could hope to exercise alone. The number of possible political interests is virtually without limit. Of these, only a finite number actually become organized for collective political action, and an even smaller number achieve significant political clout.

A political interest brings together individuals who might otherwise have little in common in terms of their attitudes and beliefs. What they have in common is a material stake in how some political conflict is resolved. Wheat farmers, automotive workers, university professors, east coast fishermen, pulp and paper companies, and small business people are all examples of political interests. Their participation in politics as an organized group is based on considerations of material well-being. Indeed, the interests that the members of such groups have in common are primarily economic ones.

A political identity is broader than an interest. An identity is a state of mind, a sense of belonging to a community that is defined by its language, ethnic origins, religion, regional location, gender, or some other social or cultural characteristics. One can be a French Canadian, or a westerner, or a woman, or the member of some other social or cultural group, and be conscious of the fact, without this having any special political relevance. Identities such as these become politically relevant when those who share them make demands on the state—or when the state recognizes their group identity as a reason for treating them in a particular way. Some political identities emerge spontaneously in society, while others are forged and promoted by the state. Governments in Canada have come to play an increasingly active role in defining and promoting political identities in this country, a role that has generated much controversy.

The *nation* has been a particularly crucial political identity in Canadian politics. It is probably the single most powerful political identity in the world today—although religious identity surpasses it in some societies. The meaning of the term 'nation' is hotly disputed. It is perhaps no accident that *The Canadian Encyclopedia* does not even take a stab at defining it, settling instead for a definition of *nationalism*. 'Nationalism', it states, 'is the doctrine or practice of promoting the collective interests of the national community or state above those of individuals, regions, special interests or other nations.... In the first 25 years after WWII, 66 new nations were created.'[6]

Embedded in this definition of nationalism is a claim—not universally shared—about what constitutes a nation. Most of the '66 new nations' it refers to were former colonies whose populations were divided on ethnic and linguistic lines. For example, Nigeria achieved independent statehood in 1960 and immediately had to grapple with political conflicts between its three major communities—Yoruba, Ibo, and Hausa. The members of these communities did not share a sense of belonging to the same nation. Closer to home, organizations like the Parti Québécois and the Société de St-Jean Baptîste argue that French-speaking Quebec constitutes a nation that is distinct from the rest of Canadian society. They define the term 'nation' as a community united by common linguistic, historical, and even racial (although here modern nationalists usually tread lightly) ties. For Quebec nationalists, the concept of a single Canadian nation is nonsense (see Box 1.4).

Nationalism is usually accompanied by territorial claims. The nation is associated with some particular territory—'the homeland', 'la patrie'—that is argued to belong to the members of the nation. Quebec nationalists have asserted such claims, but so, too, have organizations representing Aboriginal Canadians, many of which are grouped together under the Assembly of First Nations. The territorial demands of organizations claiming to represent nations boil down to a demand for self-government, a demand that those making it usually justify as the democratic right of any 'people' to self-determination.

But a sense of place—a regional consciousness—may produce political demands that stop far short of independence and self-determination. A regional identity may be based on a variety of cultural, economic, institutional, and historical factors that distinguish the inhabitants of one region of a country from those of other regions. This identity may influence the political behaviour of those who share it, but their political demands generally will be less sweeping than those made by nationalist groups. When regionalism enters politics, it usually takes the form of demands for fairer treatment by the national government, better representation of the region in national political institutions, or more political autonomy for

---

Box 1.4 What Is a Nation?

'A nation is a community of persons bound together by a sense of solidarity and wishing to perpetuate this solidarity through some political means. Contributing to this solidarity are common "objective" factors such as history, territory, race, ethnicity, culture, language, religion and customs and common "subjective" factors such as the consciousness of a distinct identity, an awareness of common interests and a consequent willingness to live together. Because of the existence of such factors, there is a special relationship among members of a nation which enables them to cooperate politically more easily among themselves than with outsiders.' Canada, *The Task Force on Canadian Unity* (1979).

'A nation ... is no more and no less than the entire population of a sovereign state.' Pierre Elliott Trudeau, *Federalism, Nationalism, and Reason*.

'A nation is a community of people who became aware of themselves as history has made them, who treasure their own past, and who love themselves as they know or imagine themselves to be, with a kind of inevitable introversion.' Jacques Maritain, *Man and the State*.

'The simplest statement that can be made about a nation is that it is a body of people who feel that they are a nation; and it may be that when all the fine-spun analysis is concluded this will be the ultimate statement as well.' Rupert Emerson, *From Empire to Nation*.

regional political authorities—all of which stop short of the usual catalogue of nationalist demands.

Cultural and social identities are not inherently political. The differences that exist between religious, ethnic, language, regional, or gender groups—to name only a few of the most important social-cultural divisions in the world today—may give rise to political conflicts when they are associated with inequalities in the *economic status* and *political power* of these groups. In other words, identities acquire political consequences when the members of a group, the 'identity-bearers', believe that they experience some deprivation or injustice because of their social-cultural identity, and when a 'critical mass' of the group's membership can be persuaded to take political action based on their self-identification as women, or French Canadians, or westerners, or whatever the identity happens to be. Political identities may not be primarily economic, but they usually have an economic dimension. Even when the stakes appear to be mainly symbolic—for example, the long-standing political debate over special status for Quebec in Canadian federalism—material considerations generally lurk behind the demands that the representatives of a social or cultural group make on the state.

Why particular identities surface in politics, while others remain 'pre-political', is a question that can only be answered by looking at the particular circumstances of any society. The persistence of regional, ethnolinguistic, and religious identities in the modern world and the emergence of gender inequality onto the political agendas of virtually all advanced industrial societies have confounded the earlier belief of many social scientists, and all socialists, that class divisions would come to dominate the politics of advanced capitalism. The term 'class' (like most of the concepts discussed in this chapter) means different things to different people. When used as in the labels 'upper class' or 'middle class', it refers to a social status that is determined by such measures as the societal prestige of a person's occupation, an individual's income, or even his or her behaviour. Since Karl Marx's time, many social scientists have defined class as being primarily an economic concept. According to this usage, a person's class membership is determined by one's relationship to the means of economic production—the main division in society being between those who control the means of production and those who must sell their labour to earn a livelihood.

No one seriously argues that modern day capitalism is characterized by a simple division between the owners of capital—the *bourgeoisie*—and their workers—the *proletariat*— as Marx predicted would happen. The very terms 'bourgeoisie' and 'proletariat' have a sort of antiquated ring in an age when liberal political reforms and market economic reforms have been sweeping through the formerly Communist countries of Eastern Europe and what was the Soviet Union. But those who insist that class divisions, however complicated they may be today, are determined by whether one wields or is subject to economic power also maintain that class is inevitably the major source of political conflict in society. The material interests of classes on different sides of the capital divide are, according to them, fundamentally opposed. The fact that most members of society do not believe this to be true only demonstrates the cultural dominance of dominant class values. Those who understand class to mean social status are much less likely to take the position that class divisions are the chief lines of political conflict.

In some societies, class identity is a powerful force in politics. Political parties make calculated appeals to class interests and draw on different classes for their electoral support.

This is not particularly true of Canada. The sense of belonging to a class is relatively weak in Canadian society. Other political identities, especially ethnolinguistic and regional ones, have overshadowed class in Canadian politics. Some commentators argue that this should be taken at face value—that the linguistic and regional interests of Canadians are simply more vital to them than is something as abstract as class. Others maintain that the consciousness of belonging to a class whose interests are at odds with those of other classes has been suppressed in various ways by parties and élites who have vested interests in the suppression of class awareness and action.

Continuity and Change in Politics

When Canadian Confederation was being discussed at Charlottetown and Quebec City in 1864, French-English relations and the relationship between the national and provincial governments were on the table. They are still on the table today. Other issues like 'reproductive rights', what to do with the waste produced by households and industry, and how to pay for public pensions in an aging society—which are all part of the contemporary political agenda—were not even imagined by those who drafted the Confederation agreement. The basic institutions of parliamentary democracy in Canada have remained the same since the middle of the nineteenth century. But the way in which elections are fought, how interest groups attempt to influence public policy, and the relationships between the various branches of government have all undergone enormous change. The formal division of constitutional powers between Ottawa and the provinces has not been altered in any fundamental way since it was first laid out in 1867. And yet both levels of government legislate on a far wider range of matters, spend and tax at rates unthinkable a hundred years ago, and co-operate through a dense network of administrative and financial relations that has developed mainly since the Second World War.

Change is a fundamental characteristic of the human condition and of societies. But so, too, is continuity. The questions that Aristotle, Plato, and Thucydides asked about politics between 500 and 300 BC are still being asked today. If present-day Canada does not bear much of a resemblance to ancient Athens, it is nonetheless true that many of the most elementary issues of governance are the same. We should not, however, underestimate their differences. Economic and technological changes have not only transformed societies, they have also redrawn their political maps. Where pressures for political democracy have become irresistible, this has not been due primarily to an intellectual conversion on the part of society's ruling élites. The economic-technological changes that gave rise to the modern city and to an industrial working class also produced demands for the extension of full democratic citizenship to the previously excluded masses.

Politics is usually a contest between those who advocate change and those who prefer to see more of the same. Change is likely to be viewed as a threat by those whose status, income, or privileges are tied to existing practices and institutions. Those who are aware that they have something to lose, and who are willing to act to protect it, are often referred to as *vested or special interests*. This is usually considered a term of opprobrium, at best synonomous with 'selfish', and at worst on a par with 'reactionary'.

Change may, however, be viewed as an opportunity to accomplish something desirable. Those who want to see the status quo changed through political reform are not necessarily less self-interested than the vested interests they criticize. But they believe that current social practices or public policies prevent them from achieving goals that they value. The advocates of reform and the defenders of the status quo have one thing in common. They will both invoke communal values—'justice', 'equality', 'freedom', 'jobs', 'economic growth', 'peace'—in arguing their case.

In the real world, political conflicts seldom take the form of a straightforward fight between one side committed to change and another side dug in to defend its privileges. This is a caricature of how politics actually unfolds. Even on an issue like abortion, where the conflict usually is portrayed as a two-sided struggle between 'Right to Life' and 'pro-Choice' groups, the actual constellation of interests and positions is much more complex. In fact, the politics of abortion may appear to be an exception to our claim that political conflict generally pits the defenders of the status quo against the advocates of reform. After all, none of the sides in the abortion controversy appears to be satisfied with the current situation. Instead, they are all clamouring for various sorts of reform. Nonetheless, when dissecting political conflict we generally find that some interests are pushing for change while others are either protective of the status quo or at least opposed to the sorts of changes that the pro-reform forces have in mind.

When political change occurs, it is likely to be explained in one of two ways. On the one hand, it may be attributed to socio-economic changes that create pressures for state action and the opportunity for political reform. This is a *materialist* explanation of political change. On the other hand, political reform may be explained as the result of a shift in societal attitudes and beliefs—a shift that may be more or less general throughout society, or that mainly characterizes political élites. This is an *ideological* explanation of political change.

The materialist and ideological explanations of what triggers political reform are not mutually exclusive. They do, however, emphasize different putative causes of change. This may best be understood by considering the political impact of the contemporary feminist movement (this subject is discussed in greater detail in Chapter 12). Laws dealing with issues that span abortion, publicly subsidized day care, equal pay for work of equal value, and the definition and official treatment of pornography in films and magazines have all been influenced, to a greater or lesser degree, by the feminist movement. So, too, have the hiring practices of both public and private organizations, the lending practices of banks, the content of school textbooks and university curricula, and the factors at play in selecting candidates and leaders for political parties—to mention only a few of the social changes that can be linked to the political movement for gender equality.

What has caused these changes? Is it because society has become more aware of gender-based inequalities and less tolerant of practices and institutions that treat women as inferior to men? Is the explanation, therefore, an ideological one, linked to a spreading popular acceptance of the political discourse of gender rights pioneered in the 1960s by such early feminists as Betty Friedan (*The Feminine Mystique*), Germaine Greer (*The Female Eunuch*), and Kate Millet (*Sexual Politics*)? Or does the explanation in fact lie in such material factors as changing birth control technology, which has facilitated sex without reproduction, leading to smaller families and an increase since the 1960s of the female participation rate in the labour force? Combined with the dramatic leap in the rate of divorce and the consequent explosion in the number of single-parent families headed by women, these material changes in social and economic structures have helped make gender inequality an issue. According to this materialist explanation, the political and social reforms associated with the women's movement have only been possible because changes in the family and the economy have produced an increasingly wide and obvious gap between the economic needs and social roles of women, on the one hand, and their opportunities and rights, on the other. Into this gap have flooded political demands for reform and a heightened social awareness of gender inequality as a problem.

So have changes in material conditions prompted changing ideas, or have shifting views about the sexes generated material changes in institutions like the family and the workplace? The complex reality is likely to provide support for both the ideological and materialist views.

A second issue that divides those who seek to understand the processes of change and continuity in politics is the significance of political reform. Some argue that developments like the extension of full political citizenship rights to all adults, the growth of the 'welfare state', and the more recent emergence of equality rights issues onto the political stage of advanced industrial societies signify democratic progress. Democracy may remain flawed, dominated by élites and special interest groups, but the general trajectory of politics and society over the last couple of centuries has been in the direction of greater equality. We may call this the *onward march of democracy* view.

Others maintain that these same political reforms have had much less impact on political, social, and economic relations than the 'onward march of democracy' view suggests. Reform, they argue, has failed to change the fundamental social and economic inequalities that determine the distribution of political power in society. We may call this the *limits to democracy* argument. It assumes two main forms, one associated with class analysis and the other with the feminist critique of political democracy.

The differences between the 'limits to democracy' and the 'onward march of democracy' assessments of political reform are based largely on the way they conceive of politics. The class analysis and feminist perspectives tend to view all human relationships—from the bedroom to the boardroom—as being charged with political significance. The formal political equality of citizens, competitive elections, guarantees of individual rights and freedoms, and social legislation that others point to as proof of democracy's onward march are more likely to be viewed from the Marxist and feminist perspectives as cosmetic surgery that leaves the skeleton and musculature of inequality untouched. According to class analysis, the capitalist economy limits the possibilities for democratic reform. Feminist theory contends that the limits to democracy are due to the patriarchal, i.e., male-dominated, character of society and culture.

This book does not provide definitive answers for those who wish to know whether the story of Canadian democracy is one of progress toward ever higher levels of equality and protection for rights and freedoms, or whether the achievement of democracy remains stalled for the reasons social critics suggest. It does, however, attempt to provide the reader with the information and critical perspectives necessary to arrive at such a judgement.

Box 1.5 Democracy on the March, or Stalled?

On the march …

'[It is not true] that every change brings ineluctable progress. More nations have moved from being democracies to tyrannies in the last forty years than have moved the other way. But the trend appears to be reversing, and we hear the cry for democracy repeated in many corners of the world. Still, there is reason to be cautious: institutions are subject to decay, man is subject to temptation; greed, envy, and rage stalk democracy's best intentions. Each step on the road to a technological innovation may take humankind down a yellow-brick road to doomsday.' Patrick Watson and James Barber, *The Struggle for Democracy*.

or stalled …

'The most important fact about advanced capitalist societies … is the continued existence in them of private and ever more concentrated economic power. As a result of that power, the men—owners and controllers—in whose hands it lies enjoy a massive preponderance in society, in the political system, and in the determination of the state's policies and actions.

'The trouble does not lie in the wishes and intentions of powerholders, but in the fact that the reformers…are the prisoners, and usually the willing prisoners, of an economic and social framework which necessarily turns their reforming proclamations, however sincerely meant, into verbiage.' Ralph Miliband, *The State in Capitalist Society*.

PART TWO

The Societal Context of Politics

American culture casts a long shadow over Canada, as the looming towers of Detroit across the river from Windsor's Canada Broadcasting Corporation remind us. (*Stephen Brooks*)

Ideas constitute an important element of political life. This chapter surveys some of the key issues pertaining to the role of ideas in Canadian politics and discusses the political ideas of Canadians. The following topics are examined:

- ❖ Ideologies, values, and institutions.
- ❖ Fragment theory.
- ❖ Formative events.
- ❖ Economic structures and political ideas.
- ❖ The interplay of political institutions and values.
- ❖ The political ideas of Canadians.
- ❖ Community.
- ❖ Freedom.
- ❖ Equality.
- ❖ Citizen expectations for government.

CHAPTER TWO

Ideological and Institutional Roots

In 1982 Canada's best-known popular historian, Pierre Berton, wrote a book with the promising title *Why We Act Like Canadians*.[1] It was written as a series of letters to an imaginary American friend by the name of 'Sam'. The fact that Berton addressed his explanations of what he calls Canada's 'national character' to an American was no accident. Canadians—English-speaking Canadians at least—have always struggled to escape the long shadow cast by American culture. *Why We Act Like Canadians* could have easily been titled 'Why We Are Not Americans'. It is virtually impossible to discuss the political ideas and institutions of English Canada without reference to those of the United States.

The same is not true of French Canada. Language and history combine to ensure the distinctiveness of French-Canadian society. Investigations into their 'national identity' have long been as popular in French Canada as in English Canada. But they seek to explain the values and institutions of French Canadians in terms of forces that have little to do with the United States. Instead, most analyses of French-Canadian culture focus on the internal dynamics of that society and on the effects that French-English relations have had on the development of French Canada.

It is impossible to discuss questions of culture and ideas in Canada without immediately becoming ensnared in controversy. Use of the terms 'English Canada' and 'French Canada' will offend some Canadians who feel left out by these labels, or who believe that there is only one Canada, politically, culturally, and otherwise. A term like 'national character', used so confidently by Pierre Berton, is certain to bring down the wrath of most academics, who argue that it is a bogus caricature of something much more complex and diverse. Before we discuss the values and institutions that characterize Canadian politics we must clarify what it is we want to explain, and what concepts will help us achieve this.

Ideologies, Values, and Institutions

Ideas assume various forms in political life. When they take the form of a set of interrelated beliefs about how society is organized and how it ought to function—an interpretative map for understanding the world—this is an *ideology*. An ideology spills beyond the boundaries of politics to embrace beliefs and judgements about other social relationships, including economic ones. It is this holistic character of ideologies that distinguishes them from more limited political value systems. The fact that most people are not aware of having ideological leanings, and might be puzzled or even startled at being labelled a 'conservative', a 'liberal', or a 'socialist', does not mean that ideology is irrelevant to their political beliefs and actions. When the politics of a society are described as 'pragmatic' and 'non-ideological', this usually indicates that a particular ideology dominates to such a degree that it has become the conventional wisdom.

Ideas also enter politics in the form of *political culture*. The classic definition of this controversial concept is 'the particular distribution of patterns of orientation toward political objects among the members of the nation'.[2] As this definition suggests, a political culture has a more limited scope than does an ideology. Individuals may share an ideological outlook, but differ in their beliefs about and feelings toward specific political objects. In Canada, research on political culture has focused primarily on the differences that exist between the politically relevant attitudes and beliefs of French and English Canadians and on the question of whether English-speaking Canada is characterized by regional political cultures. To determine whether significant and persistent differences exist, political scientists have attempted to measure such things as levels of political knowledge and participation, feelings of political efficacy (a person's sense of whether his or her participation in politics matters) and alienation (variously defined as apathy, estrangement from the political system, or the belief that politics is systematically biased against one's interests and values), attitudes toward political authority and the different levels of government, and the sense of belonging to a particular regional or linguistic community.

The third way in which ideas are relevant for politics is through individual *personality*. One of the most often repeated claims about Canadians is that they are less likely to question and challenge authority than are Americans. Canadians are, it is argued, more deferential. We examine this claim later in the chapter. Several of the standard questions used in studies of political culture, such as those dealing with political efficacy, trust in public officials, and emotional feelings toward political authorities, tap politically relevant dimensions of personality. Much of the research on the political consequences of individual personality traits has focused on the relationship between a person's general attitudes toward authority and non-conformity, on the one hand, and, on the other, their political attitudes on issues like the protection of civil liberties, toleration of political dissent, the group rights of minorities, and attitudes toward public authorities. The main conclusion of this research is that general personality traits show up in an individual's political ideas and action.

One way of categorizing political ideas—perhaps the most popular way—is to describe them as being *left wing, right wing,* or *centrist*. These labels are used to signify the broader ideological premises believed to lie behind an action, opinion, or statement. For example, a newspaper editorial slamming welfare fraud and calling for mandatory 'workfare' would be called right wing by some, as would a proposal to cut taxes for the affluent or to eliminate public funding for abortions. Proposals to increase the minimum wage, ban the use of replacement workers during a strike or lockout, or increase spending on assistance for developing countries are the sorts of measures likely to be described as left wing. Centrist positions, as the term suggests, fall between the right and left wings of the political spectrum. They attempt to achieve some middle ground between the arguments and principles of left and right. The centre is, virtually by definition, the mainstream of a society's politics, and those who occupy this location on the political spectrum are likely to view themselves as being non-ideological.

Right and left are shorthand labels for conflicting belief systems. These beliefs involve basic assumptions about how society, the economy, and politics operate, as well as ideas about how these matters *should* be arranged. Generally speaking, to be on the right in Anglo-American societies means that one subscribes to an *individualistic* belief system. Such a person is likely to believe that what one achieves in life is due principally to his or her own efforts, that the welfare of society is best promoted by allowing individuals to pursue their own interests, and that modern government is too expensive and too intrusive. To be on the left, however, is to prefer a set of beliefs that may be described as *collectivist*. This person is likely to attribute greater weight to social and economic circumstances as determinants of one's opportunities and achievements than does someone on the right. Moreover, those on the left have greater doubts about the economic efficiency and social fairness of free markets and have greater faith in the ability of government to intervene in ways that promote the common good. Although those on the left may be critical of particular actions and institutions of government, they reject the claim that the size and scope of government need to be trimmed. Smaller government, they would argue, works to the advantage of the affluent and privileged, at the expense of the poor and disadvantaged.

In reality, the politics of left and right is more complicated than these simplified portraits suggest. For example, while opposition to abortion generally is viewed as a right-wing position, many who subscribe to all the elements of right-wing politics listed above support easy access to abortion. These people, often labelled *libertarians*, believe that individuals should be allowed the largest possible margin of freedom in all realms of life, including those that involve moral choices. The libertarian right is, however, smaller and less of a political force than the socially conservative right. Social conservatives are distinguished by such stands as opposition to abortion, support for capital punishment and stiffer jail sentences, and rejection of forms of pluralism that they believe are corrosive of traditional values. The wellsprings of their conservatism are quite different from those of libertarianism, but their shared antipathy for the modern welfare state and their preferences for markets over state planning in economics cause libertarians and social conservatives to be grouped together on the right. The fissures in this alliance, and the difficulties with the right-left categorization of political ideas, become apparent when the issue is one of personal morality (e.g., abortion, homosexuality, religious teachings in public schools).

Despite its limitations, and the fact that labels like 'right' and 'left' are more often used to dismiss and discredit one's opponents in politics than to inform in a dispassionate way, the right-left spectrum taps a crucial and enduring truth of modern politics. This involves the character of the good society and how best to achieve it. We have said that the underlying struggle is essentially one between collectivist and individualist visions of the good society. These visions differ in how they view the conditions that promote human dignity and in their conceptions of social justice. For example, it is often said that one of the cultural characteristics that distinguishes Canadians from Americans is our greater propensity to sacrifice individual self-interest to the good of the community. In this connection Canada's health care system is invoked like a mantra whenever Canadian-American cultural differences are discussed and fears are expressed by Canadian nationalists that Canada is sliding down the slope toward American values and public policies (see Box 2.1). What the watchdogs of Canadian-style health care are really saying is that the more collectivist Canadian health care model provides greater dignity for individuals and is fairer than the more individualistic American system.

Defenders of the American health care system often retort that Canadian health policy is a form of socialism. *Socialism* is one of a trio of ideologies that have greatly influenced the politics of Western societies since the American and French revolutions. The other two are *liberalism* and *conservatism*. The importance of these ideologies in defining the contours of political life is suggested by the fact that major and minor political parties in many Western democracies continue to use the names liberal, conservative, and socialist.

In Canada, the two parties that have dominated politics for most of the country's history, the Liberal Party and the Progressive Conservative Party (simply the Conservative Party before the party was rechristened in 1942), have their roots in the ideological divisions of

---

Box 2.1   What Makes a Canadian?

What are Canadian values? Well, a few years ago, a famous Texan coined the term 'a kinder and gentler' nation. Well, that is what we in Canada are. That is what we want to remain.

Our most important values as a nation are tolerance and sharing. We know that government cannot and should not do everything. But we also know it can and must be a force for good in society. And during times of great change, government has an obligation to help people adapt.

Most important, we know that citizenship has responsibilities. Individual rights are important in Canada. Very important…. But just as important are the responsibilities we have for each other and for our community. That is why health care is so important in Canada.

There is a wide consensus in our country about preserving our distinctive state-funded health care system called Medicare. Under our system, you can go to the doctor of your choice. You are admitted to a hospital if you need to be. Period. Not if you have enough money. Or the right private plan. The fact is that no one in Canada needs to worry about medical bills. It is one of our proudest achievements. Canadians want to keep Medicare. And we will.

I believe that is one thing that makes us a 'kinder, gentler' society.

Prime Minister Jean Chrétien,
speaking to the American Society of Newspaper
Editors, 6 April 1995.

the nineteenth century. Over time, however, the labels have lost much if not all of their informative value. Today, the ideological distance between a Liberal and a Conservative is likely to be small. Indeed, already at the beginning of the twentieth century the astute French observer André Siegfried remarked that the Liberal and Conservative parties were virtually indistinguishable in terms of their ideological principles. They and their supporters shared in the dominant liberal tradition that pervaded Canada and the United States.

At the heart of this tradition was the primacy of individual freedom. *Classical liberalism*—liberalism as understood until the middle of this century—was associated with freedom of religious choice and practice, free enterprise and free trade in the realm of economics, and freedom of expression and association in politics. These liberal values constituted a sort of national ethos in the United States, where they were enshrined in the Declaration of Independence and in the American Bill of Rights. In the colonies of British North America that would become Canada in the late nineteenth century, liberalism's dominance was somewhat more tentative than in the United States. This was due to the streak of conservatism that was kept alive by some of the élites in colonial society, notably the Catholic Church, the Church of England, and the British colonial authorities.

Classical conservatism was based on the importance of tradition. It accepted human inequality—social, political, and economic—as part of the natural order of things. Conservatives emphasized the importance of continuity with the past and the preservation of law and order. They were wary of innovation and opposed to such basic liberal reforms as equal political rights for all men (even liberals did not come around to the idea of equal political rights for women until this century). Unlike liberals, who located the source of all just rule in the people, conservatives maintained that God and tradition were the true founts of political authority. Consequently, they supported an established church and were strong defenders of the Crown's traditional prerogatives against the rival claims of elected legislatures.

Although no party having the label 'socialist' has ever achieved the status of being even an important minor party in either Canada or the United States, socialist ideology has been influential in various ways. *Classical socialism* was based on the principle of equality of condition, a radical egalitarianism that distinguished socialist doctrine from liberalism's advocacy of equality of opportunity. Socialists supported a vastly greater role for the state in directing the economy, better working conditions and greater rights for workers vis-à-vis their employers, and reforms like public health care, unemployment insurance, income assistance for the indigent, public pensions, and universal access to public education that became the hallmarks of the twentieth-century welfare state.

The usefulness of these three 'isms' as benchmarks for reading the political map is no longer very great. There are two main reasons for this. First, all three of these classical ideologies, but especially liberalism and conservatism, mean something quite different today from what they meant 100 or 200 years ago. For example, contemporary liberalism does not place individual freedom above all else. Instead, modern liberals are distinguished by their belief that governments can and should act to alleviate hardships experienced by the poor and the oppressed. They are more likely to worry about minority group rights than individual freedoms, or at any rate to see the improvement of the conditions of disadvantaged minorities as a necessary step toward the achievement of real freedom for the members of these groups. Modern liberalism has also become associated with support for multiculturalism and openness toward non-traditional lifestyles and social institutions.

The doctrine of classical conservatism has disappeared from the scene in contemporary democracies, leaving what has been called the conservative outlook or 'conservative mind'.[3] Modern conservatives tend to embrace the economic beliefs that once were characteristic of liberals. And like classical liberals they defend the principle of equality of opportunity. They are more likely to place the protection of personal freedoms before the advancement of minority rights. As in earlier times, conservatism is generally viewed as the ideology of the privileged in society. It is worth noting, however, that conservative politicians and political parties receive much of their support from middle-class voters whose hands are far from the levers of economic power and social influence.

Of the three classical ideologies the meaning of socialism has changed the least. There is today, however, much less confidence among socialists that state ownership of the means of economic production and distribution is desirable. Modern socialists, or *social democrats* as they often call themselves, temper their advocacy of an egalitarian society with an acceptance of capitalism and the inequalities that inevitably are generated by free-market economies. The defence of the rights of society's less fortunate members, which has always been characteristic of socialism, is today carried out largely under the banner of other 'isms', including feminism, multiculturalism, and environmentalism. In Canada and the United States these other collectivist-egalitarian belief systems have more of an impact on politics than does socialism.

A second reason why the traditional trio of 'isms' is no longer a reliable guide to politics has to do with the character of political divisions in modern society. The aristocracy of land and title and the deferential social norms that nurtured classical conservatism belong to the past. They live on as the folklore of castles and estates in the once rigidly hierarchical societies of Europe, in the continuing pomp of hereditary royalty, and in Britain's House of Lords. Otherwise, classical conservatism has no legitimacy in the middle-class cultures of Western societies. In the United States the structures and values that supported classical conservatism never existed, and in Canada they achieved only a precarious and passing toehold.

The struggles of liberalism in the eighteenth and nineteenth centuries, and of socialism in the nineteenth and twentieth, have largely been won (though some argue that they have been eroded in recent years by the forces of economic globalization). Liberals fought for free-market reforms and the extension of political rights and freedoms, first to the new propertied classes created by the Industrial Revolution and then more widely to the (male) adult population. They fought against conservatives who dug in to protect the political privileges of an hereditary aristocracy and the economic dominance of the traditional land-owning classes. Socialists fought for more government control over the economy, workers' rights like collective bargaining and limits on the hours of work, and the welfare state. They fought against both the vestiges of conservatism and liberalism's emphasis on individualism.

The classical ideologies were formed and evolved in response to one another as well as to the social and economic conditions in which they were rooted. Today, Canadians, Americans, and Western Europeans live in affluent middle-class societies that bear little resemblance to those of the nineteenth century, when Europe was a tilting ground for the rivalries between conservatism, liberalism, and socialism. As the character of Western societies has changed, so, too, have the ideologies that slug it out in their politics.

Does this mean, as some have argued, that the traditional ideologies are obsolete, unsuited to the realities of modern society? This is the 'end of ideology' thesis that American sociologist Daniel Bell put forward in the 1960s. 'In the western world', he argued, 'there is today, a rough consensus among intellectuals on political issues: the acceptance of a Welfare State; the desirability of decentralized power; a system of mixed economy and of political pluralism.'[4] Many, from Camille Paglia to Preston Manning, agree. Manning dismisses the traditional 'isms' and the left-centre-right ideological grid as outmoded ways of thinking about politics. He has described his own ideological orientation as 'social conservatism', a label that suggests a blend of principles from previously warring ideological camps.

It is a great mistake, however, to underestimate the continuing importance of ideology in politics. Although the traditional 'isms' now must jostle with feminism, environmentalism, multiculturalism, and other 'isms' on a more crowded playing field, and despite the changes that have taken place in the meanings of the classical ideologies, they continue to be useful, though certainly not infallible, guides to understanding political ideas. The right v. left or individualism v. collectivism dichotomy is probably the most useful. In the real world, however, we should seldom expect to find that the ideas of an individual, or those associated with a group or political party, can be neatly categorized as one or the other.

To illustrate this point, consider the case of Reform Party leader Preston Manning. Manning is usually described by those in the media, his political opponents, and even by many of his supporters as 'conservative' or 'right wing'. This is, however, an overly simple

The Canadian political mood seems to have shifted to the right in recent years, as Ontario's New Democratic Party government discovered in that province's 1995 election. (Roy Peterson, *Vancouver Sun*)

and even misleading description of Manning's political ideology. As former Reform Party research director Tom Flanagan explains, Manning's political beliefs combine free enterprise economics and a religiously inspired social conscience in the framework of western Canadian populism to create what Manning himself describes as 'social conservatism'. Manning explicitly rejected media portrayals of him as 'Newt of the North' after his 1995 meeting with Republican House Leader Newt Gingrich, insisting that his own brand of conservatism was in the more compassionate collectivist tradition of Canada. As Flanagan argues, 'Manning holds many opinions that most people would call conservative, but they are not supported by an overall conservative philosophy.... He is certainly not a socialist or even a liberal, but in ideological terms he could be leader of a centrist party with a favourable orientation to business.'[5]

Explaining Ideas and Institutions

Until recently, explanations of Canadians' political ideas, and of the institutions that embody them, could be grouped into three broad camps. These were: fragment theory, the role of formative events, and economic explanations. A fourth approach that emphasizes the historical balance between statist and participatory tendencies in politics has recently been developed by historian Gordon Stewart. Each of these perspectives stresses a different set of causes in explaining the origins of Canadians' political ideas and institutions and the forces that have shaped their development.

Fragment Theory: European Parents and Cultural Genes

Canada, along with other New World societies, was founded by immigrants from Europe. Native communities already existed, of course, but the sort of society that developed in Canada had its roots and inspiration in the values and practices of European civilization. Those who took the decision to emigrate to the New World—or who had it made for them, as was true of the convicts sent from Britain to Australia—did not represent a cross-section of the European society from which they came. They were unrepresentative in terms of their social class (the privileged tended to stay put in Europe), their occupations, and in some cases their religion. Moreover, immigration tended to occur in waves, coinciding with particular epochs in the ideological development of Europe. New World societies were 'fragments' of the European societies that gave birth to them. They were fragment societies because they represented only a part of the socio-economic and cultural spectrum of the European society from which they originated, and also because their creation coincided with a particular ideological epoch. The timing of settlement is crucial. Along with whatever material possessions immigrants brought with them, they also brought along their 'cultural baggage': values and beliefs that they acquired in Europe and transplanted into the New World. As David Bell and Lorne Tepperman observe, '[t]he "fragment theory" sees the culture of founding groups as a kind of *genetic code* that does not determine but sets limits to later cultural developments.'[6]

But why should the ideas of the founders carry such weight that they shape the political values and beliefs of subsequent generations? Fragment theory is rather weak on this

Table 2.1 Liberalism, Conservatism, and Socialism: Classical and Contemporary Versions

I. CLASSICAL

	Liberalism	*Conservatism*	*Socialism*
a. Characteristics of the Good Society	Individual freedom is maximized; politics and economics are free and competitive; achievements and recognition are due to personal merit and effort; a capitalist economy will produce the greatest happiness for society and maximize material welfare; personal dignity depends on the individual's own actions.	The traditional social order is preserved; individuals are members of social groups that are linked together by a web of rights and obligations; those born in privileged circumstances have an obligation to those below them on the social ladder; there is a natural social hierarchy based on inherited status; personal dignity depends on one's conformity to the norms and behaviour of one's social group.	Social and economic equality are maximized; private ownership of property is replaced by its collective ownership and management; competition is replaced by co-operation; the welfare of society is maximized through economic and social planning; personal dignity depends on work and one's solidarity with the working class.
b. Nature of Government	All just government rests on the consent of the governed; party system is competitive; the state is subordinate to society; government should be small and its scope limited; the elected legislature is the most powerful component of the state; separatism between church and state.	The rights and responsibilities of those who govern derive from God and tradition; the state's fundamental role is to preserve social order; the state is superior to society and is owed obedience by all citizens and groups; the Crown is the most powerful component of the state; the size and scope of government are small by modern standards, but are not limited by liberalism's suspicion of the state; the state recognizes an official church.	All just government rests on the consent of the governed and the principles of social and economic equality; the state should control crucial sectors of the economy; government has a responsibility to redistribute wealth from wealthy to the less fortunate classes; government is large and its scope wide; a socialist state is the embodiment of the will and interests of the working class; no officially recognized religion.

| c. Chief Supporters | Industrialists, merchants, property-owning individuals. | Landed aristocracy, established church, military officers and agents of the Crown whose status and income depended on maintenance of the traditional social hierarchy. | Organized workers, intellectuals. |

II. CONTEMPORARY

	Liberalism	*Conservatism*	*Socialism*
a. Characteristics of the Good Society	Individual freedom is balanced by protection for disadvantaged elements in society and recognition of group rights; capitalism must be regulated by the state to ensure the social and economic well-being of the majority; social diversity should be recognized and promoted through public education, hiring, and the policies of governments; social entitlements are respected, including a certain standard of living and access to health care and accommodation; personal dignity is based on freedom and social equality.	Individual freedom is more important than social equality, and should not be sacrificed to the latter; state regulation of capitalism should be kept to a minimum and should not be used to promote any but economic goals; social diversity is a fact, but is not something that should be actively promoted by government; individuals should be responsible for their own lives and policies that encourage dependency on the state should be avoided; personal dignity depends on one's own efforts and is undermined by collectivist policies and too much emphasis on promoting social and economic equality.	Social and economic equality are the most important values; individual rights must be subordinated to collective goals; small-scale capitalism has its place, but state economic planning and active participation in the economy are still necessary to promote both economic competitiveness and social fairness; the environmental consequences of all public and private actions must be considered; systemic discrimination based on gender, race, and ethnicity is eliminated through government policies; personal dignity depends on social and economic equality.

b. Nature of Government	The state has a responsibility to protect and promote the welfare of the disadvantaged; the post-WWII welfare state is a necessary vehicle for ensuring social justice; government should reflect the diversity of society in its personnel and policies; the state should not be aligned with any religious group.	The state's primary function should be to maintain circumstances in which individuals can pursue their own goals and life plans; government should be small and the level of taxation low in order to minimize interference with individual choice; government should not remain neutral between different systems of morality, but should promote traditional values through the schools and through support for the traditional family.	The state should redistribute wealth in society and ensure the social and economic equality of its citizens; some modern socialists argue that political power should be decentralized to community-level groups as the best way to ensure democratic responsiveness and accountability; the state should reflect the society in its personnel and policies; traditional value systems are based on systemic discrimination and oppression, and government has a responsibility to eradicate these values.
c. Chief Supporters	Many middle of the road advocacy groups within the feminist, environmental, and multicultural movements; public-sector workers; middle-class intellectuals in the universities and the media; the national Liberal and Progressive Conservative parties and the Bloc Québécois.	Business groups; middle-class workers in the private sector; the Reform Party; the Alberta and Ontario Conservative parties.	More extreme advocacy groups within the feminist, environmental, and multicultural movements; some elements in the NDP and within organized labour.

point, arguing that the fragment's ideological system 'congeals' at some point—the ideology of the founders becomes the dominant ideology—and that immigrants who arrive subsequently have little choice but to assimilate to the dominant values and beliefs already in place. The transmission of the fragment culture from generation to generation presumably depends on social structures and political institutions that date from the founding period and embody the dominant ideas of the founding immigrants.

Canada is viewed as a two-fragment society. French Canada was founded by immigrants from France who brought with them their Catholicism and *feudal* ideas about social and political relations. Feudal society is characterized by fairly rigid social classes, connected to one another by a web of mutual rights and duties based on tradition and by the exclusion of most people from the full right to participate in politics. According to French-Canadian historians like Fernand Ouellet, this was the ideological and social condition of New France when the colony was conquered by British forces in 1759.[7] Cut off from the social and political developments unleashed by the French Revolution (1789)—emigration from France, with the exception of some priests, virtually dried up—French Canada's ideological development was shaped by its origins as a feudal fragment of pre-revolution France. Institutions, chiefly the Catholic Church, the dominant social institution in French Canada until well into the twentieth century, operated to maintain this pre-liberal inheritance.

The 'cultural genes' of English Canada are, according to fragment theory, very different. English Canada was originally populated by immigrants from the United States. These were the so-called Loyalists, those who found themselves on the losing side of the American War of Independence (1776). They migrated north to British colonies that were overwhelmingly French-speaking.[8] The 'cultural baggage' they carried with them has been the subject of much debate, but the general view seems to be that they held predominantly *liberal* political beliefs. The liberalism that emerged in the eighteenth century was built around the idea of individual freedom: freedom in politics, in religion, and in economic relations. One of its crucial political tenets was the idea that government was based on the consent of the people. So why did the Loyalists leave the United States, a society whose political independence was founded on liberal beliefs?

The defenders of fragment theory offer different answers to this question. Some argue that the liberalism of the Loyalists was diluted by *conservative* or *Tory* political beliefs: deference toward established authority and institutions, an acceptance of inequality between classes as the natural condition of society, and a greater stress on preserving social order than on protecting individual freedoms.[9] Others reject the view that Tory values were ever a legitimate part of English Canada's political culture, arguing that this belief system had no roots in the pre-revolutionary American colonies and therefore could not have been exported to English Canada through the Loyalist migration.[10] The Loyalists were 'anti-American Yankees' who had rejected American independence because of their loyalty to the British Empire and to the monarchy and their dislike of republican government (or, as they were more likely to put it, 'mob rule'). Their quarrel was not with liberal ideology, as shown by the fact that they immediately clamoured for elected assemblies and the political rights they had been used to in America. Bell and Tepperman thus argue that:

Forced to leave their country, the Tories, or Loyalists, suffered profound doubts. Expulsion kept the Loyalist from basing a fragment identity on the liberal principles of John Locke. Made to give up his real identity, the Canadian Loyalist invented a new one. As a substitute, it was not quite good enough, of course. How could it be, when he had continuously to deny its true nature, liberalism? 'The typical Canadian,' an Englishman observed a hundred years ago, 'tells you that he is not, but he is a Yankee—a Yankee in the sense in which we use the term at home, as synonymous with everything that smacks of democracy.' The Loyalist in Canada is thereafter always a paradox, an 'anti-American Yankee.' Only one path leads out of his dilemma: creating a myth that helps him survive. In this myth, he insists that he is British.[11]

The debate over how important non-liberal values were among the Loyalists is not merely academic. Contemporary analyses of English Canada as a more deferential and conservative society than the United States often trace this alleged difference back to the original ideological mixtures of the two societies. A second reason why the debate matters involves the explanation for Canadian socialism. Some of those who contend that conservative values were an important and legitimate component of English Canada's original cultural inheritance go on to argue that the emergence of socialism in Canada was facilitated by, first, the fact that liberalism never achieved the status of a national creed (as it did in the United States) and, second, the fact that social class was not a foreign concept in English Canada.[12] Conservatism and socialism, according to this view, are two varieties of collectivism.

Formative Events: Counter-revolution and the Conquest

Societies, like human beings, are marked by certain major events at critical periods in their development. These events are 'formative' in the sense that they make it more probable that a society will evolve along particular lines instead of along others. In the world of politics, these formative events are associated with both ideas and institutions. For example, the American Revolution was fought in the name of liberal values and was followed by the adoption of a constitution and structures of government that enshrined the victors' preference for dispersed political power, a weak executive, and guarantees for individual rights. The institutions put in place after the Revolution embodied eighteenth-century liberal values of individual freedom and limited government. They shaped the subsequent pattern of American politics by promoting and legitimizing behaviour and issues that conformed with these values.

The main exponent of the formative events theory of political culture is American sociologist Seymour Martin Lipset. He first introduced it by arguing that the political development of the United States has been shaped by its revolutionary origins, while that of English Canada has been shaped by its *counter*-revolutionary origins. Lipset writes:

Americans do not know but Canadians cannot forget that two nations, not one, came out of the American Revolution. The United States is the country of the revolution, Canada of the counterrevolution. These very different formative events set indelible marks on the two nations. One celebrates the overthrow of an oppressive state, the triumph of the people, a successful effort to create a type of government never seen before. The other commemorates a defeat and a long struggle to preserve a historical source of legitimacy: government's deriving its title-to-rule from a monarchy linked to church establishment. Government power is feared in the south; uninhibited popular sovereignty has been a concern in the north.[13]

Many of those who found themselves on the losing side of the American Revolution—the Loyalists—migrated north. They were the founders of an English-speaking society that originated in its rejection of the new American republic. This original rejection would be repeated several times: in the War of 1812; in the defeat of the American-style democratic reforms advocated by the losers in the 1837–8 rebellions in Lower and Upper Canada; in the 1867 decision to establish a new country with a system of government similar to that of Great Britain. The political history of Canada, including many of the major economic and cultural policies instituted by Canadian governments, reads largely as a series of refusals in the face of Americanizing pressures.

Is rejection of American political values and institutions proof of the greater strength of conservative values in English Canada? Some of those who agree with Lipset about the importance of formative events do not agree that counter-revolutionary gestures signify *ideological conservatism*. David Bell and Lorne Tepperman have argued that Loyalism concealed an underlying *ideological liberalism*. They acknowledge that the Loyalists were not anti-government and that Canadians ever since appear to have been more willing to use the state for social, economic, and cultural purposes than have their American neighbours. But, they argue, a fondness for government is not inconsistent with liberal values. It is only in the United States, where the Revolution was directly about the tyranny of government, that liberalism acquired a strongly anti-government character.[14]

If Loyalism was not a conservative ideology, what was it? Bell and Tepperman argue that Loyalism was essentially a self-justification for not being American. Faced with the paradox of being cast out of a society whose political values they shared, the Loyalists had a serious identity crisis. They resolved it by insisting on their Britishness and by constant criticisms of American values and institutions. This anti-Americanism is a component of Loyalism that endures even today. It explains, according to Bell and Tepperman, English Canada's centuries-old national identity puzzle.

What 1776 represents for English Canada's political development, the British conquest of New France in 1759 represents for that of French Canada. The Conquest has always occupied a central place in French-Canadian nationalism, testifying to French Canadians' own awareness of its significance. The motto on Quebec licence-plates, 'Je me souviens' ('I remember'), is in fact an oblique reference to the time before the Conquest, when French-speaking Canadians presumably were free from the oppression of Ottawa and English Canadians. Particularly under Parti Québécois governments in Quebec it has been common for the Conquest to be mentioned in official government documents on subjects ranging from language to the economy and federal-provincial relations.

There is no agreement as to how the Conquest has affected the ideological development of French Canada on this question. Some, like historian Michel Brunet and sociologist

Marcel Rioux, have argued that the Conquest cut off the development of a French-speaking bourgeoisie—Francophones were rarely found in Canada's corporate élite until only a few decades ago—thereby depriving French Canada of the class that elsewhere was the main carrier of liberal political values. The mantle of social leadership, and the task of defining French-Canadian society, eventually fell on the Catholic Church and the ideologically conservative politicians who accepted the clerics' interpretation of that society as Catholic, French-speaking, non-liberal, and agrarian (in about that order of importance).

Others, like historian Fernand Ouellet and political scientist Louis Balthazar, maintain that there was no fledgling bourgeoisie, and therefore no catalyst for liberal political reform, in the first place. French Canada, they argue, was essentially a feudal society at the time of the Conquest. It fixated at this pre-liberal/pre-capitalist stage because it was cut off from the future, not because French Canada was deprived of something that it once possessed.

History did not, of course, stop at the Conquest. The crushed 1837 rebellion in Lower Canada (Quebec) signalled the defeat of the politically liberal *patriotes*, and consolidated the dominance of the conservative ideology. This ideology would ultimately collapse by the end of the 1950s, finally brought down by the weight of the enormous social and economic transformations that the conservatives had ignored and even denied. Since then, conservative ideology has had little credibility in Quebec, but the memory of the Conquest continues to be a favourite starting point for Quebec nationalists.

Economic Structures and Political Ideas

From a class analysis perspective, both fragment theory and the formative events explanation are 'hopelessly idealistic'.[15] This is because they locate the sources of political values and institutions primarily in ideas—the 'cultural baggage' of fragment theory and the cultural mindset or *idée fixe* associated with the notion of formative events. An economic interpretation of values and structures, by contrast, explains culture and the institutions that embody and perpetuate it as the products of class relations. These class relations are themselves rooted in the particular system of economic production and distribution—the *mode of production* as Marxists generally call it—that is found in a society at any point in time. Ideas and institutions change in response to transformations in the economic system and in the class relations associated with this system. The dominant ideas and existing political arrangements of a society are not, however, merely the shadows cast by economic phenomena. But what sets this approach apart from the other two we have examined is the belief that *culture and institutions are the embodiments of power relations whose sources lie in the economic system*.

How is political culture produced? By whom? For whom? With what effects? How do political institutions embody and reinforce the power relations that characterize society? These are the questions addressed by those who approach political values and institutions from the angle of economically determined class relations. They argue that the dominant ideas of a society are inevitably those of its most powerful class, i.e., those who control the system of economic production and distribution. This is because important means of forming and disseminating ideas and information are controlled by the dominant class, such as the privately owned mass media. Others, including the schools, mainstream religious organizations, and the state, accept and propagate the values of this class for reasons more subtle than ownership. Chief among these reasons is their support for *social order* and their rejection of tendencies and ideas that fundamentally challenge the status quo. None of these major institutions is in the business of overturning society. They depend on a stable social order to carry out their respective activities and to satisfy their particular organizational needs. But the social order they support, and whose values they accept, embodies a particular economic system and the power relations it produces. Defence of established institutions and values is not, therefore, a class-neutral stance.

Why would the members of subordinate classes embrace values and beliefs that, according to this class perspective, are basically justifications for the self-interest of the dominant class? The answer has two parts. First, those who are not part of the dominant class—and by definition this would include the majority of people—may be the victims of *false consciousness*. This concept, first used by Karl Marx, involves the inability of the subordinate classes to see where their real interests lie. For example, deference to established authority and belief in a hereditary aristocracy's natural right to rule—ideas that defend the privileges of the dominant class in a feudal society—would seem to reinforce the subordinate social position of those who are not fortunate enough to be born into the ruling aristocracy. In liberal societies, the widespread belief that opportunities to move up the socio-economic ladder are relatively open to those who are willing to work hard is argued by some to reinforce the dominant position of that small minority who control the economy and who account for most of society's wealth. After all, they argue, there is abundant empirical evidence that significant barriers to socio-economic mobility exist, that a good deal of poverty is passed on from generation to generation, and that those at the top of the socio-economic pyramid constitute a largely self-perpetuating élite. And yet we learn in school, through the mass media, and in countless other ways that equality of opportunity, not systemic inequality, is a characteristic feature of our society.

The second reason why, according to this class perspective, members of subordinate classes accept the ideas of the dominant class as 'common sense' is because these ideas conform, to some significant extent, to their personal experience. Democratic claims about the fundamental equality of all persons have a false ring in societies where some people are denied a share of this equality because they are Black or female, for example. But in a society in which, under the constitution, there are no second-class citizens and where everyone has the right to vote and participate in politics and enjoys equal protection under the law, claims about equality may appear to be valid. Or consider the liberal belief, discussed earlier, that opportunities to acquire wealth and social standing are relatively open. There is, in Canada and in other liberal societies, enough evidence of this mobility to make the proposition appear true. While some people never escape the socio-economic circumstances they are born into, many others do. There is enough proof that hard work and/or intelligence pays off in terms of material success to make liberalism's claim about what determines a person's socio-economic status a credible one. As Patricia Marchak observes, 'the propagation of an ideology cannot occur in a vacuum of experience; there must be a fair amount of congruence between personal experience and ideological interpretation for the propaganda [read, "dominant ideology"] to be successful.'[16] Where this congruence is either weak or totally absent, the dominant class must rely on force to uphold its rule.

This idea that a certain degree of congruence between the dominant values and beliefs of a society and the lived experience of most of its members must exist, otherwise the ideas of the dominant class will be exposed as pure self-interest, is important. It means that what some have called 'false consciousness' cannot be totally false. Ideological systems that are not anchored in the social and economic realities of those subject to them are just not viable. We can understand this better by looking at the case of Quebec and the ideological changes associated with that province's 'Quiet Revolution' of the 1960s.

As recently as the 1950s, the dominant ideology in French-speaking Quebec was conservative. It was an ideology based on the concept of *la survivance* (survival): conserving the religious and linguistic heritage of French Canada in the face of assimilationist pressures. While possessing the formal structures of political democracy, Quebec's political life was dominated by autocratic politicians, rampant patronage, and social institutions—notably the Church and conservative newspapers—that encouraged submission to established authority.[17] Functions like education and social services, which in virtually all industrial democracies were already under state control, were still in the hands of the Church. Even the province's Francophone labour unions were predominantly confessional, linked to a Church whose ideas about industrial relations were shaped largely by its concern for preserving social harmony. In short, the dominant ideology and the social institutions that embodied it were conservative.

This conservatism, linked as it was to the social dominance of the Church and to a sharply limited role for the provincial state, was increasingly out of step with the industrial society that had been evolving in Quebec throughout the twentieth century. Those who advocated reforms that entailed a more interventionist role for the Quebec state, such as public control over education and social assistance, and whose vision of Quebec was of a secular industrial society, necessarily found themselves in conflict with the spokespersons for the conservative ideology. The reformist elements in Quebec politics had on their side the fact by the 1950s the typical Québécois was a city-dweller who worked in a factory, store, or office,[18] and a new middle class of university-educated Francophone professionals was gaining numerical strength in the province.[19] This new middle class was the leading force behind the expansion of the Quebec state that took place in the early to mid-1960s. Ultimately, the lack of 'congruence' between the values of the conservative ideology and the personal experience of most Québécois brought about the collapse of one dominant ideology and its replacement by one more in tune with those social groups—the new middle class and the growing Francophone business community—who have dominated Quebec politics since the Quiet Revolution.

The Interplay of Political Institutions and Values

Canadian politics is often said to be more élitist than the politics of the United States. Deals struck between élites, particularly between the Prime Minister and provincial premiers, in which social groups and elected legislatures often have little input, are a routine feature of the Canadian political scene. Some, like S.M. Lipset, argue that the greater deference of Canadians toward authority, and their weaker commitment to liberal values, explains why Canadian politics is more élitist. Lipset ascribes this difference to the formative events that shaped the political institutions, symbols, and attachments of the two societies, while fragment theory emphasizes the ideological differences between the founding communities and the Tory tinge of the Loyalists who left the United States for Canada. But both of these explanations maintain that contemporary differences in the political cultures of English Canada and the United States have their roots in earlier ideas and political institutions.

The class perspective is less likely to attribute much significance to the claim that Canadian politics is more élitist. Instead, a class analysis focuses on the identical role that liberal-democratic ideology and institutions play in buttressing the social and economic dominance of each society's capitalist class. National differences do exist, and they can often be traced to the particular value inheritance, political structures, and social composition of Canada and the United States. But they are overshadowed by the influence that structures of economic power—class relations—have on a society's political ideas and institutions.

An alternative to these three explanations of political culture has recently been developed by historian Gordon Stewart. In *The Origins of Canadian Politics*,[20] Stewart argues that the pattern of contemporary Canadian politics was formed in the crucible of the mid-1800s. During this period, when the system of *responsible government* was achieved, the more élitist tendencies usually attributed to Canadian politics were embedded in the institutions and practices of political life. Responsible government is government by a Prime Minister and cabinet that are accountable to, and can be removed by, a majority of the legislature. What was at stake during this critical period was the precise balance between the executive, i.e., the cabinet, and the legislature. Stewart argues that the balance was ultimately resolved in favour of a relatively strong executive whose dominance was consolidated through close control over partisan patronage and the bureaucracy. He agrees with the proposition that Canadian politics is more élitist than that of the United States. But Stewart locates the source of this difference in the unique institutional arrangements and political practices adopted in each country. These, more than the early value differences between Americans and Loyalists, between revolutionaries and counter-revolutionaries, have reached into the future to shape political culture.

At the heart of Stewart's interpretation of political culture is the struggle between statist and participatory tendencies in liberal democracy, a struggle he traces back to the conflict between 'court' and 'country' pressures in Britain during the late seventeenth and early eighteenth centuries. The 'court' position defended centralized political power, a strong executive, and the traditional prerogatives of the Crown. The 'country' position was opposed to a strong executive, favouring instead a powerful legislature capable of acting as a check on the executive's power. This 'country' position was embodied in demands for the protection of individual liberties and property rights against infringements by the state, and was associated with the interests of local economic élites who came into conflict with the 'court' faction over issues like taxation.[21]

The terms 'court' and 'country' sound rather archaic to a late twentieth-century ear. Nevertheless, the conflict they describe is no less relevant today than it was in the past. It is a conflict over the state's power in relation to societal groups. The American choice was to create a relatively weak state whose powers were limited by constitutional guarantees of individual rights and freedoms, and by dispersing state power between the various branches of government (the system of checks and balances) and between levels of government (federalism). Canada, Stewart argues, opted for a significantly different arrangement when the issue of the legislature's relationship to the executive was being resolved. A powerful legislature and an enfeebled executive appeared too much like the American democracy that the Loyalists had rejected, and at the same time appeared to be a disloyal rejection of the symbols and institutions of monarchical power that existed in the colonies of British North America. But the pressures to democratize government—to widen the range of participation in public policy-making—were irresistible. What eventually emerged from this struggle was a compromise that retained a powerful executive while rendering it more responsive to the elected legislature. But making the executive more responsive did not mean limiting the powers of government. Instead, it meant opening up the network of government patronage—the positions, contracts, and honours dispensed by the public authorities—to those groups represented in the legislature.

Stewart accepts the claims that Canadian politics has been more élitist than in the United States and that Canadians have been less hostile to a large and interventionist state than their American counterparts. The explanation for these differences in political culture lies, he argues, in the greater strength of statist forces in Canada when the institutional relationship between the executive and the legislature was being forged. The political party system that developed within Canada's system of parliamentary government reinforced these statist tendencies. This was due to the fact that patronage, the 'spoils of power', served as the glue that held together the Liberal and Conservative parties, seeping into every corner of the public sector until well into the present century. While there is nothing uniquely Canadian about patronage, Stewart argues that it dominated Canadian politics for the first several decades after Confederation to a greater extent than was the case in either the United States or Britain during this era. The legacy of this period is a Canadian tradition of strong party leaders, strong executive dominance over the legislature, and an élitist style of policy-making that finds its epitome in the deal-making that takes place between the Prime Minister and premiers, often with little or no real legislative or popular input. It is, in short, a deferential political culture.

The Political Ideas of Canadians

What do Canadians believe about politics? Is it true that they value social order more, and individual freedom less, than their American counterparts? Does French Canada, and more particularly French-speaking Quebec, constitute a 'distinct society' in terms of its values and beliefs? Is it reasonable to talk about the political ideas of English-speaking Canadians, or are the regional differences in political culture too great to warrant such an approach?

There are many possible ways of approaching the subject of political culture. In the following pages we will organize our analysis under four themes: community, freedom, equality, and attitudes toward the state. These tap crucial dimensions of political culture, while at the same time allowing us to explore the differences and similarities between French- and English-speaking Canadians, between different regions of the country, and between Canadians and Americans. The evidence we will use includes both survey research data on attitudes and measures of actual behaviour—of individuals, groups, and governments—from which values can be inferred.

Community

'Canadians', someone has written, 'are the only people who regularly pull themselves up by the roots to see whether they are still growing.' This search for a national identity unites successive generations of Canadians. Indeed, as the above remark suggests, it may be that the obsessive and often insecure introspection of Canadians is itself one of the chief characteristics of the Canadian identity (in English Canada, at least).

The roots of this preoccupation with national identity go back to the Conquest and the American War of Independence. The Conquest laid the basis for a society in which two main ethnolinguistic communities would cohabit—communities whose values and aspirations would often be at cross-purposes. The American War of Independence, as discussed earlier, was followed by the emigration of Loyalists from the United States to the British colonies that would become Canada. Founded by those who rejected the republican democracy to the south, English Canada would constantly compare itself to that society and seek to explain and justify its separate existence.

In more recent years these two historical pillars of Canada's identity 'crisis' have been joined by newer challenges to the *political community*. These have come from Aboriginal Canadians and from some ethnic minorities who reject what they argue is their marginalization within Canadian society. Lacking a confident unifying sense of national identity, Canadian society has been buffeted by identity politics and the often irreconcilable definitions of Canada—sometimes proposing the dismemberment of the country as we know it—advanced by various groups.

The term 'political community' implies, quite simply, a shared sense of belonging to a country whose national integrity is worth preserving. This is something less than nationalism, which defines a community by its language, ethnic origins, traditions, or unique history. And it is not quite the same as patriotism, which one associates with a more fervent and demonstrative love of country and its symbols than is usually considered seemly in Canada. Political community is, rather, what historian W.L. Morton once described as 'a community of political allegiance alone'.[22] National identity, in such a community, is free from cultural and racial associations. Instead, national identity is essentially political—a sense of common citizenship in a country whose members have more in common with one another than with the citizens of neighbouring states and who believe that there are good reasons for continuing to live together as a single political nation. The term 'political nationality' is used by Donald Smiley to refer to precisely this sort of non-ethnic, non-racial sense of political community.[23]

The importance of national identity and a sense of political community in politics is nowhere better illustrated than in the break-up of the former Soviet Union and Yugoslavia after the end of the Communist Party's monopoly over power. Nationalist aspirations and bitter animosities that had been kept in check under totalitarian rule were unleashed, undermining any possibility that these countries could retain their pre-reform boundaries. There was, quite simply, no popular basis for political community in these formerly Communist political systems. Once democratic institutions were in place, their break-up was inevitable.

The spectre of Canadian troops laying siege to Hull, or of armed barricades where the Trans-Canada highway crosses the border between Ontario and Quebec, probably seems like a lurid fantasy to the minds of most Canadians. The great national bust-up, if it comes about, would almost certainly be acrimonious. But it is unlikely that the sort of civil war unleashed by the break-up of Yugoslavia into Serbia, Croatia, and Bosnia would occur if Quebec were to declare its independence. Not everyone agrees. In public statements toward the end of 1991 Gordon Robertson, former Chief Clerk of the Privy Council under Pierre Trudeau, raised precisely the spectre of the former Yugoslavia in arguing that the break-up of Canada could very well be violent.

A more imminent possibility, perhaps, is that of another violent confrontation between Native Canadians and federal or provincial authorities, such as occurred at Oka, Quebec, during the summer and autumn of 1990. A group of Mohawk Warriors, protesting the planned expansion of a golf course on land they claimed as their own, barricaded a road leading to the golf course. The confrontation eventually escalated, resulting in the death of one Quebec police officer, a sympathy blockade by Mohawks of an important commuter bridge near Oka and other sympathy blockades of rail lines and roads by other Indian bands in communities across the country, riots involving the white townspeople of Oka and members of the local Mohawk band, intervention by thousands of Canadian troops, and even United Nations observers.[24] Fears of another Oka were raised in 1995 when small groups of Natives occupied land that they claimed was sacred at Lake Gustafsen, BC, and Ipperwash Provincial Park in Ontario. Violence broke out in both cases and a Native was shot dead at Ipperwash.

Outbursts of violence on the scale of Oka are not typical of Canadian politics. But they are not unknown. Indeed, Canada's sense of community has often seemed terribly fragile, threatened by French-English tensions, western grievances against Ontario and Quebec, and, most recently, conflicts between the aspirations of Native Canadians and the policies of federal and provincial governments. This apparent fragility needs to be viewed alongside evidence suggesting that the country has been relatively successful in managing (repressing, critics would say) the tensions that have threatened it. The existing constitution dates from 1867, making it one of the oldest and most durable in the world. Moreover, the territorial integrity of the country has (so far) remained unshaken by either civil war or secession. This is not to understate the importance of the rifts in Canada's sense of community. But the problems of Canadian unity and identity should be viewed from a broader perspective.

There are four major challenges to the Canadian political community. These are:

- French-English relations;
- Native demands for self-government;
- American influence on Canadian culture;
- Regional tensions.

The first two have occasionally been associated with political violence and calls for the redrawing of territorial boundary lines. They represent clear challenges to the Canadian political community, as we defined this earlier. The third challenge, that of American influence, has assumed forms that are less obviously territorial. Nevertheless, its impact on the Canadian political community has been great. We will examine American influences separately in the section on 'Independence' in Chapter 3.

The fourth challenge, regional tensions, has been an important factor in Canadian politics from the country's inception. We would argue, however, that regional grievances and conflicts have never threatened the territorial integrity of Canada. Westerners and, less stridently, eastern Canadians have long complained about policies and institutions that favour the interests of Ontario and Quebec. But their resentment has never boiled over to produce politically significant separatist movements in these regions or popular defection from the *idea* of Canada. The importance of regionalism will be discussed in Chapter 5.

For most of Canada's history, relations between the Francophone and Anglophone communities have not posed a threat to the political community. The differences and tensions between Canada's two major language groups have been managed through political accommodations between their political élites. This practice arguably goes back to the Quebec Act of 1774. Official protection was extended to the Catholic Church and Quebec's civil law system just when the British authorities were worried about the prospect of political rebellion in the American colonies spreading north. The tradition of deal-making between French and English Canada acquired a rather different twist in the couple of decades prior to Confederation, when the current provinces of Ontario and Quebec were united with a common legislature. The practice of dual ministries, with a leader from both Canada East (Quebec) and Canada West (Ontario), quickly developed, as did the convention that a bill needed to be passed by majorities from both East and West in order to become law. The federal division of powers that formed the basis of the 1867 Confederation continued this deal-making tradition. The assignment to the provinces of jurisdiction over education, property and civil rights, and local matters was shaped by Quebec politicians' insistence on control over those matters involving cultural differences.

This tradition of élitist deal-making has continued throughout Canada's history at two different levels. Nationally, the federal cabinet and national political parties, particularly the Liberal Party of Canada, have been important forums where the interests of Quebec could be represented. But as the powers of the provincial governments have increased, the ability to represent the interests of French and English Canada within national institutions has become less important than whether compromises can be reached between the governments of Canada and Quebec.

The *modus vivendi* that for a couple of centuries prevented French-English conflicts from exploding into challenges to the idea of a single Canada seemed to come unstitched during the 1960s. Quebec independence, which previously had been a marginal idea that surfaced only sporadically in the province's politics, became a serious proposition advocated by many French-speaking intellectuals and apparently supported by a sizable minority of Québécois. The independence option spawned a number of organized political groups during the 1960s. In 1968, most of them threw their support behind the pro-independence Parti Québécois (PQ). Since then, the debate over whether the province should remain in Canada, and if so on what terms, has been one of the chief dimensions of Quebec political life.

In attempting to understand how great a threat Quebec separatism has posed to the Canadian community, we will consider two measures. They are political violence and public attitudes.

Political Violence

Canadians are not accustomed to the violent resolution of political disputes. There have been only two political assassinations since Confederation, the first when D'Arcy McGee was shot down on the muddy streets of Ottawa in 1868 and the second in 1970 when Quebec's Minister of Labour, Pierre Laporte, was strangled to death by members of the Front de libération du Québec. *The World Handbook of Social and Political Indicators* ranks Canada well down the list of countries in terms of riots, armed political attacks, deaths from domestic political violence, and government sanctions to repress or eliminate a perceived threat to the state. Non-violent protest has occupied a more prominent place in Canadian politics, as one would expect in any genuine democracy. But even here, protest demonstrations historically have been much rarer in Canada than in most other advanced industrialized democracies.[25]

Violence has not, however, been either absent or unimportant in Canadian politics. Much of that violence has involved labour disputes or workers' protests where the police or military were called in to protect the interests of employers and the capitalist social order. The violent suppression of the Winnipeg General Strike in 1919 and the use of the Regina police in 1935 to break up the 'On to Ottawa Trek' of unemployed workers during the depth of the depression are perhaps the two most noteworthy instances of such violence. The forcible detention of many Japanese, German, and Italian Canadians during World War Two is another instance of state political violence. Indeed, in most of these cases the state decided to use violence to settle some conflict or deal with some perceived menace. The most significant instances of political violence instigated by groups or individuals against the state have been related to the French-English conflict and, more recently, the status of Canada's Native population.

The almost tribal animosities that have existed between French and English Canadians have crystallized around violent events on several occasions. The hanging of the Francophone Métis leader Louis Riel in 1885, after the military defeat of his provisional government in the territory of Saskatchewan, provoked denunciations of the Conservative government and its leader, Sir John A. Macdonald, from many Francophone leaders. Although they did not sympathize with the rebellion that Riel led, Francophones felt that the government's unwillingness to commute Riel's execution sentence was influenced by anti-French prejudice. Violence broke out again in 1918 over the conscription issue. French Canadians believed that Canada's involvement in World War One was motivated by the colonial attachments that English Canadians still felt for Britain, and they opposed the imposition of conscription. Anti-conscription riots broke out in Quebec City during the spring of 1918, the culmination of simmering recriminations and animosities between French and English Canadians over Canada's relationship to the British Empire.

The 1960s saw renewed violence, this time a spate of bombings and vandalism directed at symbols of the federal government's authority and Anglophone domination in the province of Quebec. This was mainly the work of the FLQ, a very small group of people who achieved national prominence when they kidnapped British trade commissioner James Cross and Quebec cabinet minister Pierre Laporte in October, 1970. The federal government reacted by invoking the War Measures Act, under which normal civil liberties were suspended. About 500 people were eventually detained under the authority of the Act, although none of them were ultimately charged. Laporte's body was found shortly after imposition of the Act. Cross was released by the FLQ a few weeks later in exchange for safe passage out of the country for his captors.

The October Crisis, as the affair came to be called, was unique in Canada's political history. It was the only occasion when the War Measures Act has been invoked during peacetime. The government of Pierre Trudeau argued that civil order was teetering on the verge of collapse in Quebec and that there existed a state of 'apprehended insurrection'. Most commentators argue that Ottawa's reaction was excessive, even in the unfamiliar circumstances of political kidnappings and uncertainty that existed at the time. Excessive or not, the October Crisis needs to be placed in its proper perspective. The political kidnappings were the work of a tiny band of political extremists whose tactics enjoyed little support among Quebec nationalists. Although there was some sympathy for the goals of the FLQ, this evaporated after the murder of Pierre Laporte.

Perhaps the most revealing lessons to be drawn from the October Crisis involve the attitude of the Canadian public and the actions of the state when confronted with political violence. Canadians were overwhelmingly supportive of the decision to invoke the War Measures Act and both opposition parties in the House of Commons supported the government's actions. The state, faced with a challenge to its authority, reacted with its own violence, rounding up hundreds of Quebec nationalists who had absolutely nothing to do with the militant FLQ. Kenneth McNaught argues that this is a recurring pattern in Canadian history, the 'stringent suppression of violence when it occurs or is threatened and lenience toward the instigators once the crisis has been weathered'.[26]

Public Attitudes

'Égalité ou indépendance!' (Equality or independence!) The sentiment is familiar to any contemporary Quebec-watcher. The slogan did not, however, originate with the PQ. *Egalité ou indépendance* was the title of a booklet written by Daniel Johnson, leader of the Union Nationale and Premier of Quebec, 1966–8, and served as his party's campaign slogan in the 1966 election. But neither Johnson nor the Union Nationale was committed to separatism. With the birth of the Parti Québécois in 1968, the province acquired a political party whose leader, René Lévesque, and platform were committed to taking Quebec out of Canada. Daniel Johnson's rhetoric and René Lévesque's commitment represented and helped catalyze an important change in Quebec politics. This change involved the idea of Quebec independence. Before the mid-1960s independence was a marginal idea in the province's politics, supported by many Québécois intellectuals but not taken seriously by the main political parties or by the public. Since then, the idea of independence has been supported by a significant portion of the Quebec citizenry, including, many would argue, a majority of Francophones.

According to public opinion polls, the level of popular support for Quebec independence has ranged between a low of about 20 per cent to a high of nearly 60 per cent over the last few decades (see Figure 2.1). Without reading too much into the numbers, we may say that there appears to be a durable core of support for the idea of Quebec independence. The level of support varies over time and also depending on what sort of independence is envisaged by the pollster's question. Support for 'sovereignty-association'—a term generally understood to mean a politically sovereign Quebec that would be linked to Canada through some sort of commercial union or free trade agreement—is always higher than for outright political and economic separation. It is clear that many Québécois are conditional separatists. Indeed, even among PQ supporters there has always been much less enthusiasm for complete separation than for separation plus economic association.[27]

Figure 2.1 Support for Quebec Independence, 1978–95

"If a referendum was held today regarding Quebec sovereignty, would you vote for or against Quebec sovereignty?"

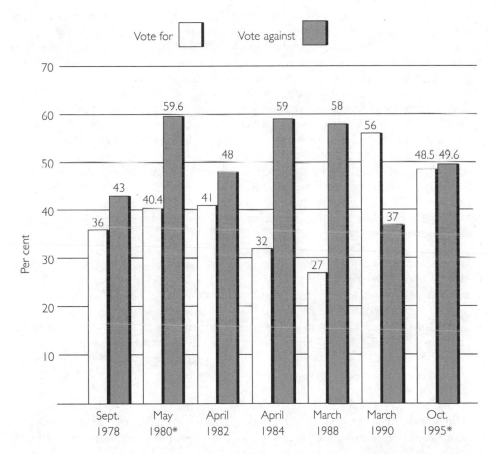

*The results for 1980 and 1995 are based on the referendum questions for each of those years.

Note: The columns for each year may not add up to 100 per cent because "don't know" and "no response" are not included.

Source: Adapted from Simon Langlois, *La société québécoise en tendances, 1960–1990* (Québec Institut québécois de recherche sur la culture, 1990), 649.

When the PQ was first elected to office in 1976, it was clear that Quebec voters were not casting their ballots for separatism. The PQ was committed to holding a referendum on Quebec independence, so that non- and soft-separatists were able to vote for the party without fear that a PQ government would necessarily mean Quebec independence. Indeed, a survey conducted during the 1976 campaign revealed that only about half of those intending to vote for the PQ actually favoured independence.[28] When the PQ sought re-election in 1981, it ran on its record in office rather than on its goal of Quebec independence. In fact, the PQ promised not to hold another referendum during its next term. As in 1976, the PQ's 1981 victory could not be interpreted as a vote for separatism. Instead, the PQ's strategy of distancing itself from the controversial independence issue was an important element of its success on both occasions.

The first direct challenge to the Canadian political community came in May of 1980, when the PQ government held its promised referendum on sovereignty-association. The referendum was very carefully—if complicatedly—worded. It stressed that what was being proposed was not a radical break from Canada but a negotiated political independence for Quebec, which would maintain economic ties to Canada.

> The Government of Quebec has made public its proposal to negotiate a new arrangement with the rest of Canada, based on the equality of nations; this arrangement would enable Quebec to acquire the exclusive power to make its laws, administer its taxes and establish relations abroad—in other words, sovereignty—and at the same time to maintain with Canada an economic association including a common currency; no change in political status resulting from these negotiations will be effected without approval by the people through another referendum; on these terms, do you give the Government of Quebec the mandate to negotiate the proposed agreement between Quebec and Canada? Yes. No.

Despite the PQ's careful strategy, Quebec voters rejected the sovereignty-association option by a vote of 59.6 per cent ('Non') to 40.4 per cent ('Oui'). Even among Francophones, a majority voted against Quebec independence.[29] Advocates of Quebec separatism were quick to point out that sovereignty-association was more popular among younger than older voters. Time, they argued, would eventually turn the tide in favour of independence. It is not clear, however, that this interpretation is sound. The fact that the 'oui' option was most popular among those who entered adulthood in the nationalist 1960s and early 1970s—Quebec's 'baby-boomers'—could mean that the politically formative experiences of this generation were rather exceptional.

In fact, however, it appears that younger Francophone Québécois are as supportive of independence as the generation preceding them. This was demonstrated in the 30 October 1995 Quebec referendum, where an estimated 60 per cent of Francophones voted for the PQ's independence option. University-age Francophones were perhaps the most fervently nationalist group during the referendum campaign. Those who comforted themselves after the 1980 referendum by saying that the *indépendantistes* were the product of an unusual nationalist ferment during the 1960s and 1970s were proven wrong. The narrow victory for the No side—50.6 vs. 49.4 per cent—was achieved because of overwhelming opposition to independence from non-Francophones. A solid majority of Francophones, however, opted for independence.

Or did they? Despite the PQ promise to put the issue of Quebec independence squarely to the voters, instead of hiding behind such reassuring phrases as 'sovereignty-association', the 1995 question was far from being a model of clarity. It read:

Do you agree that Quebec should become sovereign, after having made a formal offer to Canada for a new Economic and Political Partnership within the scope of the Bill respecting the future of Québec and of the agreement signed on 12 June 1995? Yes. No.

Moreover, the Yes side's chief campaign poster featured the Canadian 'Loonie' coin in place of the letter 'O' in the word 'Oui'. Throughout the campaign the PQ and other supporters of independence attempted to reassure soft nationalists that citizens of an independent Quebec could continue to use Canadian currency, carry Canadian passports (in addition to new Quebec ones), and enjoy free trade with the rest of Canada. Apparently, many Yes supporters even believed that after independence they would continue to elect representatives to the Canadian Parliament! In circumstances like these, it is difficult to discern the precise meaning of 60 per cent support among Francophones for independence, except that it clearly signifies a good deal of unhappiness with existing constitutional arrangements.

Accustomed to the challenge that Quebec separatism poses to the political community, most Canadians were probably surprised when the Oka crisis revealed the existence of another challenge to the idea of a single Canada. In fact, however, the armed confrontation at Oka had several precedents. Violent confrontations between Natives and whites punctuate Canadian history, going back to the near extermination of the Beothuk Indians of Newfoundland in the 1700s. Some of the major episodes of violence between Natives and Whites are described in Table 2.2.

These violent clashes are linked by a common thread: the struggle between the traditional independence of Native communities and the authority of, first, European colonial authorities and, then, of the Canadian state. Native resistance to the rule of White authorities, and the efforts of the White authorities to establish their rule and crush Native resistance, span over three centuries of Canadian history. But the struggle between Native aspirations for autonomy and the authority of the White community has only occasionally produced flashpoints of violence. Long periods of apparent peace have been more characteristic of Native-White relations. We say 'apparent peace' because even during these periods the conflict between the aspirations of many Native communities and the demands and restrictions imposed on them by the Canadian state was only dormant, waiting to be catalysed by some issue or incident. The confrontation at Oka turned out to be just such an incident, galvanizing Native groups and throwing into sharp relief the issues of Native land claims and demands for self-government.

We cannot deal with these matters in any detail here.[30] The land claims issue is essentially about who has the right to control territory to which various Native communities claim an historical right. Treaties signed by Ottawa and Native groups after Confederation, which were intended by the non-Native leaders to extinguish Native claims to these territories in exchange for reserves, money, and other benefits, do not cover all of Canada. In fact, an enormous area encompassing much of the North and both the western and eastern extremities of the country was not covered by treaties. Moreover, about 40 per cent of status

Table 2.2 Major Violent Confrontation between Natives and Whites

Date	Native Group and Location	Event
1700s (Newfoundland)	Beothuk	Many were killed by Europeans.
1763	Seneca (area near Detroit)	Led by Pontiac, Huron and Ojibway tribes rebelled against British rule in several bloody confrontations.
circa 1794	Shawnee and other tribes (Ohio River Valley)	Led by Shawnee war chief Tecumseh, several Indian tribes attempted unsuccessfully to resist White settlement and control of the Ohio Valley.
1869–70	Métis (Manitoba)	In the Red River Rebellion, Métis fought for provincial status and guaranteed land and cultural rights.
1885	Métis and Plains Indians (Saskatchewan)	In the North-West Rebellion, a series of battles took place between Métis and Indian forces, on one side, and White militia volunteers and soldiers, on the other.
1990	Mohawk (Quebec)	This armed confrontation at Oka resulted in one death and riots as Natives protested the expansion of a golf course on land that they claimed was theirs by historical right.
1995	Shuswap (British Columbia) Chippewa (Ontario)	Armed confrontations took place at Lake Gustafsen, BC, and Ipperwash Provincial Park in Ontario. In both cases a small group of Natives occupied land they claimed was sacred. A Native was shot dead at the Ipperwash stand-off.

Indians[31] are not members of bands that have signed treaties with Ottawa. Having never been vanquished militarily or given up their territorial rights through a treaty, they claim that the land their ancestors inhabited still belongs to them.

Land claim negotiations have progressed at a snail's pace for decades, leading most Native groups to conclude that Ottawa really has not been serious about settling these claims. The issue had only slightly intruded onto public consciousness until the Oka confrontation, when the Mohawk Warriors claimed to be an independent nation with an historical right to the land on which the local municipality planned to extend a golf course. This claim to be a sovereign nation, outside the authority of Canadian law, was more extreme than most Native demands for self-government. And it was a claim that was steadfastly rejected by the federal government and most Canadians. '[N]ative self-government', Prime Minister Brian Mulroney declared at the time, 'does not now and cannot ever mean sovereign independence. Mohawk lands are part of Canadian territory, and Canadian law must and does apply.'[32] Liberal Prime Minister Jean Chrétien has also rejected the claims of some Natives that they stand outside the authority of Canadian law.

Freedom

'Live free or die.' So reads the motto on licence plates in the state of New Hampshire. Individual freedom is said to be part of the American political creed, symbolized in such icons as the Statue of Liberty and Philadelphia's Liberty Bell and in such historical documents as the Bill of Rights and the Declaration of Independence. Canadians, it is usually claimed, are more willing than Americans to limit individual freedom in pursuit of social order or group rights. Is this true?

The greater stress on individual freedom and suspicion of government control in the United States than in Canada is corroborated by many types of evidence. One of these is literature. Writers like Henry David Thoreau, Jack Kerouac, and Allan Ginsberg embody a powerfully individualistic current that runs through American culture. There is no Canadian Thoreau, whose writings about civil disobedience and the need to resist the demands of society as the price to be paid for a life of virtue and freedom have had an important influence on the libertarian tradition in American politics. Individualism and freedom are also powerful themes in American popular culture. The films of Eastwood, Stallone, and Bronson are among the most popular in a genre that, though not uniquely American, is exported by Hollywood to the rest of the world and represents for the world an archetypically American character. This is the loner who is indifferent to social conventions and the law and whose virtue and attractiveness rest on these traits. Marlon Brando's brooding performance in *The Wild One* and Peter Fonda in *Easy Rider* were in this tradition. More recently, Nicolas Cage captured the spirit of this radical individualism in David Lynch's film, *Wild at Heart*.

Americans' more passionate love affair with freedom is evident in the very different character of the gun control debate in Canada and the United States. When Liberal Justice Minister Alan Rock introduced a law proposing tougher restrictions on gun ownership and a national registry for all firearms, opposition in Canada focused on such matters as whether the legislation would really reduce the use of guns in committing crimes and whether the legislation reflected urban Canada's insensitivity and even hostility to the values and lifestyles of hunters and rural communities. Few people argued, and not many seriously believed, that a fundamental freedom was jeopardized by this legislation.

In the United States, however, proposals to restrict the sale and ownership of firearms invariably face objections from those who see these restrictions as threatening individual freedom. It is a mistake to assume that these objections are merely the cynical ravings of National Rifle Association devotees and white supremacists who wrap themselves in the Second Amendment's guarantee of the 'right to bear arms'. Many Americans believe that gun ownership is a right, not a privilege that governments bestow on citizens. One often hears the argument that restrictions on gun ownership will leave citizens helpless to defend themselves, not simply against criminals but against the state! This argument would be met with blank stares of incomprehension in Canada. But in the United States, even many of those who do not agree that individual freedom would be placed at risk by restrictions on private gun ownership at least understand the premises and beliefs that lie behind this argument.

Mistrust of the state is as old as the American War of Independence. It is woven into the American constitution's system of checks and balances; it was behind the adoption of a Bill of Rights before the ink had scarcely dried on that constitution; and it was also part of the case for federalism that, as James Madison argued in the famous *Federalist Papers*, no. 51, was expected to help check the emergence of any political majority large enough to threaten individual and minority rights. Pride in their system of government and greater patriotism than in most other democracies have also co-existed in the American political culture with a mistrust of government that has its roots in both the revolutionary experience and the individualistic spirit of Americans. Thus many Americans, and not just those who dress in khaki on the weekends and participate in the civilian militias that are perhaps a uniquely American phenomenon, understand the argument that government may be the problem or the enemy and that citizens have a right to defend themselves and should not have to rely on government to do it for them. Canadians are much less likely to share these views.

The state is viewed more benignly north of the Canada-United States border. As Seymour Martin Lipset observes, 'If [Canada] leans toward communitarianism—the public mobilization of resources to fulfill group objectives—the [United States] sees individualism—private endeavor—as the way an "unseen hand" produces optimum, socially beneficial results.'[33] Canadian writer Pierre Berton makes the same point when he maintains that 'We've always accepted more governmental control over our lives than ...[Americans] have—and fewer civil liberties.'[34]

Attitudinal data provide a basis for generalizations about the value attached to freedom in the two societies. Using questions that require people to choose between the protection of individual liberty and the defence of social order, Americans consistently give more freedom-oriented responses (see Table 2.3).

Americans' greater stress on individual freedom is often credited to their individualist culture. Canadians, on the other hand, are often portrayed as less assertive about their rights as individuals, and more concerned than Americans with social order. When presented with a list of six words—tolerant, independent-minded, peaceful, aggressive, clean, and sexy— and asked to choose which one best describes the ideal American or Canadian, 64 per cent of Americans chose either independent-minded (52 per cent) or aggressive (12 per cent). Only 41 per cent of Canadians selected these two ideal characterizations (38 per cent independent-minded; 3 per cent aggressive). Fifty-four per cent of Canadians thought that tolerant (38 per cent) and peaceful (16 per cent) were the features of an 'ideal Canadian', compared to only 33 per cent of Americans (21 per cent tolerant; 12 per cent peaceful).[35]

Equality

If the Loyalists have left a Tory imprint on Canadian politics, we would expect to find that Canadians place a lower value on equality than do Americans. Tories, after all, believed that

Table 2.3 Support for Liberty and Order in Canada and the United States

| | Canadians | | | Americans |
	Francophones	Anglophones	All	
a. 'It is better to live in an orderly society than to allow people so much freedom they can become disruptive.' (percentage agreeing)				
	77	61	65	51
b. 'The idea that everyone has a right to their own opinion is being carried too far these days.' (percentage agreeing)				
	45	33	37	19
c. 'Free speech is just not worth it if it means we have to put up with the danger to society of radical and extremist views.' (percentage agreeing)				
	38	35	36	28
d. 'Free speech ought to be allowed for all political groups even if some of the things that these groups believe in are highly insulting and threatening to particular segments of society.' (percentage agreeing)				
	63	47	51	60

e. 'In times of crisis, do you believe government should or should not have the power to declare a national emergency and remove all civil rights?'

	Canada	United States
Should	48	41
Should not	49	56

Sources: Items a to d from Paul M. Sniderman et al., 'Liberty, Authority, and Community: Civil Liberties and the Canadian Political Culture' (Centre of Criminology, University of Toronto, and Survey Research Center, University of California, Berkeley, 1988), figures 9A-9D. Item e is from the Maclean's-Decima Poll, 'Portrait of Two Nations', Maclean's, 3 July 1989, 32.

the organization of society along class lines was a natural and desirable state of affairs. They were apt to sneer at American democracy as 'mobocracy'. A long line of sociologists, political scientists, and historians, going back to Alexis de Tocqueville and other Europeans who visited North America in the nineteenth century, have generally agreed that America's political culture is more egalitarian and Canada's more hierarchical.

Whatever the historical accuracy of this characterization might have been, it is no longer obviously true. As Figure 2.2 shows, Canadians appear to value equality *more* than do Americans. They are much more likely to support public policies, like a publicly funded health care system and a guaranteed minimum income, that are intended to narrow the gap between the poor and the well-off. A comparative study of the development of the welfare state in Canada and the US corroborates this difference. Robert Kudile and Theodore Marmor argue that ideological differences between the two societies are the main reason for the earlier enactment and more generous character of welfare state policies in Canada,

Figure 2.2 Equality in Canada and the United States

1. *Socio-economic equality*
   'Do you view the following as an absolute right that can never be taken away, or as a limited right, one which in certain circumstances can be limited by government?'
   a) A publicly funded health care system available to all, regardless of financial situation.

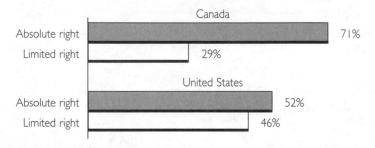

   b) A guaranteed minimum income for everyone.

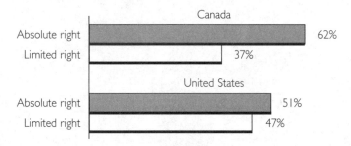

2. *Equality vs. individual freedom*
   a) Too much liberalism has been producing increasingly wide differences in peoples' economic and social life. People should live more equally. (percentage agreeing with the statement)

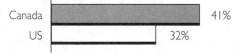

   b) Certainly both freedom and equality are important, but if I were to make up my mind for one of the two, I would consider equality more important, that is, that nobody is underprivileged and that class differences are not so strong. (percentage agreeing with the statement)

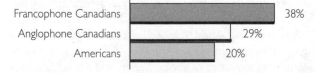

3. *Racial and ethnic equality*

   a) 'Would you be happy, indifferent or unhappy if one of your children married someone from a different racial background?'

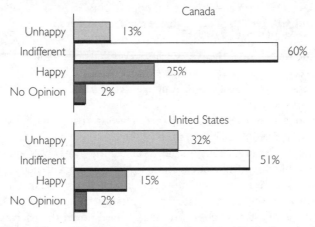

   b) 'What would you think is better for Canada/the United States: that new immigrants be encouraged to maintain their distinct cultures and ways, or to change their distinct culture and ways to blend with the larger society?'

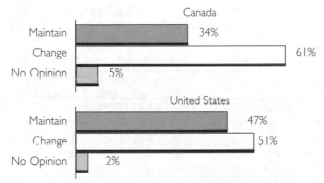

Sources: Parts 1 and 3 are adapted from Maclean's-Decima Poll, 'Portrait of Two Nations', *Maclean's*, 3 July 1989, 48–9. Part 2 is based on data reported in S.M. Lipset, *Continental Divide: The Values and Institutions of the United States and Canada* (Toronto: C.D. Howe Institute, 1989), 157–8.

observing that 'In every policy area it appears that general public as well as élite opinion…[has been] more supportive of state action in Canada than in the United States.'[36]

    Canadians are more likely than Americans to value equality of results, whereas Americans are more likely than their northern neighbours to value equality of opportunity. Numerous cross-national attitudinal surveys confirm this observation.[37] In Canada egalitarianism has its roots in a more collectivist tradition; in the United States it draws on a more individualistic tradition. The value differences between the two societies are shaded rather than starkly contrasting, as parts 1 and 2 of Figure 2.2 show. Nevertheless, they help to explain Canadians' apparently greater tolerance—historically at any rate—for state measures targeted at disadvantaged groups and regions. Lipset's conclusion seems a fair one: 'Canadians are committed to redistribution egalitarianism, while Americans place more emphasis on meritocratic competition and equality of opportunity.'[38]

In Canada, more than in the United States, debates over equality have been about group rights-equality between different groups in society, not equality between individuals. This difference goes back to the founding of the two societies. While the American constitution made no distinction between groups of citizens, the Quebec Act of 1774 incorporated protection for religious rights and the British North America Act of 1867 provided protections for both religious and language rights.

A by-product of Canada's long tradition of recognizing group rights, many have argued, is greater tolerance of cultural diversity than one finds in the United States. This is the familiar, if exaggerated, theme of the Canadian 'mosaic' versus the American 'melting pot'. Although there is considerable historical evidence to suggest that non-French, non-British groups have felt less pressure to abandon their language and customs in Canada than have non-English-speaking groups in the United States, rates of cultural assimilation have been high in both societies. Moreover, Canadian governments have shown themselves to be as capable as their American counterparts of discriminating against ethnic and religious communities. For example, in both countries many people of Japanese origin were deprived of their property and kept confined to camps during World War Two. The religious practices of Doukhobors, Hutterites, Mennonites, and Jehovah's Witnesses have at various times brought them into conflict with either Ottawa or provincial governments. And in both Canada and the United States immigration policy has historically discriminated against non-White, non-European peoples—although this is no longer a fair characterization of policy in either country.

Despite evidence that in Canada, too, tolerance of cultural diversity has known limits, these limits have been less restrictive than in the United States. The treatment of Canada's Native peoples, for example, has been less harsh and less violent than that of America's Native minorities. And there is nothing in Canada's history that compares to the official discrimination and the physical violence directed against American Blacks for much of that country's history. An official policy of multiculturalism has existed in Canada since 1971 and was entrenched in the constitution in 1982.[39] Moreover, Canada's constitution appears to provide a firmer basis for affirmative action programs and other state activities that have as their goal 'the amelioration of conditions of disadvantaged individuals or groups including those that are disadvantaged because of race, national or ethnic origin, colour, religion, sex, age or mental or physical disability.'[40] And we have already seen that more Canadians than Americans are likely to choose 'tolerant' as the word that they feel best describes the ideal citizen of their country.

Nonetheless, some evidence runs counter to the commonly held view that cultural tolerance is greater in Canada than in the United States. A 1989 Maclean's-Decima poll found that Canadians were less positive than Americans toward new immigrants retaining their distinctive cultures (see Figure 2.2). Pollster Allan Gregg interprets this as evidence of a backlash against the non-White, non-European immigrants who have comprised the vast majority of immigrants to Canada since the 1970s.[41] But non-Europeans, particularly people of Asian origin, have for years accounted for most new immigration to the United States.

Why a backlash in Canada but not in the United States? We should not attach too much significance to a single survey question, asked at one point in time. On the other hand, the greater tolerance expressed by Americans should at least suggest the need to reflect critically on old stereotypes of assimilationist Americans and tolerant Canadians.

Debates over gender equality have been an important part of the political scene since the 1960s. In both Canada and the United States attitudes on the appropriate roles and behaviour of men and women have changed sharply in the direction of greater equality. The visible signs of this change are everywhere, including laws on pay equity, easier access to abortion, affirmative action to increase the number of women employed in male-dominated professions, the ways in which females are portrayed by the media, and greater female participation in the political system. These are all indirect measures of attitudes toward gender equality. Although they do not provide a direct indication of cultural values, we might reasonably infer these values from the actions of governments and private organizations. Comparing Canada to the United States using such measures, we come up with a mixed scorecard. The differences between the two societies tend not to be very large, Canada being 'more equal' on some counts, the United States on others.

As in the case of the other dimensions of equality we have examined, there is no evidence to support the claim that Canadians value equality less than Americans do. Indeed, in terms of recognizing group rights, it is fair to say that Canadian governments have gone at least as far as their American counterparts. In one important respect, however, Canadians are unequivocally more committed to an egalitarian society than are Americans. This involves racial equality. Part 3(a) of Figure 2.2 confirms that racist sentiments are more pervasive in the United States than in Canada. This difference clearly has its roots in the very different histories of the two societies. Those who argue that Canadian society historically has placed greater emphasis on hierarchy and ascriptive status, and the United States on equality and achievement, forget that racial inequality was the great blindspot of American liberalism. Canadians can thank the fact that they had no slavery-based plantation economy in their past, for racism is less ingrained in their society than in that of the United States.

Citizen Expectations for Government

Canadians, it has often been argued, are more likely than Americans to look to government to meet their needs. They are, moreover, more likely to accept state actions that they dislike, instead of mobilizing against such policies and the governments that institute them. Thomas Jefferson's declaration that 'That government is best which governs least' is a less accurate encapsulation of Canadian political culture than is the title of a Canadian poetry anthology, *A Government Job at Last*.[42]

This view of Canadians as both more demanding of the state and more passive toward it appears to be backed up by a good deal of evidence. On the expectations side, Canadian governments do more than American ones to redistribute wealth between individuals and regions of the country; their intervention in the health services sector is far more extensive than in the United States; they own corporations whose activities range from producing electricity to television broadcasting, while American governments generally content themselves with regulating privately owned businesses in these same industries; and they are much more actively involved in promoting particular cultural values, especially those associated with bilingualism, than are most governments in the United States. Overall, the state accounts for a larger share of gross national expenditure in Canada than in the United States, and by most appearances government is more intrusive in Canadian society.

What about the evidence for Canadians' alleged passivity in the face of government actions that they dislike? Here, the comparatively élitist nature of policy-making, including the ability of governments to pass laws that either could not get through the American legislative system or only in a much diluted form, is said to demonstrate the greater acquiescence of Canadians in the decisions of their political leaders. For example, in both countries the persistence of large public-sector deficits became an important political issue in the 1980s. But whereas a major part of the Canadian government's response was to increase taxes, which included broadening the range of taxed goods and services through the politically unpopular Goods and Services Tax, proposals for increased taxes remained non-starters in American politics. The middle-class tax revolt embodied in California's 'Proposition 13', which swept across much of the United States during the late 1970s and early 1980s, had no analogue in Canada despite generally higher levels of provincial and local taxation in this country.

To use another example, in Canada it was a decision of the House of Commons—actually, a series of decisions[43]—that eliminated capital punishment, despite widespread public support for the death penalty. In the United States, elected politicians have been more responsive to their constituents' views on this issue, and the death penalty exists in most states. Those limitations that have been placed on capital punishment, including its suspension for several years, have been due primarily to American Supreme Court decisions and not to legislative action.

Canadians' greater faith in government compared to the more sceptical attitudes of Americans owes a good deal to a collectivist ethos that sets Canadians and their history apart from the United States. It is this ethos that Canadian nationalists are invoking when they argue that Canada's public health care system and more generous social programs reflect the 'soul' of this country and that their dismemberment would send Canadians down the allegedly mean-spirited path of American individualism. Some of Canada's most prominent thinkers, including George Grant and Charles Taylor, have argued that the collectivist ethos and greater willingness of Canadians than Americans to use the state to achieve community goals are central to the Canadian political tradition.

In *Lament for a Nation*, Grant argued that the Canadian political tradition was marked by a communitarian spirit that rejected the individualism of American-style liberalism. He traced the roots of this spirit to the influence of conservative ideas and the British connection, which helped to keep alive a benign view of government as an agent for pursuing the common good. This distinctive national character was, Grant believed, doomed to be crushed by the steamroller of American liberalism and technology, which, he maintained in later works, would ultimately flatten national cultures throughout the capitalist world.

Grant's 'lament' was in the key of what has been called *red Toryism*. Red Tories are conservatives who believe that government has a responsibility to act as an agent for the collective good and that this responsibility goes far beyond maintaining law and order. Grant and others in this tradition espouse, for example, state support for culture as through the Canadian Broadcasting Corporation. Red Tories since Grant are comfortable with the welfare state and the principle that government *should* protect the poor and disadvantaged. Red Toryism involves, its critics would claim, a rather paternalistic philosophy of government and state-citizen relations. Defenders, however, maintain that it is compassionate and a true expression of a collectivist national ethos that distinguishes Canadians from their southern neighbours.

Charles Taylor is not a red Tory. Canada's most internationally acclaimed living philosopher is firmly on the left of the political spectrum. He agrees with Grant about the importance of collectivism in Canada's political tradition. Taylor has always been extremely critical of what he calls the 'atomism' of American liberalism, a value system he believes cuts people off from the communal relations that nurture human dignity. Like most Canadian nationalists, he believes implicitly in the moral superiority of Canada's collectivist political tradition.

Taylor is one of the leading thinkers in the contemporary movement known as *communitarianism*. This is based on the belief that real human freedom and dignity are only possible in the context of communal relations that allow for the public recognition of group identities and that are based on equal respect for these different identity groups. Taylor argues that the key to Canadian unity lies in finding constitutional arrangements that enable different groups of Canadians to feel that they belong to Canada and are recognized as constituent elements of Canada. He calls this rather fuzzy formula the recognition of 'deep diversity'. This would include, presumably, official recognition of Quebec as a distinct society, constitutional acknowledgment of a Native right to self-government, and a willingness to allow different communities to belong to Canada in different ways. To some this might sound like a recipe for dismantling whatever fragile sense of Canadian community already exists. Taylor insists, however, that one-size-fits-all notions of community do not work in the modern world.

Canadians' pride in what they believe to be their country's superior quality of life has co-existed in recent years with a widespread sense of economic insecurity and anxiety about the future. (Roy Peterson, *Vancouver Sun*)

Politics unfolds against a backdrop of social and economic conditions. This chapter focuses on the following aspects of Canadian society:

❖ Material well-being.

❖ Equality.

❖ Quality of life.

❖ Independence.

CHAPTER THREE

The Social and Economic Setting

Speaking before an audience of American newspaper editors in Texas in 1995, Prime Minister Jean Chrétien referred to Canada as a 'kinder and gentler nation'. He said that Canadians' most important values were tolerance and sharing. Canada, he said, because of its bilingualism and multicultural character, 'has been referred to by some as the first "post-nationalist" country'.[1] Although he did not mention it to his American audience, he may have been tempted to crow a bit about Canada's first-place ranking on the United Nations' human development index (a measure that combines literacy rates, formal education levels, average longevity, and real purchasing power). Prime Minister Chrétien certainly found other occasions for boasting about Canada's ranking by the UN, including during the 1995 Quebec referendum.

Canadians are indeed fortunate. But that good fortune is not shared by all Canadians. Over four million Canadians fall below the poverty line, the low-income point established by Statistics Canada. More revealingly, hundreds of thousands of people use the food banks that have proliferated in Canada since the 1980s. Some of these people would probably dispute Prime Minister Chrétien's characterization of Canada as a 'kinder and gentler nation'. Within months of the Prime Minister's Texas speech, violence broke out between Aboriginal Canadians and police forces in British Columbia and Ontario, stirring the still fresh memories of the violent confrontation at Oka, Quebec, in the summer of 1990. And in the autumn of 1995 the Prime Minister found himself doing battle against Quebec separatists who obviously were unimpressed with his description of Canada as the 'first "post-nationalist" country'. There seemed to be more trouble in paradise than the Prime Minister had confided to the American newspaper editors.

In this chapter we will examine the social and economic setting of Canadian politics. At various points comparisons will be made between Canada and other countries, between regions in Canada, between various points in Canada's history, and between actual conditions and some idealized standards that have been applied to the performance of Canada's political system. Our goal in this chapter is not, however, chiefly to judge. Instead, our main purpose is to understand the societal context that influences, and is influenced by, politics and public policy. In doing so we will be selective, focusing on aspects of Canadian society and the economy that are closely associated with several general values that most Canadians consider to be important. These include the following:

- material well-being;
- equality;
- quality of life;
- independence.

Obviously, these values will be interpreted differently by different people. Disagreements aside, we have selected these values for two related reasons. First, they represent public purposes that most of us expect governments to preserve or promote. Second, political controversies are frequently about one or more of these values—disagreements over how to achieve them; over what value(s) should give way, and by how much, when they conflict; about whether they are being adequately met, and so on. It makes sense, therefore, to focus on these dimensions of the social and economic setting of Canadian politics.

Political issues and outcomes are not determined in any simplistic manner by such things as the extent and nature of inequalities in Canadian society or the level of material well-being, any more than political ideologies and institutions translate directly into political behaviour and public policy. Like ideology and institutions, the social and economic settings of politics establish boundaries to political life. They do so by determining the sorts of problems a society faces, the resources available for coping with these problems, the nature and intensity of divisions within society, and the distribution of politically valuable resources between societal interests.

Material Well-Being

Canada is an affluent society. This simple fact is sometimes obscured by the news of fresh layoffs, plant closings, slipping competitiveness, and chronic government deficits. For most of the last couple of decades, the average real purchasing power of Canadians was the second highest in the world, topped only by that of Americans. Today Canadians stand sixth (see Figure 3.1). Affluence affects both the opportunities and problems faced by policy-makers. The problem of poverty, for example, assumes a very different character in an affluent society like Canada from that in a poorer society like Mexico or a destitute one like Sudan. Not only does Canada's poverty problem look rather enviable from the standpoint of these other countries, but the means that governments in Canada have available to deal with this problem are far greater than those that can be deployed by the governments of poorer societies. The very definition of what constitute public problems, warranting the attention of

Figure 3.1 Per Capita PPPs* (\$US) for OECD Countries, 1992

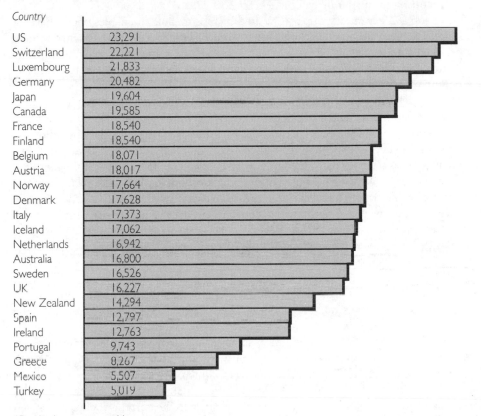

Country

Country	PPP
US	23,291
Switzerland	22,221
Luxembourg	21,833
Germany	20,482
Japan	19,604
Canada	19,585
France	18,540
Finland	18,540
Belgium	18,071
Austria	18,017
Norway	17,664
Denmark	17,628
Italy	17,373
Iceland	17,062
Netherlands	16,942
Australia	16,800
Sweden	16,526
UK	16,227
New Zealand	14,294
Spain	12,797
Ireland	12,763
Portugal	9,743
Greece	8,267
Mexico	5,507
Turkey	5,019

*Purchasing power parities.

Source: Organization for Economic Co-operation and Development, *OECD Economic Surveys: Australia 1995* (Paris: OECD, 1995).

government, is also influenced by a society's material conditions. Environmental pollution, a prominent issue on the public agendas of affluent societies, tends to be buried under the weight of other pressing social and economic problems in less affluent societies.

Within the élite club of affluent societies, cultural and institutional differences are probably more important as determinants of the public agenda and government response to them than are their differences in material well-being. But the particular characteristics of a national economy, factors upon which material affluence depends, are significant influences on the politics and public policies of any society. These characteristics include the sectoral and regional distribution of economic activity, the level and distribution of employment, characteristics of its labour force, the profile of its trade with the rest of the world, and so on. Despite enjoying one of the highest standards of living in the world, Canadians have seldom been complacent about their affluence. Fears that Canada's material well-being may rest on fragile footings have long been expressed. These fears have become increasingly urgent over the last decade, as Canadians have attempted to come to grips with what global economic restructuring means for their future.

A secure job at a decent rate of pay is desired by most people. It enables one to plan for the future and achieve the goals that one has for oneself and one's family. Unemployment can be personally and socially devastating. The political importance of employment is seen in the fact that it is regularly mentioned by Canadians as one of the most important issues facing the country. Governments react with rhetoric, gestures, and policies. These policies may not succeed in maintaining employment at a socially acceptable level—indeed, they may not even be intended to reduce unemployment—but no government would pass up an opportunity to express its commitment to increasing jobs and its sympathy for the unemployed.

What does Canada's employment record look like? Compared to other advanced industrialized democracies, Canada has done fairly well. The national level of unemployment has fluctuated between about 6 and 13 per cent over the last couple of decades, being about 7 to 9 per cent in most years. This may not impress Japanese, Swiss, or West Germans, all of whom have enjoyed average unemployment rates of between 2 and 4 per cent over this period. Canada's unemployment rate, however, has been only slightly above the average for OECD countries.[2] Moreover, the economy's ability to create new jobs has been among the best. This has been important because Canada's labour force has grown more rapidly than those of most other advanced industrial democracies.

Looking at the distribution of employment across sectors of the Canadian economy, one finds that Canada closely resembles the world's other major capitalist economies. A little over 70 per cent of workers are in service industries (sales, communications, transportation, tourism, finance, public administration, etc.), about 20 per cent are employed in the manufacturing sector, and the remaining 5–6 per cent work in primary industries like farming, fishing, forestry, and mining. These shares are very similar to those in our major trading partner, the United States. Over time, the service sector's share of total employment has grown dramatically, from about 40 per cent at mid-century to the current level of over seven in ten jobs. The shares in the primary and secondary sectors have obviously declined, more sharply in primary industries than in manufacturing. These employment trends have led many to worry that the Canadian economy is 'de-industrializing'. In fact, however, these employment trends are broadly similar to those that have characterized all of the world's major capitalist economies over the past several decades.

The last few years have seen the emergence of a politically important debate over the relative value to an economy of service versus manufacturing jobs. Some argue that service industries also produce value, and so there is no reason to worry about a shrinking manufacturing base. Others argue that the manufacturing sector is especially important and that a point can be reached—and may already have been reached in economies like those of Canada and the United States—where further decline of the manufacturing base undermines the overall competitiveness of the economy and drags down real incomes.[3]

Equality

One of the most persistent images that Canadians have of their society is that it has no classes. This image becomes translated into the assertion that Canadians are all relatively equal in their possessions, in the amount of money they earn, and in the opportunities which they and their children have to get on in the world....

That there is neither very rich nor very poor in Canada is an important part of the image. There are no barriers to opportunity. Education is free. Therefore, making use of it is largely a question of personal ambition.[4]

This may well have been the image held by most Canadians when sociologist John Porter wrote *The Vertical Mosaic* (1965). It is doubtful whether Canadians today are as confident that their society is one without serious inequalities. Charges of discrimination made by women's groups, Aboriginals, visible minorities, homosexuals, and other minorities—charges that were muffled until a few decades ago—are common today. The passage of provincial human rights codes and of the Charter of Rights and Freedoms, and the proliferation of human rights officers—ombudsmen, race relations officers, equity officers, and so on—have contributed to this sharpened awareness of inequality. But these reforms were themselves inspired by a growing sense that existing policies and institutions did not adequately protect the equality of citizens and that, in some cases, laws and institutions actually perpetuated inequality.

For various reasons, then, Canadians are probably more aware of inequalities today than they were a few decades ago. But despite this heightened awareness, most Canadians still cling to the belief that their society is basically middle class. This belief—which, we hasten to add, is not totally false—springs from the dominant liberal ideology. Individualism and a belief that opportunities to get ahead in life are open to those with the energy and talent needed to take advantage of them are at the core of this liberal ideology. To say that society is basically middle class means, from this ideological perspective, that it is essentially classless. The fact that some people are extraordinarily wealthy and some others are quite destitute needs to be set alongside an even more prominent fact, i.e., that most Canadians occupy a broad middle band in terms of their incomes and lifestyles.

Wealth is unevenly divided in all societies. Few people believe that the sort of levelling implied by Karl Marx's aphorism, 'From each according to his abilities, to each according to his needs', is desirable. But many people are disturbed by the jarring contrast between conspicuous luxury and destitution in their society. The gap between rich and poor is not as great in Canada as in some other industrialized democracies. Nevertheless, it is considerable and persistent. Moreover, some groups bear the brunt of poverty much more heavily than others.

Figure 3.2 shows that the distribution of income in Canada has remained pretty much unchanged for decades. The richest one-fifth of the population receives close to 44 per cent of all income, while the poorest one-fifth accounts for just under 5 per cent. If social security benefits are left out of the picture, the inequality gap is even wider, the bottom fifth of Canadians accounting for barely 1 per cent of earned income. Compared to the distribution of income in other advanced capitalist societies, Canada's is fairly typical. The distribution of income is more equal than in some countries, such as the United States, but less equal than in others, such as Japan and Sweden.

The distribution of income is only part of the story in any assessment of equality. The other part involves the extent of poverty. 'Poverty' is to some degree a relative concept,

Figure 3.2 Distribution of Income in Canada (total money income), 1957, 1993

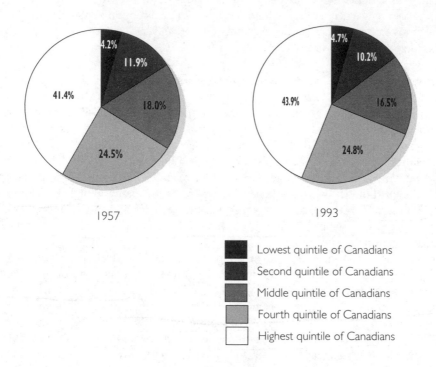

1957

1993

Lowest quintile of Canadians

Second quintile of Canadians

Middle quintile of Canadians

Fourth quintile of Canadians

Highest quintile of Canadians

Source: Statistics Canada, *Income After Tax, Distributions by Size in Canada*, cat. 13-210, annual.

meaning something different in an advanced industrialized society like Canada than in a developing country like Nigeria. In Canada, poverty is usually measured using Statistics Canada's definition of what constitutes an income that is so low that an individual or household lives in 'straightened circumstances'. This is generally referred to as the poverty line, currently defined to mean that more than 56.2 per cent of income (20 percentage points above the national average) is spent on food, clothing, and shelter. Although the number of Canadians whose incomes fall below the poverty line varies from year to year, the figure has fluctuated between about 14 and 17 per cent over the last decade. Two of the groups hardest hit by poverty in Canada are Native Canadians and women. Consider the following facts:

Native Canadians

• The employment rate for Natives is the lowest of any ethnic group, at about two-thirds of the national level. To put this a bit differently, the unemployment rate among Natives is usually between two and two and one-half times the national level.

- The employment rate for Natives living on reserves is only half the Canadian rate.
- About one-half of all status Indians obtain most of their income from employment, compared to roughly 70 per cent of all Canadians.
- Native incomes are about two-thirds the Canadian average.

Women

- Women are more likely than men to be poor. The poverty rate for women is about 25 per cent higher than that for men.
- Over one-quarter of elderly women, compared to about 14 per cent of men, fall below the poverty line (1993).
- Over 60 per cent of single-parent families headed by women fall below the poverty line, about five times the level for those headed by men.
- The poverty rate among single-parent families headed by young mothers is absolutely crushing. For mothers under 25 it is 90 per cent. Among those aged 25–44 it is 58 per cent (1993).
- About half of single women aged 65 or over fall below the poverty line.

Why are these groups particularly susceptible to poverty? The answers are too complex to be explored fully here. A few of the contributing causes may, however, be mentioned. In the case of Native Canadians, discrimination certainly plays a role in explaining their higher jobless rate and lower incomes. Lower levels of education are also a factor. But as John Price notes, these causes are considerably less important than 'cultural heritage, choice of occupation and residence far from the main centres of the economy'.[5] Likewise, poverty among women results from a complex set of causes.[6] These include their segregation in lower-paying occupations, their lower participation rate in the labour force, and the greater number of women than men who work part-time.

Inequality also has an important regional dimension in Canada. Income levels and employment rates vary dramatically and persistently between provinces, as well as between regions within provinces. Personal incomes in the poorest provinces (Newfoundland, New Brunswick, and PEI) are only two-thirds to three-quarters of the Canadian average. If transfer payments from government to individuals and households are excluded from the calculation, incomes in these poorest provinces drop to between 50 and 70 per cent of the national average. Figure 3.3 shows that inter-regional variation in average personal incomes has narrowed over the last few decades. This has been due mainly to government transfers that provide greater income benefits to the residents of the poorer provinces than to those of the richer ones. On the other hand, the gap between the highest and lowest regional rates of unemployment has widened (see Figure 3.4).

One of the important dimensions of equality, and one of the chief influences on it, is socio-economic mobility. This refers to the ability of individuals, families, and groups to move from one social or economic position to another. Socio-economic mobility implies the existence of hierarchically arranged differences in society, such as those that exist between income groups and occupations. These differences exist in all societies to a greater or lesser extent. Where socio-economic mobility is high, movement up and down the social ladder is

Figure 3.3 The Gap Between the Richest and Poorest Provinces, 1954–94

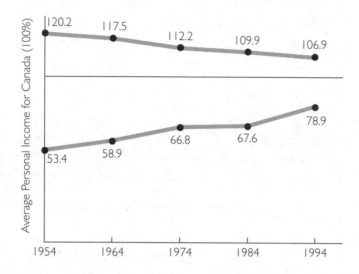

Note: The two provinces used in this comparison are Ontario and Newfoundland.

Source: Statistics Canada, *Provincial Economic Accounts.*

common and the barriers to entry into high-paying occupations, prestigious status groups, or powerful élites are relatively low. This is what students of mobility call an open society. In a closed society there is relatively little intergenerational movement on the social ladder and barriers to entry into privileged social and economic groups are high.

Most Canadians believe that theirs is a relatively open society, and compared to many it is. But an enormous amount of evidence shows that social stratification in Canada remains high and real opportunities to climb the socio-economic ladder are much lower than the conventional wisdom suggests. The 'vertical mosaic' that John Porter analysed three decades ago has been opened up, but gender, ethnicity, race, and family background continue to exert a tremendous downward pull on mobility.

This may be demonstrated in many ways. Data from a national survey of social mobility and status achievement in Canada indicated that the socio-economic backgrounds of individuals explain about one-third of the differences between people in their level of educational attainment.[7] Educational attainment was found to be strongly related to the educational achievements of one's parents and the occupation of one's father. Education is highly correlated with income, and several years of post-secondary education are, of course, necessary to qualify for some of the most prestigious and high-paying professions in Canada. Recent studies confirm that access to these privileged professions is far from open. Glasbeek

Figure 3.4 Regional Unemployment Rates, 1966–93

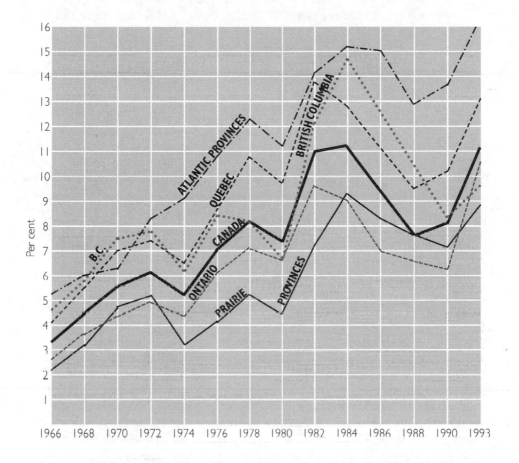

Source: Statistics Canada, *Canadian Economic Observer*, Historical Statistical Supplement 1994/94, cat. 11-210.

and Hasson note that law students still come 'disproportionately from the wealthier classes of societies'.[8] The sons and daughters of physicians—but especially the sons—continue to be far more likely than the children of others to enter medical schools and become physicians themselves. Looked at from the other end of the socio-economic ladder, those born into a relatively poor family where the parents' level of education and occupational status are low are far less likely than the children of middle- and upper-class parents to achieve higher incomes and higher-status occupations as adults.

Can we at least say that mobility has increased over time? Perhaps, although researchers disagree on this issue. There is no doubt that most Canadians are better off than their ancestors were a couple of generations ago. This is what sociologists call structural mobility. But it is not clear that exchange or circulation mobility, i.e., people changing their positions relative to one another, has increased significantly. John Goyder argues that 'there has been a trend toward greater circulation mobility in Canada, but the effect is tiny'.[9]

What about élites in Canadian society? John Porter argued that they were largely self-perpetuating, recruiting new members chiefly from those groups already dominant within them. Does this continue to be true? Academic and journalistic examinations of Canada's corporate élite agree that this group is highly unrepresentative of the general population and that access to it appears to be much greater for those from certain backgrounds than from others. The most systematic studies of the social characteristics of the corporate élite have been carried out by sociologists John Porter and Wallace Clement. Porter's study was based on data for 1951 and Clement's on data for 1972.[10] They both found that this élite (which they defined as the directors of Canada's dominant corporations) was overwhelmingly male, about a third had attended private schools like Upper Canada College or Ridley, most had upper-class backgrounds (50 per cent in 1951 and 59.4 per cent in 1972), those with non-Anglo-Saxon ethnic origins were under-represented (comprising 13.8 per cent of Clement's 1972 group, compared to 55.3 per cent of the Canadian population), and about half (51.1 per cent in 1972) belonged to one or more of the six most prominent private clubs in Canada. The picture they sketched was one of a self-perpetuating group whose social backgrounds and adult activities set them sharply apart from the general population.

The corporate élite operates as a social network that reproduces itself largely through self-recruitment. Education at élite schools adds to what John Porter calls the 'social capital' of its members, reinforcing élite ties that are maintained in the adult world of business. Club membership provides a complement to the boardroom, a social setting that is very much part of the personal relations essential in business life. It is for this reason that the question of private club membership has become a matter of political controversy in recent times. Women's groups especially have charged that the exclusively male character of these clubs reinforces men's dominance of the business world by excluding women from its social network.

Evidence suggests that access to the corporate élite is no more open today than in the past. Using data from 1991, Milan Korac replicated the analysis of Porter and Clement. He reported findings that are almost identical to those of these two earlier studies. For example, men constituted 92 per cent of the corporate élite; 42 per cent had attended exclusive private schools; those from non-Anglo-Saxon backgrounds were still grossly under-represented (only 22.1 per cent of the economic élite, compared to 74.7 per cent of the population); and well over half of the economic élite belonged to one or more of the Toronto Club, the Mount Royal Club, the Rideau Club, and the St James Club.[11]

Access to the political élite is certainly more open than in the past. Traditionally, Canada's major political parties were dominated by males of either British or French ethnic origins. They still are, but the representation of females and Canadians of non-British, non-French origins has increased sharply over the last couple of decades (see Chapter Twelve for data on female representation). The election of Audrey McLaughlin as NDP leader in 1989 marked the first time a woman had been chosen to lead a national political party, and was followed by the 1993 selection of Kim Campbell as leader of the Conservative Party and the unexpected 1995 election of Alexa McDonough as the new NDP leader. A handful of women have led provincial political parties and one, Catherine Callbeck of PEI, has been elected premier of a province. Several of Canada's major cities have had female mayors, going back to the middle of this century. The continuing domination of Canada's political élite by males from the two so-called charter groups, albeit less strikingly than in the past, is less the result of deliberate discrimination against the members of other groups than a product of systemic discrimination.

Why do inequalities like those that we have described in the preceding pages exist? What consequences do they have for Canadian politics and society? These are complex questions. Several factors contribute to inequality: deliberate discrimination, systemic discrimination, choice, and politics.

Deliberate Discrimination

The prejudice that one person feels toward the members of some group or groups becomes deliberate discrimination when it is acted upon. For example, the landlord who refuses to rent to someone he suspects of being homosexual is discriminating against that person and against all members of that group. Deliberate discrimination is characterized by the intent to discriminate. The intent that underlies social prejudice and bigotry is, however, often hard to prove. While there is no doubt that this sort of discrimination is widespread in Canadian society, we would argue that it is less important in explaining inequality than the next three causes.

Systemic Discrimination

This is discrimination without conscious individual intent. It is the discrimination that inheres in traditions, customary practices, rules, and institutions that have the effect of favouring the members of one ascriptive group over another. For example, a controversy erupted several years ago over the refusal of the Royal Canadian Mounted Police to permit a Sikh constable to wear the turban that his religious beliefs required him to wear. Here was a case where the uniform regulations of the RCMP effectively discriminated against the members of a particular group. Another example would be height and/or weight requirements for certain jobs. Because women are typically smaller than men, it could be argued that these requirements are discriminatory. Everyone recognizes, of course, that some job requirements may be reasonable and cannot be jettisoned even if they have the effect of discriminating against certain groups.

The examples mentioned above merely scratch the surface of systemic discrimination. A further example will help to demonstrate just how deeply rooted systemic discrimination may be. Our society is one in which most people learn that child-rearing is primarily a female function. This assumption is deeply embedded in our culture and its social practices and is even reinforced through the law. What results is a situation where the opportunities effectively open to men and women are not equal. They may appear to be the product of individual choice, particularly where the constitution proclaims the equality of men and women. But these individual choices are shaped by the weight of social practices and cultural values that have the effect of discriminating between males and females.

Choice

Individual choice also contributes to inequality. For example, a status Indian who decides to stay on the reserve reduces his or her opportunities of finding a job, and if one does find employment it probably will pay less than a job in the city. Native reserves are usually far from centres of population and economic activity, so that there is an economic cost that accompanies the choice of life on the reserve. Likewise, if one decides to live in Cape Breton, northern Ontario, Newfoundland, or many other regions of Canada, there is a greater probability that one will be unemployed or earn less than someone else who went down the road to Toronto or Calgary.

We hasten to add that mobility choices like these are not always easy. A person who grows up in the poverty and deprived environment that characterize most Indian reserves may neither perceive nor have much choice about his or her future. Only by applying a rather generous meaning to the word may one conclude that someone from a second-generation welfare family has much individual choice regarding education and future career opportunities. Nevertheless, individual choice is a factor that contributes to inequality.

Politics

Although debates over equality generally draw on the rarefied language of rights and justice, this should not conceal the fact that they are essentially political struggles. How much inequality is acceptable, or, to put it differently, how much equality is enough? Are there circumstances where some forms of discrimination might be reasonable because they are necessary to protect or promote other values? What groups should be targeted for affirmative action—why, for example, do many affirmative action schemes consider Punjabis to be a visible minority but not Chinese? Why Sikhs, but not Jews?

Fairness and equality are cultural notions. A century ago only a small minority of Canadians regretted the fact that women were without most of the rights that are taken for granted today. Poverty was once believed to be primarily the fault of the person suffering from it, an explanation that absolved society, the economic system, and governments from blame for the suffering of many whose greatest offence was to be born into the sort of circumstances that make a life of poverty very likely. As values and beliefs change, a society's notions of what is fair may also be transformed.

Value shifts of this sort are almost certain to be accompanied, and influenced, by political struggles. If Canadians are more conscious today of the discrimination that has been practised against the country's Aboriginal peoples, it is because of the efforts of Aboriginal groups to bring these inequalities to the public's attention and influence government policy. The social policies that redistribute wealth from more affluent to less affluent Canadians did not emerge overnight: they have been built up (and, more recently, chipped away at) gradually over time in response to struggles between conflicting interests and values. Political parties, interest groups, individuals, and various parts of the state may all be participants in these struggles.

The structure of the state matters, too, affecting what sorts of inequalities are dealt with by governments and influencing the opportunities and resources available to different interests. It is likely, for example, that Canadian governments have long targeted more money at regional economic inequalities than have American governments because of the particular division of powers between Ottawa and the provinces under Canada's constitution and the relatively greater leverage of the provincial governments than of the state governments in the United States. To use another example, the entrenchment of the Charter of Rights and Freedoms in the Canadian constitution has had an enormous impact on the prominence of equality rights issues, the strategies that groups use to achieve their goals, and the treatment of certain groups. The interplay of interest, ideas, and institutions that is politics plays a key role in determining what inequalities get on the public agenda and how they are dealt with.

Quality of Life

The United States, still the world's wealthiest society, has one of the world's highest rates of homicide and a drug problem that costs thousands of lives and billions of dollars annually, to say nothing of the enormous misery associated with it. It also has a high rate of alcoholism, thousands of homeless people, and a high level of marriage break-up (which translates into many single-parent families, usually headed by women, and a high incidence of child poverty), to mention only a few of the social pathologies of that rich society. Canadians often take smug pride in being less afflicted by these problems. But Canada's high standard of living, like that of the United States, is also tarnished by problems that undermine the quality of life (QOL) experienced by millions. These problems often become politicized as

Each generation is shaped by a different set of experiences, and is likely to view politics through the lens of its own interests and values. (Roy Peterson, *Vancouver Sun*)

groups demand that governments take action to deal with them. In some cases government policies are blamed for having caused or contributed to a QOL problem. For example, Native groups and those sympathetic to their demands argue that the appallingly bad quality of life experienced by many Native Canadians is due to unjust and discriminatory policies. While the QOL in Canada is comparatively high, the picture is not uniformly bright for all groups. Native Canadians, in particular, experience conditions far below what most Canadians would consider decent and acceptable in a society as wealthy as ours.

One way of measuring the QOL in a society is to ask people how satisfied they are with their lives. Pollsters have done this for decades. But the results tell us little except that most people claim to be satisfied with their lives, while a persistently large minority are not satisfied. Attitudinal data like these tell one nothing about the causes of dissatisfaction or the sorts of problems that actually undermine the QOL in a society. To get at these one must rely on objective measures that may reasonably be construed as reflections of QOL. We will look at mortality, crime, suicide, alcoholism, and destitution.

Compared to other advanced industrialized societies, Canada does relatively well on all of these measures. Its mortality rate of 7.3 per 1,000 members of the population and the infant mortality rate of just under 7 per 1,000 are about normal for such societies. Average life expectancy is 77.4 years, surpassed only by Japan, Iceland, and Switzerland.

In terms of violent crime, Canada is unexceptional. A study prepared by the Canadian Centre for Justice Statistics placed the Canadian homicide rate for the years 1975–9 seventh in a list of fourteen countries.[12] Canada's current rate of about two homicides per 100,000 population compared to a rate of about nine per 100,000 in the United States. Although rates vary from year to year, the statistics do not support the popular assumption that murders have become more common. Canada's homicide rate has actually declined since the mid-1970s.[13]

Statistics on other violent crimes like rape, domestic violence, and assault are difficult to interpret. This is partly because of changes in reporting procedures that can produce an increase or decrease from one year to the next without there being any real change in the actual incidence of the offence. Changes to the law and public attitudes may also affect crime statistics. For example, rape charges and convictions are dramatically higher today than a couple of decades ago. This increase is mainly due to the greater willingness of victims to come forward, a willingness that is due to a combination of changed social attitudes and reforms to the law on sexual assault. Interpretation problems aside, the data do not suggest that Canada is an exceptionally dangerous place to live. It certainly is much safer than the United States and it compares favourably to many other advanced industrial democracies.[14]

Suicide and alcoholism and other drug abuse are social pathologies that are symptomatic of a low QOL. Suicide accounts for about 4 per cent of deaths among Canadians between the ages of 15 and 69, exceeded only by cancer (36 per cent), circulatory system malfunction (30 per cent), and accidents (10 per cent).[15] As in other countries, the rate of successful suicide is considerably higher among men than women, at about twenty-three per 100,000 population compared to six per 100,000.[16] And although the rate has remained stable for females, it has increased by about 30–40 per cent for males since the 1960s.[17] On the other hand, Canada's suicide rate is only about one-third that of Hungary and a little over half the Swiss rate. There is enormous international variation, suggesting that suicide is closely related to culture. For example, Mexico's rate is just over one per 100,000, Italy and the United Kingdom have rates around eight per 100,000, while Hungary and Austria top the list at about forty and twenty-five, respectively. Canada's rate of about fourteen per 100,000 falls in the middle.

It is conservatively estimated that about 4 per cent of adult drinkers in Canada, or over 600,000 people, are alcoholics.[18] This figure is based on the mortality rate from cirrhosis of the liver, national cirrhosis rates being highly correlated with alcohol consumption levels. Alcoholism in Canada is about average for Western industrialized countries. The level is dramatically lower than in such countries as Hungary, Germany, Italy, and France. Abuse of other non-medical drugs generally is not considered to be a major problem in Canadian society. The social and economic costs associated with their use are certainly much less than those produced by alcohol and tobacco consumption.

Advanced industrial societies all have in place a 'safety net' of social programs to protect individuals and households from destitution. Nevertheless, some people fall between the cracks. When the safety net fails to catch a significant number of those who, for one reason or another, cannot make ends meet, this is surely an indication that the QOL experienced by some people falls below acceptable standards of human decency. We would argue that homelessness and the demands placed on food banks are two indicators of holes in the social safety net.

The extent of homelessness is difficult to pin down for the obvious reason that the homeless, unlike those who have a fixed address, cannot be enumerated, telephoned, or otherwise kept track of with any accuracy. Nevertheless, there are abundant signs that homelessness is a problem experienced by thousands of Canadians and, moreover, that the number of homeless people has increased over the last several years. A 1990 report published by the Canada Mortgage and Housing Corporation estimated that there were about 14,000 homeless persons in Toronto alone during the late 1980s.[19] The Canadian Council on Social Development reckons the number of homeless in Canada to be somewhere between 100,000 and 250,000.

The number of Canadians who rely on food banks for part of their needs has also increased. The Canadian Association of Food Banks estimates that in 1991, 300 food banks across Canada were providing food to approximately 600,000 people on a monthly basis. About three-quarters of food bank users rely on welfare or old age security as their main source of income. Refugees, the disabled, and those with no income and often no home account for another 10 per cent. Over 10 per cent of users are the working poor.[20]

Demands on food banks are largely cyclical, increasing during periods of higher than usual unemployment. But there appears to be a more permanent component to food bank demand that has grown larger as governments have retreated somewhat from providing adequate social assistance for those in need. This component is created by the gap between the income that social assistance provides and the cost of paying for life's necessities. The wideness of this gap varies across the country because social assistance benefits are determined by the individual provinces and, second, because of regional variations in the cost of living. But the gap is wide in all provinces (see Figure 3.5). As social assistance benefits fail to keep pace with increases in the cost of living, the demand on food banks inevitably will increase. Given this increase on the 'normal' demand for food banks, an increase in the level of unemployment pushes an already strained system to the breaking point.

Figure 3.5 The Welfare Gap, by Province, 1994

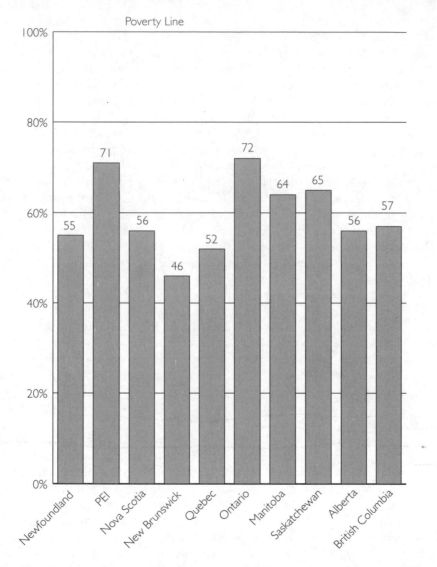

Note: The welfare gap is the difference between total welfare income (social assistance benefits, child tax benefits, and federal and provincial sales tax credits) and the Statistics Canada poverty line for each province for a couple with two children. It does not take into account the value of welfare benefits such as subsidized accommodation, day care, dental coverage, etc.

Source: Based on data in National Council of Welfare, Welfare Incomes 1994 (Ottawa: Supply and Services, Summer, 1995), table 3.

Canada is an affluent society. Its social pathologies are fairly typical of those experienced by other advanced industrial societies. The surrogate measures of the QOL that we have examined suggest that the United Nations is certainly right in rating Canada as one of the world's best countries in which to live. But the QOL is sharply lower for one group, namely, Native Canadians. Consider these facts:

- Life expectancy for status Indians is about ten years less than for the Canadian population as a whole.
- Infant mortality rates are twice as high among Natives as among non-Natives.
- Native death, illness, and accident rates are all about three times national levels. Most deaths of status Indians under 45 are caused by violence rather than illness.
- Although less than 3 per cent of the population are Native Canadians (defined to include Indians, Inuit, and Métis), about 18 per cent of those in prisons are Native.[21] Natives also comprise almost one-fifth of all murder victims and over one-fifth of all murder suspects in Canada.[22]
- The suicide rate among Natives is well over twice the Canadian rate. For the Inuit it is about three times the national rate.
- Alcoholism is much more prevalent among Natives than non-Natives. It has been estimated that 50–60 per cent of accidents and deaths among status Indians are alcohol-related.[23]
- Many Natives live in overcrowded conditions. About one-fifth of Indian dwellings are crowded (defined as more than one person per room), the figure rising to about one-third on reserves. As of the 1986 census, the level of overcrowding on reserves was about sixteen times the Canadian rate.

Independence

A democracy requires self-government. This means that public policies affecting the lives of citizens should be taken by people whom these same citizens have elected and who are accountable to them for their policies. The first major step toward self-government in Canada was taken in 1848 when the principle of responsible government was recognized in the colonies of Nova Scotia and the United Canadas (followed by the other British North American colonies soon afterwards). Responsible government meant that the governor, himself chosen by the British colonial office, was obliged to select cabinet ministers who were members of the elected legislature. A cabinet without the support of a majority in the legislature would be required to resign.

Self-government advanced another step with Confederation. The British North America Act of 1867 (now called the Constitution Act, 1867) created a new country out of the colonies of Nova Scotia, New Brunswick, and the United Canadas, and transferred to its federal and provincial legislatures the exclusive right to make laws for Canada and its provinces. Full self-government was almost achieved. We say 'almost' because certain powers were withheld from Canadian governments and, therefore, from the voters who elected them. These included:

- *The power to enter into foreign treaties.* Under section 133 of the BNA Act this remained the responsibility of the British government. Treaty-making power was formally transferred to Canada in 1931 by the Statute of Westminster.
- *The power to amend the constitution.* This also remained in the hands of the British Parliament. The BNA Act that created Canada and established the powers of the federal and provincial governments was a British law. It could only be changed by passing another British law. This situation remained unchanged until 1982, when the BNA Act of 1867 and all its amendments were patriated. Britain's authority to pass laws applying to Canada was ended, and a procedure for amending the constitution in Canada was established (see Chapter 5).
- *The power to interpret the constitution.* At Confederation, the highest court for the colonies of British North America was the Judicial Committee of the Privy Council (JCPC). The JCPC was, in fact, a committee comprised of members of the British House of Lords. The BNA Act, 1867 left the JCPC's authority over Canada intact. This continued until 1949, when the Supreme Court of Canada become the final appellate court for this country and, as such, Canada's constitutional umpire.

Step by step the Canadian state achieved the full powers of self-government it exercises today. With the passage of the Constitution Act, 1982, the last formal impediment to political sovereignty was removed. But the issue of political sovereignty has been far less controversial in the modern politics of Canada than those of economic and cultural sovereignty. The real limitations on Canadian independence, many have argued, have not come from the vestiges of colonialism that have gradually been removed from Canada's constitution, but have been and are imposed by economic dependence on, first, Great Britain and then the United States and by the 'colonization' of Canada by American cultural industries. Formal political sovereignty, according to Canadian nationalists, is empty so long as the country's economic and cultural destinies are controlled by others.

In the real world, however, no self-governing democracy is totally independent of external influences. Trade, military alliances and animosities, and contemporary mass media are some of the chief factors that create a web of interdependence between modern societies. The question is not, therefore, whether political life in Canada or in any other country is unaffected by influences from outside. Instead, the question is whether the nature and extent of these external influences undermine the political independence of a country.

If one looks at Canada's economic relations with the rest of the world, both historically and today, there is no denying our enormous dependence on foreign sources of investment capital, imports, and markets for Canadian exports. Some of the main features of Canada's international economic relations are listed in Box 3.1.

This dependence must, however, be put into perspective. Several advanced industrial democracies, including the Netherlands, Belgium, Sweden, and Germany, rely on trade for a greater share of their national income than does Canada. These countries are members of the European Union, which imposes considerably greater limitations on the policy-makers of its member states than the free trade agreement imposes on Canadian and American governments. What is unique about Canada is the extent to which our trading relations depend on a single partner, i.e., the United States. Among advanced industrialized economies, only

---

BOX 3.1 Canada's Economic Links to the World

Past…

- Much of the money used to build the roads, railways, and canals of Canada's early commercial economy was borrowed from foreign, mainly British, investors.

- At Confederation, Canada was already heavily in debt to foreign investors.

- It is estimated that about 450 American companies had established subsidiaries in Canada by 1913.

- By the 1920s, the United States surpassed Britain as the major source of foreign investment in Canada.

- The level of foreign ownership in Canada peaked in 1971 at 37 per cent of corporate non-financial assets. The level was close to 60 per cent for manufacturing industries.

Present…

- Foreign investors control about one-fifth of corporate non-financial assets in Canada.

- About one-quarter of Canada's gross domestic product comes from trade. Over 70 per cent of that trade is with the United States.

- Canada is still a net importer of capital. But over the last couple of decades Canadian investment abroad has increased from about one quarter of the value of foreign investment in Canada (1970) to about 60 per cent (1990).

Japan comes close to this level of dependence on a single trading partner (close to half of Japanese exports are purchased by the United States).

In terms of investment, Canada remains heavily dependent on foreign capital. But this dependence has weakened over the last couple of decades at the same time as Canadian investment abroad—and therefore our penetration of other economies—has increased. Indeed, as a result of the increasing globalization of business and investment, Canada has come to look more and more like several other advanced industrial economies in terms of its level of foreign ownership. Again, however, Canada is rather unique in the degree to which it is dependent on a single source of foreign investment, i.e., the United States.

Culturally, Canada has always lived in the shadow of the United States. Physical proximity, a common language, and shared values have facilitated the flow of cultural products—books, magazines, films, television programs, and records—between the two countries. Economics has ensured that this flow has been mostly from the United States to Canada. This is because of the much greater domestic audience/readership available to American producers, which enables them to produce high-quality mass-appeal products that are attractive to advertisers. Advertising revenue is the main or sole source of income for most privately owned media businesses (films, records, and books are the chief exceptions). The Canadian dilemma was summed up succinctly by the Canadian Task Force on Broadcasting Policy, one in a long line of government inquiries into the problem of defending Canadian culture (whatever it might be) from the American onslaught. The Task Force estimated that for the $133 million that Canada's English-language private broadcasters spent on foreign programs in 1984-85, they received a production value of $3–5 billion.[24]

The result has been predictable. American-made films, television programs, popular music, and magazines spill over into Canada's English-language market. In fact, they dominate all of these Canadian markets. American books also do very well in the English-Canadian market, with authors like Danielle Steele, John Grisham, and Stephen King topping the bestseller lists both north and south of the border. Newspapers are the main exception to the rule of American dominance. This is because of provisions in Canada's Income Tax Act that heavily favour Canadian-owned newspapers and, second, because for most people newspapers are primarily sources of local information.[25]

Let us return to our initial questions. Is Canada's political independence undermined by the country's economic dependence on the United States and by the enormous influence of American mass media in English Canada? In what ways? Is the Canadian predicament so different from that faced by many other industrialized democracies in today's interdependent world?

The answer to the first question is clearly 'yes'. Canadian policy-makers, at all levels, must be sensitive to the actions and possible reactions of governments in the United States. Moreover, many of the public policy matters they deal with, from trans-boundary pollution to interest rates, are affected by circumstances in the United States, circumstances over which Canadians and their governments can exert little, if any, control. Canada's economic and cultural linkages with the United States affect us in too many ways to be listed here. The fact that about three-quarters of our international trade is with the United States obviously means that our economy will be highly vulnerable to the state of the American economy and to changes in the exchange rate between the Canadian and American dollars. The fact that Canadians are raised on a heavy diet of American films, television programs, and magazines will certainly affect the images and ideas in their heads (see Box 3.2). To the extent that these American cultural imports erode distinctively Canadian values (whatever these may be, or might have been), one may argue that they also erode the cultural basis for a Canadian society and public policies that are different from those of the United States.

BOX 3.2 The Long Shadow of American Culture

- American magazines account for close to two-thirds of sales in English Canada.

- About two-thirds of television viewing time in English Canada is spent watching American programs. This increases to about 90 per cent in the case of drama and comedy viewing time.

- Canada's feature film and television production industries depend on a life support system of government subsidies, channelled through the Income Tax Act, the Broadcast Fund, and the state-owned Canadian Broadcasting Corporation and National Film Board. Despite this, few genuinely Canadian films reach the box office market.

- An American television series can be purchased by a Canadian broadcaster for less than 5 per cent of what it costs to produce, a mass appeal film for 1–2 per cent of its production costs.

Faced with a challenge from a larger, more powerful economy and a predatory mass culture, governments typically respond with protectionist policies. They attempt to protect domestic industries or local culture through import restrictions, subsidies to domestic producers, regulations affecting business practices and cultural industries, and so on. Canadian policy-makers have resorted to all of these measures, as have policy-makers elsewhere. To cite but one example, Canadian cultural policy is determined largely by the rules that the Canadian Radio-television and Telecommunications Commission (CRTC) imposes on broadcasters. The CRTC establishes and enforces a dense thicket of regulations governing Canadian content over radio and television, regulations that have a very simple bottom line: to ensure that more Canadian music and television programming reaches the airwaves than would be the case if market forces were allowed to operate without restriction.

Finally, is the Canadian 'dilemma' really so different from that of other small and middle-sized democracies? After all, *Forrest Gump* and *The Lion King* were box office hits in Western Europe, just as they were in North America. Macdonald's restaurants span the globe, so much so that the standardized cost of a 'Big Mac' is used by the respected business newspaper, *The Economist*, as a measure of the cost of living in different countries. Direct broadcast satellites, Ted Turner's Cable News Network, international credit cards, and the multinational corporation have shrunk the globe, so that no country is free from some other's cultural or economic incursions. Is Canada really such a special case?

The answer to this question will inevitably be coloured by one's own values. How much dependence on another economy is too much? Is dependence on one of the world's economic powerhouses preferable to a more diversified trade profile with weaker or less reliable economies? Has Canada had much choice but to rely on, first, the British and then the American economy?

On the cultural front, if most Canadians prefer American films, television programs, magazines, and music over home-grown alternatives, should their governments interfere? It stretches credulity to suggest that protectionist measures like the Canadian content quotas imposed on radio stations are a response to listener demands. Obviously they are not. And anyway, what are the differences in Canadian culture that policy-makers want to preserve? Does protectionism preserve these values, or just the industries that depend on the state's cultural life support system?

All countries are subject to external influences that limit the independence of their elected governments. Canada is not unique in this regard. Nevertheless, one may fairly say that these influences are felt somewhat more powerfully in Canada than in most other countries. We would not go as far, however, as those Canadian nationalists who claim that economic and cultural ties to the United States undermine Canadian democracy. A self-governing democracy does not require the freedom from external influence that nationalists argue would be desirable for Canada. There is almost certainly an element of anti-Americanism—a dislike of American culture, institutions, and public policies—that contributes to the Canadian nationalist critique of American influence. More importantly, however, their arguments are based on an outdated ideal of national autonomy that bears increasingly little resemblance to today's world of interdependent states. Indeed, the constraints faced by Canadian policy-makers are in many respects slight compared to those that the European Union imposes on its member states.

BOX 3.3 The Canadian Identity Crisis:
An American Reflects on the 1988 Canadian Election

Whither Canada? That is the question millions of Americans, as usual, have not been asking in recent weeks, as Canadians fought a bitter election campaign over the fate of a free trade agreement with the United States. But at least some have felt guilty about it. Now that Canadians have implicitly approved the agreement by reelecting Prime Minister Brian Mulroney, we can put all thoughts of Canada aside without guilt.

But should we? I think not. Canada needs us. Indeed it may be that in briefly threatening to reject this obviously sensible treaty, Canada—as is so often the case with staged suicide attempts—was simply trying to draw attention to itself. The entire election was a cry for help....

Anyone who has ever conversed with Canadians will have witnessed their psychological torment. They combine a deep professed disdain for south-of-the-border culture—our crime, our squalor, our imperial bravado, our skeletal social welfare system—with an even deeper need for approval from Americans. Clearly they're all torn up inside. They desperately want love, but are unable to supply it in return.

There is only one cure for the complex neurosis. We must give Canadians what they secretly want. We must embrace them, adopt them, love them, annex them. In short, we must make Canada the 51st state. Or, perhaps, the 51st through 54th states, depending on the best arrangement of stars in the revised American flag.

Michael Kinsley,
'Canada's Secret Wish',
Washington Post, 23 November 1988, A21.

PART THREE

The Structures of Governance

The Fathers of Confederation at Charlottetown, 1864. (National Archives of Canada/C733)

Constitutions are at the heart of democratic politics. This chapter examines key features of the Canadian constitution. It includes the following topics:

- ❖ Functions of a constitution.
- ❖ Rights and freedoms.
- ❖ Parliamentary government.
- ❖ Responsible government.
- ❖ Ministerial responsibility.
- ❖ Parliamentary and constitutional supremacy.
- ❖ Judicial independence.
- ❖ The House of Commons and the Senate.
- ❖ The biases of British parliamentary government.
- ❖ Changing the constitution.
- ❖ Citizen participation in constitutional reform.

CHAPTER FOUR

■ The Constitution

A constitution is an essential ingredient of democratic politics. But the existence of a constitution does not by itself ensure that politics is democratic. South Africa, for example, had for decades a constitution that denied the Black majority of that country rights equal to those of the White minority. The People's Republic of China has a constitution under which the violent suppression of the peaceful protesters at Tiananmen Square and staged political trials for dissidents were perfectly lawful. Closer to home, the fact that constitutional government was well established in Canada did not prevent the federal government from depriving thousands of Japanese Canadians of their rights as citizens during World War Two. A constitution is no guarantee that human rights will be respected, that group rights will be protected, or that political opposition to those who govern will be tolerated. Without a constitution, however, the concepts of rights and limited government do not even exist.

A *constitution* is the fundamental law of a political system. It is 'fundamental' because all other laws must conform to the constitution in terms of *how they are made* and in terms of their *substance*. A constitution is a necessary condition for democratic politics. Without it there is no civilized way of resolving conflicts, nor is there a way of predicting either the powers of government or the rights of citizens.

A constitution is expected to establish order, allowing for the peaceful settlement of differences. Early liberal thinkers like Thomas Hobbes, John Locke, and Jean-Jacques Rousseau all used the concept of the 'state of nature'—a pre-political condition—to illustrate the impulse behind constitutional government. The state of nature, wrote Hobbes, was a state of chaos in which no individual could feel secure in the possession of his property or life. It is this insecurity that leads people to demand a constitution where there is none and to accept the necessity of a constitution even if they find it difficult to agree on its precise components.

In modern societies the alternatives to constitutional government are anarchy—the sort of chaos and civil strife that have existed in some of the newly independent republics created after the break-up of the former Soviet Union—or totalitarianism. Where anarchy reigns, there are no generally accepted rules for resolving the differences between factions of the population. The state does not exist. Under totalitarianism the state exists, but because its powers are unlimited and all realms of social and economic life are subordinate to it, it makes no sense to talk of a constitution. If the rules of a board game can be changed at will by one of the players, then it is nonsense to speak of rules. So, too, with a constitution: if its terms are purely arbitrary, it ceases to be a constitution in anything other than name.

The rules that make up a constitution deal with two sets of relations. One of these involves the relationship between citizens and the state. A constitution *empowers* the state to act, to pass laws on behalf of the community. At the same time most constitutions *limit power*. They do this by identifying those individual rights, and in some cases group rights, that the state cannot infringe. The other set of relations encompassed by a constitution involves the distribution of functions and powers between different parts of the state. After all, modern government is a complex mechanism. This mechanism is often analysed under three main functional headings: the legislature (making the law); the executive (implementing the law); and the judiciary (interpreting the law). But the reality of the modern state is more complicated than this tripartite division of powers suggests. Whatever the degree of complexity, the rules that govern the relations between the various parts of the state are an important component of the constitution.

In a federal state like Canada, where the constitution divides law-making powers between a national and regional governments, the rules governing the relations between these two levels are also part of the constitution. This third aspect of the constitution has overshadowed the other two for most of Canada's history. Indeed, before 1982, when the Charter of Rights and Freedoms was entrenched in the constitution, the relations between individuals and the state in Canada were defined by the courts mainly in terms of federal and provincial legislative powers (see Chapter 5).

A constitution, then, is a set of rules governing political life. These rules may take three forms: written documents; the decisions of courts (called the *common law*); and unwritten conventions. 'Conventions' are those practices that emerge over time and are generally accepted as binding rules of the political system. An example would be the convention that the leader of the party that captures the most seats in a House of Commons election is called on to form a government. In Canada the first two components of the constitution—written documents and the common law—together comprise *constitutional law*. Conventions, while part of the constitution, do not have the status of constitutional law, at least not in Canada. This distinction was made by the Supreme Court of Canada in a 1981 ruling (see Box 4.1). It should not be interpreted to mean that constitutional law is more important than constitutional conventions. What it does mean, however, is that the rules of constitutional law are enforceable by the courts, whereas constitutional conventions are not.

Box 4.1   What Is a Constitutional Convention?

...[M]any Canadians would perhaps be surprised to learn that important parts of the Constitution of Canada, with which they are the most familiar because they are directly involved when they exercise their right to vote at federal and provincial elections, are nowhere to be found in the law of the Constitution. For instance it is a fundamental requirement of the Constitution that if the Opposition obtains the majority at the polls, the Government must tender its resignation forthwith. But fundamental as it is, this requirement of the Constitution does not form part of the law of the Constitution....

The main purpose of constitutional conventions is to ensure that the legal framework of the Constitution will be operated in accordance with the prevailing constitutional values or principles of the period....

The conventional rules of the Constitution present one striking peculiarity. In contradistinction to the laws of the Constitution, they are not enforced by the courts....

It is because the sanctions of convention rest with institutions of government other than courts, such as the Governor General or the Lieutenant-Governor, or the Houses of Parliament, or with public opinion and, ultimately, with the electorate that it is generally said that they are political.

Supreme Court of Canada,
Attorney General of Manitoba et al. v. Attorney
General of Canada et al., 28 September 1981.

Constitutional Functions

A constitution does more than provide a basis for non-violent politics. It also performs several more specific functions that include the following.

Representation

All modern democracies are representative democracies, in which politicians make decisions on behalf of those who elect them. But this still leaves enormous room for variation in how the population is represented, who is represented, and how representatives are selected.

A constitution describes both the *basis* of political representation and the *method* by which representatives are chosen. The basis of democratic representation may be by population, by territory, or by group. Representation by population is based on the principle of 'one person, one vote'. Under such a system, all elected members of the legislature should represent approximately the same number of voters. This arrangement is most likely to allow the preferences of a simple majority of the population to be translated into law. Although virtually all modern democracies incorporate some form of 'rep by pop' in their constitutions, many temper majority rule by representing regions as well. For example, the American constitution gives each state the right to two senators, despite the fact that the population of the largest state is about forty times that of the smallest. Representation in Canada's Senate is also by region: Ontario, Quebec, the western provinces, and the Atlantic provinces each have twenty-six seats, while the northern territories have two senators. Federalism is a form of government that embodies the principle of territorial representation. It does so by giving regional governments the exclusive right to pass laws on particular subjects.

A constitution may also accord representation to groups. New Zealand's constitution, for one, guarantees a certain number of seats in that country's legislature to representatives of the Maori minority. In Canada, suggestions for Senate reform have included proposals to guarantee seats for women and for the representatives of Aboriginal Canadians. The defeated 1992 Charlottetown Accord would have ensured that Quebec, whose share of Canada's population has been falling steadily, would maintain one-quarter of all seats in the House of Commons, which is about the province's current share. This was, one might argue, a thinly disguised guarantee for Francophone group representation. Proposals like these are based on a collectivist political philosophy.

A constitution also establishes the methods by which the holders of public office are selected. Election and appointment are the two basic methods, but each allows for a wide variety of procedures that affect who is represented and how responsive public officials are to the popular will. For example, it is typical for members of the judiciary to be appointed for life, a practice that is expected to insulate them from popular passions and the transitory preferences of elected governments. An elected legislature is a standard feature of democratic political systems and, for that matter, of non-democratic ones. But many constitutions divide the legislative power between an elected chamber and an appointed one, as in Canada, the United Kingdom, and Germany.

Finally, the electoral process itself has a crucial influence on representation. As we will see in Chapter 7, the single-member constituency system used in Canada discourages political parties from directing their appeals at a narrow segment of the national electorate. Unless that segment happens to be concentrated in a particular region, such a strategy will not pay off in elected members. A system of proportional representation, whereby a party's percentage of the popular votes translates into a corresponding share of seats in the legislature, has a very different effect. It promotes a splintering of the party system and allows for the direct representation of such interests as avid ecologists in Germany, orthodox Jews in Israel, and racists in France. In a system like Canada's, these groups would have to rely on whatever influence they could achieve within one of the larger political parties or else turn to non-electoral political strategies.

Power

The simple fact that constitutional government exists means that the state is empowered to act and that its actions may be backed up by the full weight of public authority. A constitution, therefore, provides the basis for the legitimate exercise of state power. But it also *limits* and *divides* power, at least under a democratic constitution. For example, a constitutional requirement that elections be held periodically restrains state power by making those who wield it accountable to, and removable by, the electorate. The existence of separate branches of government under the constitution, or of two levels of government as in the case of federalism, divides state power between different groups of public officials. How power is divided among the various parts of the state, or between the national and regional governments, is not determined solely by the constitution. But constitutional law and conventions both affect the extent and distribution of state power.

Rights

A right is something that a person is entitled to, like the right to vote or the right not to be held against one's will without a reason being given. Constitutions vary greatly in the particular rights they assign to individuals and to societal groups. At a minimum, a democratic constitution establishes the basic right of citizens to choose their government. But most constitutions go beyond this to guarantee—although not without limit—such rights as the individual's right to free speech, freedom of association, and freedom of religion and conscience, as well as legal rights like freedom from arbitrary detention and illegal search and seizure. These are rights that limit the state's power *vis-à-vis* the individual either by making that power dependent on popular consent (democratic rights) or by establishing an individual's right not to be interfered with by the state (personal liberty).

Rights may also empower individuals by requiring the state to either protect or promote their interests. For example, a right to freedom from discrimination provides individuals with a constitutional remedy in cases where they have been discriminated against because of their sex, race, ethnic background, or whatever other basis of discrimination is prohibited by the constitution. The state is obliged to protect their interests. As a practical matter, this may involve judicial decisions that remedy a private wrong (for example, requiring a minor hockey association to permit females to play in the same league with males). But the protection of equality may also see the state involved in more sweeping activities like affirmative action or racial desegregation on the grounds that these steps are necessary to alleviate discrimination.

Constitutions may also recognize the special status of particular groups, thereby giving to the members of such groups rights that are not enjoyed by others. For example, Canada's constitution declares that both French and English are official languages with 'equality of status and equal rights and privileges as to their use in all institutions of the Parliament and government of Canada.'[1] This is a *positive* right in the sense that it obliges the state to assume particular linguistic characteristics and, therefore, to protect actively the rights of French- and English-speakers—at least in matters that fall under Ottawa's jurisdiction. A constitution that recognizes the special status of particular religious denominations, as the Israeli constitution recognizes the Jewish religion, the Iranian constitution the Moslem religion, or the British constitution the Church of England, empowers the members of these religious groups to varying degrees by giving them state-protected rights that are not held by other denominations.

Community and Identity

When Pierre Trudeau wrote that 'A nation ... is no more and no less than the entire population of a sovereign state',[2] he was arguing that a constitution establishes a community, and in an obvious sense it does. A constitution is the set of fundamental rules that govern political life *in a particular territory*. Its rules are operative within that territory and not elsewhere, so that it establishes a formal bond among all those who live in that territory. Individuals in Rimouski, Quebec, and in Kitimat, British Columbia, are part of the same constitutional system and share a formal political status as Canadians. Even if they perceive their differences to be more important than what they share, this does not diminish the fact that they have legal membership in the same constitutional community.

Carrying the same national passport and being eligible to vote in the same elections may seem a rather weak basis for a *sense of community*, a sentiment that transcends the cold, formal ties of common citizenship. The fact of being citizens of the Soviet Union, for example, did not erase the strongly nationalist sentiments of Ukrainians, Estonians, and other ethnic communities within that country. For many members of these groups, the Soviet constitution and the political community it created were things to regret, not to rejoice over. Likewise in Canada, a significant minority of the population—Quebec separatists—rejects the Canadian political community and would prefer to live under a different constitution creating an independent Quebec.

A constitution may, therefore, inspire negative or positive feelings among the members of a political community, or it may leave them feeling indifferent. These feelings may be associated with the political community that a constitution creates—Canada, the United States, the Soviet Union—but they may also be associated with the particular institutions, values, and symbols embedded in a constitution. For example, the monarchy and other institutions and symbols redolent of Canada's colonial past have historically been an aspect of the Canadian constitution that has divided Canadians of French origin from those of British origin.

Official bilingualism and constitutional proposals that would recognize Quebec as a 'distinct society' within Canada have been two of the most divisive constitutional issues in recent years. On the other hand, some features of the constitution unite, rather than divide, Canadians. There is, for example, overwhelming support among all regions and social groups for the Charter of Rights and Freedoms. In general, we may say that a constitution generates a shared identity among the citizens of a country to the extent that most people have positive feelings toward the political community it creates and the values it embodies. On these counts, Canada's constitution has had a mixed record of successes and failures.

National Purpose

When the first permanent white settlement was established at what today is Quebec City, it operated under a royal charter that proclaimed the Catholic mission of the French colony. Aside from being an outpost of political and economic empire, it was to be a beachhead of Christianity, from which Catholicism would spread to the rest of the continent. The constitution of New France was therefore linked to a communal goal, to a sense of purpose and direction for society.

This is not so rare. The constitution of the former Soviet Union was full of references to building a socialist society. The constitutions of the Islamic Republic of Iran and of Pakistan both declare that society should conform to Moslem religious teachings. The most controversial part of the failed Meech Lake reforms to Canada's constitution, the recognition of Quebec as a 'distinct society', would have transformed Quebec nationalism from a political reality to a constitutionally entrenched fact. This was because the Quebec legislature and government would have been constitutionally required to 'preserve and promote' the distinct character of the province, which the distinct society proposal made clear was the French-speaking character of Quebec.

The constitutional document that created Canada, the Constitution Act, 1867, also included a number of provisions that embodied a national purpose. This purpose was the building of a new country stretching from the Atlantic to the Pacific oceans and an integrated economy tying together this vast territory. The nation-building goal is evident in the anticipation that other parts of British North America would eventually be admitted into Canada,[3] in the prohibition of barriers to trade between provinces,[4] and even in the constitutional commitment to build the Intercolonial Railway, a project described as 'essential to the Consolidation of the Union of British North America, and to the assent thereto of Nova Scotia and New Brunswick'.[5] The Constitution Act, 1982, commits Ottawa and the provinces to the promotion of equal opportunities for Canadians and the reduction of economic disparities between regions of the country.[6] It is hard to know, however, if such declarations of national purpose are merely symbolic recognitions of current policy or whether they might someday acquire more practical significance.

Canada's Constitution

As constitutional documents go, Canada's is a fairly lengthy one. In fact, it is not one document but a series of laws passed between 1867 and 1982. Together they are both longer and more detailed than the United States' constitution. Even so, the written documents of Canada's constitution provide only a fragmentary and even misleading picture of how the constitution actually works. Many of the most basic features of the constitution—including most of those that deal with the democratic accountability of government to the people—are nowhere to be found in these documents. On the other hand, some of what is included in the written constitution would, if acted on, probably result in a constitutional crisis!

The most useful way of analysing a constitution is to approach it from the angle of each of the relationships governed by constitutional rules. As noted earlier, these relationships include: (1) those between individuals and the state; (2) those between the various institutions of government; and (3) those between the national and regional governments. The first category involves rights and freedoms, the second deals with the machinery and process of government, and the third category is about federalism. A constitution also includes a fourth category of rules that establish what procedures must be followed to bring about constitutional change. Federalism is dealt with in the next chapter. We turn now to an examination of the other three dimensions of Canada's constitution.

Rights and Freedoms

Since 1982 Canada's constitution has included formal distinctions among fundamental political freedoms, democratic rights, mobility rights, legal rights, equality rights, and language rights. These are the categories set down in the Charter of Rights and Freedoms. Most of the rights and freedoms enumerated in the Charter were, however, part of Canada's constitution before 1982. In some cases they can be found in the Constitution Act, 1867. In others, they were established principles of the common law. The inclusion of these rights and freedoms in the Charter has, however, made an important difference in Canadian politics. Groups and individuals are far more likely today than in the pre-Charter era to reach for the judicial lever in attempting to protect their rights. Second, these rights have been more secure since the Charter's passage. This has been due to the courts' willingness to strike down laws and practices on the grounds that they contravene the Charter's guarantees of rights and freedoms.

Fundamental Freedoms

Fundamental political freedoms are guaranteed in section 2 of the Charter. These include freedom of religion, belief, expression, the media, assembly, and association. During the pre-Charter era these freedoms, or *political liberties* as they are often called, were part of the common law and of Canada's British parliamentary tradition. The preamble to the Constitution Act, 1867, declares that Canada is adopting 'a Constitution similar in Principle to that of the United Kingdom'. Individual freedoms were part of the British constitution and thus became part of Canada's. Even before the Charter, then, political freedoms occupied a place in the Canadian constitution. Their protection by the courts, however, was rather tenuous. Except in a few instances, the courts were unwilling to rule that a freedom was beyond the interference of government: period. Instead, civil liberties were defended using the federal division of legislative powers as the basis for striking down a particular government's interference with individual freedom.

Democratic Rights

The basic democratic right is the opportunity to vote in regular elections. This right predated Confederation. It was embodied in the Constitution Act, 1867, through those sections that establish the elective basis of representation in the House of Commons and in provincial legislatures (ss. 37 and 40), through the requirement that the legislature meet at least once a year (ss. 20 and 86), through the right of citizens to vote (s. 41), and through the five-year limit on the life of both the House of Commons and provincial legislatures, thereby guaranteeing regular elections (ss. 50 and 85). All of these sections are now 'spent', having been superseded by sections 3, 4, and 5 of the Charter.

Mobility Rights

Mobility rights were not explicitly mentioned in Canadian constitutional law before 1982. Section 121 of the Constitution Act, 1867, prohibits the provincial governments from imposing tariffs (i.e., an import tax) on commodities coming from other provinces, but there is no mention of restrictions on the movement of people. Such restrictions are now prohibited by section 6 of the Charter. This guarantee of individual mobility rights was prompted by Ottawa's fear that some provincial governments were undermining the idea and practice of Canadian citizenship by discriminating in favour of their own permanent residents in some occupational sectors and by imposing residency requirements as a condition for receiving some social services. The Charter does, however, permit both of these types of discrimination. It allows 'reasonable residency requirements as a qualification for the receipt of publicly provided social services',[7] and permits affirmative action programs favouring a province's residents 'if the rate of employment in that province is below the rate of employment in Canada'.[8] It is doubtful whether section 6 of the Charter has had any significant impact on provincial practices that limit the mobility of Canadians.

Legal Rights

Most rights-based litigation, both before and since the Charter's passage, has been based on individuals' and corporations' claims that their legal rights have been violated. Legal rights involve mainly procedural aspects of the law, such as the right to a fair trial, the right not to be held without a charge being laid, and the right to legal counsel. Before these rights were entrenched in the constitution through the Charter, they were recognized principles of the common law and constitutional convention. For example, the field of administrative law was based largely on the principles of *natural justice*: hear the other side, and no one should be a judge in his or her own case. These were accepted parts of Canada's democratic tradition and constitution even before they were entrenched in section 7 of the Charter. And like political freedoms, democratic rights, and equality rights, these legal rights were included in the Canadian Bill of Rights passed in 1960. In addition, the rights of accused parties were set forth in Canada's Criminal Code. It is apparent, however, that the constitutional entrenchment of legal rights has made an important difference. The courts have been much bolder in striking down parts of laws and in overturning administrative and police procedures than they were in the pre-Charter era. For example, a successful legal challenge to Canada's abortion law only became possible when the right to 'security of the person' was explicitly recognized in section 7 of the Charter.[9] More generally, Charter decisions have expanded the legal rights of the accused, convicted criminals, and immigrants.

Equality Rights

Equality rights are entrenched in the constitution through section 15 of the Charter. They embody the *rule of law* principle that everyone should be treated equally under the law. But the Charter extends this principle to expressly prohibit discrimination based on race, national or ethnic origin, colour, religion, sex, age, or mental or physical disability.[10]

The particular headings in this list are important, given that Canadian courts historically have preferred to base their rulings on the precise text of laws and the constitution. Women's groups and those representing the physically and mentally disabled clearly believed that the wording of the Charter made a difference, and both fought hard—and successfully—to have the original wording of section 15 changed. The Canadian Bill of Rights did not include age or mental/physical disability in its catalogue of equality rights. In the United States, the Fourteenth Amendment of that country's constitution states simply that everyone is entitled to 'due process of law' and 'equal protection of the laws'.[11] The generality of these provisions has not prevented the United States Supreme Court from finding a constitutional basis for affirmative action programs and racial desegregation in American schools.

In Canada, the Charter explicitly declares that affirmative action is constitutional.[12] Thus, the equality rights section of the Canadian constitution is designed to cut two ways. It provides individuals with grounds for redress if they believe that the law discriminates against them. But it also provides a basis for laws that treat different groups of people differently—some would say that this is the definition of discrimination—in order to improve the condition of disadvantaged individuals or groups.

Equality rights are also important features of provincial bills/charters of rights. Since 1975 every province has had such a bill. Quebec's is probably the most extensive, including even certain economic and social rights. These rights are administered and enforced by provincial human rights commissions.

Language Rights

At Confederation, the issue of language rights was dealt with in three ways. Section 133 of the Constitution Act, 1867, declares that both English and French are official languages in the Parliament of Canada and in the Quebec legislature, and in any court established by either the national or Quebec government. Section 93 of that same Act declares that rights held by denominational schools when a province became part of Canada cannot be taken away. As a practical matter, Catholic schools in a province like Manitoba or even Ontario were often French-speaking, and most English-language schools in Quebec were Protestant. Consequently, what were formally denominational rights in section 93 were effectively language rights as well. This did not help when it came to their protection—or non-protection. The third, and in practical terms the most important language rights provision of the Constitution Act, 1867, is section 92. This assigns to the provinces jurisdiction over 'all Matters of a merely local or private Nature in the Province' (s. 92.16). Combined with exclusive provincial jurisdiction over education (s. 93), this has given provincial governments the tools to promote or deny, as the case may be, the language rights of their Anglophone or Francophone minorities.

The Constitution Act, 1982, extends language rights in several ways. These include the following:

- The declaration of the official equality of English and French, found in section 133 of the Constitution Act, 1867, is repeated and broadened to encompass 'their use in all institutions of the Parliament and government of Canada' (s. 16) and services to the public (s. 20(1)).
- The New Brunswick legislature's earlier decision to declare that province officially bilingual is entrenched in the Constitution Act, 1982. The official status of English in the legislature and courts of Quebec and Manitoba is reaffirmed (s. 21).
- The right of Anglophones and Francophones to have their children educated in their mother tongue is entrenched, subject to there being sufficient demand to warrant the provision of such services out of public funds (s. 23).

Language rights would have been given an additional twist if the Meech Lake Accord (1987) or Charlottetown Accord (1992) had become constitutional law (see Chapter 5). The most controversial feature of both accords was the recognition of Quebec as a 'distinct society'. The wording of this section clearly linked this distinctiveness to the predominantly French-speaking character of Quebec. The 'distinct society' clause went on to oblige the province's legislature and government to 'preserve and promote the distinct identity of Quebec'. Some critics of the 'distinct society' clause argued that it would promote the concentration of French in Quebec, with harmful consequences for the status of the French-speaking minorities in the other provinces and for the English-speaking minority in Quebec (see Box 4.2).

Aboriginal Rights

Aboriginal rights are also included in Canada's constitution. Their explicit recognition dates from the passage of the Charter in 1982. Section 25 declares that the rights and freedoms set forth in the Charter shall not be construed so as to 'abrogate or derogate' from whatever rights or freedoms the Aboriginal peoples of Canada have as a result of any treaty or land claim settlement. Section 35(1) appears to limit Aboriginal rights to the status quo that existed in 1982, stating that 'The *existing* aboriginal and treaty rights of the aboriginal peoples of Canada are hereby recognized and affirmed' (emphasis added). There is no hint of recognizing Native claims to self-government.

**Box 4.2 The End of Bilingualism? Trudeau's View
of the 'Distinct Society' Clause**

Those Canadians who fought for a single Canada, bilingual and multicultural, can say goodbye to their dream: we are henceforth to have two Canadas, each defined in terms of its language. And because the Meech Lake accord states in the same breath that 'Quebec constitutes, within Canada a distinct society' and that 'the role of the Legislature and government to preserve and promote (this) distinct identity ... is affirmed,' it is easy to predict what future awaits anglophones living in Quebec and what treatment will continue to be accorded to francophones living in provinces where they are fewer in number than Canadians of Ukrainian or German origin.

Indeed, the text of the accord spells it out: In the other provinces, where bilingualism still has an enormously long way to go, the only requirement is to 'protect' the status quo, while Quebec is to 'promote' the distinct character of Quebec society.

In other words, the Government of Quebec must take measures and the Legislature must pass laws aimed at promoting the uniqueness of Quebec. And the text of the accord specifies at least one aspect of this uniqueness: 'French-speaking Canada' is 'centred' in that province. Thus Quebec acquires a new constitutional jurisdiction that the rest of Canada does not have, promoting the concentration of French in Quebec. It is easy to see the consequences for French and English minorities in the country, as well as for foreign policy, for education, for the economy, or social legislation, and so on.

Pierre Elliott Trudeau,
'Nothing left but tears for Trudeau',
Globe and Mail, 28 May 1987, A7.

Parliamentary Government in Canada

The whole edifice of British parliamentary government is built on profound silences in constitutional law. These silences touch on the most fundamental principles of democracy and on practices that are essential to the orderly functioning of government. Such matters as the selection of the Prime Minister, which party has the right to form a government, the relationship between the Crown and the government and between the government and the legislature, the rights of the political opposition, and the role of the judicial branch of government cannot be understood from a simple reading of the constitution. Nevertheless, for all of these matters there exist rules that are generally agreed upon, and which are vital parts of the constitution—so vital, in fact, that when they are challenged, the political system faces a crisis.

British parliamentary government was exported to Canada during the colonial period. Its main features have remained largely unchanged since the middle of the nineteenth century, when the British North American colonies achieved the right to self-government in their domestic affairs. The Constitution Act, 1867, explicitly reaffirms this British parliamentary inheritance, declaring that Canada has adopted 'a Constitution similar in Principle to that of the United Kingdom'.[13] While this might appear to be a somewhat nebulous phrase, Canada's founders understood very clearly what it meant. The constitution of the United Kingdom was, and remains today, a set of political traditions rather than a series of constitutional documents. Those who founded Canada took these traditions as their starting point and grafted onto them certain institutions and procedures—particularly federalism—for which British parliamentary government provided no guide.

Parliament

The distinguishing feature of British-style parliamentary government is the relationship between the various institutions that together comprise Parliament. *Parliament* consists of the monarch and the legislature. The monarch, currently Queen Elizabeth II, is Canada's head of state. According to the strict letter of the constitution, the monarch wields formidable powers. These include which party will be called on to form the government, when Parliament will be dissolved and a new election held, and the requirement that all legislation—federal and provincial—must receive royal assent before it becomes law. In fact, however, these powers are almost entirely symbolic, and the role is primarily a ceremonial one. When the monarch is not in Canada (which is most of the time), her powers are exercised by the Governor General. At the provincial level, the lieutenant-governors are the Queen's representatives.

The power that resides formally in the monarchy is in reality held by the Crown's advisers, the *privy council*. The privy council formally includes all members of the present and past cabinets. However, only present members of cabinet exercise the powers of the privy council, and these people are usually elected members of the legislature. At the head of the cabinet is the Prime Minister. The structure of Canada's Parliament is shown in Figure 4.1.

Parliament comprises, then, both the *executive* and *legislative* branches of government. Those who actually exercise the executive power are drawn from the legislature. In deciding

Figure 4.1 The Structure of Parliament in Canada

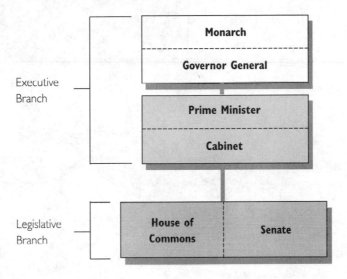

Note: The structure is basically the same at the provincial level, with two differences. The monarch's powers are exercised by a lieutenant-governor and the legislature consists of a single elected chamber.

who among those elected members of Parliament (MPs) and appointed senators will become members of the government, the rule is quite simple. The leader of the political party with the most seats in the elected House of Commons has the right to try to form a government that has the support of a majority of MPs. If at any time the government loses its majority support in the House, tradition requires that it resign. At this point a fresh election would be called or, if there is a possibility that another party could put together a government that would be supported by a majority of MPs, the Governor General could call on the leader of that party to try to form a government.

Responsible Government

In order to govern, therefore, the Prime Minister and cabinet require the confidence of the elected House of Commons. This constitutional principle is called *responsible government*. If a government loses the confidence of the House—this would be through either a defeat on an important piece of legislation or on a motion of no confidence proposed by an opposition party—it loses the right to govern. This may appear to place enormous power in the hands of MPs, capable of making and breaking governments at will. It does not. The reason why the constitutional theory of responsible government does not translate into governments tremulous before their legislatures is because of *party discipline*. This is another tradition of British parliamentary government, according to which the MPs of a party generally

Party discipline, an unwritten convention of Canadian parliamentary procedure, undermines the legislature's control over the government. (Roy Peterson, *Vancouver Sun*)

vote as a unified block in the legislature. In Canada, however, party discipline is conformed to more rigidly than in the UK.

Of the thirty-five governments elected between 1867 and 1993, only five fell because of a defeat in the legislature. In all five cases these were *minority governments*: governments that depended on the support of another party's MPs in order to win votes in the legislature. But even in these apparently precarious circumstances, it was usually the government that finally determined when an election would occur. On only one occasion has a government been defeated in the Commons and then had its request for a dissolution of Parliament and a fresh election denied. That was in 1926, and the denial provoked a constitutional crisis over the appropriate role of the Governor General. There was at least the chance of history repeating itself when the Progressive Conservative government's budget was defeated in 1979. The government had been in office a mere nine months, and the possibility of a minority Liberal government supported by the NDP was not totally outrageous. As it happened, however, Governor General Ed Schreyer granted Prime Minister Clark's request for a new election, although Schreyer claimed afterward that he seriously considered asking the Leader of the Opposition to try to form a government.

Responsible government is not just a constitutional relic. It operates today, but not in the narrow sense of legislatures making and defeating cabinets. Instead, it suffuses the parliamentary process in the form of the *rights of the legislature* and the corresponding *obligations of the government*. The legislature has the right to scrutinize, to debate, and to vote on policies proposed by the government. In order to carry out these activities, the legislature has the general right to question the government and to demand explanations for its actions and for those of bureaucratic officials who act in the government's name. The government, for its part, has a constitutional obligation to provide opportunities for legislative scrutiny of its policies and to account for its actions before Parliament. These rights and obligations are to a large extent codified in the *standing orders*—the rules that govern parliamentary procedure.

Responsible government, then, is part of the living constitution. But its formal definition bears little resemblance to the reality of modern parliamentary government. Disciplined political parties and dominant prime ministers ensure that cabinets seldom are defeated at the hands of un-cooperative legislatures. But if the ultimate sanction that underlies the notion of responsible government has been lost—it really only operated for a brief period in Canadian history, between 1848 and 1864 in the legislature of the United Canadas[14]—the practice of cabinet government that is accountable to the elected legislature remains.

Ministerial Responsibility

The accountability of the government to the legislature is the reason behind another principle of British parliamentary government, that of *ministerial responsibility*. It entails the obligation of a cabinet minister to explain and defend policies and actions carried out in his or her name. This individual accountability of cabinet ministers rests on a combination of constitutional law and parliamentary tradition. Section 54 of the Constitution Act, 1867, gives to cabinet the exclusive right to put before the legislature measures that involve the raising or spending of public revenue. In practice, such measures are introduced by particular members of the government. For example, changes to the tax system are proposed by the Minister of Finance. The constitution also requires that any legislation involving raising or spending public money must originate in the elected House of Commons. This reflects the liberal-democratic principle of no taxation without representation. Only the people's elected representatives, legislators who can be removed in a subsequent election, should have the right to propose laws that affect voters' pocketbooks. The accountability of ministers is, therefore, to the people's elected representatives.

Two fundamental principles of British parliamentary government, i.e., strong executive authority and democratic accountability, come together in the concept of ministerial responsibility. Strong executive authority is a tradition that dates from an era when the monarch wielded real power and the principle that these powers depended on the consent of the legislature was not yet established. When the legislature finally gained the upper hand in the seventeenth century, the tradition of strong executive power was not rejected. Instead, it was tamed and adapted to the democratic principle that government is based on the consent of the governed. Since then, individual ministers and cabinet as a whole have exercised the powers that, symbolically, continue to be vested in the Crown. But they do so in ways that enable the people's elected representatives to vote on their proposals and to call them to account for their policies (see Figure 4.2).

In recent times the constitutional principle of ministerial responsibility has come under increasing pressure. The enormous volume of decisions taken in a minister's name and the fact that much of the real power to determine government policy has passed into the hands

Figure 4.2 The Constitutional Roots of Ministerial Responsibility

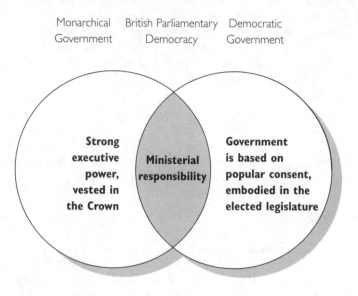

Monarchical Government   British Parliamentary Democracy   Democratic Government

Strong executive power, vested in the Crown

Ministerial responsibility

Government is based on popular consent, embodied in the elected legislature

of unelected officials mean that no minister can be well informed about all the policies and actions undertaken within his or her ministry. According to some, the solution is to locate accountability where decision-making power really lies. This is reasonable for most actions and decisions. But elected members of the government must remain directly accountable for the general lines of policy and for major decisions, otherwise a vital link in the chain of accountability that joins the people to those who govern is lost.

Parliamentary Supremacy versus Constitutional Supremacy

Another central feature of British parliamentary government is that of *parliamentary supremacy*. This means that Parliament's authority is superior to that of all other institutions of government. In concrete terms, this means that the courts will not second guess the right of Parliament to pass any sort of law, on any subject. Parliament embodies the popular will, and unpopular laws can always be defeated by changing the government at the next election. In a federal system like Canada's there is one complication. Law-making powers are divided between the national and provincial governments. But so long as Ottawa acts within its spheres of constitutional authority, and the provincial governments within theirs, both the federal and provincial parliaments are supreme.

This was the situation in Canada until 1982. When called on to determine whether a law was constitutional or not, the courts almost always referred to the federal division of powers set down in the Constitution Act, 1867. If a legislature was not intruding on the constitutional territory of the other level of government, its actions were by definition constitutional. The only exception to this rule was in the case of laws or actions that ran afoul of procedural rules of the common law, like the principles of natural justice. The substance of laws, on the other hand, would not be questioned.

Parliamentary supremacy was dealt a major blow by the Charter. Those who opposed the Charter argued that entrenching rights and freedoms in the written constitution would result in a transfer of power from legislatures to the courts. This is indeed what has happened. Since 1982 the Supreme Court has struck down numerous federal and provincial laws on the grounds that they violate the guarantees set forth in the Charter. The defenders of parliamentary supremacy claim that a system of court-protected rights and freedoms is fundamentally undemocratic. Their reasoning is that it substitutes the decisions of non-elected judges for those of the people's elected representatives.

What is beyond doubt is that parliamentary supremacy has been replaced in Canada by constitutional supremacy. The Constitution Act, 1982, makes this very clear. Section 32 declares that the Charter applies to both the federal and provincial governments and to all matters under their authority. Section 52(1) of the Constitution Act, 1982, is even more categorical. It states that 'The Constitution of Canada is the supreme law of Canada, and any law that is inconsistent with the provisions of the Constitution is, to the extent of the inconsistency, of no force or effect.' A vestige of Parliament's former superiority is retained, however, through s. 33 of the Charter. This is the so-called 'notwithstanding clause', which enables either Parliament or a provincial legislature to declare that a law shall operate even if it violates the fundamental freedoms, legal rights, or equality rights sections of the Charter. Such a declaration must be renewed after five years, otherwise the constitution reasserts its supremacy.

Judicial Independence and the Separation of Powers

The role of the judicial branch of government is based on constitutional convention rather than law. The Constitution Act, 1867, includes several sections that deal with the system of provincial courts, including how judges shall be selected, how they may be removed, when provincial Superior Court judges must retire (age seventy-five), and who will determine judicial salaries.[15] But there is no mention of the Supreme Court of Canada or of any other federal courts. Instead, section 101 authorizes Parliament to establish a 'General Court of Appeal for Canada', which it did in 1875 (the Supreme Court of Canada) and again in 1970 (the Federal Court of Canada).

Canadian constitutional law is silent on the powers, indeed on the very existence and composition, of this country's highest court of appeal. Nor is the relationship between the judicial and other branches of government described in much detail. This stands in sharp contrast to the American constitution, in which lengthy descriptions of the powers of Congress (the legislative branch) and the President (the executive branch) are followed by Article III on the judicial branch of government. In Canada, however, the role of the judiciary is based largely on constitutional convention and statute law. The fundamental principles that underlie that role are *judicial independence and separation of powers*.

Judicial independence means that judges are to be free from any and all interference in their decision-making. Former Chief Justice Brian Dickson declared that the core of this principle involves 'the complete liberty of individual judges to hear and decide the cases that come before them'.[16] It is particularly important that judges be protected from interference by the government. Despite the fact that the principle of judicial independence is deeply embedded in Canada's political culture, and enshrined in laws on contempt of court and in guidelines for ministerial conduct, doubts have been raised over whether these protections are adequate. The fact that court budgets are determined by governments represents, in the eyes of some, a potential limitation on judicial autonomy.[17]

The principle of separation of powers guarantees the special role of the judiciary. This role is to interpret what the law and the constitution mean when disputes arise. As in the case of judicial independence, this principle relies more on cultural norms, statute law, and constitutional convention than it does on constitutional law. There is, however, at least one important reference to the role of the judicial branch in the constitution. This is section 24 of the Constitution Act, 1982, which declares that the enforcement of the Charter shall be through the courts. The perception that the courts represent a check on the powers of Parliament and the provincial legislatures—a perception that has taken hold since the Charter's passage in 1982—reflects an Americanizing trend in Canadian politics. The concept of checks and balances between the three branches of government is basic to the American constitution. It is not, however, part of British parliamentary democracy.

The separation of the judiciary's role from that of Parliament is not watertight. The ability of the federal and provincial governments to refer a resolution or draft legislation to the courts for a decision on its constitutionality does not, strictly speaking, respect the principle of separation of powers. These constitutional reference cases enable governments to use the provincial and Canadian Supreme Courts to receive advisory opinions before acting, or to thrust a politically volatile issue into the hands of judges. The separation of powers is also breached when judges step outside their role as interpreters of the law's meaning to advocate some position or reform. This occasionally happens (see Box 4.3).

Box 4.3 'Inject Female Values into Judiciary, Supreme Court Judge Urges'

The time is long overdue for the introduction of female values into a judiciary permeated by a male approach to the world, says the first woman appointed to the Supreme Court of Canada

In a speech that delved boldly into public policy, Madam Justice Bertha Wilson proposed that judicial task forces be struck across Canada to find ways to neutralize male bias and thus humanize the law.

She also stressed the need to reform certain criminal laws that are so ludicrous they 'cry out for change'. Sexism courses for judges are also badly needed, Judge Wilson said.

Female values would bring imagination, sympathy and a broader context to the legal system, the judge said in her speech Thursday night at Osgoode Hall Law School at York University in Metro Toronto.

Judge Wilson said these values would balance the fiercely competitive bent men built into the court system in the days when women were systematically shut out of politics and law.

Globe and Mail, 10 February 1990, A5.

Relations between the House of Commons and the Senate

When the founders designed Canada's Parliament, they took the bicameral structure of Britain's legislature as their model. Accordingly, the legislative branch was comprised of two bodies, an elected House of Commons (the lower house) and an appointed Senate (the upper house). A literal reading of the constitution suggests that their powers are roughly equal. The major difference is that money bills must be introduced in the House of Commons. In fact, however, the superiority of the elected House of Commons has been clear from day one. The unelected character of the Senate has always sat uneasily in Canada's democratic political culture. This fact, along with the brazen patronage of most government appointments to the Senate, undermined its legitimacy.

The superiority of the House of Commons over the Senate is reinforced by several constitutional conventions. Probably the most important of these involves the selection of the Prime Minister and other members of the government. Constitutional law does not require that they be drawn from the House of Commons, but it is unthinkable today that the Prime Minister not be an elected MP. It occasionally happens that one or two senators are appointed to cabinet, but this usually is because the party in power has few (or no) MPs from a particular region of the country. And occasionally the Prime Minister will appoint to cabinet someone who is neither an MP nor a Senator.[18] By tradition, however, this person will very soon afterward seek election to the House of Commons. The whole system of democratic accountability would crumble if the Prime Minister and other members of the government were not elected officials, removable by the electorate.

Another convention that reinforces the House of Common's superiority is found in the legislative process itself. All bills must pass both the Senate and the House of Commons before they become law. Moreover, the stages through which a bill must pass are identical in both houses of Parliament. But until recently, it was generally accepted that the Senate did not have the right to obstruct or reject the will of the elected House of Commons. On occasion the Senate would suggest minor revisions to legislation, sending it back to the House of Commons for reconsideration. After the 1984 election of the Progressive Conservative government, however, the Senate—dominated by people appointed during over two decades of almost unbroken Liberal government—became more recalcitrant. On legislation dealing with such matters as drug patents, government spending, unemployment insurance, the Goods and Services Tax, and the Canada–United States Free Trade Agreement, the Senate delayed and in some cases rejected bills coming from the House of Commons. Constitutional law gives senators this right: constitutional convention suggests that they should not try to exercise it (see Box 4.4).

The Biases of British Parliamentary Government

Along with people and the English language, Westminister-style parliamentary government has been one of Britain's chief exports. It is one of the main legacies bequeathed to that country's former colonies, Canada included. We have described the major features of British parliamentary government, as adapted to Canadian circumstances. Let us now consider whether this system tends to favour certain interests and outcomes more than others.

Box 4.4 Showdown in the Legislature

The battle between the House of Commons and the Senate over unemployment insurance reforms appeared no closer to resolution yesterday as both sides claimed to be vindicated by a ruling from the Speaker of the Commons.

Speaker John Fraser decided yesterday that the Progressive Conservative government was procedurally powerless to stop the Liberal controlled Senate's fight against the UI legislation—a decision that Liberal senators interpreted as a victory for them.

However, Mr. Fraser also said that the Commons had moral and democratic principles on its side, and warned that the Senate could be paving the way for a constitutional crisis if it stands firm in its opposition to the UI changes.

'Should the Senate choose to further insist on its amendments, the two Houses may well be unable to resolve their differences and be faced with a serious constitutional crisis,' he said.

Globe and Mail, 27 April 1990, A1.

In discussing ministerial responsibility we noted that the pre-democratic tradition of strong executive authority was never abandoned under British parliamentary government. Instead, it was adapted to the democratic principle that government is based on the consent of the people, a principle embodied in the powers of an elected legislature and in the doctrine of responsible government. When we recall that the legislature that embodied the popular will originally was elected by and accountable to only a fraction of the people, i.e., property-owning males, this adaptation does not appear very revolutionary or particularly democratic. Of course, universal male suffrage arrived by the latter half of the 1800s, and females were enfranchised early in the twentieth century, extending participatory rights to all the people and not simply a privileged group of them. This democratization of citizenship rights did not, however, fundamentally alter the non-participatory biases that were already embedded in the structure of British parliamentary government.

Following Philip Resnick's arguments in *Parliament vs. People*,[19] we may label these biases *statism*. A statist political tradition is one characterized by a relatively strong political executive and by a population that tends to be deferential toward those in power. The adoption of British parliamentary government, first in the colonial legislatures during the mid-1800s and then through the Constitution Act of 1867, mainly reaffirmed the tradition of centralized executive authority that had existed before the elected legislature's approval was needed to pass laws. This reaffirmation of strong executive power is, Resnick argues, apparent throughout Canada's founding Constitution Act. 'What our Founding Fathers were doing', he maintains,

> was consolidating an orderly ... move from direct colonial rule to House Rule.... They had a particular kind of [political] order in mind, the parliamentary system as it had evolved in Britain, combining the interests of monarchs, lords and commoners. If by the latter part of the 19th Century this system was increasingly responsive to the wishes of an electorate, restricted or enlarged, it was by no means a servant of the electorate.[20]

Some might say, that was then but this is now. Yet the institutions of government adopted through the Confederation agreement and, equally important, the expectations of the political élites who controlled the levers of state power reached forward to shape the future course of Canadian politics. Parliament was sovereign, but Parliament was not merely the people. It also included the Crown, the traditional seat of state authority whose powers came to be exercised by a Prime Minister and cabinet with few serious checks from the legislature. 'Parliamentary sovereignty', Resnick argues, 'fostered attitudes in the population which were nominally participatory but maximally deferential towards those exercising political power. The mystique of British Crown and Constitution helped make illegitimate all forms of political activity not sanctioned or channeled through parliamentary institutions.'[21] This is an important point. Resnick is arguing that the more deferential political culture of Canada, as compared to the United States, did not simply happen. It was generated to some degree by parliamentary institutions that discouraged popular participation in politics, beyond the ritual of voting, and that enshrined a sort of top-down philosophy of governance.

The evidence suggests that Resnick is right. There have, of course, been influential currents of participatory politics in Canadian history, particularly coming out of western Canada. But these populist urges have had to struggle against a parliamentary tradition that concentrates political power in the hands of the Prime Minister (or premiers) and cabinet. This style of governance is epitomized in the long tradition of élite deal-making that has characterized federal-provincial relations. But it also surfaces when this country's political leaders reject referenda or constituent assemblies on constitutional change as being 'un-Canadian' or foreign to our political tradition. Indeed, the statist political tradition fostered by British parliamentary government is apparent in a multitude of ways, large and small. 'Our governments', argues Resnick, '... become the organizers of our civic consciousness. National celebrations like Expo have to be staged; nationalist propaganda is transmitted across the airwaves, through the newspapers, along with our social security cheques.'[22] Many argue that the Canadian state's orchestration of culture has been a defensive response to the Americanizing pressures from mass media industries centred in the United States. To some degree this is certainly true. But this explanation of state-centred nationalism in Canada does not pay adequate attention to the possibility that the state's efforts may pre-empt those of groups in civil society and encourage a climate of dependence on government to, in Resnick's words, 'organize our civic consciousness'. If governments had done less, and private citizens more, to construct the identities that are part of Canadian culture, perhaps national unity would be less fragile.

Changing the Constitution

Constitutions are meant to last a very long time, but they seldom do. Among the forty-seven countries whose independence predates 1900, only about a third have constitutions that date from before 1950.[23] Canada's 1867 Constitution Act is one of the oldest and most durable. Only the United States (1787), Sweden (1809), the Netherlands (1814), and the United Kingdom (1832) have older constitutions.

A *coup d'état* is one way of changing a constitution. More peaceful means may also accomplish dramatic change, including the wholesale replacement of one constitution by a fundamentally different one. The political evolution of Eastern Europe since 1989 is testimony to this. But radical alteration of the fundamental rules and structures of government is much less common than constitutional reform. Reform aims at changing some aspect(s) of the existing constitution, leaving the basic constitutional structure intact. Limited change of this sort is generally accomplished through a formal procedure set down in the constitution. Reforms that result from such a process are called *constitutional amendments*.

When does constitutional reform become constitutional upheaval? This is difficult to pinpoint, but the line has certainly been crossed when as a result of change a constitution is no longer recognizably what it was before. For example, the 1982 Constitution Act did three main things: (1) it transformed Canada's written constitution from a set of British laws into Canadian constitutional law; (2) it entrenched the Charter of Rights and Freedoms in the constitution; and (3) it established formal mechanisms for changing the constitution. As important as these changes were, they did not amount to a new constitution. Most features of parliamentary government and of federalism remained the same. On the other hand, the replacement of parliamentary government by American-style congressional government, the elimination of federalism, or—least farfetched of all—the political independence of Quebec would in each case represent a radical transformation of Canada's constitution.

Constitutional change may also come about through the gradual evolution of principles and practices. For example, the principle that the Governor General should accept the advice of the Prime Minister on when Parliament should be dissolved and a new election called was one that emerged imperceptibly as Canada shook off the vestiges of its colonial relationship to Great Britain. It was only when this principle was breached by Governor General Lord Byng in 1926 that it became clear that this relationship between the Prime Minister and the Governor General was part of the constitution. The clear superiority of the House of Commons over the Senate on matters of legislation is another constitutional convention that became clearer with the passage of time. Those appointed to the Senate in 1867 were largely prominent politicians from the new provinces. During this early period the Senate became known as the chamber of 'sober second thought'. Over time, however, the practice of patronage appointments, the emergence of assertive provincial governments as spokespersons for regional interests, and changing ideas about democracy and representation all contributed to the Senate's decline *vis-à-vis* the Commons.

Amending the Constitution before 1982

The Constitution Act, 1867, gave Ottawa a very modest power to amend the constitution of Canada regarding matters that concerned only the federal government.[24] In practical terms, all this power amounted to was the ability to change electoral districts and boundary lines. The Act gave the provincial governments a similar power.[25] Canada's founders, however, failed to establish an amending procedure that could be used to change the division of powers and all the other important matters that could not be changed using the very limited amendment powers conferred by sections 91(1) and 92(1) of the Constitution Act, 1867. They did not even discuss such a procedure, a curious oversight in view of the fact that disagreement over the federal division of powers in the United States had just produced the American Civil War. The only clear requirement was that a request would have to be made to the British Parliament in order to change Canada's constitution. The reason for this was, of course, that the Canadian constitution was in fact a British law, originally passed as the British North America Act, 1867.

What was not clear, however, was who would have to agree here in Canada before a resolution could be sent to London. Would all provincial governments have to agree if a proposed amendment affected their powers? Did Quebec or Ontario or any other province enjoy a special right to veto amendments? Just how much provincial consent was needed to change the constitution? It was not even clear what would happen if all ten provincial legislatures and the House of Commons agreed to an amendment, but the Senate rejected it. Formally, at least, the Senate appeared to have the power to block constitutional change.

After decades of uncertainty, the issue was finally decided by the Supreme Court in 1981. The background to this decision was the stalemate in constitutional negotiations between Ottawa and the provinces. The Liberal government of Pierre Elliott Trudeau wanted to patriate the constitution, entrench in it a Charter of Rights and Freedoms, and establish a formal procedure for future constitutional amendments. Only the governments of Ontario and New Brunswick supported Ottawa's proposal. The conflict ended up in the courts when the governments of Manitoba, Newfoundland, and Quebec each decided to ask their provincial supreme courts whether Ottawa's actions were constitutional. There was some variation in the questions and wording of these provincial references. Nonetheless, they all asked whether: (1) Ottawa's proposed amendments affected provincial powers; and (2) provincial consent was constitutionally required to make such changes. Quebec's reference also asked whether that province had a special veto over amendments. These decisions were then appealed to the Supreme Court of Canada.

In its *Reference on the Constitution*[26] the Court made the following points:

- Some level of provincial consent was required for changes affecting provincial powers. This requirement was a constitutional convention, not part of constitutional law. It could not, therefore, be enforced by the courts.
- The level of required provincial consent was not at all clear. It was the Court's view that a majority of the provinces certainly had to agree, but unanimous consent was not necessary.
- In constitutional law, no province had a special right of veto over constitutional change. The Court did not give an opinion on whether such a right existed as a matter of constitutional convention.
- Ottawa did not need provincial consent before requesting the British Parliament to change Canada's constitution in ways affecting provincial powers. If the federal government chose to act without the consent of the provinces, or with the support of only a few of them, this would be legal—but at the same time unconstitutional!

Both Ottawa and the dissenting provinces claimed victory as a result of the Court's decision. Legally, the way was clear for Ottawa to act with or without the consent of the provinces. Politically, unilateral action remained a very risky option, particularly in light of the Court's acknowledgement that some level of provincial consent was required by constitutional convention. All eleven governments returned to the bargaining table, each side conscious of the constitutional turf occupied by itself and its opponents. In November of 1981, ten of them were able to reach agreement on a compromise document that became the Constitution Act, 1982. Only the PQ government of Quebec rejected the proposed changes. Despite Quebec's refusal to sign the 1981 agreement, the Constitution Act, 1982, is constitutional law in that province just as it is elsewhere in Canada. A 1982 Supreme Court decision confirmed this.[27]

Amending the Constitution since 1982

The uncertainties surrounding constitutional amendment have been largely dispelled by the Constitution Act, 1982. Part V of the Act lays down the amendment procedures. In fact, it establishes four different procedures, each of which applies to certain types of constitutional change. These procedures and when they are used are explained in Table 4.1.

Any of the four amendment procedures may be set in motion by either Ottawa or a provincial government (s. 46(1)). But because intergovernmental agreement is crucial to the success of most amendments, the most likely scenario is that the Prime Minister and the provincial premiers will first reach an agreement that will then be submitted to their respective legislatures. This was the procedure that led to the Meech Lake Accord, the first proposal for constitutional amendment under the 1982 rules. Negotiations and deal-making between governments—the pre-legislative stage of the amendment process—is as crucial now as when the amendment process was governed by convention. The new procedures have not formally expanded the opportunities for public participation, nor have they enlarged the legislature's role in the process.

Not content with the distinction of having four different procedures for amending the constitution, the ten governments who agreed to the 1982 Constitution Act included another extraordinary feature in the amendment rules. This is the 'opting-out' section (s. 40). Under this section, a provincial government that does not agree to an amendment that transfers powers relating to education or other cultural matters from the provinces to Ottawa is not obliged to give up this power. Moreover, Ottawa is required to provide 'reasonable compensation' to any dissenting province. The Meech Lake Accord would have expanded the opting-out section, guaranteeing a dissenting province the right to reasonable compensation in the case of any transfer of legislative powers from the provinces to Ottawa. In fact, this would only have enshrined in the constitution a practice that has existed in Canada since 1964.

The Meech Lake and Charlottetown Accords

The first effort at amending the constitution, using the 1982 rules, ended in acrimonious failure. The proposed amendment was in fact a group of changes collectively known as the Meech Lake Accord. The Accord was a 1987 agreement between Prime Minister Brian Mulroney and the ten provincial premiers. It was a response to a series of five demands that the Quebec government of Robert Bourassa wanted met before it was willing to sign the 1981 agreement that produced the Constitution Act, 1982. The main changes proposed by the Meech Lake Accord included the following:

Table 4.1 Amending the Constitution

PROCEDURE	REQUIREMENT	APPLICATION
1. General (ss. 38, 42)	– Resolution passed by the House of Commons and the Senate* – Two-thirds of the legislatures of the provinces that together comprise at least half the population of all the provinces	– Reduction or elimination of powers, rights, or privileges of provincial governments or legislatures – Proportionate representation of the provinces in the House of Commons – Senate – Supreme Court of Canada (except its composition) – Extension of existing provinces into the territories – Creation of new provinces
2. Unanimous consent (s. 41)	– Resolution passed by the House of Commons and the Senate* – Resolution passed by every provincial legislature	– Queen – Governor General – Lieutenant-governors – Right of each province to at least as many seats in the House of Commons as it has in the Senate – Use of the English or French language (except changes that apply only to single province) – Composition of the Supreme Court – Changing the amending procedures of the constitution
3. Ottawa and one or more provinces (s. 43)	– Resolution passed by the House of Commons and the Senate* – Resolution passed by the legislature of each province where the amendment applies	– Alteration of boundaries between provinces – Use of French or English in a particular province or territory
4. Ottawa or a province acting alone (ss. 44, 45)	– If Ottawa, a resolution resolution passed by the House of Commons and the Senate* – If a province, a resolution passed by its legislature	– Executive government of Canada, the Senate, and the House of Commons, subject to the limits established by ss. 41 and 42 of the Constitution Act, 1982

*If after 180 days the Senate has not passed a resolution already passed by the House of Commons, Senate approval is not necessary.

- *Immigration policy.* Some federal powers over immigration would be transferred to Quebec. This would have entrenched in the constitution an agreement that had been reached between Ottawa and Quebec in 1978. Any other province would also be able to assume these expanded powers.
- *Distinct society.* Quebec would be recognized as a 'distinct society', and the government and legislature of the province would have a responsibility to 'preserve and promote the distinct identity of Quebec'. The distinct identity referred to in this section was explicitly linked to the French language. As well, this section of the Accord declared that the constitution of Canada shall be interpreted in a manner consistent with the recognition of Quebec as a distinct society.
- *Supreme Court.* Provincial governments would have been given the right to nominate candidates for the Supreme Court of Canada. When filling a vacancy on the Court, Ottawa would be obliged to select from the provinces' lists of nominees and to select from the Quebec government's list of nominees in the case of the three Supreme Court positions that must be filled by members of the Quebec bar.
- *Shared-cost programs.* Any provincial government would have the right to receive reasonable compensation from Ottawa in the event that it decided not to participate in a new national shared-cost program. The only stipulation was that the provincial program would have to be 'compatible with the national objectives'.
- *Amending procedures.* Two important changes were proposed to the amending procedures of the constitution. The first would have changed the opting-out provision, discussed earlier, so that a dissenting province would be entitled to reasonable compensation to finance its own programs in the case of any transfer of legislative powers from the provinces to Ottawa. The second change involved the list of subjects requiring the unanimous consent of the provinces. The Accord would have doubled the length of this list, adding to it Senate reform, the principle of proportionate representation of the provinces in the House of Commons, any change to the Supreme Court of Canada, and both the extension of existing provinces into the territories and the establishment of new provinces.

After three years of wrangling marked by both an anti-French backlash in parts of English Canada and a revival of separatist nationalism in Quebec, the Accord expired. It was not ratified by all of the provincial legislatures before the three-year deadline imposed on the process by the constitution. What did the Meech Lake episode tells us about the new process of amending the constitution?

Both the birth and the death of the Accord suggested that not much had changed as a result of formalizing the amendment process. The proposed changes that made up the Accord represented a deal struck between eleven heads of government, a deal that was reached with no public participation or legislative debate. In fact, the Prime Minister and some of the provincial premiers were very insistent that their agreement could not be altered in any respect. It was submitted to their legislatures for ratification, not for possible modification. Groups and individuals opposed to the Accord's provisions denounced this process as being undemocratic.

The critics may have been right. But it was also clear that any change to the 1987 first ministers' agreement would have required that a new resolution be submitted to Parliament and all the provincial legislatures, and the ratification process would have to start over again. Debate and popular participation *after* an amendment resolution has been agreed to by governments are almost certain to prolong the amendment process and probably reduce the chances of reaching an agreement. But this is not an argument in favour of élitist deal-making. It is, rather, a reason for providing adequate opportunities for public involvement *before* a resolution is framed and submitted to the legislatures. As matters currently stand, these opportunities depend entirely on the readiness of the eleven governments to hold public hearings and listen to the views of interested groups.

For those who were heartened by the popular participation that contributed to the Constitution Act, 1982, particularly to the drafting of the equality rights section (s. 15) and the inclusion of provisions dealing with Aboriginal rights, the Meech Lake episode was a disappointment. Public participation was solicited very late in the process, and then only because the Accord seemed destined for defeat. Finally, the federal government decided to establish a Special Committee to hold a month of public hearings on the New Brunswick government's plan to save the Accord. Critics charged that the Special Committee's hearings were orchestrated in favour of those advocating the Accord. The Committee's report declared that 'the lesson of Meech Lake is that the Canadian people want a say in the development of their Constitution'. There was, however, little to suggest that any of the governments struggling over the Accord saw public participation as anything more than a resource to use when convenient.

The death of the Meech Lake Accord likewise suggested that the process of constitutional amendment remained largely as it was before 1982. The final several months leading up to the 23 June 1990 ratification deadline were marked by acrimonious debate and some *ad hoc* efforts to salvage the Accord, and finally ended with Quebec being largely isolated from the other provinces (see Chapter 5). There was a sense of *déjà vu* about the whole affair. Quebec had been similarly isolated in 1971 when the first Bourassa government suddenly withdrew its acceptance of the Victoria Charter amendments, and then again in 1981 when René Lévesque claimed to have been betrayed by a last-minute deal concocted by the other provinces. In each case agreement ran aground because Quebec and some of the governments of English Canada were unable to settle their differences on Quebec's status within Canada. Meech Lake came to grief because of the same obstacle that had blocked previous efforts at constitutional change.

Wrangling over the constitution did not die with the Meech Lake Accord. On the contrary, the next two years saw dozens of government-organized public hearings on the constitution and hundreds of conferences and forums organized by academics, political parties, and interest groups. Ottawa and the provinces were determined to avoid the charges of élitist deal-making that had been levelled at the Meech Lake process. In this they failed. Although there were ample opportunities for citizens and groups to express their views on constitutional reform, the proposals presented to Canadians in the 26 October 1992 referendum were widely viewed as yet another instance of the élites cutting a deal and trying to foist it on the public.

The Charlottetown Accord, as these proposals were referred to, represented the culmination of what the federal government rather misleadingly called the 'Canada round' of constitutional negotiations (the period leading up to Meech Lake having been labelled the 'Quebec round'). In fact, however, the desire to get the Quebec government's political agreement to the constitutional changes of 1982 and worry over the post-Meech Lake resurgence of support for separatism were the chief reasons why the constitutional issue dominated Canadian politics with a vengeance between 1990 and 1992. Moreover, the deal ultimately struck at Charlottetown in August, 1992, bore a striking resemblance to the Meech Lake Accord in some important respects. The main features included the following:

- a Canada clause listing the fundamental characteristics of Canadian society;
- recognition of Quebec as a distinct society;
- entrenchment of the Aboriginal right to self-government;
- an elected Senate with equal representation from the provinces and, eventually, special seats for Aboriginal representatives;
- Francophone veto in the Senate regarding bills affecting the French language or culture;
- guarantee of three Quebec judges on the Supreme Court and provincial input in the selection of judges;
- Quebec guaranteed at least 25 per cent of the seats in the House of Commons;
- entrenchment of Ottawa's right to spend money on matters within provincial jurisdiction, but with the provision that any province could opt out of any new shared-cost program and be entitled to reasonable compensation to run its own program;
- confirmation of the provinces' exclusive jurisdiction in several policy areas, and some decentralization of powers to the provinces in the areas of immigration and labour policy.

In the national referendum on the Charlottetown Accord, a majority of Canadians (54.5 per cent) rejected the proposed reforms, including provincial majorities in British Columbia, Alberta, Saskatchewan, Manitoba, Quebec, and Nova Scotia, as well as the Yukon. The result in Ontario was virtually a dead heat. During the impassioned referendum campaign it was clear that many English Canadians said 'no' to the Charlottetown Accord because they thought it gave Quebec too much, while many Francophone Quebecers rejected the deal because they believed it gave them too little! Indeed, the only serious question asked by members of the Quebec media and the province's politicians during the campaign was 'Did Quebec get enough in the Charlottetown Accord?' Although the 1992 agreement provided the Quebec government with more than had been proposed by the Meech Lake Accord, this was not enough in the nationalist political climate that prevailed in the post-Meech years.

On the other hand, a further decentralization of powers to the provinces and special status for Quebec proved to be more than most English Canadians could stomach. While it is always treacherous and somewhat misleading to talk about Quebec or any society as though it has a single set of aspirations, the failure of the Meech Lake and Charlottetown accords confirmed that a wide gap existed between those of Francophone Quebecers and their compatriots in the rest of the country.

Citizen Participation in Constitutional Reform

For most of Canada's history the only direct actors in constitutional reform were governments. This changed during the negotiations and debates that led to the Constitution Act of

1982, when a number of citizens' interest groups played an active role through lobbying government and attempting to influence public opinion. These groups, and many others inspired by the opportunities created by the Charter, were instrumental in bringing about the death of the 1987 Meech Lake Accord, which had been agreed to by the eleven first ministers in the old pre-1982 style. During the two years of consultation and negotiation that preceded the signing of the 1992 Charlottetown Accord these citizens' interest groups were very much part of the process. Informally at least, Ottawa and the provincial governments appeared to have conceded the legitimacy of a more inclusive style of constitution-making.

What they did not concede, however, was a direct role for public participation and consent. Under the old élitist policy-making style, popular consent was mediated by the heads of government. Under the more inclusive policy-making style that emerged in the early 1980s, popular consent was mediated by these heads of government *plus* certain citizens' interest groups claiming to speak on behalf of women, ethnic and racial minorities, Aboriginals, the disabled, official-language minorities, and so on. But not until the decision was taken in the late summer of 1992 to submit the Charlottetown reforms to the people in a national referendum was popular consent unmediated and the public given a direct role in the constitutional amendment process. This represented a remarkable break from Canada's élitist tradition of constitution-making. With few exceptions, mainly from western Canada, the idea of a referendum to approve constitutional change had been rejected throughout Canada's history. When a formal procedure for constitutional amendment was being debated in the 1930s, one of the country's most prominent constitutionalists dismissed the suggestion of a referendum as being inconsistent with cabinet government and a device for 'passing the buck'.[28] Frank Underhill, expressing the views of most intellectuals, argued that average citizens were generally incompetent to decide matters of constitutional change and that their elected representatives usually held more advanced views on public affairs. Legislatures, not citizens, he argued, should be required to ratify constitutional reforms.[29]

The idea of a referendum on the Meech Lake Accord surfaced from time to time in the English-language media. It was dismissed by Prime Minister Mulroney and most of the provincial premiers as being alien to Canada's political tradition. This view was as likely to be expressed by those on the social-democratic left, such as the national New Democratic Party leader, Ed Broadbent, and Manitoba's NDP Premier, Howard Pawley, as by those more to the right of the political spectrum.

But in the flood of condemnation that followed the death of the Meech Lake Accord the idea that popular ratification should be sought in any future attempt to change the constitution gathered force. Quebec's provincial government committed itself to holding a provincial referendum on whatever agreement it reached with Ottawa. British Columbia also passed a law requiring provincial ratification of reform proposals. However, most politicians remained steadfast in their opposition. Ottawa's decision to introduce legislation enabling Parliament to authorize a referendum (really a plebiscite, in that the vote would be formally non-binding) reflected practical necessity more than principled conviction. The powerful Quebec caucus of the governing Conservative Party opposed such legislation. The Minister of Intergovernmental Affairs, Joe Clark, had often expressed serious reservations about a referendum. But the fact was that Quebec and British Columbia were both committed to holding referenda, and there was a good chance that the reform proposals would be rejected in both provinces. A national referendum campaign and a favourable vote in most regions was a possible way of legitimizing reform proposals in this climate of division.

The decision to hold a referendum on the Charlottetown Accord and the decision to abide by what was, legally speaking, a non-binding popular vote appeared to mark the beginning of a new era in Canadian constitution-making. Most commentators believed so, arguing that governments would in the future find it impossible to ignore the 1992 precedent of a popular ratification vote.

Such predictions may be premature. A country's political culture and ways of conducting politics do not change abruptly as a result of a single experience. First ministers will continue to be the key players in any future effort at constitutional reform. Both political tradition and the formal amendment procedure ensure their dominance. But a repeat of the Meech Lake process—an accord negotiated and agreed to without consultation—has become virtually unthinkable. Public consultation, which inevitably privileges the leadership of organized groups, is a necessary precondition for any future agreement.

It remains to be seen, however, whether governments will feel obliged to submit future agreements to the electorate for ratification, or whether the Charlottetown experience was an aberration that has left no mark on Canada's political culture. In provinces like British Columbia and Alberta, which have more of a populist tradition than the rest of Canada, the political pressure for constitutional referenda may be irresistible. In the case of Quebec, the idea that any major change in that province's constitutional status must be approved by the electorate is now firmly established. These provinces are the ones most likely to insist on popular ratification of constitutional reform. If they do, it becomes very awkward for Ottawa not to concede a role for direct public participation through a national referendum, as happened in 1992.

Francophone minorities outside Quebec, like the one in the Ste-Anne parish of Tecumseh, Ontario, realized that their future was doubtful if Quebecers voted to separate in the 1995 referendum. (Stephen Brooks)

Canada's constitution establishes two levels of government—national and provincial—both of which have important law-making and taxation powers. This system of divided jurisdiction is known as federalism. In this chapter some of the major issues associated with federalism are discussed, including the following:

- ❖ What is federalism?
- ❖ The origins, maintenance, and demise of federal states.
- ❖ The origins of Canadian federalism.
- ❖ The federal division of powers.
- ❖ The courts and federalism.
- ❖ Quebec's impact on federalism.
- ❖ Centre-periphery relations.
- ❖ Intergovernmental relations.
- ❖ Financing federalism.
- ❖ The federal spending power and national standards.

CHAPTER FIVE

■ Federalism

When the proposal to create an independent Canada was discussed at Charlottetown (1864) and Quebec (1867), the main subject of debate was the relationship between the new national and regional governments. Two decades of self-government and the constitutional traditions imported from Britain provided the colonies with ready guideposts for most other features of the constitution. Federalism, by contrast, was uncharted territory. Most of the practical knowledge Canada's founders had of the principles and operation of federalism was based on their observation of the United States. The lessons they took from the American experience were mainly negative. Secession of the Confederacy and the bloody Civil War of 1861–5 did not inspire much confidence in the American model. Despite all this, Canada's founders opted for a federal system of government.

What Is Federalism?

A federal system of government is one in which the constitutional authority to make laws and to tax is divided between a national government and some number of regional governments. Neither the national government acting alone nor the regional governments acting together have the authority to alter the powers of the other level of government. They are co-ordinate and independent in their separate constitutional spheres. Citizens in a federal state are members of two political communities, one national and the other coinciding with the boundaries of the province, state, canton—the name given to the regional units of a federal state vary between countries—in which they reside.

Federalism is a legal term, and its existence is based on the constitution. If a single government controls all legislative and taxation powers in a country, then no amount of administrative decentralization or variation in the economic, social, or cultural characteristics of its regions will make it a federal state. Federalism is chiefly a property of constitutions, not of societies. Nonetheless, some political scientists refer to 'federal-type' societies, a tendency that has been labelled the *sociological approach* to federalism. Its most prominent advocate, American political scientist William S. Livingston, argues that '[t]he essence of federalism lies not in the constitutional or institutional structure but in the society itself.'[1] 'Federalism', Livingston declares, 'is a function of societies.'[2]

Which understanding of federalism is correct, the constitutional or sociological one? The answer must be the constitutional approach, for two reasons. First, if federalism is primarily a quality of societies, not of constitutions, then relatively few countries are not federal. After all, most societies have politically significant ethnic or linguistic minorities, often concentrated in a particular region of the country. In fact, of those political systems with federal constitutions, only India places in the world's top ten countries ranked according to their level of ethnic and linguistic diversity. Canada is 19th, Belgium is 49th, Switzerland and the United States tie at 54th place, and Australia comes in at 69th.[3]

The second reason for preferring the constitutional approach to federalism involves the dynamic of state power. A federal constitution institutionalizes regional divisions by associating them with different governments. The regionalism that is responsible for the adoption of a federal constitution in the first place is reinforced by political and administrative rivalries between the national and regional governments. Regional politics can certainly take place in the absence of a federal constitution. But the political significance of regional differences tends to be elevated by associating them with different political jurisdictions and the governments/bureaucracies that preside over them.

Federalism divides political authority along territorial lines. It is not, however, the only form of government to do so. Important policy-making and administrative powers may be exercised at the regional level even in a unitary state. The extent to which these activities are *decentralized*, i.e., placed in the hands of regional officials, or remain *centralized* at the national level is determined by the particular social, geographic, and political conditions of a country. This is also true of federal states, where the constitution provides only a partial and sometimes very misleading guide to the real division of powers between governments. Political authority is also linked to territory in *confederations* and *economic communities*. These are formal groupings of independent states that have agreed to assign certain legislative and administrative functions to a common institution or set of institutions. All member states have a say—though not necessarily an equal say—in the decision-making of such a body, while retaining their ultimate sovereignty (see Box 5.1).

The Origins, Maintenance, and Demise of Federal States

Only about twenty of the 184 member countries of the United Nations have a federal system of government. We say 'about twenty' because the determination of whether a political system is federal is not an exact science. Using the definition of federalism offered in the previous section, one can identify fifteen countries with federal constitutions, five confederal political systems, and at least one with a constitution that recognizes the autonomy of a particular region within national borders (see Table 5.1). Some of these choices may be open to

Box 5.1 Territory and Political Authority

In the unitary form of government, even when there is a good measure of administrative or legislative devolution or decentralization, sovereignty or competence resides exclusively with the central government, and regional or local governments are legally and politically subordinate to it.

In the federal form of government, sovereignty or competence is distributed between central and provincial (or state) governments so that, within a single political system, neither order of government is legally or politically subordinate to the other, and each order of government is elected by and exercises authority directly upon the electorate.

In the confederal form of government, even where there is a considerable allocation of responsibilities to central institutions or agencies, the ultimate sovereignty is retained by the member-state governments and, therefore, the central government is legally and politically subordinate to them. Furthermore, the members of the major central institutions are delegates of the constituent state governments.

An economic association, when it has common organizing institutions, is a confederal type of government in which the functions assigned by the participating states to the common institutions are limited mainly to economic cooperation and coordination.

Task Force on Canadian Unity, *Coming to Terms: The Words of the Debate* (Hull: Supply and Services Canada, 1979), 21–2.

challenge. For example, both the Mexican and Argentine governments have sometimes interfered with the autonomy of state governments. But the precise membership of the club is less important than the fact that it is a small one. Unitary government is far more popular, even in countries where regionally based political conflicts are strong.

What are the circumstances that lead to the adoption of a federal political system? Although there is no simple answer, it is possible to identify a very general condition that is present at the birth of all federal states and vital to the continued health of a federal union. This involves agreement among the regional components of the federal state that the benefits of being part of the union exceed whatever costs membership may impose. A federal state is based, therefore, on a *consensus of regions*. Students of international law and federalism disagree over whether any part of a federal state has a legal right to break away from the union. But the political facts are that when a region no longer shares the national consensus on which federalism is based, its separation becomes a real possibility.

'[F]ederalism', declares Pierre Trudeau, 'has all along been a product of reason in politics.... it is an attempt to find a rational compromise between the divergent interest-groups which history has thrown together; but it is a compromise based on the will of the people.'[4] This is why federal unions are often referred to as 'pacts', 'contracts', or 'bargains'. The key role of consent may be seen in the case of the former Soviet Union. As part of the post-World War Two deal between the Soviet Union and the US-led Western democracies, the countries of Estonia, Latvia, and Lithuania were made members of the Soviet 'federal' state against their will. Their unwilling entry into the Soviet Union, combined with the fact that Moscow dominated the regional republics through the Communist Party's monopoly on power, exposed the hollowness of the Soviet Union's federal pretensions. But with the 1989 aboli-

Table 5.1 Federal, Confederal, and Quasi-Federal Political Systems, 1995

1. Federal	2. Confederal	3. Quasi-Federal*
Argentina	Commonwealth of Independent States	Spain
Australia	European Union	
Austria	Senegambia (Senegal & Gambia)	
Belgium	Trinidad and Tobago	
Botswana	United Arab Emirates	
Brazil		
Canada		
Germany		
India		
Malaysia		
Mexico		
Saint Kits and Nevis		
Switzerland		
United States		
Venezuela		

*Catalon has the status of an autonomous region within Spain's borders.

tion of the Communist Party's legal monopoly on power and the greater autonomy enjoyed by the regional republics, the Soviet Union fell apart. Without even a minimal consensus on the desirability of maintaining the central government, and without the Communist Party and Red Army to keep them in check, republic after republic declared national independence.

Trudeau's argument that federalism is the product of reason will not convince Quebec separatists, whose view of 1867 is of a sell-out by an élite of 'cannibal kings'[5] who were willing to collaborate with the Anglo-Saxon oppressor. Nor does reason appear to be the chief factor explaining why disgruntled regions remain part of a federal union when their politicians and their people clearly believe that they are treated unfairly and exploited for the benefit of other regions—a century-old view in western Canada. Some argue that the 'reason' that leads to federal union or that sustains it may indeed be in the self-interest of some groups, but that federalism may not be reasonable from the standpoint of other groups' self-interest.

Nevertheless, the origins of federal democracies lie in compromise. Because some regions are more enthusiastic than others about the federal compromise—indeed, some may enter it only because of despair at the lack of viable alternatives—does not diminish the fact that the voluntary consent of the regions forms the basis of a federal union. Once established, however, a federal state achieves a new dynamic. The existence of a national government and the idea of national citizenship are centralizing factors that offset the decentralizing pull of regional interests. Federalism is sustained, then, not by sheer rational calculations on the part of regional populations and politicians. Instead, it is sustained by a *sense of political nationality*. According to Donald Smiley, for two decades Canada's foremost expert on federalism, political nationality 'means that Canadians as such have reciprocal moral and legal claims upon one another that have no precise counterparts in their relations with others, and that Canadians as such have a continuing determination to carry out a significant number of important common activities together.'[6] It is, in short, a sense of political community that transcends regional, ethnic, and linguistic identifications (though it does not replace or necessarily overshadow the other identities that citizens have of themselves).

Federalism is ultimately sustained by the sense of political nationality—or community—that develops around the national state. By the same token, the break-up of a federal state is sure to be presaged by the deterioration of this sense of community. Sometimes a sense of political nationality is never solidly established in the first place, as it was not in post-independence Nigeria (1961–5). In other cases a fragile political nationality may be destroyed by a particularly divisive regional conflict, as American federalism was split asunder by the slavery issue. The most stable federal systems are those where regional communities share in a sense of political nationality that dampens the decentralizing tendencies produced by regional differences. Switzerland, the contemporary United States, and Austria are good examples of this. The Swiss case in particular demonstrates the fact that regionally based ethno-linguistic divisions do not necessarily prevent the development of a strong political nationality.

To say that a weak sense of political nationality is associated with unstable federalism really just begs the question: What determines the strength of political nationality? Why do regional divisions acquire the status of independence movements in some federal states but not in others? Several factors come into play, but the most basic is regional inequality. If the citizens of a particular region feel strongly that existing federal structures discriminate against their interests economically and politically, this places a strain on the sense of political nationality. Sentiments like these are, however, very common. A 1981 survey found that only in Ontario and PEI did a majority of respondents agree that their province was treated fairly by the federal government.[7] Such feelings do not, however, prevent people from feeling positively toward Canada. A 1991 Gallup poll discovered that large majorities in all regions except Quebec thought of themselves as Canadians first and provincial citizens second.[8]

The likelihood that regional grievances may threaten the stability of federalism is greatest when they are linked to a nationalist movement. Nationalism is usually accompanied by territorial claims. These claims can range from demands for outright independence to more moderate calls for greater autonomy for the region where members of the national community are concentrated. What distinguishes nationalism from regionalism is that nationalism makes its demands on behalf of both a territory and a community that share some ethnic, linguistic, or other cultural traits. This is far more difficult to accommodate within a federal state than is a region's complaints of unfair treatment. Indeed, nationalism linked to the social and cultural characteristics of a group is fundamentally at odds with the concept of political nationality on which a viable federal state depends.

The Origins of Canadian Federalism

Canada's federal constitution was a compromise. Most of the Anglophone Fathers of Confederation favoured a unitary system of government under which all power would be in the hands of a new national parliament. They were opposed, however, by two groups. The strongest opposition came from the French-Canadian representatives of Canada East, what today is Quebec. This group, led by George-Étienne Cartier, insisted on constitutional protection for their cultural community. They believed that the most effective way to protect their interests was through a federal union that gave exclusive jurisdiction over linguistic and cultural matters to the provincial governments. Federalism was also the preferred constitutional option of Maritime politicians. Maritimers had developed strong local identities that they were unwilling to see submerged under unitary government. Besides, in an era when politics and patronage were virtually synonymous it was only reasonable that provincial politicians would want to retain control over such important sources of contracts as roads and public works, as well as bureaucratic sinecures.

Although the Anglophone politicians of Ontario and Quebec tended to be much less enthusiastic about federalism, some of them saw merit in the idea of dividing legislative powers between two levels of government. For example, Grit politician George Brown expressed the view that conflict between the English Protestant and French Catholic communities—conflict that had produced government instability and political deadlock in the legislature of the United Canadas, and that was one of the reasons behind the Confederation movement—would be reduced by assigning local matters to the provincial legislatures.[9] Ottawa would deal with matters of national interest, like trade and commerce, immigration, defence, and transportation. The presumption that sectional rivalries and local interests would not enter into deliberations on these national issues was naive, to say the least.

The forces pushing the colonies of British North America toward political union required a strong national government. Commercial interests, particularly railroad promoters, wanted unification because their ability to raise investment capital abroad was linked to Canada's credit worthiness. A larger union, with a wider revenue base and an integrated national economy, was crucial to the railroad promoters' interests and to those of the Canadian financial institutions linked to them. Likewise, a strong central government was needed if British North America was to assume the burden of its own military defence and if expansion into the sparsely populated region between Ontario and British Columbia was to be accomplished. Tugging in the opposite direction were the facts of cultural dualism and the existence of colonial administrations and regional societies that were unwilling to be completely submerged in a unitary state that would inevitably be dominated by Ontario and Quebec. Federalism was a necessary compromise between these contradictory tendencies.

What sort of federal union did the founders envisage? Obviously, different politicians had different expectations. Some, such as Canada's first Prime Minister, John A. Macdonald, anticipated that the provincial governments would be little more than glorified municipalities, subordinate to Ottawa. Others, including Oliver Mowat, who as Ontario's Premier led the movement for provincial rights during the 1870s and 1880s, clearly did not share this centralist vision.[10] Individual expectations aside, the agreement the founders reached gave what were then the most important legislative powers and sources of public revenue to the federal government. Ottawa was given authority over trade and commerce, shipping, fisheries, interprovincial transportation, currency and banking, the postal service, and several other subjects related to managing the economy. Responsibility for immigration and agriculture was divided between the federal and provincial governments, but in the event of a conflict, Ottawa's legislation would prevail. The federal government was also assigned the duty to build an intercolonial railway connecting Montreal to Halifax. Together, these powers appeared to establish Ottawa's clear superiority over the provinces in economic matters. When we consider that promoting economic growth and military defence (also a federal responsibility) were the two chief functions of the nineteenth-century state, there is little doubt that Ottawa was assigned the major legislative powers of that era.

Ottawa's superiority was also clear on the taxation front. Donald Smiley notes that customs and excise taxes—indirect forms of taxation—accounted for about three-quarters of colonial revenues prior to Confederation. The Confederation agreement made these the exclusive preserve of the federal government, which could '[raise] Money by any Mode or System of Taxation' (s. 91(3)). The provinces were restricted to the less developed field of 'Direct Taxation' (s. 92(2)), as well as royalties on provincially owned natural resources (s. 109). Not only were provincial revenue sources meagre compared to those of the federal government, the Confederation agreement also established the practice of federal money transfers to the provinces (s. 118, repealed in 1950). The dependence of the economically weaker provinces on subsidies from Ottawa began in 1867 and continues to this day (see the discussion later in this chapter).

In addition to all this, the Confederation agreement included several provisions that have been described as *quasi-federal*. They appear to establish a nearly colonial relationship between Ottawa and the provinces by permitting the federal government to disallow laws passed by provincial legislatures. Sections 55, 56, and 90 of the Constitution Act, 1867, give provincial lieutenant-governors, appointees of Ottawa, the authority to reserve approval from any Act passed by a provincial legislature for a period of up to one year or to disallow the Act at any time within a year of its passage. These were widely used powers during the first few decades after Confederation and were used periodically during the first half of the twentieth century. In most instances Ottawa was reacting to provincial economic policies that challenged its own priorities and jurisdiction. Moreover, section 92(10c) gives the federal government the authority to intervene in a provincial economy by declaring that the construction of a 'public work' (this could be anything from a road to an oil field) is in the national interest. This power has been used 470 times, but has not been used since 1961. Finally, section 93(3)(4) actually gives Ottawa the power to pass laws respecting education, an area of provincial jurisdiction. It may do so where education rights that denominational minorities held when a province entered Confederation are abrogated by provincial law. This power has never been used.

Assuming that it is even possible to sort out the founders' intentions, do they really matter? Legally, no. In interpreting the federal division of powers the courts have generally been unreceptive to arguments about what the Fathers of Confederation really had in mind.[11] Indeed, the majority ruling in the 1981 Patriation Reference declared flatly that 'arguments from history do not lead to any consistent view or any single view of the nature of the British North America Act. So, too, with pronouncements by political figures or persons in other branches of public life. There is little profit in parading them.'[12]

Politically, however, arguments about intentions can matter. The argument that has been most frequently made about Canadian federalism is that it represents a compact between French and English Canada or, alternatively, a contract between the provinces that agreed to give up certain powers to a new national government of their creation. Both the compact and contract theories of federalism maintain that the federal 'bargain' cannot be changed without the mutual consent of those who agreed to it. In the case of the compact theory, this means that Quebec—the province in which most Francophones reside and the only province in which they are in the majority—should have a veto over any constitutional change that affects either the federal distribution of powers or the relative weight of Quebec in Parliament and on the Supreme Court (where three of the nine justices must be members of the Quebec bar). This argument was rejected by the Supreme Court of Canada in the 1981 Patriation Reference and again in 1982.[13]

Those who argue that federalism is a contract between the provinces claim that each of them has the right to veto constitutional change that affects provincial powers or national representation. In fact, there are three variants of contract theory. One would restrict the right of veto to the original signatories. A second extends it to all provinces, regardless of when they joined Canada. The third takes the position that the unanimous consent of the provinces is not required to change the federal distribution of powers but that 'substantial provincial agreement' is necessary. Like compact theory, none of these variants of contract theory has any legal foundation.

The political importance of these compact/contract theories may be seen in the fact that Canadian governments were for nearly fifty years unable to agree on a formula for amending the constitution. Between the first serious attempt in 1935 and the 1982 promulgation of the Constitution Act, it proved impossible to get all the provincial governments to agree to an amendment formula. Unanimous provincial consent appeared to be a political requirement for enacting such a formula (although if one or two of the smaller provinces had been the only dissenters, this 'requirement' might have been overcome somehow). Moreover, many constitutionalists and political scientists came to assume—wrongly, it turned out—that unanimity or something close to it was also a legal requirement.

Compact and contract interpretations of Canadian federalism continue to carry political weight. The Quebec government's refusal to agree to the Constitution Act, 1982, was widely viewed as a serious blow to the constitution's legitimacy. Former Prime Minister Brian Mulroney regularly, if misleadingly, spoke of bringing Quebec into the constitution. Legally, of course, the 1982 reforms applied right across Canada. But politically the Prime Minister had a point. The Meech Lake Accord was intended to satisfy the Quebec government's conditions for signing the 1982 constitutional agreement. Both the reasons for the Meech Lake Accord and the protracted and anguished debate that preceded and followed its failure revealed that the idea of Canada as a bi-national compact was as alive, and controversial, as ever.

The Federal Division of Powers

Whatever the intentions of the founders may have been when they drafted the Constitution Act, 1867, it is clear today that both levels of government exercise wide-ranging legislative and taxation powers. Their ability to do so ultimately rests on the responsibilities assigned to them by the constitution. Canada's founders took exceptional pains to specify the responsibilities of each level of government. But a literal reading of the division of powers they decided on and the formal changes that have been made to it since then provide at best a partial and at worst a misleading guide to Canadian federalism. In some cases policy areas were unthought of when the federal division of powers was framed—electronic communications, air transportation, and environmental protection would be examples—and so are not explicitly assigned to either Ottawa or the provinces. In other cases what were minor responsibilities in the nineteenth and early twentieth centuries have assumed greater importance as a result of economic and societal changes, and of changes in the state itself.

The heart of the federal division of powers is found in sections 91 and 92 of the Constitution Act, 1867. Each of these sections contains a detailed list of enumerated powers that belong exclusively to the federal (s. 91) or the provincial (s. 92) governments. Combined with several other sections that also deal with the division of powers, this is the constitutional foundation of Canadian federalism. An examination of who holds what powers reveals that both Ottawa and the provinces have the capacity to act in most of the major policy fields (see Table 5.2).

Some of the constitutional powers listed in Table 5.2 could reasonably have been placed under more than one policy heading. The authority to tax, for example, has been used to promote economic growth, to redistribute income between groups, and to subsidize all sorts of special interests. Unemployment insurance is both an economic policy, tied to manpower retraining and a claimant's job search activities, and a social policy that has the effect of redistributing income to less affluent regions of the country. Immigration policy has always been harnessed to the needs of the Canadian economy and has also been tied to cultural policy through citizenship services and language training for immigrants.

At the same time, governments have sometimes found the authority to legislate in powers that are implied, rather than stated, in the constitution. The most important example of this involves the federal government's spending power. Ottawa spends billions of dollars annually on programs that fall under the jurisdiction of provincial and municipal governments. The federal government also provides money to universities (for research) and to school boards (for language instruction), even though these organizations fall under the constitutional authority of the provinces, and to individuals for purposes that might appear to fall under provincial jurisdiction. Ottawa's constitutional 'right' to spend money for any purpose has never been definitely established in the courts.[14] Nevertheless, the spending power today provides the constitutional basis for such major federal grants to the provinces as the Canada Health and Social Transfer (which, among other things, helps to pay for social assistance, health care, and post-secondary education) and equalization payments.

The Courts and Federalism

Only the layperson perceives constitutional terms like 'trade and commerce', 'property and civil rights', and 'direct taxation' to have straightforward meanings. This view has not been shared by constitutional lawyers, governments, and the private interests that have challenged federal and provincial laws. For these groups the federal division of powers is a dense thicket of contradictory and contested meanings and opportunities, and the interpretation attached to a particular enumerated power is often a matter to haggle over in the courts. The judicial decisions that have resulted from these disputes have played an important role in shaping the evolution of Canadian federalism.

Table 5.2 The Federal Division of Powers under the Constitution Acts

	Ottawa	Provinces
Public finance	(1867) – 91(3): authority to raise money by any 'Mode or System of Taxation' – 91(4): authority to borrow money (1982) – 36(2): commits Ottawa to the principle of equalizing public revenue levels in the provinces	(1867) – 92(2): authorizes direct taxation within the province – 92(3): authority to borrow money – 92A(4): permits provinces to use 'any mode or system of taxation' in the case of non-renewable natural resources, forestry resources, and electrical energy
Managing the economy	(1867) – 91(2): regulation of trade and commerce – 91(2A): unemployment insurance – 91(5): post office – 91(10, 12): navigation, international waters, and offshore resources – 91(14, 15, 16, 18, 19, 20): national monetary system – 91(17, 22, 23): commercial standards – 92(10c): authority to intervene in a provincial economy by declaring a public work to be in the national interest – 95: agriculture – 121: prohibits provincial taxes on imports from other provinces, thus reinforcing the concept of a national economic union (1982) – 6(2): guarantees the economic mobility of citizens anywhere within Canada, reinforcing the concept of a national economic union	(1867) – 92(9): authority to issue commercial licences – 92(10): public works within the province – 92(11): incorporation of companies with provincial objects – 92(13): property and civil rights – 92A: reaffirms provincial authority over natural resources within their borders – 95: agriculture, but federal law takes precedence – 109: establishes provincial ownership of natural resources within their borders (1982) – 6(4): permits provinces to favour provincial residents in hiring if the rate of unemployment in that province is above the national average
Social policy and the quality of life	(1867) – 91(24): Aboriginal Canadians – 91(26): marriage and divorce – 93(3, 4): authority to protect the educational rights of denominational minorities	(1867) – 92(7): hospitals – 92(12): solemnization of marriage – 93: education – 94A: public pensions

Table 5.2 continued

	– 94A: old age pensions, but provincial law prevails – 95: immigration	– 95: immigration, but federal law prevails
Cultural policy	(1867) – 133: official bilingualism of Parliament	(1867) – 92(16): all matters of a merely local or private nature – 93: education – 133: official bilingualism of Quebec legislature
	(1982) – 16(1), 19, 20: establish official bilingualism in all institutions of the federal government	(1982) – 16(2), 17(2), 18(2), 19(2), 20(2): establishes official bilingualism in all institutions of the New Brunswick government
Administration and enforcement of law	(1867) – 91(27): criminal law – 91(28): penitentiaries – 96: appointment of judges of provincial courts – 100: authority to set judicial salaries – 101: authority to establish a general court of appeal for Canada, and other federal courts	(1867) – 92(14): administration of justice and the organization of courts within the province – 92(15): authority to establish penalties for violations of provincial laws
International relations and defence	(1867) – 91(7): military and defence – 132: authority to enter foreign treaties and perform obligations under them	– Since the Supreme Court's decision in the *Labour Conventions* case of 1937, it appears that provincial consent is required to implement foreign treaty obligations involving matters of provincial jurisdiction. There is, however, no consensus on this.
Other legislative authority	(1867) – 91 (preamble): authorizes Parliament to make laws for the 'peace, order, and good government' of Canada – 91(29): matters not falling under the enumerated powers of the provinces come under Ottawa's jurisdiction	(1867) – 92(8): municipal institutions – 92(16): all matters of a local or private nature in the province

Among the many contentious sections of the constitution, the courts' interpretation of Ottawa's authority to 'make laws for the peace, order, and good government of Canada' and the federal government's 'trade and commerce' power have had the greatest impact on the division of powers. We will look briefly at each of these.

Peace, Order, and Good Government

The courts have tended to place a narrow interpretation on the federal Parliament's general authority to make laws for the peace, order, and good government of Canada. This has been reduced over time to an emergency power that can provide the constitutional basis for federal actions in special circumstances. It cannot, however, be used to justify federal laws during 'normal' times.

This narrow interpretation began with the *Local Prohibition Case* (1896). The Judicial Committee of the Privy Council ruled that the peace, order, and good government clause could not be used by Ottawa to override the enumerated powers of the provinces. The decision also marked the introduction into Canadian constitutional law of the 'national dimensions' test. Lord Watson wrote,

> Their Lordships do not doubt that some matters, in their origin local or provincial, might attain such dimensions as to affect the body politic of the Dominion, and to justify the Canadian Parliament in passing laws for their regulation or abolition in the interest of the Dominion.[15]

When does a matter acquire 'national dimensions'? This question was dealt with in a series of three decisions handed down in 1922, 1923, and 1925. In *re Board of Commerce Act and Combines and Fair Prices Act 1919* (1922), the JCPC struck down two federal laws introduced after World War One in order to prevent business monopoly and hoarding of essential commodities. For the first time the court articulated the 'emergency doctrine', according to which Parliament could pass laws under the authority of peace, order, and good government only in the case of a national emergency. Writing for the majority, Viscount Haldane declared that,

> [C]ircumstances are conceivable, such as those of war or famine, when the peace, order and good Government of the Dominion might be imperilled under conditions so exceptional that they require legislation of a character in reality beyond anything provided for by the enumerated heads in either s. 92 or s. 91.[16]

Essentially, the JCPC ruled that some national crisis must exist before federal laws can be based on peace, order, and good government doctrine. The fact that a matter has acquired 'national dimensions' would not, by itself, be sufficient to justify such exceptional legislation.

Despite the JCPC's admission that peacetime circumstances could conceivably warrant Ottawa acting under the authority of the doctrine, subsequent rulings suggested that it was really a wartime power. In the first of these decisions, *Fort Frances Pulp and Power Co. v. Manitoba Free Press* (1923), the JCPC declared that war-related circumstances were sufficient to warrant legislating under peace, order, and good government. Moreover, Viscount Haldane's opinion in *Fort Frances* indicated that the courts should be reluctant to question Parliament's judgement that a war-related emergency exists. Rulings in 1947 by the JCPC and in 1950 by the Supreme Court of Canada repeated this view.[17]

In those cases where the courts have rejected peace, order, and good government as a valid basis for federal legislation, the impugned laws were intended to deal with peacetime circumstances. The first of these was the decision in *Toronto Electric Commissioners v. Snider* (1925). Relying on the 'emergency doctrine' it had developed in the *Board of Commerce* case, the JCPC struck down Canada's major industrial relations law, the Industrial Disputes Investigation Act, 1907. The JCPC again rejected peacetime recourse in the 1937 reference decision on Ottawa's Employment and Social Insurance Act, 1935.[18] The federal government's attempt to justify this law, on the grounds that unemployment was a matter of national concern and, moreover, that it threatened the well-being of the country, was considered inadequate by the JCPC.

Confronted with broadly similar reasoning in the 1970s, the Supreme Court of Canada found that peace, order, and good government could be used to justify federal laws during peacetime. The Court was asked to rule on the constitutionality of Ottawa's Anti-Inflation Act, 1975. A majority of the Court accepted the federal government's argument that mounting inflationary pressures constituted an emergency justifying legislation that encroached on provincial jurisdiction. Not only was the 'emergency doctrine' liberated from war-related circumstances, the Court also indicated its reluctance to challenge Parliament's judgement on when emergency circumstances exist. The result, according to such constitutionalists as Peter Russell, is that Ottawa now appears to have fairly easy access to emergency powers under this doctrine.[19] Constitutionally this may be so. Politically, however, any federal government would think twice before legislating under this contentious power.

Trade and Commerce

On the face of it, Ottawa's authority over 'The Regulation of Trade and Commerce'[20] appears rather sweeping. Any economic activity or transaction would seem to fall within its scope. In fact, however, court decisions have construed the trade and commerce power to be much narrower, limited largely to interprovincial and international trade. At the same time, provincial jurisdiction over 'Property and Civil Rights in the Province'[21] has been interpreted as the provinces' own 'trade and commerce' power.

This line of judicial interpretation began with the decision in *Citizens' Insurance Co. v. Parsons* (1881). Based on its view that a broad, literal interpretation of s. 91(2) of the Constitution Act, 1867, would bring any and all aspects of economic life under the authority of Ottawa, leaving the provinces powerless to affect business, the JCPC interpreted 'regulation of trade and commerce' to include 'political arrangements in regard to trade requiring the sanction of parliament, regulation of trade in matters of interprovincial concern, and it may be that they would include general regulation of trade affecting the whole Dominion.'[22] To construe Ottawa's trade and commerce power otherwise, the JCPC argued, would be to deny the 'fair and ordinary meaning' of s. 92(13) of the Constitution Act, 1867, which assigns 'Property and Civil Rights in the Province' to the provincial governments.

The legacy of *Parsons* has been that Ottawa's authority to regulate trade and commerce has been limited to interprovincial trade, international trade, and general trade affecting the whole of Canada. But even this definition of federal jurisdiction has presented problems of interpretation. For example, what about a federal law whose principle goal is to regulate trade that crosses provincial borders, but which has as an incidental effect the regulation of some transactions that occur wholly within a province. Is such a law constitutional under s. 91(2)? Until the 1950s the courts' answer was 'no'.[23] But a series of Supreme Court decisions, culminating in *Caloil v. Attorney-General of Canada* (1971), signified a broader interpretation of Ottawa's power to regulate interprovincial trade.[24] In *Caloil*, the Court acknowledged that a federal law prohibiting the transportation or sale of imported oil west of the Ottawa Valley interfered with local trade in a province. Nevertheless, the Court upheld the federal law on the grounds that its 'true character' was 'the control of imports in the furtherance of an extraprovincial trade policy.'[25] Ottawa's authority was given an additional boost by a 1971 reference decision of the Supreme Court. In the *'Chicken and Egg'* *Reference*—no kidding, 'Chicken and Egg'—the Court ruled unconstitutional a provincial egg-marketing scheme that restricted imports from other provinces on the grounds that it encroached on Ottawa's trade and commerce power. Justice Bora Laskin, who would later become Chief Justice of the Supreme Court, referred specifically to the trend toward a more balanced interpretation of federal and provincial jurisdiction over trade.[26] Laskin went on to argue that 'to permit each province to seek its own advantage ... through a figurative sealing of its borders to entry of goods from others would be to deny one of the objects of Confederation ... namely, to form an economic unit of the whole of Canada'.[27]

The current situation may be described as *Parsons* + *Caloil* = 'trade and commerce'.

What of the *Parsons* allusion to general trade affecting the whole of Canada? Constitutional expert Peter Hogg suggests that its meaning remains obscure, but that it could conceivably provide the basis for federal laws regulating business.[28] In both *MacDonald v. Vapor Canada Ltd* (1977) and *Attorney-General of Canada v. Canadian National Transportation* (1983), the Court raised the question of when trade affects the whole country, thereby justifying, per *Parsons*, federal regulation under the trade and commerce power. It has not yet given a definitive answer.

The Impact of Judicial Decisions

Court rulings seldom put an end to conflicts between Ottawa and the provinces. Instead, they typically become part of the bargaining process between governments. Consider the following examples:

- *Employment and Social Insurance Act Reference* (1937). The JCPC struck down a federal statute establishing a program to deal with national unemployment. This was followed by negotiations between the federal and provincial governments, leading to a 1940 constitutional amendment that gave Ottawa authority over unemployment insurance.
- *Public Service Board v. Dionne* (1978). The Supreme Court confirmed Ottawa's exclusive jurisdiction to regulate television broadcasting. Immediately after the decision was handed down, the federal Minister of Communications announced Ottawa's willingness to negotiate some division of authority with the provinces.

- *CIGOL v. Government of Saskatchewan* (1978). In *CIGOL*, a provincial tax on natural gas was found to be a direct tax and therefore outside the jurisdiction of the province. When Ottawa and the provinces were negotiating constitutional reform in 1980–1, the issue of provincial control over natural resources was on the table. The result was s. 92A of the Constitution Act. It appears to permit the form of resource taxation that was ruled *ultra vires* in the *CIGOL* decision.
- *Patriation Reference* (1981). The Supreme Court ruled that Ottawa's proposal to patriate the British North America Act and to change it in ways affecting provincial powers was legal, but that it was unconstitutional in the conventional sense (see Chapter 4). The decision gave the federal government a legal victory, at the same time as the provinces were given the moral high ground. Within weeks all governments were back at the table trying to find a negotiated solution.

Evolving Federalism

It is generally believed that judicial decisions have pushed Canadian federalism in a more decentralist direction than the Fathers of Confederation planned, but that this tendency has been attenuated since 1949 when the Supreme Court became Canada's highest court of appeal. Some bemoan the judiciary's decentralizing influence, particularly that of the JCPC during Canada's first half-century. Others maintain that the limits placed on Ottawa's general legislative authority and trade and commerce power, and the broad interpretation of such provincial powers as 'property and civil rights', have reflected the political reality of Canada. As Pierre Trudeau observes, 'It has long been the custom in English Canada to denounce the [Judicial Committee of the] Privy Council for its provincial bias; but it should perhaps be considered that if the law lords had not leaned in that direction, Quebec separatism might not be a threat today: it might be an accomplished fact.'[29]

Judicial review is only one of the factors that have shaped the evolution of federalism. In fact, legal disputes over the division of powers are only symptomatic of underlying tensions that are at the root of intergovernmental conflict. These tensions have three main sources: 1) the status of Quebec and the powers of the Quebec state; 2) centre-periphery relations; and 3) the political and administrative needs of governments.

Quebec

'What does Quebec want?' The question has been asked countless times over the years by English Canadians, some of whom genuinely wanted to know and others who asked it out of exasperation, believing all along that the answer would be unacceptable. The complementary question—'What does English Canada want?'—has seldom been posed. Yet neither question makes sense in isolation from the other. To understand what Quebec wants from Canada it is also necessary to consider what the rest of Canada expects from, and is willing to concede to, Quebec.

Quebec's unique role in Canadian federalism derives from two factors. One is its predominantly French-speaking character. About 85 per cent of the provincial population claims French as their mother tongue, and about 90 per cent of all Canadian Francophones reside in Quebec. The second factor is Quebec's size. At Confederation it was the second most populous province, and Montreal was the hub of Canada's commercial and financial industries. Although its weight relative to the rest of Canada is much less today, Quebec is still the second most populous province, accounting for about 24 per cent of Canada's population. Economically, Quebec's gross provincial product and its importance as a centre for finance and manufacturing are surpassed only by Ontario.

Quebec's distinctive social and cultural fabric explain why it has made special demands on Canadian federalism. Because it is a large province with the second largest bloc of seats in the federal Parliament and because Francophones have always been able to control their provincial legislature, Quebec's demands have had a significant impact on the evolution of Canadian federalism. This impact has been experienced on two main fronts: the constitution and the financial and administrative practices of federalism. We will examine Quebec's impact on the financial and administrative dimensions of federalism later in this chapter (see 'Intergovernmental Relations').

Quebec's influence on the constitution predates the Confederation agreement. Between 1848 and 1867 Ontario and Quebec formed the United Canadas, governed by a single legislature in which the two colonies held equal representation. During this period the *double-majority* practice developed. To become law, a bill had to be approved by a majority of members on both the Ontario and Quebec sides of the legislature. This was Canada's first experience with the federal principle of regional representation. Predominantly Francophone Quebec and predominantly Anglophone Ontario were joined in a legislative partnership that required the agreement of both regional communities in order to work. It turned out, however, to be a failure.

Quebec's influence on the constitution was strongly evident in the Confederation agreement. Its representatives were the most insistent on a federal constitution for Canada, under which the provincial government would have authority over those matters considered vital to the preservation of the language, religion, and social institutions of Quebec. Indeed, for decades the clerical and political leaders of French Canada were unanimous in viewing Canadian federalism as a pact between two peoples. 'Canadian Confederation', declared Henri Bourassa, 'is the result of a contract between the two races in Canada, French and English, based on equality and recognizing equal rights and reciprocal duties. Canadian Confederation will last only as long as this equality of rights is recognized as the basis of the public right in Canada, from Halifax to Vancouver.'[30]

The equality Bourassa had in mind did not last very long. It was violated in Manitoba, where the status of French in the provincial legislature and the educational rights of Francophone Catholics were swept away a couple of decades after that province entered Confederation. It was also violated in Ontario, where Regulation 17 (1913) banned French instruction from the province's public schools. These developments contributed to the identification of French Canada with Quebec, the only province in which Francophones were in the majority and where they could effectively defend their rights and preserve their culture.

The constitutional consequences of limiting French Canada to the boundaries of Quebec became apparent by the middle of the twentieth century. As Ottawa became increasingly involved in areas of provincial jurisdiction, particularly through its spending power but also by monopolizing the field of direct taxation between 1947 and 1954, the Quebec government became more and more protective of what it argued were exclusive provincial powers under the constitution. But not until the Quiet Revolution of the 1960s, marking the eclipse of the conservative anti-statist nationalism that had dominated Quebec politics for more than a century, was Quebec's resentment toward Ottawa's encroachment onto provincial territory matched by aggressive constitutional demands. The first major indication of this occurred during the federal-provincial negotiations on a public old age pension scheme (1963–5). Quebec Premier Jean Lesage stated that his government would only agree to a constitutional amendment giving Ottawa the authority to pass pension legislation if Quebec were able to opt out of the federal plan. Ottawa agreed, and so was born the Canadian practice of provinces being able to opt out of a federal shared-cost program without suffering any financial loss.

Quebec's constitutional demands appeared to become even more ambitious a few years later. The 1966 provincial election saw the Union Nationale party run on the slogan 'Québec d'abord!' (Quebec first!) The party's leader, Daniel Johnson, had authored a book entitled *Égalité ou indépendance,* and in the election campaign the Union Nationale called for major constitutional reform that included the transfer of virtually all social and cultural matters to the province, constitutional recognition of Canada's bi-national character, and exclusive provincial control over the major tax fields then shared with Ottawa. In fact, however, these demands were not pursued with much vigour during the party's five years in power (1966–70). The one constitutional issue on which the Union Nationale government did confront Ottawa was that of international representation for Quebec. But as Kenneth McRoberts observes,

> In purely symbolic terms Quebec's demands seemed very significant, Quebec was seeking to assume what many regarded as the trappings of sovereignty. Yet … these demands did not directly attack the real distribution of power and responsibilities to the extent that various Lesage demands, such as a separate Quebec Pension Plan, had.[31]

Despite the lack of substantive change in Quebec's constitutional status and powers during this period, the province's nationalist undercurrent was gaining momentum. The creation of the Parti Québécois in 1968, under the leadership of René Lévesque, brought under one roof most of the major groups committed to the eventual political independence of Quebec. The Liberal Party of Quebec remained federalist but advocated what amounted to special status for Quebec within Canadian federalism. 'Un fédéralisme rentable' (profitable federalism) was the passionless way in which Liberal leader Robert Bourassa explained Quebec's commitment to Canada.

Constitutional negotiations between Ottawa and the provinces had been ongoing since 1968. The 1970 election of a Liberal government in Quebec appeared to provide an opportunity to bring these talks to a successful conclusion. But when the eleven governments got together at Victoria in 1971, it became apparent that Quebec's price for agreeing to a constitutional amendment formula and a charter of rights was higher than Ottawa was willing to pay.[32] The impasse was over social policy. Quebec demanded constitutional supremacy in an area in which Ottawa operated several major programs, including family allowances, unemployment insurance, manpower training, and old age pensions. Moreover, the Quebec government wanted the fiscal means to pay for provincial policies in these fields. Ottawa went some way toward meeting these demands. The Trudeau government refused, however, to concede the principle of provincial supremacy over social policy and would not provide a constitutional guarantee that provinces would receive financial compensation for operating their own programs in these areas. The federal-provincial compromise reached in Victoria fell apart days later in Quebec, where the deal was widely seen as constitutional entrenchment of an unacceptable status quo.

After Quebec's rejection of the Victoria Charter, the Bourassa government adopted a piecemeal strategy for changing federalism, negotiating with Ottawa on single issues like family allowances, social security, and telecommunications. It was unsuccessful, however, in extracting any major concessions from a federal government that believed provincial powers were already too great and was staunchly opposed to special status for Quebec.

A rather different strategy was followed by the PQ government of René Lévesque after it came to power in 1976. The PQ was committed to holding a provincial referendum on its option of political sovereignty for Quebec, combined with some form of economic association with the rest of Canada. But instead of simple confrontation with Ottawa, the Lévesque government pursued an *étapiste* (gradualist) strategy of providing 'good government'—which required some degree of co-operation with Ottawa because of the intricate network of intergovernmental programs and agreements—while attempting to convince the Quebec population that its best interests lay in sovereignty-association. The two governments co-operated on dozens of new capital spending projects, on management of the economy, and on immigration policy. The PQ government even participated in federal-provincial talks on constitutional reform in 1978–9.[33] All of this occurred against the background of the looming referendum on the PQ's separatist option.

Sovereignty-association was rejected by Quebec voters in May of 1980. But they re-elected the PQ to office in 1981. Thus, a PQ government participated in the constitutional negotiations toward 'renewed federalism' that the federal Liberal government had initiated after the Quebec referendum. But it was also a PQ government that refused to sign the final product of these talks, the November, 1981, accord that became the Constitution Act, 1982. The PQ refusal was hardly surprising in light of the fact that none of the demands that Quebec governments had made since the 1960s were included in the 1981 constitutional accord. Indeed, the province's Liberal opposition also found the accord to be unacceptable. The constitution had undergone its most dramatic reform since its passage in 1867, but the provincial government of the country's second largest province and home to 90 per cent of Canada's Francophones had not agreed to these changes. Although the legality of the Constitution Act, 1982, was not in doubt, its political legitimacy was.

This was the situation when Robert Bourassa and the provincial Liberals were returned to power in 1985. Their election appeared to reflect the muted tenor of Quebec nationalism in the post-referendum era. Change had also taken place in Ottawa. Prime Minister Brian Mulroney, elected in 1984, did not share Pierre Trudeau's view that the provinces were already too powerful for the good of the national economy and political unity. Nor was he viscerally opposed to some form of *statut spécial* for Quebec, as Trudeau was. Conditions seemed propitious, therefore, for 'bringing Quebec into the constitutional family'—a phrase favoured by Prime Minister Mulroney.

It was not to be. The Quebec government put forward a package of five demands that had to be met before it would agree to the constitutional reforms passed in 1982. These proposals were agreed to by Ottawa and all of the provincial premiers on 30 April 1987, forming the basis for what became known as the Meech Lake Accord (the contents of the Accord were explained in Chapter 4). Premier Bourassa's claim that the Accord represented the bare minimum Quebec needed before agreeing to the 1982 reforms was not seriously questioned. Even so, the Accord provoked intense opposition in English Canada, particularly the provision that recognized Quebec as a 'distinct society'. Last-ditch efforts to save the Accord before its 23 June 1990 ratification deadline focused largely on allaying fears that the distinct society clause would take precedence over the Charter of Rights and Freedoms in Quebec. Various proposals were made that would have left no doubt about the Charter's pre-eminence. They were all rejected by the Quebec government. The final compromise was a legal opinion appended to the Accord. Six constitutional experts expressed their view that the Charter was in no way diminished by the distinct society clause. This was not, however, the message that Quebec politicians communicated to their constituents.

Manitoba and Newfoundland failed to pass the Meech Lake Accord before the 23 June deadline. But even before the death of the Accord, the apparent unwillingness of English Canada to concede Quebec's minimum demands for constitutional change had contributed to a resurgence of Quebec nationalism. The sovereignty option acquired widespread respectability in Quebec. Polls taken in June of 1990 showed that a majority of Québécois supported political independence and many of the province's Francophone business leaders spoke confidently about the economic future of a sovereign Quebec. In the aftermath of the Meech Lake failure the PQ and the province's Liberal government agreed that the only reasonable course for Quebec would be to determine its constitutional future by itself and negotiate the terms of this future with the Canadian government. There was less agreement on where they expected these negotiations to lead.

Two years later, however, Quebec was back at the table with Ottawa and the provincial governments, joined this time by the leaders of Canada's major Aboriginal organizations. The agreement they arrived at in Charlottetown contained most of the main elements of the Meech Lake Accord. Indeed, it went beyond Meech in also proposing that Quebec be forever guaranteed 25 per cent of the seats in the House of Commons and that on matters affecting the French language or culture a majority of Francophone senators would be required for approval. In addition to provisions targeted specifically at Quebec, the 1992 Accord proposed what many believed was a significant devolution of policy responsibilities to the provinces in matters ranging from labour market development and training to culture.

Quebecers solidly rejected the Charlottetown Accord in the 26 October 1992 referendum, as did provincial majorities in five other provinces. Separatists rejoiced in the outcome, but in no way could Quebec's solid 'no' be interpreted as a vote for separatism. It was more plausibly viewed as rejection of a deal that did not go far enough toward satisfying Quebec's demands for more powers and recognition of Quebecers' distinctive collective identity. Of course, many English Canadians said 'no' to the Charlottetown Accord because they thought it went too far in these directions. *Plus ça change, plus c'est la même chose!*

In the wake of the Charlottetown Accord's rejection, politicians of all stripes fled from the constitutional issue. Indeed, the whole question of constitutional reform was conspicuously absent from the Liberal Party's 'Red Book', its official statement of policy positions and promises. Nor was it an issue in the 1993 federal election campaign, at least outside Quebec. In Quebec, however, these matters were kept before the voters by the Bloc Québécois, under the leadership of Lucien Bouchard. The Bloc's *raison d'être* was, of course, to achieve political independence for Quebec. Their success in capturing fifty-four of Quebec's seventy-five seats in the House of Commons may not have been a surrogate vote for separation, but it certainly demonstrated the depth of Quebec voters' dissatisfaction with the federal government and existing constitutional arrangements.

Despite their obvious wish to avoid the constitutional quagmire, the Liberals were forced to confront the issue as a result of the 1994 election of the PQ in Quebec. The PQ was committed to holding a referendum on Quebec independence within a year of their election. When the referendum campaign began in September of 1995, the *indépendantiste* side got off to a sputtering start. There appeared to be little enthusiasm among Québécois for the PQ's separatist vision, and early polls showed the No side to be leading by a margin of as much as 20 percentage points. The federalist campaign relied on messages intended to convince Quebecers that they would suffer economically if the province voted Yes. Federal Minister of Finance Paul Martin, Jr, and prominent business spokespersons warned Quebec voters that the days after separation would be dark ones.

About halfway through the campaign, however, leadership of the Yes side passed from Quebec Premier Jacques Parizeau to Bloc Québécois leader Lucien Bouchard. Support for independence took off, no doubt due in large measure to Bouchard's charismatic style and unsurpassed ability to connect emotionally with Francophone Quebecers, but also due to what in retrospect can be seen to have been a terribly uninspired campaign by the federalists. Prime Minister Jean Chrétien chose to stay on the sidelines until the last couple of weeks of the campaign when polls showed the Yes side to be leading. His previous refusal to make any concrete constitutional offer to Quebec wavered during the week before the vote, when he suggested that he supported constitutional recognition of Quebec as a distinct society and a Quebec veto over constitutional reform. On 30 October 1995, the Yes side emerged with the narrowest of victories: 49.6 per cent against independence, 48.5 per cent for, with spoiled ballots accounting for the rest.

The federal government's reluctance to deal with the issue of constitutional reform and Quebec's demands before the 1995 referendum forced its hand was due in great measure to its realization that Canadians' reactions to the constitutional issue tended to range from indifference to deep hostility. But as their uncertain performance in the referendum campaign showed, the Liberals' silence may also have been due to their inability to formulate a positive response to the sovereignty option proposed by Quebec nationalists.

This inability can be traced to the Liberal model of federalism that took shape during the Trudeau era. Although not centralist in any absolute sense—Canada is surely among the least centralized federal systems in the world—it assumes that a strong central government is essential to the maintenance of Canadian unity. Moreover, this model is in general opposed to what is called 'asymmetrical federalism', i.e., the constitutional recognition of differences in the status and powers of provincial governments; in particular, it is against constitutional entrenchment of special status for Quebec. The Constitution Act of 1982, particularly the Charter and the denial of a right of constitutional veto to any single province, embodies this vision of federalism.

This model is, of course, hotly contested. The main challenge comes from Quebec nationalists, not only from separatists but also from Quebec's nationalist-federalists. This latter group, which includes the Liberal Party of Quebec, maintains that constitutional reforms, including, at a minimum, recognition of Quebec's special responsibility for the protection and promotion of the French language in Canada and a Quebec veto over constitutional change, are necessary to keep Quebecers interested in Canadian federalism. The federal Liberals, since Trudeau stepped down as party leader in 1984, have shown a willingness to concede much of what the nationalist-federalists demand, as seen in the party's support for the Meech Lake and Charlottetown Accords. However, their enthusiasm for these constitutional reforms has been tempered both by a realization that they receive mixed reviews among voters in Ontario and generate downright hostility in western Canada, and by a vestigial loyalty among many Liberals to Trudeau's brand of no-special-status-for-Quebec federalism.

In the wake of the close call experienced by federalists in the 1995 Quebec referendum, where a clear majority of Francophones voted for the sovereigntist option, the federal Liberal Party showed that it was ready to cut the cord connecting it to the Trudeau era. Only weeks after the referendum the Liberal government introduced a motion recognizing Quebec as a distinct society, assigning the province a veto over constitutional change (Ontario and British Columbia were also assigned veto power, as were the prairie and Atlantic regions if at least two provinces representing more than 50 per cent of the regional population opposed a proposed amendment), and transferring to Quebec some authority for job training. The first two of this trio of reforms have clear constitutional implications. The federal motion would not, of course, change the written constitution. However, to the extent that Ottawa allows its behaviour to be governed by what the Liberal government characterized as a constitutional offer to Quebecers, it does change the constitution in an informal way.

This, in fact, marks a return to a tradition of Canadian federalism that predates Pierre Trudeau's entry into federal politics. It is a tradition familiar to students of the British constitution and of Canadian federalism alike, whereby constitutional change is not the result of formal amendments to the written constitution but of developments in policy and practice whose status is greater than that of ordinary laws but not quite that of tablets brought down from Mount Sinai.

Centre-Periphery Relations

Canada spans five and a half time zones and occupies the second largest land mass of any country, and yet the narrow belt that runs between Windsor and Montreal—the 'industrial heartland' of Canada—is home to over 55 per cent of Canada's population and generates over 60 per cent of national income and production. Ontario and Quebec together account for just under 60 per cent of the 295 seats in the House of Commons. No national political party can hope to form a government without considerable support from the voters of at least one, and usually both, of these provinces. They comprise Canada's centre, in terms of both their political and economic power.

Predictably, the provincial governments of Ontario and Quebec carry greater weight in Canadian federalism than do those of the other provinces. The other eight provincial gov-

---

Box 5.2 What Future for an Independent Quebec?

Sunshine?...

Because Canada, far from taking pride in and proclaiming to the world the alliance between its two founding peoples, has instead consistently trivialized it and decreed the spurious principle of equality between the provinces;

Because starting with the Quiet Revolution we reached a decision never again to restrict ourselves to mere survival but from this time on to build upon our difference;

Because we have the deep-seated conviction that continuing within Canada would be tantamount to condemning ourselves to languish and to debasing our very identity;

Because the respect we owe ourselves must guide our deeds;

WE, THE PEOPLE OF QUEBEC, DECLARE IT IS OUR WILL TO BE IN FULL POSSESSION OF ALL THE POWERS OF A STATE: TO LEVY ALL OUR TAXES, TO VOTE ON ALL OUR LAWS, TO SIGN ALL OUR TREATIES AND TO EXERCISE THE HIGHEST POWER OF ALL, CONCEIVING, AND CONTROLLING, BY OURSELVES, OUR FUNDAMENTAL LAW.

We, the people of Quebec, through the voice of our Assemblée nationale, proclaim: Quebec is a sovereign country.

From the preamble to the 1995
Quebec referendum question.

Or gloom?...

A lone Quebec would not get Canada's credit rating overnight; whatever its debts, it would have to service them at higher rates of interest. Capital might flee; enough, some federalists think, to force Quebec to create liquidity by inventing its own currency willy-nilly. Certainly the new country would start life with a trade deficit, to be financed how? Even assured of free trade, potential direct investors might opt for less dirigisme and lower taxes elsewhere. And, though Quebec now has its own confident business class, head offices might flee from Montreal to Toronto.

None of this proves that it cannot be done. But clearly the joys of independence could include painful belt-tightening. If most Quebeckers, knowing this (which the PQ has not told them), are ready for it; if they really believe Quebec cannot get a fair deal as part of Canada; if they are willing (as the PQ claims to be, but patently is not) to ensure a fair deal for Quebec's own minorities; then so be it. All who believe multicultural societies can flourish, all who value Canada as such, will be sorry; but the issue is one for today's Canadians. Those are big ifs.

Editorial in *The Economist*, 16 September 1995.

---

ernments preside over regions whose interests have usually been subordinated by Ottawa to those of central Canada. In this sense, these other provinces constitute Canada's peripheries, situated on the edge—sometimes precariously so—of national politics. Resentment against central Canada and the federal government has deep roots in the politics of these provinces, particularly in the West. Their litany of grievances includes, to mention only a few: tariff policy that for a century protected manufacturing jobs and corporate profits in Ontario and Quebec; the perceived insensitivity of the country's Toronto- and Montreal-based financial institutions when it comes to western interests; Ottawa's treatment of the petroleum

Balancing the interests of the different provinces is no easy task, as any Canadian prime minister can attest. (Roy Peterson, *Vancouver Sun*)

resources that are concentrated in the West, investment and spending decisions by the federal government; official bilingualism and what westerners in particular perceive to be Ottawa's favouritism toward Quebec's interests. No one can seriously doubt that the peripheral provinces have a case. As Donald Smiley has written, 'there are dangers that Canadian problems will be resolved almost entirely within the framework of the heartland of the country with the progressive alienation from national affairs of those who live on the peripheries.'[34]

The fact that the federal principle of regional representation is embodied in the Canadian Senate and is practised assiduously by prime ministers in selecting cabinet ministers and in making certain other federal appointments has not provided these regions with what they believe to be an adequate voice in national politics. *Intrastate federalism*—the representation and accommodation of regional interests within national political institutions—has been an abysmal failure in Canada. Deprived of significant influence in Ottawa, the peripheral regions of the country have tended to rely on their provincial governments for the protection and promotion of their interests.

The fact that more MPs are elected from Ontario and Quebec than from all the other provinces combined has always been the root cause of Ottawa's tendency to favour central Canadian interests. This political factor has been reinforced by the ideological bias of Canadian politics, a bias that has tended to interpret Canadian history and identity in terms of experiences more germane to central Canada than to the peripheral regions. The very concept of 'Canada' has usually been associated with a counter-revolutionary or Loyalist tradition based on a rejection of the values and political institutions of the United States (see Chapter 2) and with the cultural dualism so important to the political history of central Canada. Neither of these experiences is central to the identity and political consciousness of western Canadians.[35] In the East, too, the national myths, symbols, and identities associated with 'Canada' often have had little relationship to the experience of Maritimers.[36]

The dominance of Ontario and Quebec in national politics and the subordinate status of the interests and cultural values of the peripheral regions of the country have always been reflected in relations between Ottawa and the provincial governments of the peripheries. For example, although Ottawa has exercised its constitutional power to disallow provincial laws 112 times, only a few of these were laws passed by Ontario or Quebec.[37] When Manitoba joined Confederation in 1870 it did so without control over public lands situated in the province.[38] Ottawa retained control in order to promote its own nation-building strategy relating to railway construction and western settlement. Similarly, when Saskatchewan and Alberta became provinces in 1905 they did not immediately acquire control over public lands and natural resources within their borders.[39] Ottawa kept these powers to itself, using the argument that this was necessary to accomplish its immigration and settlement objectives for western Canada. All of these provinces received subsidies from Ottawa as compensation for the revenue they were deprived of by not controlling public lands and, in Alberta and Saskatchewan, natural resources. Their governments did not consider this to be adequate recompense for the quasi-colonial status imposed on them by Ottawa.

There is nothing subtle about the disallowance power, or about denying some provinces constitutional powers possessed by other provincial governments. Today's list of grievances against Ottawa is comprised of less blatant forms of policy discrimination against the interests of the peripheries. Among the items perennially on this list are claims that Ottawa does too little to support prairie grain farmers and the east coast fishing industry, and that the federal government's spending decisions unfairly favour Ontario and Quebec. Even in provinces like Alberta and British Columbia, which are wealthy by Canadian standards, a sense of powerlessness in the face of central Canadian dominance is a major component of their provincial politics. 'The West', observes Alberta historian Doug Owram, 'has never felt in control of its own destiny. None of the wealth of recent years has eased this feeling. In fact, the tremendous wealth of the region merely sharpens the contrast with the political powerlessness that exists on the national level.'[40]

State Interests and Intergovernmental Conflict

The fact that Quebec is overwhelmingly Francophone, while the other provinces are not, gives it a special set of interests that any Quebec government feels bound to defend. Likewise, grain farming in Saskatchewan, petroleum in Alberta, the automotive industry in Ontario, and forestry in British Columbia shape the positions taken by the governments of these provinces on taxation, trade, and other policies affecting these interests. Each province comprises a particular constellation of economic, social, and cultural interests that together influence the demands its provincial government makes on federalism. Intergovernmental conflict, then, is to some extent the clash of conflicting regional interests.

This is, however, only part of the explanation. Governments do not simply reflect societal interests. They actively shape these interests through their policies, sometimes deliberately and other times inadvertently. Moreover, governments have their own political and administrative interests, the pursuit of which may have nothing to do with the interests of those they represent. 'Canadian federalism', Alan Cairns argues, 'is about governments, governments that are possessed of massive human and financial resources, that are driven by purposes fashioned by élites, and that accord high priority to their own long-term institutional self-interest.'[41] This state-centred interpretation of federalism maintains that conflicts between governments are likely to be generated, or at least influenced, by the 'institutional self-interest' of politicians and bureaucrats.

The evidence in support of this view is overwhelming. Intergovernmental turf wars, over their respective shares of particular tax fields and over which level will have jurisdiction over what matters, often seem remote from the concerns of Canadian citizens. But looked at from the state's point of view, how revenue sources and legislative competence are divided between levels of governments affects the ability of politicians to pursue their interest in re-election, career advancement, and personal prestige and their own conception of the public interest. So, too, with bureaucratic officials, we may assume that they are not indifferent toward matters that influence the future of the organizations and programs to which their personal career fortunes and ambitions, and their own conception of the public interest, are tied.

When the political-administrative needs of governments are reinforced by the demands of provincially oriented economic interests this may give rise to what has been called *province-building*. As the term suggests, this is the provincial counterpart to the nation-building orientation of Sir John A. Macdonald's post-Confederation government. Province-building has been defined as the 'recent evolution of more powerful and competent provincial administrations which aim to manage socioeconomic change in their territories and which are in essential conflict with the central government.'[42] The concept generally has been associated with the provincial governments of Alberta and Quebec.[43] The Ontario government is as 'powerful and competent' as these other provincial states, and no one would accuse Ontario governments of being indifferent toward the direction of 'socioeconomic change' within their borders. Ontario's pivotal status in Canadian politics, however, based on its large population and economic importance, has meant that it generally has been able to count on a sympathetic hearing in Ottawa. With the exception of the NDP government of Bob Rae (1990–5), overt 'fed-bashing' has not been a popular blood sport among that province's politicians, simply because it has not been necessary for the achievement of their goals. In other respects, however, Ontario governments have not lagged behind their more aggressive counterparts, and in fact have often been at the forefront in expanding the political-administrative reach of the provincial state.

Intergovernmental Relations

The constitution, we have seen, does not establish a neat division of legislative and taxation powers between Ottawa and the provinces. All of the chief sources of public revenue—personal and corporate income taxes, payroll taxes, sales taxes, and public-sector borrowing—are shared between the two levels of government. Likewise, both the federal and provincial governments are involved in all the major policy fields. Defence and monetary policy come closest to being exclusive federal terrain, although provincial governments do not hesitate to express their views on such issues as the location of armed forces bases, major defence purchases, and interest rates. On the provincial side, snow removal, refuse collection, and sidewalk maintenance are the sorts of local activities that are free from federal involvement. But not entirely: the money that Ottawa transfers annually to the provinces affects the amounts that provincial governments pay to their municipalities, thereby having an impact on municipalities' ability to carry out these local functions.

Divided jurisdiction has given rise to a sprawling and complicated network of relations linking the federal and provincial governments. This network has often been compared to an iceberg, only a small part of which is visible to the eye. The 'visible' tip of intergovernmental relations involves meetings of the Prime Minister and provincial premiers (first ministers' conferences) and meetings of provincial premiers. These meetings always generate considerable media attention, and some part of their proceedings usually takes place before the television cameras. Less publicized, but far more frequent, are the hundreds of annual meetings between federal and provincial cabinet ministers and bureaucrats. Many of these meetings take place in the context of ongoing federal-provincial structures like the Continuing Committee on Economic and Fiscal Matters, established in 1955, or the Economic and Regional Development Agreements negotiated between Ottawa and the less affluent provinces. Others are generated by the wide range of shared-cost activities that link the two levels of government, from major spending programs such as the Canada Health and Social Transfer and Equalization to smaller federal subsidies such as for official minority-language education.

Executive federalism is the term often used to describe the relations between cabinet ministers and officials of the two levels of government. The negotiations between them and the agreements they reach are usually undertaken with minimal, if any, input from either legislatures or the public. The secrecy that generally cloaks this decision-making process, combined with the fact that the distinction between federal and provincial responsibilities is often blurred by the deals it produces, has generated charges that executive federalism is undemocratic. It is undemocratic because it undermines the role of elected legislatures whose role, if they have one at all, is usually limited to ratifying *faits accomplis*. Second, agreements to finance jointly the cost of a program, or to share a particular tax field or legislative power, make it difficult for citizens to determine which level of government should be held responsible for what policies. Third, executive federalism provides no meaningful opportunities for public debate of intergovernmental issues that affect the standard of health care services, welfare, post-secondary education, local taxation, and other matters of real concern to citizens. Political parties, interest groups, and individual Canadians are generally excluded from a decision-making process dominated by cabinet ministers and intergovernmental affairs specialists of the two levels of government.

In addition to these indictments of executive federalism, Donald Smiley lists three others.[44]

- *It distorts the political agenda.* Executive federalism has a territorial bias. It reinforces the significance of territorially concentrated interests and of the provincial governments that represent them, at the same time as it undervalues the importance of other interests.

- *It fuels government expansion.* Competitive relations between Ottawa and the provinces have produced inefficient duplication, as each level of government has its own bureaucracy to pursue similar goals.
- *It perpetuates intergovernmental conflict.* The increasing sophistication of executive federalism, conducted through specialized bureaus staffed by intergovernmental affairs specialists, reduces the likelihood of resolving federal-provincial disputes. These intergovernmental affairs offices, which exist in all provinces and at the federal level, and the experts that staff them tend to perceive issues in terms of the powers and jurisdiction of their particular government. Intergovernmental conflict is in a sense institutionalized by the fact that what is perceived to be at stake is the power/resources/ prestige of one's government.

In the face of this lengthy catalogue of allegations, executive federalism and its practitioners are left to rely on the defence of necessity. Overlapping powers are an unavoidable fact of life under Canada's federal constitution. In light of this, is it realistic to imagine that complex administrative and financial agreements can be negotiated in public forums? And besides, much of policy-making is carried on in a closed fashion, dominated by cabinet ministers and bureaucratic élites. Why condemn executive federalism for traits that are deeply embedded in Canadian policy-making generally?

Financing Federalism

From the very beginning, money has been at the centre of intergovernmental relations. The Confederation agreement included an annual per capita subsidy that Ottawa would pay to all provincial governments.[45] Moreover, the new federal government agreed to assume liability for the debts of the provinces as they stood in 1867.[46] Taxation powers were divided between the two levels of government, with Ottawa receiving what were at the time the major sources of public revenue.

These financial arrangements have never been adequate. At the root of the problem is the fact that the provinces' legislative responsibilities proved to be much more extensive and expensive than the founders had anticipated. Provincial governments attempted to fill this gap between their revenues and their expenditure requirements through an increasing array of provincial taxes. Licence fees, succession duties, and personal and corporate income taxes were all used to increase provincial revenues. In addition, the provinces pressed Ottawa for more money. Indeed, only two years after Confederation the federal subsidy paid to Nova Scotia was increased. An important precedent was thereby established: federal-provincial financial relations are determined by governments, not by the constitution.

Today, provincial and local revenues exceed those of the federal government (see Figure 5.1). The revenue position of the provinces improved steadily between the 1950s and the 1970s, as Ottawa conceded *tax room*—i.e., an increasing share of particular revenue sources like the personal income tax—to aggressive provincial governments. But at the same time, provincial dependence on subsidies from Ottawa remains as great as ever because the rate of growth in combined provincial and local spending has outstripped the growth in their own source revenues. Transfer payments from Ottawa (and borrowing on the public credit) have made up the difference. In the case of the poorest provinces, money from Ottawa cur-

Figure 5.1 Public Finance in Canada: Revenue and Expenditure as Percentages of GDP for Each Level of Government, 1950 and 1994

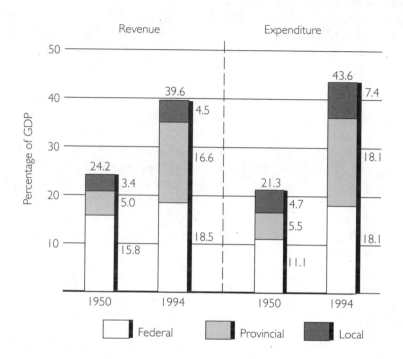

Note: Transfer payments are assigned to the level of government that actually spends the money.

Sources: Figures provided in Department of Finance, *Quarterly Economic Review,* Annual Reference Tables; and Statistics Canada, *Canadian Economic Observer,* Historical Statistical Supplement 1994–5, cat. 11-210.

rently accounts for about half of their total revenue. Part of this dependence has been encouraged by Ottawa through *shared-cost programs,* provincially administered programs where Ottawa's financial contribution is geared to how much a province spends. In the past Ottawa agreed to match provincial spending dollar for dollar. Until 1995 the major shared-cost program in Canada was the Canada Assistance Plan, which financed welfare and other provincial social services. The federal budget of that year replaced CAP with the Canada Social Transfer to the provinces, the amount of which is not geared to provincial spending. Federal grants for health care and post-secondary education also were launched on a shared-cost basis, but were converted by Ottawa into *block funding programs* through the Federal-Provincial Fiscal Arrangements Act of 1977. The federal government argued, reasonably enough, that the shared-cost formula did not encourage the provinces to control program costs. Under block funding, Ottawa's financial contribution is geared to the previous year's subsidy plus an amount calculated on the basis of growth in the recipient province's gross product. Ottawa is not obliged to match provincial spending, and indeed the effect of the switch to block funding has been to transfer an increasing share of the burden of health care and post-secondary education costs onto the shoulders of the provinces.

What could possibly be wrong with the provinces carrying more of the costs for programs that fall under their constitutional jurisdiction? First, provincial governments argue that Ottawa encouraged them to spend more on social services by offering to share program costs on a matching basis. It is unfair, they claim, for the federal government to try to back out of financing policy areas whose growth it encouraged. Second, the provinces' ability to increase their own source revenues to compensate for reduced federal transfer payments is limited by the fact that they share all of the major taxes fields with Ottawa. Unless the federal government is willing to give up some tax room (i.e., some of its share of total tax revenue from a particular source) to the provinces, provincial governments face the hard choice of increasing the total tax burden on their citizens, charging or increasing user fees (e.g., tuition fees), or cutting back on program expenditures. Third, any reduction in Ottawa's commitment to financing provincial social services hurts the poorer provinces more than it does the wealthier ones. The Maritime provinces in particular depend on federal transfers in order to offer a level of social services comparable to that in other provinces.

Some of the money that Ottawa transfers to the provinces carries conditions as to how it must be spent. These are called conditional grants. Transfers that have no strings attached to them are called unconditional grants. Important examples of both include the following:

- Provincial social assistance programs must be based exclusively on need and must not make previous residency in the province a condition for receiving benefits.
- The block transfer that Ottawa makes to the provinces under the Canada Health and Social Transfer must be spent on health care, post-secondary education, and social services previously covered under the CAP.
- The Canada Health Act, 1984, includes a provision that reduces Ottawa's payment to provincial governments that permit physicians to extra-bill their patients. Ottawa's contribution to provincial health care spending is, therefore, subject to some conditions.
- Equalization grants are paid to provincial governments whose per capita tax revenues (according to a complex formula negotiated between Ottawa and the provinces) fall below the average of the two most affluent provinces. Equalization grants account for about one-quarter of all federal transfers to the provinces and about a quarter of the total revenue of the poorest provincial governments. It carries no conditions as to how it must be spent.

Figure 5.2 provides a breakdown of federal transfers to the provinces.

The adequacy of federal transfers is not the only issue that has set Ottawa against the provincial governments. Another long-standing complaint of the provinces is that shared-cost programs distort provincial spending priorities because of the enticement of matching federal grants. Ottawa's spending power, they argue, permits undue federal interference in matters of provincial jurisdiction. The government of Quebec has been most insistent about this. Indeed, during the 1950s the provincial government of Maurice Duplessis refused to accept federal money for the construction of Quebec's portion of the Trans-Canada highway

Figure 5.2 Composition of Federal Transfers to Provincial Governments, 1993–4

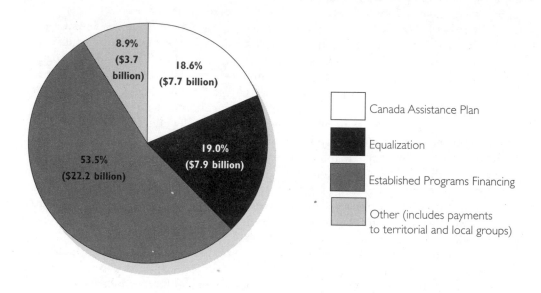

Source: Department of Finance, *Information for Decision-Making* (October 1994).

and for universities, and was not even compensated for the fact that Canadian taxpayers residing in Quebec were paying for these programs in the other provinces. In 1965 the Quebec government of Jean Lesage opted out of the new Canada Assistance Plan (although Quebec has never been freed from the fairly minimal program standards that Ottawa sets) and some other conditional grant programs, receiving compensation in the form of tax room surrendered by Ottawa to the province. Both the Meech Lake and Charlottetown Accords included a provision that would have obligated Ottawa to provide 'reasonable compensation' to any provincial government choosing not to participate in a new national shared-cost program, so long as the province's own program was 'compatible with the national objectives'. Critics argued that this opened the door for an erosion of national standards in social policy. Defenders claimed that this particular section merely constitutionalized a long-standing practice in Canadian federalism.

The Federal Spending Power and National Standards

In the 1990s it has become popular to vilify certain provincial governments, particularly the Klein government in Alberta and the Harris government in Ontario, for having undermined national standards in social programs. In fact, however, one of the major threats to national standards comes from Ottawa's shrinking financial commitment to provincially administered social programs. Liberal Finance Minister Paul Martin proclaimed his 1995 budget a 'new vision of Confederation'. Changes announced in that budget, combined with developments on the health care front, suggest that the federal Liberal government is continuing down a path already travelled, albeit tentatively, by the previous Conservative government.

The major change announced in the 1995 budget was the replacement of shared-cost programs that pay for welfare and social services under the CAP and EPF funding for health and post-secondary education with a single block transfer called the Canada Health and Social Transfer. In fact, however, the CHST institutionalizes the *ad hoc* freezes and caps on transfers that both Liberal and Tory governments imposed from the early 1980s. It does so, in Ottawa's words, by ensuring that 'the amounts transferred will not be determined by provincial spending decisions (as under cost-sharing)'.[47] Caps and freezes also had this effect, the difference being that Ottawa could always excuse what were effectively transfer cuts by citing their 'temporary' nature. The CHST appears to put the decisive nail in the coffin of shared-cost programs and thus to mark a retreat from Ottawa's commitment to national standards, a commitment that depends on the federal spending power.

The appearance may, however, be deceptive. The Liberals' determination to rein in federal transfers to the provinces has not been matched by a corresponding rhetoric of decentralization. On the contrary, the Liberal government has refused to concede an inch on the issue of national standards, particularly in regard to the health care system. Their message to the provinces has been this: We will give you fewer and fewer dollars with which to pay for your health care services, but we will continue to set conditions on how those services must operate. The Liberals' resolve has been put to the test by the Conservative government of Alberta, which has allowed the establishment of private clinics where patients, for a price, can jump the queue they would otherwise face in the publicly funded system. At the end of the day, however, all Ottawa can do is withhold some of the health care dollars it would otherwise transfer to Alberta or any other transgressing province. This may be a penalty without much sting. As economist Paul Boothe observes, 'The amount of money coming from Ottawa compared to the total health budget is trivial.'[48] In the case of Alberta he reckons that in 1995 federal cash transfers amounted to only 13 per cent of provincial revenue, with the federal share expected to fall even further. And even if the Liberals prove willing to withhold dollars from a Klein government in Alberta, would they show the same nerve in a confrontation with Ontario's Conservative provincial government?

In explaining the advantages of the CHST, the 1995 budget documents state that it would 'end the intrusiveness of previous cost-sharing arrangements'.[49] More specifically, the transition to block funding under the CHST was argued to have the following beneficial effects:

- Provinces will no longer be subject to rules stipulating which expenditures are eligible for cost-sharing or not.
- Provinces will be free to pursue their own innovative approaches to social security reform.
- The expense of administering cost-sharing will be eliminated.
- Federal expenditures will no longer be driven by provincial decisions on how to provide social assistance and social services, and to whom.[50]

Provinces would not, however, be free to do whatever they please under the new fiscal arrangements. The Liberal budget mentioned health care and social assistance as two areas where national standards would be maintained. In the case of social assistance this amounted only to an interdiction on minimum residency requirements. In regard to health care, the Liberals insisted that provinces would have to respect the principles of the Canada Health Act.

It is hard to avoid the conclusion that the Liberal government was in an advanced state of denial. It refused to recognize the fatal contradiction between the philosophy of national standards, whose chief instrument was the federal spending power, and the policy of reducing Ottawa's cash transfers for provincial social services. Under the CHST, federal cash transfers to the provinces are projected to decline from $16.9 billion in 1994–5 to $10.3 billion in 1997–8. Equalization payments, on the other hand, are set to increase over this period by an estimated 16 per cent. But equalization payments are not tied to any national program standards. Nonetheless, the dependence of some provincial governments on equalization could generate a compliant mindset. This possibility does not exist in the case of Alberta, British Columbia, and Ontario, which do not receive equalization, or in Quebec, though obviously for different reasons.

The Liberals' approach to fiscal federalism has been motivated by the red ink of federal budgets. The erosion of the federal spending power that the CHST represents—an erosion that was already under way under the Tories, but in a more *ad hoc* way through spending freezes and caps—does not embody a philosophy or vision of federalism. Instead, it represents a necessary expedient that was forced on the government by the perceived need to reduce social spending, the single largest chunk of program spending.

The Liberals' dilemma is that the 'soul' of the party remains committed to the idea of national standards set and enforced by Ottawa. Thus, Liberal government spokespersons have insisted that fewer federal dollars for provincial social services do not signal a retreat from Ottawa's tutelary role in these matters. Precisely how Ottawa will enforce compliance on un-cooperative provincial governments whose financial dependence on the feds becomes ever weaker is not clear. The exigencies of deficit management have pushed the Liberals toward a more decentralized structure of fiscal federalism, but it is evident that their hearts are not in it.

For many Canadians, government appears to be remote and mysterious. (Greg Vickers)

Modern government is a complicated affair. This chapter examines the key components of the machinery of government, including the following topics:

- ❖ The Monarch and Governor General.
- ❖ The Prime Minister and cabinet.
- ❖ Central agencies.
- ❖ The bureaucracy.
- ❖ Departments.
- ❖ Public enterprise.
- ❖ Regulatory agencies.
- ❖ The legislature.
- ❖ The courts.
- ❖ How a law is passed.

CHAPTER SIX

The Machinery of Government

Like a Rube Goldberg invention, modern government appears to be an unwieldy and complicated apparatus. Many of its parts seem to perform no useful function, and the overall impression is one of un-coordinated and often pointless activity. It appears to have been assembled piece by piece, without much planning and without discarding old parts to make room for new ones. The purpose of the machinery is easily lost sight of in its Byzantine complexity, and it seems certain that there must be a more efficient way of doing whatever the apparatus is intended to accomplish.

But for all its inelegance and appearance of muddling, the machinery does produce results. Laws are passed, regulations are applied, applications are dealt with, cheques are issued, and the innumerable other specific tasks performed by government are carried out. How well these tasks are done, whether some of them should be done at all, and what other things should be done by public authorities are important questions. But before we can answer them, we need an understanding of the machinery itself—of its individual parts, the functions they perform, and the relations between them.

In this chapter we will focus on state institutions at the national level. But Canadians also encounter the machinery of government at the provincial and local levels, where the state's activities affect their lives in ways that often seem more direct and significant than those of Ottawa. Hospitals, doctors' services, schools, rubbish collection and disposal, water treatment, police, roads and urban mass transit: these are all primarily the responsibilities of provincial and local governments. Together, provincial and local governments out-spend and out-tax the federal government.

An organization chart published by the government of Canada in July, 1995, includes 184 separate boxes, each representing a distinct component within the federal state. To simplify matters, political scientists usually group these structures under three headings that correspond to what, in democratic theory, are the three branches of government. These branches are the *legislature*, whose responsibility is the making of laws, the *executive*, whose role is the implementation of laws and the administration of public affairs, and the *judiciary*, which interprets the law when its meaning is disputed (see Figure 6.1). We may call this the *constitutional theory* approach. It provides an adequate guide to the formal constitutional division of responsibilities within the state, but it conveys a very distorted impression of the actual functions and activities of the three branches of government.

In this chapter we examine the machinery of government from a perspective that combines the constitutional theory approach with an attempt to identify the actual functions of the chief structures within each branch. These functions include representation, communication, agenda-setting, decision-making, and maintaining social order.

The Executive Branch

The Monarch and Governor General

Canada is a constitutional monarchy. The monarch, currently Queen Elizabeth II, embodies the authority of the Canadian state. Any action of the government of Canada is taken in the

Figure 6.1 The Formal Organization of Canadian Government

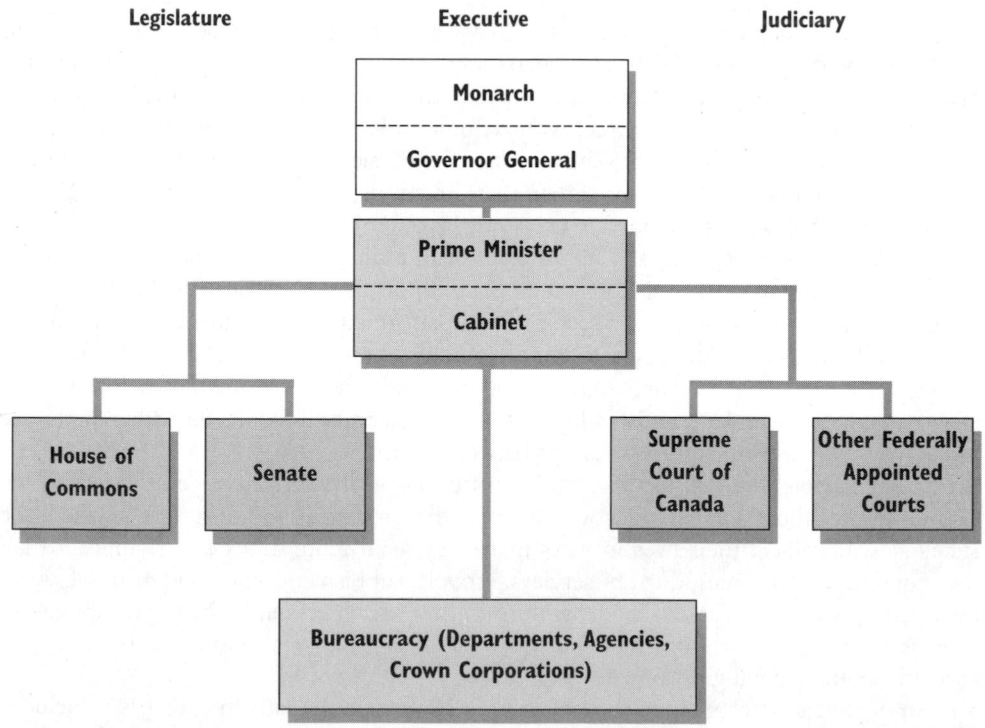

Queen's name.[1] The monarch is responsible for appointing the Prime Minister and for deciding when Parliament will be dissolved and a new election held. When she is not in Canada, which is of course most of the time, her duties are carried out by the Governor General, currently Romeo Leblanc. Although the strict letter of the constitution suggests that the role of the monarch in Canada's system of government is a formidable one, most Canadians realize that the Queen and Governor General perform mainly symbolic functions. The real decision-making powers of the executive are exercised by the Prime Minister, who is the head of government, and cabinet.

In matters such as the selection of the Prime Minister and the dissolution of Parliament, constitutional convention is far more important than the discretion of the monarch. For example, when one party wins a majority of the seats in an election, the choice of Prime Minister is automatic. Even when no party has a majority, it is understood that the leader of the party with the most seats will be given the first opportunity to try to form a government that has the support of a majority in the legislature. If, however, it is clear that the members of the other parties will not support a government led by this person, the monarch's representative may turn directly to the leader of another party. This happened in Ontario after the 1985 provincial election. Whatever the legislative scenarios appear to be, it is understood that a newly elected legislature must at least be given the opportunity to meet. The monarch's representative cannot simply decide that there is no point in convening the legislature and that a new election should be held straight-away.

Likewise in the case of dissolving Parliament, the monarch's discretion is limited by constitutional conventions that have developed over time. Normally, the Prime Minister's request that Parliament be dissolved and a new election held will be granted automatically. It is remotely conceivable, although highly improbable, that in circumstances of minority government the monarch's representative could refuse such a request and instead ask the leader of another party to try to form a government. The last time this happened was in 1926, when Governor General Lord Byng refused Prime Minister Mackenzie King's request for a new election. This refusal provoked a minor constitutional crisis. Since then, the view of most constitutional experts has been that the monarch's representative is required to accept the 'advice' given by the Prime Minister.

The monarch and Governor General play no significant role either in setting the government's policy agenda or in the subsequent decision-making process. Royal assent to legislation is virtually automatic. It has never been withheld from a law passed by Parliament. On the occasions when the monarch's provincial representatives, the lieutenant-governors, used the disallowance and reservation powers, this was almost always at the behest of the elected government in Ottawa.[2]

What role, then, does the monarchy play in Canada's system of government? We have said that the monarch's role today is primarily a symbolic one. This does not mean that the functions performed by the Queen and Governor General are unimportant. The ceremonial duties that are part of government must be performed by someone, and it may be that assigning them to a head of state who is above the partisan fray reduces the possibility of too close an association between the political system itself—the state—and the leadership of particular political factions within it. As James Mallory argues, '[the monarchy] denies to political leaders the full splendour of their power and the excessive aggrandizement of their persons which come from the undisturbed occupancy of the centre of the stage.'[3] Perhaps, but it must be admitted that these state functions are performed by an elected president in countries like the United States and France without there being much evidence that this has imperilled those democracies. On the other hand, both the American and French political systems have legislative checks on executive power that do not exist in a British parliamentary system. Mallory may, therefore, be correct in his belief that a non-elected head of state serves as a buffer against the self-aggrandizing tendencies of elected politicians. Paradoxically, then, a non-democratic institution, i.e., an unelected head of state, may contribute to the protection of a democratic social order.

But the monarchy has not always been an uncontroversial pillar of stability in Canadian politics. Despite the constitutional fact that the monarch's status in Canada's system of government is that of the King or Queen of Canada, not of the United Kingdom, the institution of monarchy has been perceived by some as an irritating reminder of Canada's colonial ties to Britain and of the dominance of Anglo-Canadians in this country's politics. This was particularly true during the 1960s, when royal visits to Quebec acted as lightning rods for the anti-federalist grievances of Quebec nationalists. Ancient memories of Anglo domination and Franco subordination have faded, but they have not disappeared. The failure of the Meech Lake Accord in 1990 led many Francophone politicians to call for the cancellation of the Queen's scheduled visit to Montreal. When French-English tensions run high, the issue of which groups in Canada are symbolically represented by the monarch resurfaces. Despite occasional imbroglios over royal visits, we should not exaggerate the institution's contribution to national disunity.

The Prime Minister and Cabinet

In contrast to the passive and principally symbolic roles of the monarch and Governor General, the Prime Minister and cabinet are at the centre of the policy-making process. The PM is the head of government in Canada. By convention, this person is the leader of the dominant party in the House of Commons. One of the PM's first duties is to select the people who will be cabinet ministers. In the vast majority of cases these will be other elected members of the House of Commons, although it occasionally happens that a senator or two are appointed to cabinet to give the government representation from a region where the governing party has elected few or no members, or because of the special abilities of a senator. In the British parliamentary tradition, cabinet members are always drawn from the same political party as the PM. In recent years, the size of the federal cabinet has ranged from a low of twenty-three to a high of almost forty members. Provincial cabinets are somewhat smaller.

The power of the PM and cabinet rests on a combination of factors. One of these is the written constitution. Section 11 of the Constitution Act, 1867, states that 'There shall be a Council to aid and advise in the Government of Canada, to be styled the Queen's Privy Council for Canada.' Section 13 of that Act goes even further to specify that the actions of the monarch's representative in Canada, the Governor General, shall be undertaken 'by and with the Advice of the Queen's Privy Council for Canada'. The privy council is essentially the cabinet, under the leadership of the PM. Although, formally, anyone who has ever been a member of cabinet retains the title of privy councillor after leaving government, only those who are active members of the government exercise the powers referred to in the constitution.

These powers include control over the budget. Section 54 of the Constitution Act, 1867, requires that any legislation or other measure that involves the raising or spending of public revenue must be introduced by cabinet. In fact, cabinet dominates the entire legislative agenda of Parliament, not just money matters. MPs who are not members of the cabinet do have the right to introduce private members' bills, but the meagre time allocated to considering these bills and the operation of party discipline combine to kill the prospects of most such initiatives.

More important than these written provisions of the constitution, however, are constitutional conventions relating to the PM and cabinet. Although the position of Prime Minister is not even mentioned in the written constitution, it is understood that the person who leads the dominant party in the House of Commons has the power to decide the following matters:

- who will be appointed to, or removed from, cabinet,
- when a new election will be held;
- the administrative structure and decision-making process of government;
- the selection of persons to a wide array of appointive positions, including deputy ministers, judges of all federal and provincial courts, senators, members of federal regulatory agencies and of the boards of directors of federal Crown corporations, ambassadors, etc.

These are formidable powers. They help to explain why the Prime Minister is always the pre-eminent figure in Canadian government, even when his or her decision-making style is a collegial one that encourages the participation of other members of cabinet. The PM's pre-eminence is reinforced by constitutional conventions on accountability. Although individual cabinet ministers are separately accountable to Parliament for the actions of their departments and the entire cabinet is collectively accountable for government policy, the PM cannot avoid personal accountability for the overall performance of government and for all major policies. The opposition parties and the media ensure that the PM takes the heat for these matters.

Responsible government is another constitutional convention that strengthens the power of the PM and cabinet. As we noted in Chapter 5, responsible government encourages party discipline. This means that the elected members of a party will tend to act as a unified bloc on most matters, particularly when voting on budget measures and important government legislation. If the members of the governing party break ranks, the government will fall. Party discipline, therefore, ensures that members of the governing party will normally be docile in their support of the government's policies. And when the government has a majority in both the House of Commons and the Senate, the automatic backing of the government party's backbenchers (i.e., MPs who are not cabinet ministers) enables the Prime Minister and cabinet to move their legislative agenda through Parliament without serious impediment. Cabinet dominance may be attenuated, however, during periods of minority government and when different parties control the House of Commons and the Senate.

The weakness of Canada's political party organizations is another factor that reinforces the dominance of the PM and cabinet. Parties, particularly the Liberal and Progressive Conservative parties, are geared primarily toward fighting election campaigns. They usually have little influence on the policies adopted by the party leadership when it forms the government. There are two main reasons for this. One is the parties' efforts to attract a broad base of support. This requires that the party's leadership be allowed a large margin to manoeuvre in communicating the party's policies to different groups. A second reason involves the absence, except in the case of the NDP, of formal affiliations between the parties and organized interests. Since 1961 the NDP has been formally affiliated to the Canadian Labour Congress. Formal affiliations usually have the effect of narrowing a party's electoral appeal and increasing the weight in a party's internal affairs—including leadership selection and policy-making—of the affiliated group(s). But when in power provincially, NDP governments have not been willing to tie themselves rigidly to the party's platform.

Statute law is not an important source of prime ministerial power. It provides, however, a significant legal basis for the authority and responsibilities of individual cabinet ministers. The statute under which a government department, agency, or Crown corporation operates will always specify which minister is responsible for the organization's actions. Legislation may also assign to a particular minister special powers over a part of the bureaucracy, such as a right of approval or veto of all or some category of the organization's decisions, or the right to order an agency or Crown corporation to base its decisions on particular guidelines or to act in a specific way. In fact, this sort of intervention is more likely to come from the PM and cabinet acting collectively, rather than being the initiative of an individual minister.

The constitutional and statutory foundations of prime ministerial and cabinet powers are reinforced by the relationship between the political executive and the media. This relationship is close and mutually dependent. The PM and members of cabinet regularly speak 'directly' to the people or to targeted publics via the media. Even when presenting or defending the government's policies in the House of Commons, they are aware of the wider audience to whom their words and behaviour are communicated by television cameras and the parliamentary press corps. For their part, journalists typically turn first to the PM and the responsible ministers when reporting on politics. In doing so, the media contribute to the personalization of politics and, more particularly, to the popular identification of government with the PM and cabinet. These tendencies have become even more pronounced as a result of the visual character of television—the medium that most Canadians depend on for national news[4]—and modern electioneering techniques that focus on the party leaders.

The reality of direct communications between the PM and cabinet and the public has undermined the role of the legislature and political parties. When public sentiment can be gauged through public opinion polls and when the PM and cabinet ministers can speak to either the general public or targeted groups via the media and personal contacts, there is no perceived need to communicate through government MPs and the party organization. The result is that Parliament is often little more than a procedural sideshow. This infuriates some constitutional purists, for whom Parliament is the proper conduit between the state and society. They argue that the practice of responsible government, the bedrock of the British parliamentary system, is subverted by direct communications between the government and the people. But the fact is that responsible government is already subverted by party discipline. And, in any case, there is no reason to believe that a diminished communications role for Parliament and MPs has reduced the democratic accountability of government from what it was before images of the Prime Minister and other government members flickered nightly across television screens.

The communications role of the Prime Minister and cabinet is related to their representative functions. From the beginnings of self-government in Canada, cabinet formation has been guided by the principle that politically important interests should, whenever possible, be 'represented' by particular cabinet ministers. Adequate representation of different regions and even particular provinces has always been considered important, as well as representation of Francophones. The numerical dominance of Anglophones has always ensured that they would be well represented in any government. Representation from the business community—the Minister of Finance has often been a person with professional connections to either the Toronto or Montreal corporate élite—and the inclusion of ministers perceived to be spokespersons for particular economic interests, particularly agriculture and occasionally labour, have also been significant factors in making appointments to particular cabinet positions. Some representational concerns, such as the inclusion of various religious denominations, have diminished in importance while others, like the representation of women and of non-French, non-British Canadians, have become increasingly significant.

Representational concerns also surface in the case of the PM. These concerns are particularly important when a party is choosing its leader. Candidates are looked at, by party members and the media, in terms of their likely ability to draw support from politically important regions and groups. At a minimum, an aspiring leader of a national political party cannot be associated too closely with the interests of a single region of the country. Moreover, he or she must be at least minimally competent in French. In practical terms, this means being able to read parts of speeches in French and to be able to answer questions in French. Given the numerical superiority of Anglophone voters, it goes without saying that any serious leadership candidate must be able to communicate well in English.

Being the leader of a national political party or even Prime Minister does not automatically elevate a politician above the factional strife of politics. Conservative Prime Minister John Diefenbaker (1957–63) was never perceived as being particularly sensitive to Quebec's interests, despite the fact that his party held a majority of that province's seats in the House of Commons between 1958 and 1962. Liberal Prime Minister Pierre Elliott Trudeau (1968–79, 1980–4) was never able to convince western Canada—not that he always tried very hard—that he shared their perspectives on Canadian politics. For westerners, Trudeau and the Liberals represented the dominance of 'the East' and favouritism toward Quebec. Conservative Prime Minister Brian Mulroney (1984–93) was more successful than Trudeau in drawing support from all regions of the country. But he, too, came under attack, particularly from the West, for allegedly neglecting western interests in favour of those of central Canada, particularly Quebec. In the end, the political weight of Ontario and Quebec is such that any PM, regardless of his or her background, is bound to be accused of favouring central Canada. The alternative is to risk losing the support of the region that accounts for 60 per cent of the seats in the House of Commons.

Representation is about power. The PM and cabinet wield considerable power through the machinery of government, which is why representation in the inner circle of government is valued by regional and other interests. This power is based on the agenda-setting role of the PM and cabinet and on their authority within the decision-making process of the state.

Each new session of Parliament begins with the Speech from the Throne, in which the Governor General reads a statement explaining the government's legislative priorities. This formal procedure is required by the constitution.[5] Although a typical Throne Speech will be packed with generalities, it will also contain some specific indications of the agenda that Parliament will deal with over the ensuing months.

Budgets represent a second way in which the Prime Minister and cabinet define the policy agenda. Every winter, usually around late February, the Minister of Finance tables the *estimates* in the House of Commons. This is what students of public finance call the *expenditure budget*. It represents the government's spending plans for the forthcoming fiscal year (1 April–31 March). Given that most public policies involve spending, changes in the allocation of public money provide an indication of the government's shifting priorities. The government can also use the expenditure budget to signal its overall fiscal stance. Increased spending may be part of an expansionary fiscal policy. Spending restraint and cutbacks, more typical in recent years, may signal the government's concern that the total level of public spending and the size of the public-sector deficit are damaging the economy.

From time to time, usually every one to one and a half years, the Minister of Finance will present in Parliament the government's plans to change the tax system. This is the *revenue budget*, and it, too, is a means by which the government sets the policy agenda. The revenue budget is one of the chief instruments of macroeconomic policy, geared toward achieving politically acceptable levels of economic growth, inflation, and unemployment. But it is also used as a tool of industrial policy, to influence activity in particular sectors and regions of the economy. As Figure 6.2 shows, cabinet and cabinet committees, particularly the Treasury Board, are central players in the budget-making process.

Even when the bills and budget proposals of government have not originated in cabinet—they often have been generated within some part of the bureaucracy—or when they appear to be simple reactions to politically or economically pressing circumstances, these initiatives must still be accepted and sponsored by the government. In deciding which initiatives will be placed before Parliament, the priorities among them, and the strategies for manoeuvring policies through the legislature and communicating them to the public, the government influences the policy agenda.

Agenda-setting is part of the decision-making process in government. It is a crucial part, being that early stage during which public issues are defined and policy responses are proposed. The role of the PM and cabinet at this and other stages of the policy process is institutionalized through the formal structure of cabinet decision-making. Between 1968 and 1993 the key committee of cabinet in terms of establishing the government's policy and budget priorities was the Priorities and Planning (P&P) Committee. It was chaired by the Prime Minister and included only the most influential members of cabinet. Since the reduction in the size of cabinet to twenty-three members under former Prime Minister Kim Campbell, a reduction maintained under Jean Chrétien, P&P has disappeared. There no longer is the need for an élite within the élite, as there was in the days when cabinets usually had thirty to thirty-five members. The structure of cabinet decision-making has been streamlined under the Chrétien Liberals to include only four permanent subcommittees of cabinet: Economic

Figure 6.2 The Expenditure Management System, 1995

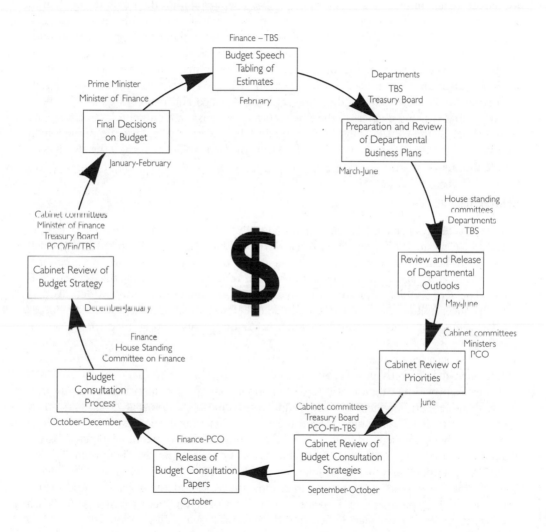

Source: Canada, Treasury Board, 'The Expenditure Management System of the Government of Canada' (1995).

Development, Social Development, Treasury Board, and the Special Committee of Council. *Ad hoc* committees are created and disbanded as circumstances require.

Ministerial control over the bureaucracy is another dimension of cabinet's decision-making authority. The word 'control' should be used carefully, however. Ministers are rarely involved in the day-to-day running of the departments that fall under their nominal control. Moreover, policy initiatives are more likely to be generated within the bureaucracy than to spring from the fertile imagination of the responsible minister. Inevitably, most ministers, most of the time, act as cabinet advocates for the interests of their departments, their budgets and programs, and the groups that depend on them. We should not succumb, however, to the caricature of wily, powerful bureaucrats manipulating their hapless political 'masters'—a caricature popularized by the British television program *Yes Prime Minister*. Departments and other parts of the bureaucracy are created and restructured as a result of cabinet initiatives, and changes to their budgets and programs are often undertaken in spite of bureaucratic opposition. Anyone who doubts this need only look at the reduction in bureaucracy carried out in the 1990s by the Klein government in Alberta and the Harris government in Ontario.

Central Agencies

Cabinet has always been a decision-making body. But when Sir John A. Macdonald and the first cabinet met in 1867, they dealt with a workload that was only a fraction of that which faces government today. There were only a handful of departments, no Crown corporations, and no regulatory agencies, and federal-provincial relations were still relatively uncomplicated. The scope and complexity of contemporary government are vastly wider. To deal with the sheer volume of information that comes before cabinet and the hundreds of separate decisions that it takes annually, cabinet needs help. This help is provided by central agencies.

Central agencies are parts of the bureaucracy whose main or only purpose is to support the decision-making activities of cabinet. More concretely, this means that they perform such functions as providing cabinet with needed information, applying cabinet decisions in dealing with other parts of the bureaucracy, and communicating cabinet decisions and their implications to the public, other governments, or other organizations within the federal state. The general character of their policy role, their direct involvement in cabinet decision-making, and their ability to intervene in the affairs of departments have led political scientists Colin Campbell and George Szablowski to refer to the senior officials of central agencies as 'superbureaucrats'.[6] The five organizations usually considered to have central agency status are the Department of Finance, the Privy Council Office, the Treasury Board Secretariat, the Prime Minister's Office, and the Federal-Provincial Relations Office.

Department of Finance

The Department of Finance plays the leading role in the formulation of economic policy. Its formal authority is found in the Department of Finance Act, 1869, and in the Financial Administration Act. The authority that the law confers on Finance is reinforced by the department's informal reputation within the state. It has always been a magnet for 'the best and the brightest' within the public service because of its unrivalled status in all aspects of economic policy-making.

The Finance Department has what amounts to almost exclusive authority over the preparation of the revenue budget and the periodic White Papers on tax reform that signal government's future policy intentions. Whatever input other parts of the bureaucracy and interests outside of government have is at the discretion of the Minister of Finance and the department.[7] New initiatives in taxation and trade policy and in managing the level of government spending and debt will often be generated within Finance. Even when a new policy idea originates elsewhere, it is unlikely to reach the legislation stage if Finance is steadfastly opposed.

Finance officials are able to influence the entire spectrum of government policy through their role in the annual formulation of the expenditure budget. They are involved at the very beginning of the expenditure budget process, providing projections on the future state of the economy and the fiscal framework within which spending choices will have to be made. A Finance forecast of weak economic activity and lean taxation revenues will impose across-the-board restraint on departments jostling for scarce funds.

The Treasury Board Secretariat

The Treasury Board Secretariat (TBS) is an administrative adjunct to the Treasury Board, which in turn is the only cabinet committee that has a statutory basis.[8] The Treasury Board is guardian of the purse strings, government employer, and the chief agency in making personnel and administrative policy within the federal government. Its authority is, in a word, extensive. In performing its responsibilities, the Treasury Board draws on the support of the TBS, which includes within it the Office of the Comptroller General of Canada (OCG). The functions of the OCG include departmental audits, establishing and enforcing accounting standards in government, and the evaluation of particular programs.

TBS officials formulate the expenditure outlook that, along with the economic outlook and fiscal framework developed by Finance, is the starting point in the annual expenditure budget exercise. The expenditure forecasts provided by TBS are used by cabinet in making decisions on the allocation of financial resources between competing programs. The involvement of TBS officials does not stop here. Along with the spending committees of cabinet, they assess the spending proposals and plans that departments are required to submit each year. Preparation of the main estimates, the detailed spending plans that the government tables in the House of Commons each winter, is the responsibility of the Treasury Board.

The Privy Council Office

The Privy Council Office (PCO) is essentially the cabinet's secretariat. It was formally created by order-in-council in 1940. The position of Chief Clerk of the Privy Council was put on a statutory basis in 1974, without any specification of the duties associated with this position. The authority of this person, who is the highest-ranking member of the federal bureaucracy, and the influence of the PCO derive mainly from their intimate and continuous involvement in cabinet decision-making.

In their study of central agencies, Campbell and Szablowski argue that the PCO is the lead agency for 'strategic planning and formulation of substantive policy'.[9] The PCO's role is 'strategic' because it is situated at the confluence of all the various policy issues and decisions that come before cabinet. In terms of its organization, the PCO is divided into a number of secretariats that provide support services for the various committees of cabinet. These services range from such mundane functions as scheduling and keeping the minutes of committee meetings to activities that carry the potential for real influence, such as providing policy advice and dealing directly with government departments. Perhaps more than any other single component of the bureaucracy, the PCO is capable of seeing 'the big picture' of government policy. This picture embraces policy *and* political concerns. A former head of the PCO, Gordon Robertson, has summarized the different roles of the PCO and the Prime Minister's Office in the following way: 'The Prime Minister's Office is partisan, politically oriented, yet operationally sensitive. The Privy Council Office is non-partisan, operationally oriented yet politically sensitive.'[10]

It was under Prime Minister Pierre Trudeau that the PCO acquired the policy orientation and influence that Robertson ascribes to it, and which have characterized the PCO since then. Many of roughly 300 officials who work in the PCO are policy experts or professional managers, usually career bureaucrats who have come to the PCO from the departmental bureaucracy or from another central agency. They represent an alternative source of policy advice to that which comes from the senior officials of government departments.

The Federal-Provincial Relations Office

Perhaps the most surprising thing about this central agency is that it did not exist before 1975. Federal-provincial relations did not suddenly become complex and the political stakes high in the 1970s. Before the Federal-Provincial Relations Office (FPRO) was created, its functions had been carried out within the PCO. What, then, prompted Prime Minister Pierre Trudeau to create a new agency to deal with intergovernmental affairs? According to Colin Campbell, the reason had to do with a staffing problem. Trudeau wanted to appoint Michael Pitfield as Chief Clerk of the Privy Council but was faced with the dilemma of what to do with Gordon Robertson, Pitfield's predecessor and perhaps the most widely respected official in the public service. The solution was to create the Federal-Provincial Relations Office and to appoint Robertson as the first secretary to the cabinet for Federal-Provincial Relations.[11] The episode provides a nice illustration of the role played by serendipity in government decision-making.

After its launch, and despite the prestige of its first head, the FPRO never achieved the influence of such other central agencies as Finance, the TBS, and the PCO. Indeed, only two years after the FPRO was established, the cabinet position of minister for federal-provincial relations and the cabinet committee on federal-provincial relations were abolished. The FPRO was to have been the support staff for this minister and the secretariat to this committee. Their elimination did not result in the dismantling of the FPRO. It has continued to provide information and advice to cabinet committees on issues that have an intergovernmental dimension. The precise functions performed by the FPRO depend on the Prime Minister. For example, the FPRO played a major role in the development of the Meech Lake Accord proposals. Its lesser stature compared to Finance, the PCO, and the TBS is largely due to the fact that the FPRO does not hold a monopoly over advice on federal-provincial matters. The other central agencies, including the Prime Minister's Office (see below), also have input into these matters.

The Prime Minister's Office

Unlike the other central agencies, the Prime Minister's Office (PMO) is staffed chiefly by partisan appointees rather than by career public servants. The PMO is the Prime Minister's personal staff, performing functions that range from handling the PM's correspondence and schedule to speech writing, media relations, liaison with ministers, caucus, and the party, and providing advice on appointments and policy. Gordon Robertson's observation that the PMO is 'partisan, politically oriented, yet operationally sensitive'[12] captures well the role of this central agency. It serves as the PM's political eyes and ears, and has the added distinction of being able to speak on behalf of the PM. The PMO is headed by the PM's chief of staff. No other non-elected official is in such regular contact with the PM.

During Pierre Trudeau's first government, the PMO seem destined to assume a major role in the formulation of policy. Trudeau created a number of 'regional desks' whose role was to monitor political issues in the various regions and to provide advice on these issues, including partisan appointments. The PMO also carried out major reviews of Canadian foreign policy and defence policy under Ivan Head, Trudeau's own external affairs adviser within the PMO. These reforms were abandoned after 1972. Nevertheless, the potential always exists for the PMO to play a more active role in the formation of policy, should the Prime Minister decide that this is appropriate.

The Bureaucracy

For policies to have an impact, they must be implemented. The unemployment insurance (UI) program, for example, depends on the administrative efforts of thousands of public servants employed in Canada Employment Centres across the country, the adjudicative work of hundreds of UI appeals commissioners, and the Unemployment Insurance Commission, which is responsible for making and applying regulations under the Unemployment Insurance Act. Educational policy is implemented through bureaucratic structures at the federal (student loans, support for research), provincial (ministries of education), and local (school boards) levels. Policies aimed at supporting Canadian industry are administered through a staggering array of separate programs—with their own budgets and bureaucracies—at all levels of government.

Policy implementation is the role of the bureaucracy. Implementation is not, however, an automatic process of converting legislative decisions into action. Unelected officials often wield enormous discretion in applying laws and administering programs. Moreover, their influence is not restricted to the implementation stage of policy-making. It begins at the agenda-setting stage, when problems and possible responses are being defined. Bureaucratic influence is felt at numerous points in the decision-making process that precedes the actual introduction of a bill in Parliament. Often, the decision-making process has no parliamentary stage, or at least Parliament has minimal involvement in the process. Here, the power of unelected officials is seen in its most naked form.

The original meaning of the word 'bureaucracy'—*bureaucracie*, coined by the French writer Vincent de Gournay in the mid-1700s—involved rule by unelected officials. The first formal definition of the word appeared in 1798 in the Dictionary of the French Academy. It read: 'Power, influence of the heads and staff of governmental bureaux.' Ever since, the political power of unelected officials has been a chief concern of those who study bureaucracy.

'Downsizing' government has been in fashion in recent years. (Roy Peterson, *Vancouver Sun*)

The Structure of Canadian Bureaucracy

According to the federal government's own count, it directly employs roughly 500,000 people working in about 400 different organizations.[12] This is not, however, the whole picture of Canadian bureaucracy. Together, the provincial governments employ about 650,000 people, and local governments employ roughly another 330,000.[13] These governments also have complex organizational structures and a collective debt that in recent years has been escalating more rapidly than Ottawa's. No analysis of bureaucracy is complete without a consideration of the provincial and local levels. Nevertheless, we will restrict our attention to the federal bureaucracy for no better reason than space does not allow for a comprehensive treatment of the subject.

The bureaucracy may be divided into three main components: the public service (chiefly departments); independent and semi-independent agencies and tribunals; and Crown corporations. Their distinguishing features include the following.

Public service. About half of the federal public sector falls under this category. It includes all statutory departments (the number of which was reduced by reorganization from thirty-two to twenty-three under former Prime Minister Kim Campbell) and other organizations whose members are appointed by the Public Service Commission and are employees of the Treasury Board. This is the part of the bureaucracy that falls most directly under the authority of cabinet.

Agencies and tribunals. These are organizations that perform a wide variety of regulatory, research, and advisory functions. Among the most widely known federal regulatory agencies are the Canadian Radio-television and Telecommunications Commission (CRTC), which regulates communications and broadcasting, the National Transportation Agency (air, water, and rail transportation), and the National Energy Board (energy when it crosses provincial and international boundaries). It is important to note that many important areas of regulation, including trucking, telephone communications in all provinces except Ontario and British Columbia, public utilities within provincial boundaries, and labour relations, are controlled by provincial governments.

These organizations have a greater degree of independence from government than those that fall under the public service. With few exceptions their members are not appointed by the Public Service Commission, nor are they employees of the Treasury Board. The precise degree of autonomy enjoyed by an agency or tribunal varies, but in some cases it is almost total.

Crown corporations. These are organizations that, in most cases, perform commercial functions and typically operate at 'arm's length' from the government of the day. They hire their own employees, determine their own internal administrative structures, and in many instances behave much like privately owned businesses. In recent years some of the largest of these corporations, notably Air Canada, Canadian National, and Petro-Canada, have been privatized.

These three categories do not cover the entire federal bureaucracy. Some relatively small but important parts of that bureaucracy, including the Auditor-General's Office and the Commissioner of Official Languages, are independent of cabinet and report directly to Parliament. The Royal Canadian Mounted Police also has a distinct legal status, as does the Canadian Armed Forces.

Together, this vast administrative apparatus has responsibility for implementing public policy. At the most mundane level—the level where virtually all of us have made personal contact with the state—officials deal with passport applications, meat inspections, public queries regarding unemployment insurance benefits, job seekers at Canada Employment Centres, and a vast number of similarly routine administrative tasks. But at the top of the bureaucratic pyramid are men and women whose relationship to public policy is much more active. Senior officials within the departmental bureaucracy, particularly deputy ministers and assistant deputy ministers, interact frequently with cabinet ministers and officials in central agencies. They are called on to testify before committees of the legislature. These officials often deal directly with the representatives of organized interests. They are universally acknowledged to have influence in shaping public policy, although the extent of their influence is a matter of debate (see Box 6.1).

The bureaucracy is not a uniform structure. One can identify several different functions performed by organizations within the administrative system. These include:

- the provision and administration of services to the public, often to narrow economic, social, or cultural clientele groups;
- the provision of services to other parts of the bureaucracy;
- the integration of policy in a particular field or the generation of policy advice;

Box 6.1 A Former Top Bureaucrat Describes His Job

The Privy Council Office provides non-partisan, public service support to the Prime Minister and the Cabinet. Under the direction of the Clerk of the Privy Council and Secretary to the Cabinet, the Office assists the head of government in meeting his other responsibilities for keeping the Ministry united and on course. In this context, the Prime Minister looks to the PCO for advice and support in choosing the principal ministerial and official office-holders, in establishing and balancing ministerial mandates, in providing the machinery that the Cabinet requires to serve the process of collective decision-making, in providing management for the public service, and in giving general direction to government policy. In addition, when Governments change, the Privy Council Office ensures a smooth transition from one administration to the next.

Paul Tellier, Clerk of the Privy Council
(personal communication, 1991).

- the adjudication of applications and/or interpretation of regulations (such as product safety standards, or the determination of what constitutes morally offensive scenes of sex or violence in films);
- the disbursement of funds to groups or individuals, as with the grants to artists and cultural organizations administered by the Canada Council;
- the production of a good or the operation of a service that is sold to buyers.

These functions are not mutually exclusive. A large and organizationally complex department like the federal Department of Transport is involved in service delivery, the regulation of transport standards, and the development of policy. Almost all government departments, regardless of their primary orientation, have a policy development capacity. During the 1970s this was formalized—although not necessarily enhanced—with the creation of policy analysis units, usually at the assistant deputy minister level. An informal policy advisory capacity, however, has always existed at the level of senior officials. This role is based on their expert familiarity with the programs administered by the department and on the fact that, typically, they remain within a particular policy field longer than their nominal superiors in cabinet. The turnover rate for deputy ministers and other senior bureaucrats has increased since the era of the Ottawa 'mandarins'[14] from the 1940s to the 1960s, when a coterie of top officials whose careers were associated with particular parts of the bureaucracy exercised an extraordinary influence on the direction of federal policy. The more recent emphasis has been on senior officials as managers, whose management skills are transferable across policy fields. Combined with the more rapid turnover of deputy ministers since the early 1980s, it is often argued that the policy influence of senior bureaucrats has diminished.

In fact, it would be more accurate to say that this power has become more diffuse. The days when a mere handful of key deputy ministers could dominate the policy-making process are gone. Today, bureaucratic influence is distributed more widely, in large part because of the increased importance of central agencies like the Treasury Board Secretariat and the Privy Council Office, but also because it is rare for a deputy minister to remain in charge of a particular department for more than a few years. Nevertheless, there is little doubt that senior bureaucrats continue to be key players in policy-making.

The passing of the mandarinate and the development of central agencies as an alternative source of expert policy advice to cabinet have not undermined the fundamental basis of bureaucratic influence on policy. This influence rests on the following factors:

- Departments are repositories for a vast amount of information about current and past programs and about the day-to-day details of their administration. While the aphorism 'Knowledge is power' is too simplistic and implies a sort of rationality that usually is not characteristic of policy choices, ministers invariably depend on the permanent bureaucracy for advice on policy. Senior bureaucrats occupy strategic positions in the policy process because of their ability to shape the information and recommendations reaching the minister.
- The relationship of a department to the social or economic interests that benefit from the programs it administers is a source of departmental influence on policy. Departmental officials clearly are not indifferent in their sympathies toward conflicting societal interests. Moreover, the bureaucracy is an important target for professional lobbyists and interest group representatives who wish to influence policy.
- The special relationship a deputy minister has with his or her minister reinforces the policy influence of the bureaucracy. Given the competing pressures on a minister's time, the deputy minister inevitably assumes the job of senior manager of the department over which a cabinet minister nominally presides. In many instances the chief responsibility for policy direction also will be assumed by the deputy minister.
- Most laws contain provisions delegating to bureaucrats the authority to interpret the general terms of the law in its application to actual cases. This is also true of other statutory instruments that have the force of law (for example, the thousands of orders-in-council that issue from cabinet each year). The task of implementation—applying the law to actual cases—is not a neutral one. In some cases this discretion is exercised at a low level in the bureaucratic hierarchy (for example, decisions by local customs officials on whether a particular videocassette constitutes obscene material and therefore should be prohibited entry into Canada).

To summarize, the bureaucracy enters the policy process both early and late. Bureaucrats are the people who actually administer the programs established by law. In doing so they regularly exercise considerable discretion, a fact that often leads special interests to focus at least part of their attention on the bureaucracy. Departmental officials are also involved in the early stages of the policy process because of the intimate knowledge they have of existing programs and the daily contact between bureaucrats and the groups that 'consume' the programs they administer. Moreover, the annual expenditure budget, which provides a fairly reasonable indication of a government's policy priorities, is based largely on the information provided by departments. New legislation is invariably influenced by the input of senior permanent officials. These officials are both managers and policy advisers, and they are very clearly part of the inner circle of policy-making that extends outward from cabinet.

On top of all the other expectations held for bureaucracy in democratic societies, it is also expected to 'represent' the population. This means that the composition of the bureaucracy should reflect in fair proportion certain demographic characteristics of society. Affirmative action programs and quota hiring are the tools used in pursuit of this goal. The basic reasoning behind arguments for 'representative' bureaucracy is that it will have greater popular legitimacy than one that is not and that its representative character will help ensure that the advice bureaucrats give to politicians and the services they provide to their clienteles are sensitive to the values and aspirations of the governed.

As reasonable as this may sound, the idea and implementation of representative bureaucracy have always been problematic. Which groups should be singled out for representation? What constitutes 'fair proportion'? To what extent are other values like efficient performance and equal rights for all compromised by such a policy? Can the idea of a representative bureaucracy be squared with that of a politically neutral one?

Problems aside, it is clear that a grossly unrepresentative bureaucracy can pose problems. The fact that comparatively few French Canadians were found at the senior levels of the federal bureaucracy was already a controversial matter in the 1940s, 1950s, and 1960s and led to major public service reforms and Canada's first policy of representative bureaucracy under Lester B. Pearson and Pierre Elliott Trudeau. On the other hand, most students of British bureaucracy agree that the strongly upper-class character of that country's public service did not prevent it from co-operating with the post-World War Two Labour government in implementing reforms opposed by the upper class. Nor has the unrepresentative and élitist character of the French bureaucracy been considered a major problem in that country.

One thing is certain: governments that have instituted policies of affirmative action and quota hiring have done so chiefly for political reasons, not because the intellectual arguments offered in support of such policies are demonstrably true. Among the most important political reasons is national unity. In Canada it has long been recognized that the merit principle, which ignores the ascriptive characteristics of individuals and looks only at their job-related achievements and skills, should not interfere with what one writer called 'a tactful balance of national elements'.[15] Until fairly recently, this balancing act chiefly involved ensuring adequate Francophone representation in the management ranks of the bureaucracy. Indeed, it is fair to say that until the 1970s this was the only serious representational factor taken into account in public service recruitment and promotion. John Porter's analysis of the senior federal bureaucracy during the 1950s showed that only the British, French, and Jewish ethnic groups were significantly represented, and those of British origin were clearly dominant. Women and what are today labelled visible minorities were almost completely absent from the senior levels of the public service.

As the ethnic composition of Canadian society has changed—people of non-British, non-French ancestry now comprise over one-quarter of the population—and especially as the discourse of collective rights and group identities has achieved greater prominence, the old concern with 'fair' linguistic representation has been joined by efforts to recruit and promote women, visible minorities, Aboriginal Canadians, and the disabled. Affirmative action programs are established by the Treasury Board and monitored by the Public Service Commission. During the 1980s their programs relied mainly on a system of employment targets rather than on mandatory quotas for group representation. Ottawa and the provincial governments continue to use targets and incentives to encourage senior managers to hire and promote members of designated groups, but they also use quota systems—euphemistically labelled 'employment equity' policies. Some interpret 'fair representation' as a proportion of the bureaucracy equal to a group's share of the population. This is, for example, the position taken by the New Democratic Party and feminist organizations in Canada. To this day, however, Canadian governments have not attempted to implement this vision of fairness.

The Legislature

The legislature is a study in contrasts. Its physical setting is soberly impressive, yet the behaviour of its members is frequently the object of derision. Its constitutional powers appear to be formidable, yet its actual influence on policy usually is much less than that of the cabinet and the bureaucracy. All major policies, including all laws, must be approved by the legislature, but the legislature's approval often seems a foregone conclusion and a mere formality. One of the two chambers of the legislature, the House of Commons, is democratically elected—and controlled by the iron hand of party discipline. The other, the Senate, has long had an unenviable reputation as a sinecure for party hacks and other appointed unworthies.

The contradictions of the legislature have their source in the tension between traditional ideas about political democracy and the character of the modern state. Representation, accountability to the people, and choice are the cornerstones of liberal-democratic theory. An elected legislature that represents the population either on the basis of population or by region—or both—and party competition are the means by which these democratic goals are to be accomplished. But the modern state, we have seen, is characterized by a vast bureaucratic apparatus that is not easily controlled by elected politicians. As the scale and influence of the non-elected parts of the state have grown, the inadequacies of traditional democratic theory—centred around the role of the legislature—have become increasingly apparent.

Is there an alternative? A more representative and democratically responsive bureaucracy is sometimes viewed as the solution to the problem of power without accountability. Reforms in this direction are certainly useful. They cannot, however, substitute for elections that enable voters to choose those who will represent them. If one begins from the premise that the free election must be the cornerstone of political democracy, the role of the legislature is crucial.

One way of ensuring that the legislature better performs its democratic functions is to improve its representative character. Possible ways through which this could be done include reform of the political parties' candidate selection process, a system of proportional representation (see Chapter 7), or a reformed Senate. Another option is to tighten the legislature's control over the political executive and the non-elected parts of the state. This may be done by increasing the legislature's access to information about the intentions and performance of the government and bureaucracy, providing opportunities for legislative scrutiny and debate of executive action, and enabling legislators to influence the priorities and agenda of government.

Canada's legislature has two parts, the House of Commons and the Senate. Representation in the elected House of Commons is roughly according to population—roughly, because some MPs represent as few as 30,000 constituents while others represent close to 200,000. Each of the 295 members of the House of Commons is the sole representative for a constituency (also known as a 'riding').

Senators are appointed by the government of the day when a vacancy occurs. They hold their seats until age seventy-five. Representation in the Senate is on the basis of regions. Each of the four main regions (Ontario, Quebec, the four western provinces, and the Maritimes) has twenty-four seats. Newfoundland has six and there is one from each of the Yukon and Northwest Territories. Eight temporary seats were added by the Mulroney government in 1988 to overcome Liberal opposition in the Senate to the Goods and Services Tax, thus raising the total number of senators for a while from 104 to 112. In recent years there have been suggestions that senators be elected and that a certain number of Senate seats be reserved for women and Aboriginal Canadians.

In law, the powers of the House of Commons and the Senate are roughly equal. There are, however, a couple of important exceptions. Legislation involving the spending or raising of public money must, under the constitution, be introduced in the House of Commons. And when it comes to amending the constitution, the Senate can only delay passage of a resolution already approved by the Commons. But all bills must pass through identical stages in both bodies before becoming law (see the appendix at the end of this chapter).

Despite the similarity of their formal powers, the superiority of the elected branch is well established. For most of its history, the Senate has deferred to the will of the Commons. This changed after the 1984 election of a Conservative majority in Parliament. On several occasions the Liberal-dominated Senate obstructed bills that had already been passed by the Commons. When the Senate balked at passage of the politically unpopular GST, the government decided it had had enough. Using an obscure constitutional power, it appointed eight new Conservative senators, thereby giving the Conservative Party a slender Senate majority.

The legislature performs a number of functions that are basic to political democracy. The most fundamental of these is the passage of laws by the people's elected representatives. Budget proposals and new policy initiatives must be placed before Parliament for its approval. The operation of party discipline ensures that bills tabled in the legislature are seldom modified in major ways during the law-passing process. This does not mean, however, that Parliament's approval of the government's legislative agenda is an empty formality. The rules under which the legislature operates ensure that the opposition parties have opportunities to debate and criticize the government's proposals.

Robert Jackson and Michael Atkinson argue that those involved in the pre-parliamentary stages of policy-making anticipate the probable reactions of the legislature before a bill or budget is tabled in Parliament.[16] Criticism is unavoidable—the role of the opposition in the adversarial British parliamentary system is, after all, to oppose. But in drafting legislative proposals, policy-makers can and do attempt to avoid supplying their critics with gratuitous ammunition. Other functions performed by the legislature include scrutiny of government performance, constituency representation, debate of issues, and legitimation of the political system.

Scrutinizing government performance. Various regular opportunities exist for the legislature to prod, question, and criticize the government. These include the daily Question

Period, the set-piece debates that follow the Speech from the Throne and the introduction of a new budget, and Opposition Days, when the opposition parties determine the topic of debate. Committee hearings and special parliamentary task forces also provide opportunities for legislative scrutiny of government actions and performance, although the subjects that these bodies deal with are mainly determined by the government. Party discipline is another factor that limits the critical tendencies of parliamentary committees, particularly during periods of majority government.

Representation. The House of Commons is both symbolically and practically important as a contact point between citizens and government. Symbolically, the elected House embodies the principle of government by popular consent. The partisan divisions within it, between government and opposition parties, have the additional effect of affirming for most citizens their belief in the competitive character of politics. At a practical level, citizens often turn to their elected representatives when they experience problems with bureaucracy or when they want to express their views on government policy.

Unlike the elected Commons, the Senate does not perform a significant representational role in Canadian politics, despite the fact that senators are appointed to represent the various provinces. The unelected character of Canada's upper house and the crassly partisan criteria that prime ministers have usually relied on in filling Senate vacancies have undermined whatever legitimacy senators might otherwise have achieved as spokespersons for the regions. Provincial governments, regional spokespersons in the federal cabinet, and regional blocs of MPs within the party caucuses are, in about that order of importance, vastly more significant in representing regional interests.

Debate. The image that most Canadians have of Parliament is of the heated exchanges that take place across the aisle that separates the government and opposition parties. Parliamentary procedure and even the physical layout of the legislature are based on the adversarial principle of 'them versus us'. This principle is most clearly seen in the daily Question Period and in the set-piece debates that follow the Speech from the Throne and the introduction of a new budget. At its best, the thrust and riposte of partisan debate can provide a very public forum for the discussion of national issues, as well as highlighting the policy differences between the parties. Unfortunately for the quality of political discourse in Canada, parliamentary debate is more often dragged down by the wooden reading of prepared remarks, heckling and personal invective, and occasional blatant abuses of either the government's majority or the opposition's opportunities to hold up the business of Parliament.

It is a mistake to believe that the purpose of parliamentary debate is to allow for a searching discussion of issues in a spirit of open-mindedness. Generally, MPs' minds are made up when a measure is first tabled in Parliament. So what is the point of the long hours spent criticizing and defending legislative proposals and the government's record, all at taxpayers' expense?

There are two reasons why legislative debate is important. First, outcomes are not always predictable. Even when the government party holds a commanding majority in Parliament or when the policy differences between government and opposition are not significant, the dynamic of debate on an issue is not entirely controllable by the government or by Parliament. Media coverage of the issue, reporting of public opinion polls, the interventions of organized interests, other governments, and even individuals who have credibility in the eyes of the media and public will all have a bearing on the trajectory of parliamentary debate.

Parliamentary debate is also important because it reinforces the popular belief in the open and competitive qualities of Canadian democracy. The stylized conflict between government and opposition parties, which is the essence of the British parliamentary system, emphasizes disagreements and differences. Adversarial politics obscures the fact that these partisan disagreements usually are contained within a fairly narrow band of consensus on basic values and that the words and deeds of the opposition, when it holds power, usually bear a strong resemblance to those of its predecessor. Parliamentary debate, therefore, produces an exaggerated impression of the open and competitive qualities of Canadian politics. This provides valuable support for the existing political system, while papering over the obstacles that non-mainstream interests face in getting their concerns and views onto the public agenda.

Legitimation. Parliament is both a legislative and a legitimizing institution. Laws must pass through the parliamentary mill before being approved, and thus Parliament deserves to be called the legislative branch of government. But it is also the legitimizing branch of government because most of the mechanisms of democratic accountability are embodied in the structure and procedures of Parliament. It represents the people. It scrutinizes the actions of government. And it debates public issues. Along with elections and judicial review of the constitution, Parliament appears to be one of the chief bulwarks against the danger that government will abuse its powers.

How well Parliament performs its democratic functions is another matter. But the structures and procedures of the legislature are built around the ideas of open government and popular consent, and the actions of government must be approved by Parliament. These factors help to legitimize the political system and the policies it produces. If, however, most people hold the view that the legislature is a farce, then its contribution to the perceived legitimacy of Canadian government would be undermined. Canadians do not hold this view. Their cynicism about the integrity of politicians does not appear to undermine their faith in parliamentary institutions.

The legislature is not the helpless pawn of the Prime Minister and cabinet. Using the rules of parliamentary procedure, opposition parties are able to prod, question, and castigate the government, all in front of the parliamentary press gallery and the television cameras in the House of Commons. The opposition's behaviour is usually reactive, responding to the government's proposals and policies, but the legislature's function as a talking shop—the *parler* in parliament—enables it to draw attention to controversial aspects of the government's performance. MPs are not quite the 'nobodies' that Pierre Trudeau once labelled them. Still, they are far from having the policy influence of their American counterparts, who, because of loose party discipline and very different rules governing the law-making process, are often assiduously courted by interest groups and the President himself.

A second way in which the legislature can influence the government of the day is through *caucus*, the body of elected MPs belonging to a particular party. When Parliament is in session, it is usual for a party's caucus to meet at least weekly. Caucus meetings provide an opportunity for the exchange of views between party leaders and backbench MPs. In the case of the government party, they may allow for debate on the policies that government MPs are expected to vote for and defend before the folks back home. This is not always a comfortable task, especially when proposed legislation is deeply unpopular with certain members' constituents.

Some insiders argue that the government caucus provides a real opportunity for backbench members to influence government policy, through frank debate behind closed doors. This may occasionally be true, but the limits on caucus's influence are readily apparent from two facts. First, extremely unpopular policies such as the GST, but which are priorities of the government, are not affected by caucus opposition. The same is true of policies that create sharp divisions in a party's caucus, such as the Liberal government's 1995 gun control law. If the policy is a high priority, the prospect that a caucus revolt will defeat or substantially change it is extremely remote. Members who fail to toe the line are likely to experience the fate of those Liberal MPs who voted against the government's gun law in 1995: the loss of committee assignments. Expulsion from caucus is another sanction that may be used to punish recalcitrant backbenchers. Second, caucus—like the legislature as a whole—usually enters the policy-making process late, after much study, consultation, and negotiation have already taken place. Embedded in the legislation that the members of the government party caucus are asked to vote for is a complex fabric of compromises and accommodations between government and interest groups, different agencies of government, or even Ottawa and the provinces. It is unlikely that the government will be willing to see this fabric come unravelled because of caucus opposition.

The Courts

Responsibility for Canada's judicial system is divided between Ottawa and the provinces. While the constitution gives the federal government the exclusive right to make criminal law, it assigns responsibility for the administration of justice and for law enforcement to the provinces. Consequently, all provinces have established their own court systems that interpret and apply both federal and provincial laws.

The constitution also gives Ottawa the authority to create courts. This authority was used in 1875 to create the Supreme Court of Canada. Since 1949 the Supreme Court has been Canada's highest court of appeal. Ottawa again used this constitutional power in 1971 to create the Federal Court of Canada. It has jurisdiction over civil claims involving the federal government, cases arising from the decisions of federally appointed administrative bodies like the Immigration Appeal Board, and matters relating to federal income tax, copyrights, and maritime law—all of which fall under the legislative authority of Ottawa. The structure of Canada's court system is shown in Figure 6.3.

Courts apply and interpret the law. They perform this role in matters ranging from contested driving offences to disputes over the most fundamental principles of the constitution. The decisions of judges often have profound implications for the rights and status of individuals and groups, for the balance of social and economic power, and for the federal division of powers. It is, therefore, crucial that we understand the political significance of the judicial process and the methods of interpretation typically used by the courts.

The independence of judges is the cornerstone of the Canadian judicial system. Judges are appointed by governments. But once appointed they hold their office 'during good

Figure 6.3 The Structure of Canada's Court System

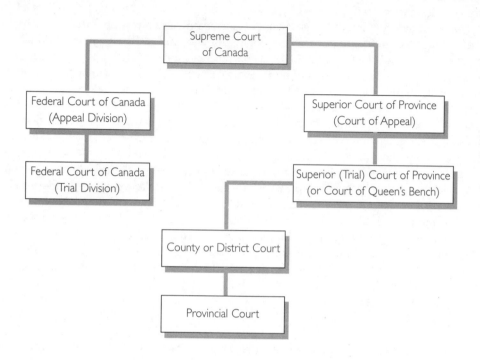

Source: Canada, Department of Justice, *Canada's System of Justice* (Ottawa: Supply and Services, 1988), 20.

behaviour'.[17] What constitutes a lapse from 'good behaviour'? A criminal or a serious moral offence could provide grounds for removal, as could decisions of such incompetence that they undermine public respect for the law and the judiciary. In such circumstances the appointing government may launch removal proceedings against a judge. In fact, however, this has seldom happened. Formal proceedings have seldom been initiated and have never been prosecuted to their ultimate conclusion, i.e., the actual removal of a judge by resolution of Parliament or a provincial legislature. Judicial independence is also protected by the fact that judges' salaries and conditions of service are established by law. Consequently, governments cannot single out any individual judge for special reward or punishment.

But as Ralph Miliband puts it, to say that judges are 'independent' begs the question, 'Independent of what?' As members of the societies in which they live—usually successful members of the middle and upper-middle classes—they cannot be neutral in the values they bring to their task. Judges, observes Miliband, 'are by no means, and cannot be, independent of the multitude of influences, notably of class origin, education, class situation and professional tendency, which contribute as much to the formation of their view of the world as they do in the case of other men.'[18] Thus, when one says that the judiciary is 'independent' this should be understood as a description of its formal separation from the executive and legislative branches of the state. When it comes to the dominant value system of their society, judges are no more independent than are the members of any other part of the state élite. Leaving aside the socio-economically unrepresentative character of the legal profession and the effects of formal training in the law, in British parliamentary systems all judges are appointed by governments.[19] One would hardly expect these governments to appoint radical critics of society, even supposing that a significant number of such individuals existed within the legal profession. Moreover, governments control promotion within the judicial system—who will be promoted from a district court to a superior court, and so on. This fact may also exert a chilling effect on unconventional judicial behaviour.

The socio-economic background of judges and the process by which they are selected both introduce conservative tendencies into the judiciary. But they are not the only factors, nor are they necessarily the most important ones, that incline the courts toward protection of the status quo. The law itself is a powerful conservative force. We are used to thinking of the law as simply 'the rules made by governments' that 'apply to everybody in society'.[20] But the law is more than this. It represents values that have accumulated over a long period of time. The concepts, meanings, precedents, and interpretive rules that shape judicial decision-making tend to inhibit sharp breaks with the past.

Judges work within the embedded premises of the law. Among the most important of these premises, in terms of their impact on the distribution of power in society, are the rights of the individual, the rights associated with private property, and the concept of the business corporation. Individualism is woven throughout the legal fabric of Canadian society. As a practical matter, respect for individual rights tends to be more important for the privileged than for the disadvantaged. While this is obviously true in the case of property rights—protection for these rights matters more to those who have something to lose than to those who do not—it has also tended to be true in matters like individual freedom of expression. For example, a 1983 Alberta court decision ruled unconstitutional a section of the federal Elections Act that prohibited advertising by organizations other than registered political parties during federal election campaigns. In the abstract this represented a victory for freedom of expression, but in practical terms the decision mattered most to well-heeled organizations with the means to pay for such advertising, such as the ideologically conservative National Citizens' Coalition, which challenged the restriction.

The powerful tug of liberal individualism on judicial reasoning was clearly demonstrated in a 1987 Supreme Court of Canada decision on the right to strike. A majority of the justices decided that 'The constitutional guarantee of freedom of association ... does not include, in the case of a trade union, a guarantee of the right to bargain collectively and the right to strike.'[21] The rights to bargain collectively and to strike were not, the court ruled, fundamental rights or freedoms that deserved the constitutional protection of section 2(d) of the Charter. 'They are', the Court said, 'the creation of legislation, involving a balance of competing interests',[22] and their scope and limitations are appropriately determined by legislatures. To put it very simply, economic rights were viewed as subordinate to political ones. The Court said as much: '[T]he overwhelming preoccupation of the Charter is with individual, political, and democratic rights with conspicuous inattention to economic and property rights.'[23] But what 'conspicuous inattention' meant in practical terms was that the existing balance of power and rights between employers and workers was considered to be correct, and that workers and unions could not count on the courts to defend their rights against governments intent on diminishing them.

In fairness to the courts, judges are not always insensitive to the structural inequalities that exist in society and in the economy. Particularly at the highest levels of the judicial system, judges are generally quite aware of the socio-economic and political consequences of their decisions. In his dissent from the majority decision in the 1987 right-to-strike case, Chief Justice Dickson observed that 'Throughout history, workers have associated to overcome their vulnerability as individuals to the strength of their employers. The capacity to bargain collectively has long been recognized as one of the integral and primary functions of associations of working people.'[24] Collective bargaining, according to Dickson, requires that workers have the right to strike. Moreover, in a 1989 decision the Supreme Court rejected the traditional liberal notion of equality as identical treatment before the law in favour of what is sometimes called *substantive equality*. This requires that individuals be looked at in terms of their group characteristics and the possible advantages or disadvantages they may have experienced as a result of these attributes. Liberal individualism does not have the field all to itself in Canadian society. Neither is it uncontested in judicial circles.

The biases of liberal individualism are also embedded in the judicial process. While all judicial systems are adversarial in the sense that one party (the plaintiff in civil cases; the prosecution in criminal ones) brings an action against another (the defendant), common-law systems like Canada's represent the most extreme form of this adversarial process. In civil cases the onus is placed on the individual parties—plaintiff and defendant—to make their respective cases before the court. In criminal proceedings the state is responsible for prosecuting the case against an individual or organization, but that individual or organization is responsible for his own defence. In both civil and criminal proceedings, the role of the court is to hear and weigh the evidence, not to participate actively in the development of either side to the action.

It is up to a plaintiff or defendant to make his or her most persuasive case. Their ability to do so will depend, in part, on their access to competent legal counsel. In criminal proceedings, the state will pay for legal counsel for defendants who cannot afford to hire a lawyer. Legal aid is available in all provinces for those who cannot afford the legal costs of a civil action. But these forms of subsidized legal assistance by no means equalize access to effective legal counsel. The difference between an Edward Greenspan and a court-appointed lawyer is not simply, or even mainly, their skills in the courtroom. The high-priced worthies of the legal profession are backed up by the resources of large law firms. A large corporation or a well-endowed individual can afford to pay for these resources, but they are beyond the means of most people.

'[J]udicial decisions', observe Leslie Pal and Ted Morton, 'have no intrinsic finality. A Supreme Court decision may appear on its own merits to favor one or another side of a dispute, but the final resolution of that dispute depends on the determination, organization, resources, and wit of the combatants.'[25] The truth of this was shown in the earlier discussion (Chapter 5) of court decisions on the federal division of powers. But Pal and Morton's statement is true in a more general sense. An individual may 'lose' in the courts but ultimately 'win' in another setting. For this to happen, an individual's case must involve an issue that is perceived to affect the interests of a larger group (or groups). Sympathetic media coverage and group efforts to influence public opinion and lobby government may produce legislative action that reverses or at least vitiates the effects of a judicial ruling. Court decisions should be seen, therefore, as an important part of an ongoing process of political conflict. They contribute to the trajectory of that conflict, but they seldom write the final chapter to a major political dispute.

Appendix: How a Law Is Passed

The law takes various forms. A statute passed by the House of Commons and the Senate, and given royal assent by the Governor General, is clearly a law. But decisions taken by cabinet that have not been approved in the legislature also have the force of law. These are called 'orders-in-council'. Thousands of them are issued each year, and they are published in the *Canada Gazette*. The decisions of agencies, boards, and commissions that receive their regulatory powers from a statute also have the force of law. Finally, there are the regulations and guidelines issued and enforced by the departmental bureaucracy in accordance with the discretionary powers delegated to them under a statute. These also have the force of law.

In a strictly numerical sense the statutes passed annually by Parliament represent only the tip of the iceberg of laws promulgated each year. Nevertheless, virtually all major policy decisions—including budget measures, and the laws that assign discretionary power to the bureaucracy—come before the legislature. The only exception has been when the normal process of government was suspended by passage of the War Measures Act. This happened during World War One, again during World War Two, and briefly in 1970 when Ottawa proclaimed the War Measures Act after two political kidnappings in Quebec by the Front de libération du Québec. The War Measures Act was replaced by the Emergencies Act in 1988.

During normal times the law-making process involves several stages and opportunities for debate and amendment. The steps from the introduction of a bill in Parliament to the final proclamation of a statute are set out in Figure 6.4.

There are two types of bills, namely private members' bills and government bills. Private members' bills originate with individual MPs, but unless they get the backing of government they have little chance of passing. Government bills dominate Parliament's legislative agenda. When major legislation is being proposed, a bill is sometimes preceded by a *White Paper*. This is a report for discussion, based on research by the bureaucracy (and sometimes the legislature as well), and serves as a statement of the government's legislative intentions.

Once a bill has been drafted by government, it is introduced into the Senate, or more usually, into the House of Commons. Here, it is given *first reading*, which is just a formality and involves no debate. Then the bill goes to *second reading*, at which time the main principles of the bill are debated and a vote is taken. If the bill passes second reading, it is sent to a smaller legislative committee where the details of the bill are considered clause by clause. At this *committee stage*, amendments can be made but the principle of the bill cannot be altered. The bill is then reported back to the House, where all aspects are debated, including any amendments. At this *report stage* new amendments can also be introduced. If a bill passes this hurdle it then goes to *third reading*, when a final vote is taken, sometimes after

Figure 6.4 From Bill to Statute

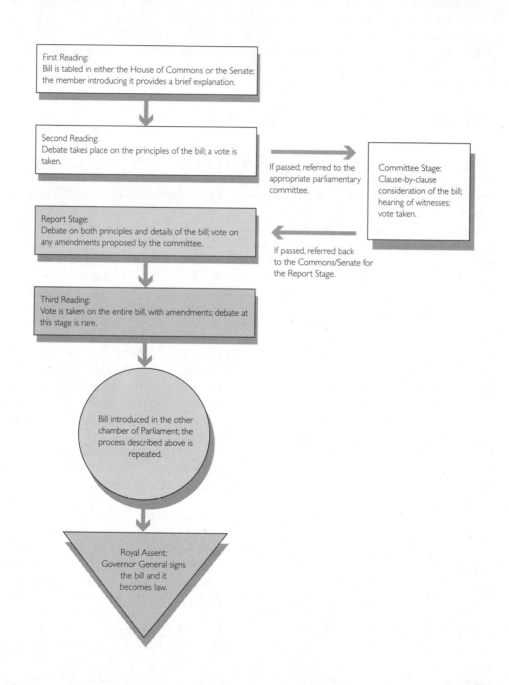

further debate. Once a bill has been passed in the House, it is then sent to the Senate where a virtually identical process takes place. If a bill was first introduced in the Senate, then it would now be sent to the House. Finally, a bill passed in both the House and the Senate can be given royal assent and become law.

PART FOUR

Participation in Politics

The national party system that Canadians had known for generations was shaken up by the 1993 election. (Party logos courtesy of the five political parties)

Political parties and elections are essential features of modern democracy. This chapter examines the characteristics and influence of these institutions in Canadian political life. The following topics are covered:

- ❖ The origins and evolution of Canada's party system.
- ❖ Brokerage politics.
- ❖ The role of minor parties.
- ❖ The electoral system and its consequences.
- ❖ Party finances and special interests.

This chapter was co-authored with Professor A. Brian Tanguay of Wilfrid Laurier University.

CHAPTER SEVEN

Parties and Elections

To most Canadians, politics is pretty much synonymous with parties and elections. For the great majority of us, the extent of our involvement in political life is limited to casting a ballot for one or more of the various candidates for public office every three or four years. Beyond that, we might take an intermittently active interest in politics, reading about the goings on in Ottawa or Victoria or Charlottetown in magazines and newspapers or watching public affairs programs on television. Much of this media coverage will inevitably focus on the actions and policies of the major political parties, or of their principal representatives (especially their leaders), thereby reinforcing our unspoken assumption that parties and elections are the cornerstones of our democratic system.

Clearly, parties and elections are essential institutions in a modern democracy. Given the size and complexity of most of the industrialized nations today, any attempt at *direct democracy*, in which citizens are regularly called upon to take part in political decision-making, would seem to be doomed to failure—except on a very local level, as in the famous town meetings that still take place in a handful of New England states. Some form of representative institution appears to be necessary, and competition among political parties in regular elections is one of the most powerful tools for holding political decision-makers accountable to the citizenry. In this sense, parties are the central intermediary structure linking the individual citizen to the modern state and its policy-making processes.[1]

Too often, though, the observation that modern democratic politics appears inconceivable without parties and elections shades off into unabashed cheerleading for the type of party system found in Canada, the United States, Great Britain, or any other self-styled democracy. The assumption that parties invariably promote democracy, that they act as an effective mechanism for participation in politics, is rarely questioned. The result is a discernible smugness about our political system—a flaw common in many introductory texts on Canadian politics. In this chapter, therefore, we take a critical look at the relationship between parties and elections on the one hand and democracy on the other. To what extent do the party and electoral systems in Canada encourage real participation by citizens in political decision-making? Do these institutions enable voters to hold politicians accountable to their wishes, as the conventional wisdom suggests? Just how democratic is party politics in Canada today?

In the current age of television politics, there are very good reasons to be sceptical about the contributions that parties and elections make to the advancement of democracy, if by the latter term we mean the active participation of citizens in formulating the decisions that govern the collectivity. There is a growing fear among critical observers of our party system that the new techniques of political marketing deployed to win elections—opinion polling, negative advertising, direct mail, thirty-second clips or 'jolts' that package a political party or its leader for consumption by television viewers, and so on—are debasing political life and transforming party competition into 'the greatest show on earth'.[2] It is impossible nowadays to conceive of election campaigns being run without the usual blitz of self-serving media hype orchestrated by a tiny clique of paid professionals who market their goods—political parties and, especially, their leaders—as though they were flogging a brand of beer or a new line of high-tech running shoes. Television politics, with its emphasis on image and style rather than policy or substance, robs elections of much of their meaning by depriving voters of a real choice between alternative visions of how the polity ought to be governed.

It would surely be premature to write the death certificate of our political parties, for in many respects they are still the central intermediary institutions between the individual citizen and the Canadian state. But their previously uncontested monopoly on representation is being eroded, and this chapter will examine some of the causes of the organizational decay of our political parties, along with some of the reasons for the growing dissatisfaction with electoral politics. Although in this chapter we take a critical look at the ways in which parties and elections promote democracy in Canada, this does not mean that we simply dismiss the significance of these institutions altogether. It used to be fashionable in some radical circles to pooh-pooh 'bourgeois democracy', as though party competition in the modern industrialized nations served no other purpose than to hoodwink the 'masses' and solidify the position of the ruling capitalist class. This is a crude and caricatured view of modern party politics. The choices offered to voters and the opportunities for citizen participation in decision-making may be limited in Canada or any other capitalist society, yet they are nonetheless real and sometimes profoundly significant.

The Origins and Evolution of Canada's Party System

The Nature of Brokerage Politics

Political parties, as organizations that seek to 'elect governmental office-holders under a given label',[3] are relative newcomers on the political scene. They emerged about the same time that the franchise was extended to males in the lower strata of liberal society (first to the middle classes and gradually to the non-propertied, wage-earning class): between 1800 and 1830 in the United States and between 1832 and 1868 in Great Britain. Prior to that time, loose factions had existed within legislatures, their bonds cemented mainly by personal loyalty to a particular leader and by the judicious distribution of governmental patronage. With the extension of the right to vote to the lower classes in society, these factions were for the first time confronted with the need to 'find ways and means of reaching their new "masters", the enfranchised lower strata'.[4] Parties, with a semi-permanent organization outside of the legislature, gradually developed to enable political entrepreneurs to mobilize this mass electorate.

The origins of Canada's two historical major political parties—the Conservatives and the Liberals—can be traced back to the shifting coalitions and alignments in the United Province of Canada in the 1840s and 1850s. Although these groups were much more amorphous and unstable than modern political parties and would not really coalesce into cohesive organizations until the 1880s, they did represent distinct political tendencies. On the one hand was the governing coalition of Liberal-Conservatives (which would eventually drop the 'Liberal' from its official name) under the leadership of Sir John A. Macdonald in Canada West and his French-Canadian counterpart, George-Étienne Cartier. This disparate organization encompassed a number of distinct groups: moderate Reformers from what was to become Ontario, moderate Conservatives (the *bleus*) from Canada East (Quebec), the commercial and industrial interests of English-speaking Quebec, and the remnants of the old ruling oligarchies in Upper and Lower Canada, the Family Compact and the Château Clique. Many of these groups had potentially conflicting interests (Catholics and Protestants, French and English, urban and rural elements), but the organization was held together largely by the political dexterity of Macdonald and by the gradual development of a unifying vision based on the nation-building program eventually enshrined in the National Policy of 1878–9. The key elements of this program were the implementation of a protective tariff designed to promote the growth of indigenous manufacturing in Ontario and Quebec, the encouragement of western settlement to open up a market for the products of central Canadian industry and to protect this territory from American encroachment, and the creation of a transcontinental railroad to ship the manufactured goods of the centre to the newly opened western territories.[5]

On the other hand was an even looser opposition coalition, comprising the Clear Grits of Canada West and the *rouges* of Canada East. Both of these groups shared a common admiration for the republican and individualist ideas of the United States and both advocated free trade with the Americans. They also shared an unrelenting hostility to the commercial and banking interests linked to Macdonald's governing party. But the two groups made for rather uneasy partners, since the Grits were vocally critical of the Roman Catholic Church. So were the *rouges*, for that matter (and their anti-clericalism placed serious obstacles in the path of electoral success in their home province of Quebec), but there was nonetheless considerable ethnic and religious tension between the two groups. Only when Wilfrid Laurier assumed the leadership of the Liberal Party in 1887 were these diverse elements moulded into a relatively cohesive political organization.

It would be a mistake to make too much of the doctrinal differences between Liberals and Conservatives during the formative years of the Canadian party system (roughly 1880 to 1920). Admittedly, the Liberals were identified with free trade and provincial rights, and after 1885 (when Riel was hanged) they appeared to be 'more sensitive to the interests of French Canada' than the Tories.[6] They were also more sympathetic to the plight of the farmer than were the Conservatives. The latter, meanwhile, were generally thought of as the party of the British connection, the party of privilege—in the sense that its leading spokesmen claimed that all healthy and stable societies are ruled by a *natural* governing élite—and the party of centralization and economic protection. But these ideological differences, far from constituting fundamental clashes of world outlooks on which the two sides sought to mobilize their supporters, were almost always subordinated to the central preoccupation of Canadian politics: *patronage*.

The scramble to control the distribution of government largesse was undoubtedly the dominant feature of Canadian politics during the 1860s and 1870s, when a number of provisions in our electoral law helped to force political life into that mould. In particular, the use of the open ballot, whereby voters simply declared their choice at the polls in the presence of a government official (and anybody else who happened to be in the room at the time!), provided numerous opportunities for bribery, coercion, and intimidation, and made it difficult for anybody whose livelihood depended on government contracts to vote against candidates supported by the ruling cabinet (see Box 7.1). Non-simultaneous or staggered elections, which permitted the government to call elections in safe ridings before having to work its way into more doubtful territory, forced candidates in many ridings to be *ministerialists*, so called because their 'politics were not to support a party but a ministry and any ministry would do'.[7] This non-partisan stance was the surest way to provide for a steady flow of government patronage into the successful candidate's constituency.

The elimination of the open ballot and deferred elections by the late 1870s, along with the gradual standardization of electoral regulations across the different provinces, did not

Box 7.1 The Open Ballot

The Liberals, for reasons that are not hard to discern, favoured the secret ballot, and every year after 1869 saw a Liberal motion for the adoption of the ballot fall by the wayside. The opportunities for bribery of voters, the coercion of employees by their superiors and of civil servants by the Conservatives, and the open interference of the clergy in Quebec, were all cited as arguments by the Liberals. The Conservatives tacitly admitted the justice of the opposition's case, but yielded nothing. One staunch party man went so far on one occasion as to observe with commendable frankness that, after all, elections could not be carried on without money, and 'under an open system of voting, you can readily ascertain whether the voter has deceived you.' The Prime Minister thought the [secret] ballot 'un-British.' Another was critical of it on the ground that it would let a dishonest elector sell his vote to two or three different parties, instead of just one. With these and other cogent reasons for preserving electoral purity, the open system of voting was allowed to last until 1874.

Norman Ward,
The Canadian House of Commons
(Toronto: University of Toronto Press, 1950), 158.

reduce the importance of patronage in federal politics—far from it. Despite the removal of some of the crasser forms of electoral corruption by the 1880s, the two federal parties still operated in a political environment characterized by the absence of civil service reform (the merit principle), a highly restricted franchise, and a weak working class (from an organizational and numerical standpoint). All of these factors, it has been suggested, predispose political parties to appeal to potential supporters through networks of patron-client relations (where votes are exchanged for certain 'favours') rather than on the basis of collectivist or solidaristic appeals (class-based ideologies).[8]

This is precisely the situation described by the French political sociologist, André Siegfried, when he visited Canada in the early part of this century. Siegfried complained that the preoccupation with questions of 'material interest' and 'public works' tended to 'lower the general level of political life' in Canada. He also noted that Canadian politics was hardly lacking in substantive issues—rivalries between Catholics and Protestants, French and English, for example—that could have been addressed by the two major parties, but that the party leaders 'prefer that they should not be talked about. The subjects which remain available for discussion are not numerous. In addition, the parties borrow one another's policies periodically, displaying a coolness in this process that would disconcert us Europeans.'[9]

Siegfried's comments on the nature of party competition in Canada, written over eighty years ago, are still remarkably relevant. If Siegfried were somehow transported back to present-day Canada, he would probably conclude that there have been few substantive changes in our party system since he published his work in 1906. The emphasis on accommodating the diverse interests—regional, linguistic, ethnic, class, religious—of the electorate through the prudent employment of 'public works' and individual material incentives is still a characteristic feature of federal and provincial politics. Elections are usually preceded by a barrage of new government programs and spending initiatives in various parts of the country ill-disguised attempts by the party in power to purchase electoral support in key ridings. As well, the nonchalant borrowing of elements of one party's program by another party, which Siegfried found so disconcerting, is still going on today. Among the more flagrant recent examples of this habit occurred in the 1974 and 1984 federal election campaigns. In the former case, Pierre Trudeau's Liberal government implemented wage and price controls in an attempt to cure inflation, only a few months after an election in which they had castigated the Conservatives and their leader, Robert Stanfield, for proposing just such a policy. In 1984, the new leader of the Conservatives, Brian Mulroney, is widely thought to have scored a decisive win in the television debate with his Liberal counterpart, John Turner, on the issue of patronage appointments. Voters were seemingly impressed by the Tory leader's display of moral outrage at Turner's feeble attempt to justify appointing a raft of Liberals to plum positions at the tail end of the Trudeau dynasty. But not long after the election, the Tories themselves were practising porkbarrel politics on a scale that made their predecessors look like rank amateurs.

During the 1993 election campaign the Liberal Party under Jean Chrétien promised to eliminate the despised GST and reopen negotiations with the Americans on the Free Trade Agreement (FTA), both of which were part of the Conservatives' legacy. To no one's surprise the Americans indicated they were not interested in renegotiating the FTA, and the Liberals retreated from their campaign bravado. In the case of the GST, after two years in power it

Box 7.2 An Early Illustration of the Brokerage Theory of Canadian Politics

...The fact that in the Dominion parties exist apart from their programmes, or even without a programme at all, frequently deprives the electoral consultations of the people of their true meaning. In the absence of ideas or doctrines to divide the voters, there remain only questions of material interest, collective or individual. Against their pressure the candidate cannot maintain his integrity, for he knows that his opponent will not show the same self-restraint. The result is that the same promises are made on both sides, following an absolutely identical conception of the meaning of power. Posed in this way, the issue of an election manifestly changes. Whoever may be the winner, everyone knows that the country will be administered in the same way, or almost the same. The only difference will be in the personnel of the government. This is the prevailing conception of politics—except when some great wave of opinion sweeps over the whole country, covering under its waters all the political pygmies....

The reason for this ... is easy to understand. Canada, we know, is a country of violent oppositions. English and French, Protestant and Catholic, are jealous of each other and fear each other. The lack of ideas, programmes, convictions, is only apparent. Let a question of race or religion be raised, and you will immediately see most of the sordid preoccupations of patronage or connection disappear below the surface. The elections will become struggles of political principle, sincere and passionate. Now this is exactly what is feared by the prudent and far-sighted men who have been given the responsibility of maintaining the national equilibrium. Aware of the sharpness of certain rivalries, they know that if these are let loose without any counter-balance, the unity of the Dominion may be endangered. That is why they persistently apply themselves to prevent the formation of homogeneous parties, divided according to race, religion, or class—a French party, for instance, or a Catholic party, or a Labour party. The clarity of political life suffers from this, but perhaps the existence of the federation can be preserved only at this price. ·

André Siegfried, *The Race Question in Canada*,
ed. Frank Underhill (Toronto: McClelland and Stewart,
Carleton Library edition, 1966
[originally published in French, 1906]), 113–14.

became apparent that what the Liberals really meant by elimination of the GST was the harmonization of this tax with its provincial counterparts into a single sales tax. This was not exactly what voters had been led to believe. These kinds of flip-flops by the older parties on key issues—and many more examples could be cited—only serve to fuel the electorate's cynicism about politics in general and their distrust of politicians in particular.

The electoral opportunism exhibited by both the Liberals and the Tories in recent years should not to be taken to mean that the two older parties have no principles or ideological commitments whatsoever. Just as was the case when Siegfried was studying the Canadian party system, in recent times Canada's oldest parties have represented somewhat distinct traditions, particularly on matters concerning federalism and Canada–US relations. With the accession of Pierre Trudeau to the party leadership in 1968, the Liberals became identified in the minds of most Canadian voters with a strong central state (hence the ongoing battles between Ottawa and the provinces over control of natural resource revenues), with economic nationalism (Petro-Canada, the National Energy Program, the Foreign Investment Review Agency), and with 'French power'. The Tories, meanwhile, came increasingly to be associated with political decentralization: Joe Clark, when he was leader of the party and briefly Prime Minister in the late 1970s, described Canadian federalism as a 'community of communities', which Trudeau sarcastically rejected as 'shopping-mall' federalism. The Conservatives also came to embrace the notion of free trade with the United States; this represented a dramatic reversal of the party positions on the subject in the late nineteenth and early twentieth centuries, when the Liberals strongly advocated continentalist economic policies. Finally, the neo-conservatism of the 1980s, spearheaded by former British Prime Minister Margaret Thatcher and former US President Ronald Reagan, found its most receptive audience among the Conservatives.

Despite these apparent differences in the policy orientations of the two older parties in recent times, Siegfried's central contention about the Canadian party system remains indisputable. Our historically dominant parties have continued to be much more flexible, opportunistic, dominated by their leaders, and wary of ideological appeals to the electorate than those in most European nations. The nature of our electoral system and the norms that govern party competition in this country are such that the Liberals and Conservatives can usually fight elections without having to worry too much about keeping their principles intact or consistent. Many observers of the Canadian party system have attached a specific label to this type of flexible, non-ideological party system: it is a *brokerage* party system. That is, the two older parties at the federal level act as 'brokers of ideas ... middlemen who select from all the ideas pressing for recognition as public policy those they think can be shaped to have the widest appeal....'[10] Each of the parties attempts to cobble together a winning coalition of voters at election time; the voting support for the two older parties, therefore, does not come from stable, well-defined social groups, as is the case in many Western European countries. Most importantly, politics in Canada lacks an obvious class dimension. Conflicts between the industrial working class and capitalists over the political and economic rights of workers, and over the distribution of national wealth, take a back seat to other issues—those arising out of religious, ethnic, and regional rivalries, for instance.

This peculiarity of Canadian politics has led some observers to describe the Canadian party system as less developed or less modern than those of most other industrial nations.

Box 7.3 The Historical Importance of the Leader in Canadian Party Politics

... it is of the first importance to the success of a party that it should be led by someone who inspires confidence, and whose mere name is a programme in itself. As long as the conservatives had Macdonald for their leader, they voted for him rather than for the party. So it is with Laurier and the Liberals of today. If Laurier disappeared, the Liberals would perhaps find that they had lost the real secret of their victories.... Canadians attach themselves rather to the concrete reality than to the abstract principle. They vote as much for the man who symbolizes the policy as for the policy itself.

Siegfried, *The Race Question in Canada*, 136.

LIBERAL REALITY — NO OPPOSITION TO THE LEADER

VIRTUAL REALITY — LEADER OF THE OPPOSITION

REALITY — OUT TO LUNCH

When Canadians think of political parties, they often associate them with their leaders. (Roy Peterson, *Vancouver Sun*)

Robert Alford, for example, declared in his classic study of voting behaviour in four Anglo democracies (the United States, Canada, Great Britain, and Australia) that Canada had the lowest level of class voting among the four nations that he examined.[11] Alford's explanation of this situation echoes the one advanced by Siegfried almost sixty years earlier: 'Class voting is low in Canada because the political parties are identified as representatives of regional, religious, and ethnic groupings rather than as representatives of national class interests, and this, in turn, is due to a relative lack of national integration.'[12] Class divisions and antagonisms are certainly not absent in Canada, Alford observed, and he predicted that once the issue of national unity had been resolved, class voting would increase and Canada would come to resemble other modern democracies, such as Great Britain.

In the thirty years since Alford's book was written, it should be noted, his prediction has simply not come true: the issue of class is still subordinated to questions of national unity and regional or ethnic grievances. The two older parties do not normally appeal to specific class constituencies and still evade class issues when possible. Moreover, the self-described left-wing party in Canada, the New Democratic Party, receives nowhere near a majority of the votes of blue-collar workers.

Brokerage theory, then, makes two fundamental claims about Canada's two historically dominant political parties: first, they do not appeal to specific socio-economic groupings, and they lack cohesive ideological visions (especially those based on class); second, the parties are flexible and opportunistic because this sort of behaviour is necessary to preserve the fragile unity of the nation. This brings to mind Siegfried's observation that there are all kinds of pressing issues in Canadian politics, but that the prudent and cautious leaders of the two main parties do not want them to be discussed, for fear of inflaming group jealousies and thereby jeopardizing the stability of the country.

An alternative explanation of the absence of class politics in Canada is advanced by Janine Brodie and Jane Jenson in *Crisis, Challenge, and Change*.[13] They argue that brokerage theory tends to view political parties as more or less passive transmission belts for societal demands. In the vocabulary of empirical social science, brokerage theorists consider parties to be *dependent variables*: their behaviour is shaped by the divisions that exist in society—in Canada's case, the most important divisions being those of language, ethnicity, region, and religion. Brodie and Jenson call for a more nuanced view of parties, one that treats them simultaneously as *dependent* (influenced by society) and *independent* (actively shaping societal demands) variables. The most important aspect of the independent, creative function of political parties in liberal democracies like Canada is their role in creating a *definition of politics*:

> through which people make sense of their daily lives. Because issues are raised and choices provided in particular ways, this cultural construction defines the content and sets the limits of partisan politics. Social problems never included within the bounds of partisan political debate remain invisible and confined to the private sector or private life for resolution. From a myriad of social tensions the definition of politics identifies and selects those susceptible to 'political' solutions. Political parties, in other words, by defining the political, contribute to the organization and disorganization of groups in the electorate.[14]

Brodie and Jenson argue that in the period immediately following Confederation, class, religion, language, and other social differences competed with each other, more or less equally, as potential support bases for the two federal parties. Since both of these parties drew the bulk of their support from the same social group—the bourgeoisie—they tended to avoid the issue of class in their competition for votes. As a strategy for differentiating their 'product' from that of the governing Conservatives, the Liberals gradually seized on the issue of ethnic, religious, and linguistic differences, and 'became the party of French Quebec (and later of other ethnic minorities) while the Conservatives solidified their base among Anglophone Canadians'.[15] In later years, the authors claim, the two traditional parties would frequently try to avoid discussing class issues such as the rights and place of workers in Canadian society by redefining them as regional or cultural concerns. The NDP, they contend, has not been able or willing to challenge the prevailing definition of politics in Canada and therefore is forced to compete with the Liberals and Conservatives under conditions that permanently handicap it and leave a significant portion of the Canadian electorate effectively disenfranchised.

Brodie and Jenson's explanation of the non-class nature of the Canadian party system is an important contribution to our understanding of politics in this country. Nevertheless, it does seem somewhat overdrawn, since it appears to downplay or minimize the pre-eminence of religious and ethnic divisions in Canadian society in the late nineteenth century and to exaggerate the extent to which the parties have been able to play up the issues of language and culture for their own electoral advantage. One very important reason that class identity came so slowly and unevenly to Canadian workers was precisely the role played by religious institutions—the Catholic Church and the Orange Order, most notably—in organizing the working class. The Orange Order appealed to workers as Scottish or Irish Protestants, while the Catholic Church stressed the spiritual mission of French-Canadian workers and was reluctant to define society in terms of antagonistic classes (as socialists did). All of this helped to ensure that for large numbers of Canadian workers, their class identity was intermingled with their ethnic and religious allegiance. A large part of the explanation of the relative unimportance of class issues in Canadian politics, therefore, must be found in the social organization of the working class itself and not simply attributed to the major parties' manipulation of the definition of politics.

Whatever the explanation of our brokerage party system, a recurrent theme in critical discussions of Canadian politics has been the need for a form of party competition that would offer voters a greater choice at election time. It has often been argued that this might be achieved through the elimination of one of the 'bourgeois' or centre parties, which would lead to a polarization of the system between a party of the right and a party of the left. In the mid-1960s, sociologist John Porter lamented the fact that 'Canada must be one of the few major industrial societies in which the right and left polarization has become deflected into disputes over regionalism and national unity'.[16] In 1970, a political philosopher and NDP activist, Charles Taylor, echoed Porter by calling for the abandonment of the Canadian tradition of seeking consensus at all costs, in order to 'open up deeper questions about power and political structures which will polarize our society into left and right....'[17] And Ed Broadbent, the former leader of the federal NDP, speculated in an interview during the 1988 election that '[i]t would be healthy for Canada to evolve the way other countries have with one party that's left of centre—like us—and a conservative party.'[18]

There are a number of reasons why the two older parties, despite their strong similarities to each other, have survived and dominated Canadian elections for most of this country's history, and why Ed Broadbent's 'dream' is not likely to be realized without a far-reaching change in the country's electoral laws or its political culture. One of the most important factors contributing to the longevity of the two historically dominant parties, apart from the rules of Canada's electoral system (examined below), has been their ability to shift to the right or the left of the ideological spectrum to head off electoral challenges from protest movements and minor parties. Let us examine the nature and role of these parties of protest.

The Role of Minor Parties in the Brokerage System

By the summer of 1991, almost three years into its second mandate, the Progressive Conservative government of Prime Minister Brian Mulroney had sunk to historic lows in public opinion polls, with barely 15 per cent of the electorate indicating that it would vote for the Tories if an election were held at that time. In fact, the Conservatives were being rivalled in voter popularity by a fledgling organization that was beginning to capture a great deal of voter and media attention: the Reform Party of Canada. Under the leadership of Preston Manning, the son of the former Social Credit Premier of Alberta, Ernest Manning, the Reform Party was founded in late 1987, primarily as a vehicle for western discontent (its original slogan was 'The West Wants In'). The Reform Party is thus the latest in a string of western protest movements—its most successful predecessors having been the Progressives in the 1920s, Social Credit and the CCF in the 1930s and 1940s, and the Western Canada

Concept in the early 1980s—that have tapped into the powerful feelings of economic and political alienation in the western provinces. These feelings originate in the firm conviction that the West is getting the short end of the stick, economically speaking: many westerners believe that existing federal arrangements allow Ontario and Quebec to siphon off the resource wealth of the West to fuel growth and prosperity in the centre. The two older parties are seen as co-conspirators in this vicious circle of exploitation, since they are beholden to the powerful economic interests in the metropolitan areas and are compelled to enact policies that favour those regions where the bulk of the seats are to be won in a federal election.

This deep-seated suspicion among westerners of central Canada and national political institutions was briefly dispelled by the 1984 federal election. Although the new Prime Minister, Brian Mulroney, was himself a bilingual Quebecer, for the first time since the Diefenbaker interlude of the 1950s a large number of prominent westerners were placed in key cabinet positions. 'At last', western voters seemed to be saying to themselves, 'we're getting a government that will understand and respond to our concerns and not treat us like second-class citizens.' Gradually, however, this guarded optimism gave way to a shattering disillusionment, as the Conservative government made a number of policy decisions that were viewed as detrimental to western interests. Without a doubt the most publicized instance of 'biased' government decision-making was Ottawa's awarding of a multimillion-

Box 7.4 Reform's Founding Vision

A new federal party, born out of western concerns and aspirations, should not be simply a negative reaction to the status quo. It should not simply be a party of protest with a litany of complaints and concerns, but rather a party of reform, with some positive alternatives to offer....

In order to ensure that we could draw support from the disaffected members of the Liberals and the NDP as well as the Conservatives, it is important that a new western political party have a strong social conscience and program as well as a strong commitment to market principles and freedom of enterprise.

A new federal party which embodies the principal political values of the West will transcend some of the old categories of left and right. It will provide a home for the socially responsible businessman and the economy conscious social activist. It should be a party whose members and leaders are characterized as people with 'hard heads and soft hearts', i.e., people who attach high importance on wealth creation and freedom of economic activity on the one hand, but who are also genuinely concerned and motivated to action on behalf of the victims of the many injustices and imperfections in our economic and social systems....

A new federal party, created initially to represent the West, should aspire to become that new national party, and nothing should be done in the early stages of its conception and birth to preclude it from eventually gaining support all across the country, particularly in those regions of Ontario, Quebec, Atlantic Canada and northern Canada which share many of our concerns and aspirations.

Excerpts from a speech by Preston Manning
to the Western Assembly on Canada's
Economic and Political Future, Vancouver, May, 1987.

dollar maintenance contract for the CF-18 fighter aircraft to a Quebec-based firm, despite the fact that Bristol Aerospace of Winnipeg had presented what federal officials acknowledged was a technically superior bid. 'This enraged not only Manitobans, but most westerners, and the CF-18 decision quickly joined the National Energy Program as a symbol of regional resentment and injustice.'[19] Many westerners drew the conclusion from this affair that no matter how many representatives they sent to the House of Commons, the system itself—especially the 'national' parties—was biased against the West. A new voice, therefore, that of a regionally based protest party like the Reform Party, was necessary to extract favourable policies from central Canada.

Although the Reform Party began its life as a strictly regional organization—its constitution originally even included a prohibition on fielding candidates east of Manitoba—it quickly capitalized on the public's growing disenchantment with so-called 'traditional' political parties to make inroads into Ontario, the bastion of central Canadian power. Table 7.1 indicates just how widespread the public disillusionment with political parties in general had become during the Tories' second mandate. One of the principal reasons for the Reform Party's appeal to Ontario voters can be traced to its critique of existing political institutions, which are attacked as being unresponsive, unaccountable, and élitist. Rigid party discipline—which various governments have promised to relax, without much noticeable effect—is singled out by both voters and the Reform Party alike as one of the biggest culprits in driving a wedge between the individual citizen and the political system. Under the Mulroney Conservatives, two Tory backbenchers who were publicly critical of the GST found themselves expelled from the party's caucus. Likewise, and despite Jean Chrétien's promise to relax party discipline, those Liberal MPs who opposed the government's 1995 gun control law were stripped of their parliamentary committee assignments. Such incidents remind voters that under the traditional parties those they elect to Parliament are expected to vote as the party brass decides, even if this collides with the strongly held desires of their constituents.

Table 7.1 Respect and Confidence in State and Societal Institutions

	1979	1985	1989	1991
Percentage expressing 'great deal' or 'quite a lot' of confidence in:				
Church/Religion	60	54	55	—
Supreme Court	57	55	59	—
House of Commons	38	29	30	—
Large Corporations	34	28	33	26
Political Parties	30	22	18	7
Labour Unions	23	21	28	21
Federal government	—	—	—	9

Source: Canadian Institute of Public Opinion, The Gallup Report, 'Confidence in Political Parties Declines', 9 February 1989; ibid., 'Government Increasingly Becoming Object of Scorn Among Canadians', 20 February 1991.

There is also a generalized suspicion, fuelled by occasional sordid conflict-of-interest scandals that have befallen governments in Ottawa and in many of the provincial capitals as well, that politicians have become overly concerned with furthering their own careers or lining their pockets at the expense of their primary duty of representing the wishes and interests of their constituents. The issue of MPs' pensions is a lightning rod for this popular sentiment. The Reform Party made much of its commitment to opt out of what it considered to be the unfairly generous terms of MP pensions, and in 1995 all but one of the party's MPs chose not to participate in the lucrative pension plan. Finally, there is declining tolerance among voters for the kind of closed-door, élitist decision-making that traditionally has characterized Canadian politics under Liberal and Conservative governments.

Responding to the widely held demands among the electorate for greater accountability and a more democratic political structure, the Reform Party has followed in the path of its populist predecessors, the Progressives and Social Credit, and called for the implementation of a number of republican reforms that would increase the individual citizen's control over his or her representatives. The Reform Party advocates greater use of referenda and citizen initiatives; the right of constituents to recall their MPs, should they be deviating too obviously from their wishes; and relaxation of party discipline, so that most votes in Parliament would be 'free' votes. The party's ideology is conservative, and it regularly finds itself alone as the sole political party advocating radical change to the policy status quo. For example, during the 1993 election campaign Reform was the only party to advocate a major reduction in Canada's annual intake of immigrants during times when the economy was weak. It was also the only party to insist that deficit reduction, to be achieved mainly through spending cuts, should be Ottawa's top priority. The party also stands alone in its opposition to official multiculturalism and bilingualism.

Although the Conservatives, Liberals, and NDP all initially tried to ignore or downplay the significance of the Reform Party, by the summer of 1991—when the report of the Spicer Commission was released, documenting the deep dissatisfaction of many Canadians with the functioning of their traditional democratic institutions, especially the political parties—this protest movement was simply too powerful to be casually dismissed as a flash in the pan. If the Conservatives and the New Democrats hoped to hold onto at least some of their traditional electoral strongholds in the Prairies, then they had to respond to the policy concerns raised by Preston Manning's organization, no matter how distasteful or 'populist' they considered the Reformers to be. This is exactly what happened during previous cycles of regional protest: the major parties were eventually compelled to head off the electoral challenge of a nascent protest movement (whether the Progressives, the CCF, or Social Credit) by endorsing policies that appealed to the new party's supporters. In the case of the Progressives, for instance, the party was opposed to the National Policy tariff (which kept the price of central Canada's manufactured goods relatively high and drove up the costs of farming) and to the discriminatory freight rates charged by the CPR (which made it cheaper to ship manufactured goods from central Canada to the West than to send grain eastward). After the Progressives' meteoric rise to prominence in the 1921 federal election, however, the protest they represented was gradually dissipated by the skilful manoeuvring of Liberal Prime Minister Mackenzie King, who made relatively minor changes in the tariff and in freight rate policy and managed to buy off some of the Progressive leaders with offers of cabinet posts in his government. This was largely the fate of the Co-operative Commonwealth Federation (CCF) as well: King sought to take the wind out of the socialist party's sails by implementing a number of social welfare policies that its supporters were advocating, including old age pensions and unemployment insurance.

'Minor' parties like the Reform Party perform an important function in our brokerage party system: they provide a much-needed source of policy innovation, goading the major parties into acting on the concerns of regions, classes, or significant social groups that they have traditionally ignored or underestimated. Walter Young, in his history of the national CCF, described the contribution of third parties to the Canadian political system in the following way:

> By providing ... the kind of ideological confrontation which is typically absent in contests between the two major parties, [minor parties] have served to stimulate the older parties and reactivate their previously dormant philosophies....Two parties alone cannot successfully represent all the interests or act as a broker—honest or otherwise. Attempts to represent a national consensus have been usually based on the assessment of a few with limited access to the attitudes of the whole. The result has been that the national consensus has in fact been the view of the most dominant voices in the old parties. And these are the voices at the centre; historically, the voices of the élite or the establishment.[20]

The 1993 Election: The End of Brokerage Politics?

Since 1993, it no longer seems appropriate to refer to the Liberal and Progressive Conservative parties as Canada's two 'major' parties. Before the 1993 election it was common to speak of Canada's 'two and one-half' party system. The Liberals and Conservatives were the parties that had a realistic chance of forming a government, while the NDP was a stable minority party on the federal scene, regularly winning 15–20 per cent of the popular vote and occasionally holding the balance of power during a period of minority government. The distinction between major and minor parties was rooted in the realities of electoral competition.

The old certainties were shattered by the 1993 election results. The Liberals won a solid majority, taking 177 of the 295 seats in the House of Commons and 41.3 per cent of the popular vote. Neither the Conservatives nor the NDP elected enough MPs to qualify for official party status in the House of Commons. On the other hand, the Reform Party jumped from one seat that had been won in a by-election to fifty-two. The Bloc Québécois, created in 1990 by the defections of several Tory and Liberal MPs after the Meech Lake failure, went from seven seats to fifty-four. Not since 1921, when the Progressives came second to the Liberals, had the national party system received such a jolt from voters.

With the Conservatives and NDP reduced to near irrelevance in the Commons and two strong opposition parties, neither of which gave signs of being interested in brokerage-style politics, it was natural that political analysts should talk of the realignment taking place in Canada's national party system. Realignment suggests a durable change, not one caused by transient and unusual factors. Those who interpreted the 1993 election results as evidence of a realignment based this reading on what they saw as voters' dissatisfaction with broker-age-style politics, the weakness of party loyalties among voters, and erosion of the NDP's support across the country. This interpretation was greeted sceptically or even rejected by others. Critics of the realignment argument pointed to such factors as the monumental unpopularity of former Conservative Prime Minister Brian Mulroney, the erosion of NDP support in Ontario where an unpopular NDP government was in power, a wave of western disaffection with the major parties, and the unusual and presumably passing phenomenon of the Bloc Québecois, spawned in the bitter wake of the 1990 defeat of the Meech Lake Accord.

Textbook writers engage in prognostication at their peril, and only time will determine who is right. Nevertheless, one might argue that the elements for a durable party realignment exist. One of these involves the low esteem in which parties and politicians are held by voters. In the words of the Royal Commission on Electoral Reform and Party Financing:

> Canadians appear to distrust their political leaders, the political process and political institutions. Parties themselves may be contributing to the malaise of voters ... whatever the cause, there is little doubt that Canadian political parties are held in low public esteem, and that their standing has declined steadily over the past decade. They are under attack from citizens for failing to achieve a variety of goals deemed important by significant groups within society.[21]

The wave of cynicism that has been building in the Canadian electorate has weakened attachments to the traditional parties.

A second element that may presage a realignment of the party system involves what might be described as the shrinking centre in Canadian politics. The traditional dominance of the Liberals and Progressive Conservatives, centrist parties that differed very little from one another in terms of their principles and policies, depended on the existence of a broad popular consensus on the role of government and on the older parties' ability to keep political debate within the familiar confines of language, regionalism, and leadership. This popular consensus has become frayed, and so the parties' ability to keep political conflict within 'safe' boundaries has been diminished.

The consensus that developed during the post-World War Two era was based on the welfare state, an active economic management role for government, and official bilingualism. The Liberals and Conservatives, but particularly the Liberal Party in its role as the government for most of this era, were the architects of the policies that were the practical expressions of this consensus. Commenting on Canada's national party system in the early 1980s, Seymour Martin Lipset argued that there was no right-wing party but that all the parties were part of the left-of-centre consensus. The British weekly *The Economist* made the same point in commenting on the 1988 election. It observed that the leaders of the Conservatives, Liberals, and NDP were 'all to the left of the American Democratic team, Mr Michael Dukakis and Mr Lloyd Bentsen....Most Canadian voters, too, are committed to a quasi-welfare state.'[22] On constitutional issues, too, the traditional parties were capable of broad agreement. This was evident in the support that all three parties at the federal level gave to both the Meech Lake Accord and the Charlottetown Accord, a unanimity that certainly was not found in the Canadian population.

Popular consensus on the Keynesian welfare state and activist government has come unravelled since the 1980s. Issues like deficit reduction, welfare reform, and lower taxes are the rallying points for dissent from the post-war consensus. Opposition to what is perceived to be state-sponsored pluralism through official multiculturalism and bilingualism provides another pole for this dissent. In broadening its organization from the West to include Ontario and eastern Canada (Reform's leader, Preston Manning, appears to harbour dreams of a breakthrough even in Quebec), the Reform Party was clearly attempting to provide a voice for this dissent, a voice that many voters believed was not being provided by the Progressive Conservative Party. Reform's second-place finish in Ontario in the 1993 election, where it captured 20 per cent of the popular vote, cannot be explained in terms of 'western alienation'. These appeared to be voters who had defected from the Conservatives in search of a party that defined the issues in a way they believed responded to the country's true problems. At the provincial level this dissent contributed to the election of the Conservatives under Ralph Klein in Alberta and Mike Harris in Ontario, provincial Conservative governments that are much closer to the outlook of the Reform Party than they are to the national Conservative Party under Jean Charest.

Only the Liberal Party succeeded in practising the old brokerage-style politics. It emerged from the 1993 election as the only truly national party, electing members from every province and territory and receiving no less than one-quarter of the votes cast in any province. The lesson may be that there is no longer enough space in the centre of the Canadian electorate to support two centrist brokerage parties. Given the national Conservative Party's long history and continuing organizational resources, as well as its strength at the provincial level, it would be rash to write its obituary. But it seems likely that the party will have to reposition itself ideologically by competing for the votes that Reform siphoned off in the 1993 election. It cannot afford to remain a near-clone of the Liberal Party, especially since the Liberals in power have created some distance between themselves and the Keynesian welfare state they were instrumental in building. The electoral success of conservative Conservatives in Alberta and Ontario suggests that the future of the national party may lie in this direction.

Some critics of the realignment interpretation of the 1993 election argue that the success of the Bloc Québécois was the chief factor that knocked the party system off its usual orbit. Assuming that the Bloc is a temporary phenomenon, they argue, the national party system will return to two-party dominance once it has passed from the scene. After all, most of those who voted for the Bloc in 1993 had voted for the Conservatives in 1984 and 1988, when the latter party captured fully half of the popular vote in Quebec. Eliminate the Bloc from the picture, they argue, and many of these voters will have nowhere to go except to the Conservatives, thereby re-establishing the Conservative Party's national status.

Perhaps. But there are a couple of serious problems with this scenario. One is that in order to recapture voters who supported the BQ in 1993, the Conservatives would have to offer Quebecers something different from the federalist philosophy of the Liberals under Jean Chrétien. It is unlikely that they could do this in a way that would appeal to nationalist sentiment in Quebec without in the process angering voters in the rest of Canada. The other problem is that re-establishing Conservative support in Quebec still would not solve the party's difficulties in the rest of Canada. Reform outpolled the Conservatives in Ontario, and in the four western provinces it received about three votes to every one vote cast for the Tories. If the popular consensus on which two-party dominance in English Canada rested really has come apart, and therefore the electoral space for brokerage politics has shrunk, then the Conservatives will require more than cosmetic surgery to regain their voter appeal west of Quebec. The challenge is made all the more difficult by the fact that the Liberals, masters of the art of borrowing ideas and policies when this is expedient, have shown a willingness to move to the right on such matters as government spending and welfare reform. Between Reform's Preston Manning and Liberal Finance Minister Paul Martin, Jr, there may not be much room for Conservative leader Jean Charest to stake out some distinctively right-of-centre turf—assuming that he even wants to!

The Electoral System and Its Consequences

The Bloc Québécois, a political party dedicated to Quebec independence, emerged from the 1993 election as Her Majesty's Official Opposition. The BQ ran candidates only in Quebec. It received just under 50 per cent of the votes cast in Quebec and won fifty-four of the province's seventy-five seats in the House of Commons. The BQ received no votes and won no seats outside Quebec. Calculated on a national basis, the BQ received 13.5 per cent of all votes cast in the 1993 election, which translated into 18.3 per cent of the seats in the House of Commons. The Reform Party received a greater share of the national vote, 18.7 per cent, but two fewer seats in the Commons (fifty-two, or 17.6 per cent of all seats). The Progressive Conservative Party received 16 per cent of the national vote but won only two of the Commons' 295 seats. To paraphrase a line from Shakespeare's *Hamlet*, something seemed rotten in the state of Canada!

To understand what happened in the 1993 election, we must first describe the Canadian electoral system, whose principal features are the same at both the federal and provincial levels. It is based on the *single-member constituency*: one person elected to represent the citizens of a particular geographic area called a constituency or riding. The candidate who receives the most votes in a constituency election becomes the member of Parliament (or provincial legislator) for that constituency. This is called a *plurality system*. A majority of votes is not necessary for election and, given the fragmentation of votes among the parties, is the exception rather than the rule.

A political party's representation in the House of Commons will depend, therefore, on how well its candidates fare in the 295 constituency races that make up a general election. It regularly happens that, nationally, the leading party's candidates may account for no more than about 40 per cent of the popular vote and yet capture a majority of the seats in the Commons. Indeed, the advocates of the single-member, simple plurality electoral system point to this as the system's chief virtue. It manages, they claim, to transform something less than a majority of votes for a party into a majority of seats, thereby delivering stable majority government. (In fact, however, the system's performance on this count has been rather mediocre. Six of the thirteen general elections between 1957 and 1993 produced minority governments.)

The chief alternative to the single-member, plurality electoral system is some form of *proportional representation*. Under a proportional system, the number of members elected by each party about coincides with its share of the popular vote. This sounds eminently fair, but proportional representation has its critics. Detractors criticize it on three main counts. First, they claim that it promotes a splintering of the party system, encouraging the creation of minor parties that represent very narrow interests and undermining the development of broad-based national parties capable of bridging sectional rivalries and the differences between special interests. Second, proportional representation is said to produce unstable government. The unlikelihood that any party will have a majority of seats and, therefore, the need to cobble together and maintain a coalition government result in more frequent elections. And even between elections, the inter-party deals that are necessary to maintain a coalition government may paralyse cabinet decision-making. Countries like Italy and Belgium, where governments seldom last longer than a year or two, are said to illustrate the horrors of proportional representation. (Curiously, proportional systems with a relatively low level of executive turnover, such as the Netherlands and Germany, are seldom mentioned by the critics.)

A third standard criticism of proportional representation is that it encourages ideological polarity and enables extremist parties to achieve representation in the legislature. To be sure, countries having proportional electoral systems tend to have more political parties than those with plurality systems, and the ideological distance between the extreme ends of the party spectrum will inevitably be greater than that separating Canada's major parties, or Democrats and Republicans in the United States (another plurality electoral system). In fact, however, the ideological distance between those parties in proportional systems that are likely to be the senior partners of any government coalition tends to be no greater than between, say, the Conservative Party and the NDP in Canada, or Labour and the Conservatives in the United Kingdom. Moreover, not everyone would agree that more, rather than less, ideological dispersion between parties is a bad thing. One might argue that it improves voters' ability to distinguish between parties on the basis of the values and policies they represent. The prospect that extremist parties will infiltrate the legislature through a proportional system is also less worrisome than is claimed by detractors. Both theory and experience suggest that the closer a party gets to membership in a governing coalition, the more moderate its behaviour will be.[23]

The 'winner-take-all' electoral system that exists in Canada is not without its own detractors. In a classic analysis, Alan Cairns identifies several consequences for Canada's party system and national unity that flow from the single-member, simple plurality system.[24] They include the following:

- It tends to produce more seats than votes for the strongest major party and for minor parties whose support is regionally concentrated.
- It gives the impression that some parties have no or little support in certain regions, when in fact their candidates may regularly account for 15–30 per cent of the popular vote.
- The parliamentary composition of a party will be less representative of the different regions of the country than is that party's electoral support.
- Minor parties whose appeal is to interests that are distributed widely across the country will receive a smaller percentage of seats than votes.

Cairns concludes that the overall impact of Canada's electoral system has been negative. The system has, he argues, exacerbated regional and ethno-linguistic divisions in Canadian political life by shutting out the Conservative Party in Quebec for most of this century and giving the impression that the Liberal Party was the only national party with support in French Canada. Cairns's article on the electoral system's effects was written in the late 1960s. If it was written today it would also mention the gross underrepresentation of the Liberals in western Canada over the last couple of decades, despite their receiving between one-quarter and one-third of western votes in most elections. As William Irvine observes, 'the electoral system confers a spurious image of unanimity on provinces. By magnifying the success of the provincial vote leader, the electoral system ensures that party caucuses will overrepresent any party's "best" province.'[25] And this is not the only quirk of our electoral system (see Box 7.5).

Historically, the party that stood to gain most from the replacement of Canada's electoral system by some form of proportional representation was the CCF/NDP. It received a smaller percentage of total seats in the Commons than its share of the national vote in every one of the seventeen elections between 1935 and 1988. This was again true in 1993, but the collapse of the NDP vote from its usual 15 to 20 per cent to just under 7 per cent was clearly more significant than the fact that the electoral system once again 'under-rewarded' the party (it won nine seats, or 3 per cent of the total). The Conservative Party, which historically was one of the chief beneficiaries of the biases in the electoral system, was the big loser in 1993, and the Reform Party also received a slightly smaller share of seats in the Commons than its share of the popular vote. William Irvine's point about the electoral system's tendency to magnify the success of the most popular party in a province and punish those parties whose share of the vote does not achieve some critical mass was certainly borne out in the 1993 election. Reform received 20 per cent of the Ontario vote, coming in second behind the Liberals' 53 per cent, but was rewarded with only one seat to the Liberals' ninety-eight. This

BOX 7.5 Lottery or Equity?[26]

The [1979] election results provide a textbook illustration of the inequities and negative consequences the existing system is capable of producing. The defeated Liberals received nearly half a million more votes, and twenty-two fewer seats, than the party that replaced them in office. Although the new Conservative government was generally favored by the electoral system, the Conservatives were harmed in Quebec. They received 432,000 votes in Quebec, more than they received in six other provinces, but only two seats. In Prince Edward Island, by contrast, 34,147 votes gave the party four seats. Thus, although the Conservatives received 10.5 per cent of their total vote from Quebec, only 1.5 per cent of their seats were from that province. The Liberals, with 15 per cent of their vote west of the Great Lakes, received only three seats, 2.6 per cent of their total seats, in the four provinces of Manitoba, Saskatchewan, Alberta, and British Columbia.

Alan C. Cairns, 'The Constitutional, Legal, and
Historical Background', in Howard R. Penniman, ed.,
Canada at the Polls, 1979 and 1980 (Washington: American Enterprise Institute, 1981), 23.

helped fuel the misperception of Reform as being merely a western party, when in fact almost one million votes representing about 38 per cent of all votes cast for the Reform Party, were from Ontario. Given the realities of political life, however, there is no reason to imagine that the Liberal Party or—should it happen—a revitalized Conservative Party would show much enthusiasm for electoral reform, let alone adopting proportional representation. Their dominance would almost certainly be eroded by such a system.

Canadians probably will just have to live with the regionally divisive effects of the existing electoral system. The best hope for overcoming the negative consequences that Cairns, Irvine, and many others have pointed to may be reform of the Canadian Senate. An elected Senate whose members would be chosen according to some system of proportional representation within each province—so that a party's share of Senate seats for a province would be determined by its share of the provincial popular vote—could go some way toward overcoming the regionally unrepresentative character of parties' caucuses in the House of Commons. This would depend, however, on the Senate becoming a more effective branch of the legislature than it is at present.

Giving it an elected basis would certainly increase its legitimacy in the eyes of Canadians and would probably improve the calibre of representatives found in the Senate. If this happened, it is easily conceivable that senators would routinely be appointed to cabinet, rather than only exceptionally so, as is currently the practice. In such circumstances no major party should have difficulty in putting together a government with a fair share of representation from all regions of the country. At the same time, an unreformed House of Commons would have the virtue of retaining the Canadian tradition of individual representatives for citizens—MPs who are accountable to electors in local constituencies. Alas, there is little in our recent political history to suggest that major reforms to the Senate, and therefore to our entire parliamentary system, can squeeze by the formidable obstacles in their path.

Party Finances and Special Interests

Throughout their history, the Liberal and Progressive Conservative parties have relied heavily on corporate contributors to finance their activities.[27] The NDP, by contrast, has depended mainly on contributions from individuals and on the financial support of affiliated trade unions. Corporate donations to the national NDP have always been minuscule.

It is difficult to attach precise numbers to party finances before 1974, for the simple reason that parties were not legally required to disclose their sources of revenue. A study done by Khayyam Paltiel for the federally appointed Royal Commission on Election Expenses (1966) estimated that, before the 1974 reforms, the older parties depended on business contributions for between 75 and 90 per cent of their incomes,[28] a figure that did not even include the value of services in kind that they received from businesses, particularly from advertising and polling firms during election campaigns.[29] Not only were the Liberals and Conservatives dependent on business for all but a small share of their revenue, most of this corporate money was collected from big businesses in Toronto and Montreal.[30] Other students of party finances have confirmed this historical pattern of dependence on big financial and industrial capital.[31]

Passage of the Election Expenses Act, 1974, signalled a watershed in Canadian party finance. The Act included spending limits for individual candidates and political parties dur-

The Ceremonial
Changing of the Troughs.
Parliament Hill, Ottawa,
October 26,1993.

NDP   TORIES   REFORM   BLOC   LIBERALS

Plus ça change, plus c'est la même chose? (Roy Peterson, *Vancouver Sun*)

ing election campaigns, changes to the Broadcasting Act requiring radio and television stations to make available to the parties represented in the House of Commons both paid and free broadcast time during election campaigns,[32] and a system of reimbursement for part of their expenses for candidates who receive at least 15 per cent of the popular vote. This last reform has the effect of subsidizing the main parties at taxpayer expense, a consequence that can only be defended on the grounds that this public subsidy helps to weaken their financial dependence on special interests.

But from the standpoint of the parties' sources of income, the most important reforms brought in by the Election Expenses Act involved tax credits for political contributions and public disclosure requirements for candidates and political parties. On the first count, changes to the Income Tax Act allow individuals or organizations to deduct from their taxable income a percentage of their donations to a registered political party or candidate, up to a maximum tax credit of $500. There is no limit on the size of political donations, but the maximum tax credit is reached with a donation of $1,150.[33] On the second count, parties and candidates are required to provide the chief electoral officer with a list of all donors who have contributed $100 or more in money or services in kind, as well as an itemized account of their expenditures. Openness has its limits, however. Parties are not required to disclose how much they spend on important activities such as fund-raising and polling, although available evidence suggests that these are very expensive inter-election functions.[34]

Perhaps the most striking consequence of the 1974 reforms has been the dramatic increase in the importance of donations by individuals. These contributions were always the mainstay of NDP finances. Now, because of the tax credit for political donations and the older parties' adoption of sophisticated direct-mail techniques of fund-raising, first developed in the United States,[35] contributions by individuals are a major source of income for all three main political parties. Contributions from individuals have exceeded business contributions to both the PC and Liberal parties in several of the years since the tax credit came into effect. The same is true of candidates' revenue. NDP candidates receive very little from corporate donors but depend heavily on trade union contributions. The Reform Party relies overwhelmingly on contributions from individuals. Figure 7.1 shows the chief sources of revenue for the Liberal, Conservative, Reform, and New Democratic parties for 1993. Figure 7.2 provides a comparison of the number and average size of individual contributions to each of the parties in the 1993 election year.

On the face of if, then, the Liberal and Conservative parties' traditional financial dependence on business appears to have been diluted. This should not blind us, however, to the continuing importance of corporate donations for the older parties. They still account for close to half of total contributions during election years and roughly 40-50 per cent between elections. Moreover, very large corporate contributions still account for a sizable share of the older parties' total revenues. If we define a large corporate donation as being at least $10,000, we find that these contributions have accounted for about 15 to 30 per cent of total contributions for both the Liberal and Conservative parties over the last few years. This is a dramatic change from the days when party 'bagmen' collected all but a small fraction of party funds from the Toronto and Montreal corporate élites.

The most important consequence of special interest contributions to parties and individual politicians may be the access to policy-makers it buys for contributors. Although cases of influence-peddling come to light from time to time, it is usually a mistake to think of political contributions as payments offered in the expectation of receiving some particular favour. There are, no doubt, instances where firms that rely on government contracts for some part of their revenue, or that hope to receive government business in the future, find it prudent to donate money to parties or candidates. But for most corporate contributors, and certainly for large donors like the banks and those leading industrial firms that are perennial contributors to the two older parties, there is no expectation of a specific *quid pro quo*.

So why do they bother? One explanation is that corporate political donations represent a sort of insurance premium. As Conservative strategist and political adviser Dalton Camp puts it:

> For the wise donor, the financing of the political system may very well be a duty and an obligation to the system, but it is, as well, insurance against the unlikely—such as the ascendancy of socialism—or against occasional political aberration, a Walter Gordon budget, say, or a Carter report on tax reform [both perceived to be anti-business policies]. When such contingencies arise, the price for access is modest indeed.[36]

What Camp calls a 'duty and an obligation to the system' might also be described as an investment in two-party dominance. Business interests are often at loggerheads with both Liberal and Conservative governments over specific policies. But generally speaking, both of

Figure 7.1 Sources of Contributions to the Liberal, Progressive Conservative, New Democratic, and Reform Parties, 1993

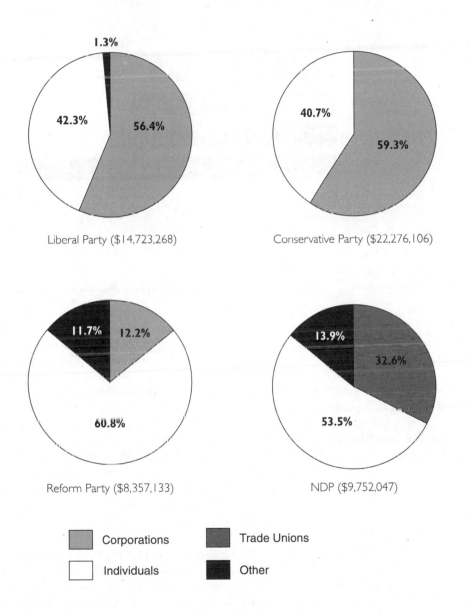

Liberal Party ($14,723,268)

Conservative Party ($22,276,106)

Reform Party ($8,357,133)

NDP ($9,752,047)

Corporations   Trade Unions

Individuals   Other

Note: The Bloc Québécois did not submit information for this period.

Source: Canada, Chief Electoral Officer, *Registered Political Parties' Fiscal Period Returns for 1993* (Ottawa: Supply and Services Canada, 1994).

Figure 7.2 Number and Average Size of Contributions by Individuals to the Liberal, Progressive Conservative, New Democratic, and Reform Parties, 1993

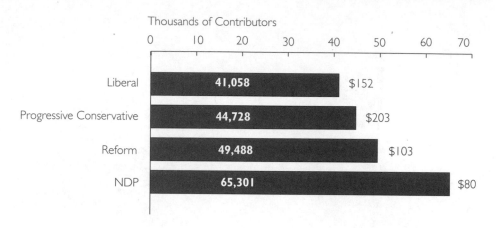

Note: The Bloc Québécois did not submit information for this period.

Source: Canada, Chief Electoral Officer, *Registered Political Parties' Fiscal Period Returns for 1993* (Ottawa: Supply and Services Canada, 1994).

the two older parties are congenial toward corporate enterprise. Business can live with either a Liberal or Conservative government and has a material interest in supporting the centrist politics that characterize the Canadian political system and in avoiding the polarization of party politics between the right and the left (as happened in the United Kingdom several decades ago).

In addition to helping finance a party system that is generally congenial to business interests, it has long been understood that donations help buy access. In the words of Dalton Camp: 'Toronto money merely [*sic!*] maintains access to the parties, keeping open essential lines of communication, corporate hotlines, so to speak, to the right ears at appropriate times.'[37] In many cases the sheer size and importance of a corporation will be sufficient to ensure a hearing when the corporation feels its interests are at stake. In any given year about half of the largest 100 industrial firms in Canada do not even contribute to either of the two older parties. It would be ridiculous to conclude that their lack of generosity cuts them off from direct access to political decision-makers. But all things being equal, contributions probably open the door a bit wider.

Is the distinction between bribery—contributions given in the expectation of a specific favour—and paying for access really a piece of hairsplitting sophistry? After all, if we acknowledge that contributions confer on the donor an advantage that is not available to those who cannot afford to donate thousands of dollars to political parties, are we not thereby acknowledging that party donations reinforce inequalities based on money? It is widely accepted that access is an important component of influence on policy. The fact that corporate donations are neither given nor received in the expectation that a particular contract or a specific legislative or regulatory output will ensue does not mean that there is no exchange. Money helps buy access. Obviously it does not always ensure a sympathetic hearing. But in a political system in which groups are clamouring to be heard so that they may make their case to those who will ultimately make policy decisions, access to political decision-makers is a valuable commodity. As Camp observes, party donations are a modest price to pay for this advantage.

The link between party contributions and access has become more controversial with the increasing prominence of 'paid access opportunities'. These are fund-raising events like dinners and cocktail parties where, for an admission price that can range up to several thousand dollars, donors receive the opportunity to rub shoulders and exchange views with party leaders and other members of the government. Money obviously acts as a filter in determining who is likely to participate in such events, as does the party's invitation list. These fund-raising events have been supplemented by an American invention—special clubs for large contributors. Both the Republican and Democratic parties have operated such clubs for years, where, for an individual contribution of thousands of dollars (higher for a corporate membership), the donor receives the chance to meet with important politicians such as congressional committee chairpersons.[38] Canada's PC Party was the first to establish such a club, its '500 Club'. The national Liberal Party operates a similar paid-admission élite network, as do many provincial parties.

In the eyes of some, paid access opportunities such as these raise an ethical question: at what point does the ability to pay for special access to political decision-makers subvert the democratic process by favouring those with the money to make their views known directly? The dilemma is captured in the remark of a one-time Liberal cabinet minister, Israël Tarte, that elections are not fought with prayers. Parties need funds to carry out their activities. Even with a tax credit for political contributions, only a small portion of all Canadian taxpayers contribute money directly to parties or candidates. The money has to come from somewhere, and such developments as paid access opportunities represent the parties' innovative search for stable sources of funds. One alternative would be to impose severe restrictions on how much money parties can spend, so that the relatively small contributions from individuals (publicly subsidized by the tax credit) and the public subsidy that candidates receive from the reimbursement provision of the Election Expenses Act would be sufficient to finance their activities. This would require that current levels of spending by the major parties and their candidates be cut back. Of course, the public subsidy to the parties could be increased. But this would serve to institutionalize the existing party system further, a criticism that has already been made of the public subsidies provided for in the 1974 reforms.

After all is said and done, we should not exaggerate the importance of corporate political contributions as a lever of influence on the behaviour of parties when in power. As Jeffrey Simpson observes:

> Even large corporations, in the era after reforms to the Elections Act, often spent more money on trade associations, the Business Council on National Issues, or lobbying firms than they did contributing to the non-socialist political parties. For them political contributions are a kind of civic duty whereas the money spent on lobbyists and the like can directly reward self-interest.[39]

These other paths of influence are discussed in the next chapter.

Appendix

Table 7.2 Summary of Election Results, 1940–93

A. Percentage of Vote* and Candidates Elected by Political Party at Canadian General Elections, 1940–93

Party	1940	1945	1949	1953	1957	1958	1962
Liberal	54.9%	41.4%	50.1%	50.0%	42.3%	33.8%	37.4%
	181	127	193	172	106	48	99
PC	30.6%	27.7%	29.7%	31.0%	39.0%	53.7%	37.3%
	40	68	41	51	112	208	116
CCF/NDP	8.5%	15.7%	13.4%	11.3%	10.8%	9.5%	13.4%
	8	28	13	23	25	8	19
Social Credit	2.7%	4.1%	3.9%	5.4%	6.6%	2.6%	11.7%
	10	13	10	15	19	—	30
Bloc Populaire	—	3.3%	—	—	—	—	—
	—	2	—	—	—	—	—
Others	3.3%	7.8%	2.9%	2.3%	1.3%	0.4%	0.2%
	6	7	5	4	3	1	1
Total valid votes	4,620,260	5,246,130	5,848,971	5,641,272	6,605,980	7,287,297	7,690,134
Total seats	245	245	262	265	265	265	265

A. Percentage of Vote* and Candidates Elected by Political Party at Canadian General Elections, 1940–93 (cont.)

Party	1963	1965	1968	1972	1974	1979	1980	1984	1988	1993
Liberal	41.7%	40.2%	45.5%	38.5%	43.2%	40.1%	44.3%	28.0%	31.9%	41.3%
	128	131	155	109	141	114	147	40	83	177
PC	32.8%	32.4%	31.4%	34.9%	35.4%	35.9%	32.5%	50.0%	43.0%	16.0%
	95	97	72	107	95	136	103	211	169	2
NDP	13.1%	17.9%	17.0%	17.7%	15.4%	17.9%	19.8%	18.8%	20.4%	6.9%
	17	21	22	31	16	26	32	30	43	9
Créditistes	—	4.6%	4.4%	—	—	—	—	—	—	—
	—	9	14	—	—	—	—	—	—	—
Social Credit	11.9%	3.7%	0.8%	7.6%	5.0%	4.6%	1.7%	0.1%	**	—
	24	5	0	15	1	6	0	0	0	—
Bloc Québécois										13.5%
										54
Reform	—	—	—	—	—	—	—	—	2.1%	18.7%
	—	—	—	—	—	—	—	—	0	52
Others	0.4%	1.2%	0.9%	1.2%	0.9%	1.5%	1.7%	3.0%	2.6%	3.6%
	1	2	1	2	0	0	0	1	0	1
Total valid votes	7,894,076	7,713,316	8,125,996	9,667,489	9,505,908	11,455,702	10,947,914	12,548,721	13,175,599	13,667,671
Total seats	265	265	264	264	264	282	282	282	295	295

Note: The election of 1945 was the first in which the name Progressive Conservative was used. The New Democratic Party first participated in the election of 1962.

* Columns may not add up to 100 per cent due to rounding.

** Less than 0.1 per cent.

B. Percentage of Vote and Candidates Elected by Party and Province, 1993

Province	Liberal	Progressive Conservative	NDP	Reform	Bloc Québécois	Others	Totals, Province
Nfld.	67.3%	26.7%	3.5%	1.0%	—	1.5%	230,590
	7	—	—	—	—	—	7
N.S.	52.0%	23.5%	6.8%	13.3%	—	4.4%	453,394
	11	—	—	—	—	—	11
N.B.	56.0%	27.9%	4.9%	8.5%	—	2.7%	385,099
	9	1	—	—	—	—	10
P.E.I.	60.1%	32.0%	5.2%	1.0%	—	1.7%	72,222
	4	—	—	—	—	—	4
Qué.	33.0%	13.6%	1.5%	—	49.3%	2.6%	3,744,201
	19	1	—	—	54	1	75
Ont.	52.9%	17.6%	6.0%	20.1%	—	3.4%	4,880,216
	98	—	—	1	—	—	99
Man.	44.9%	11.9%	16.6%	22.4%	—	4.2%	541,056
	12	—	1	1	—	—	14
Sask.	32.1%	11.3%	26.6%	27.2%	—	2.8%	486,872
	5	—	5	4	—	—	14
Alta.	25.1%	14.6%	4.0%	52.3%	—	4.0%	1,203,829
	4	—	—	22	—	—	26
B.C.	28.1%	13.5%	15.5%	36.4%	—	6.5%	1,631,994
	6	—	2	24	—	—	32
Yukon and N.W.T.	49.5%	16.8%	21.1%	10.2%	—	2.4%	38,198
	2	—	1	—	—	—	3
Totals, Party	5,647,952	2,186,422	939,575	2,559,245	1,846,024	488,453	13,667,671
	177	2	9	52	54	1	295

* Rows may not add up to 100 per cent due to rounding.

Interest groups often resort to advertising in order to influence public opinion. (Friends of Canadian Broadcasting)

Politics does not stop between election campaigns. Much of the effort to influence the actions of government is channelled through interest groups. This chapter examines their characteristics and the role they play in Canadian politics. Topics include the following:

- ❖ How many groups, representing what interests?
- ❖ The bias of the interest group system.
- ❖ Perspectives on interest groups.
- ❖ Ingredients of interest group success.
- ❖ The impact of federalism on interest groups.
- ❖ Strategies for influence.
- ❖ Advocacy advertising.
- ❖ Lobbying.

CHAPTER EIGHT

■ Interest Groups

Elections are democracy's showpiece. But as important as they are, the influence of elections on what governments do is usually rather blunt and indirect. Policies are far more likely to be determined by forces generated within the state and by the actions of organized groups outside of it than by the latest election results. Indeed, it may often seem that special interests dominate the policy-making process in democracies. Their attempts to influence government are unremitting. The resources they marshal are often impressive. And their access to policy-makers is, in the case of some organized interests, privileged. Compared to this, the role of elections and the influence of voters often appear feeble.

Interest groups or pressure groups—the terms may be used interchangeably—have been defined as 'private associations ... [that] promote their interests by attempting to influence government rather than by nominating candidates and seeking responsibility for the management of government.'[1] They arise from a very basic fact of social life, the reality of diversity in the interests and values of human beings. This diversity, in turn, gives rise to what James Madison called political factions: groups of citizens whose goals and behaviour are contrary to those of other groups or to the interests of the community as a whole.[2] If these factions, or special interests as we are apt to call them today, appear to overshadow the public interest in democracies, there is a simple explanation for this. The tug of one's personal interests—as an automotive worker, teacher, fisherman, or postal worker—tends to be felt more keenly than the rather nebulous concept of the public interest. Arguments that appeal to such general interests as consumer benefits or economic efficiency are unlikely to convince the farmer whose income is protected by the production quotas and price floors set by a marketing board. But economic interests are not the only basis for factionalism in politics.

Such group characteristics as ethnicity, language, religion, race, gender, or simply sharing certain values may also provide the basis for the political organization of interests.

Economically based or not, interest groups are distinguished by the fact that they seek to promote goals that are not shared by all members of society. Paradoxically, however, their success in achieving these goals often depends on their ability to associate their efforts with the broader public interest. 'What is good for General Motors is good for America'[3] may or may not be true. Nevertheless, the slogan makes good sense as a strategy for promoting the interests of GM, North American automobile producers, and business interests generally.

Charting the Territory

The world of interest groups is both vast and characterized by enormous variety. Although no unified, reliable list of interest groups exists for Canada or any other democracy, some idea of the sheer number of groups may be had from the directory *Associations Canada*.[4] Its 1994–5 edition lists roughly 20,000 organizations, not all of which would meet the criterion of attempting to influence government action. Many groups focus exclusively on non-political activities like providing services and information to their members. But several thousand perform political functions for their members on a regular or occasional basis.

Almost every imaginable interest is represented by an organization. There are several hundred women's associations across Canada,[5] close to 1,000 environmental groups, over 2,000 business associations, perhaps 500 organizations representing agricultural interests, about 200 that focus on Aboriginal issues[6]—the range of organized interests and the sheer number of groups within each general category of interests are enormous. Impressive as these figures may seem, they do not provide a complete map of Canada's associational system. They do not, for example, include those transitory groups that emerge briefly around a single issue and then disappear from the scene. Nor do they include international organizations that may attempt to influence the actions of Canadian governments. But however we draw its boundaries, the universe of organized interests is vast.

While it is impossible to say exactly how many of these associations qualify as interest groups, there can be no doubt that a large number of them are politically active. One way to get a sense of this is to look at the list of groups that make representations to a legislative body or government-sponsored commission considering some issue. For example, several hundred groups made representations and submitted briefs to the Royal Commission on the Economic Union and Development Prospects for Canada (1982–5).[7] Over 600 groups and individuals submitted briefs to the Commission on the Political and Constitutional Future of Quebec (1990–1).[8] Alternatively, one may look at the composition of some politically active organizations. Approximately 600 women's organizations are represented by the National Action Committee on the Status of Women, which lobbies governments on their behalf. The Canadian Chamber of Commerce, one of whose main functions is to influence government policies, represents over 500 community and provincial chambers of commerce and boards of trade, as well as close to 100 trade and professional associations and many international organizations (like the Canada–Taiwan Business Council). In short, the size of the interest group system is considerable.

The Bias of the Interest Group System

> The notion that the pressure system is automatically representative of the whole community is a myth....The system is skewed, loaded and unbalanced in favor of a fraction of a minority.[9]

It goes without saying that some interest groups are more influential than others. But which ones are the most powerful? Why? Is the interest group system biased 'in favor of a fraction of a minority', as E.E. Schattschneider claims?

Schattschneider argues that the interest group system—he calls it the pressure system—has a business and upper-class bias. Writing about American politics in the early 1960s, he observed that business associations comprised the single largest group of organized interests in American society, they were far more likely than other interests to lobby government, and they tended to spend much more money on attempting to influence policy-makers than other interest groups. Moreover, Schattschneider cites impressive evidence demonstrating that 'even non-business organizations reflect an upper-class tendency'.[10] He explains the business and upper-class bias of interest group politics as being a product of both superior resources and the relatively limited size and exclusive character of these special interests. 'Special-interest organizations', he argues, 'are most easily formed when they deal with small numbers of individuals [or corporations] who are acutely aware of their exclusive interests.'[11] This awareness of special interests vital to one's material well-being or the well being of one's organization is characteristic of trade associations like the Canadian Petroleum Association, the Canadian Bankers' Association, or a broader-based business organization like the Canadian Manufacturers' Association, and also characterizes producer and occupational groups like the Quebec Dairy Association and the Ontario Medical Association. It is less likely to characterize organizations that represent more general interests.

Most social scientists and political journalists agree with Schattschneider. Charles Lindblom argues that business occupies a 'privileged position' in the politics of capitalist societies. In *Politics and Markets*,[12] Lindblom attributes this pre-eminence to business's superior financial resources and lobbying organization, greater access than other groups to government officials, and, most importantly, propagandistic activities that—directly through political advertising and indirectly through commercial advertising—reinforce the ideological dominance of business values in society.

One of the key factors most often cited by those who argue that business interests are politically superior is the *mobility of capital*. Investors enjoy a wide although not absolute freedom to shift their capital between sectors of the economy and from one national economy to another. The epitome of this mobility is found in the multinational corporation—an enterprise whose activities span a number of national economies and whose international character often is used as a lever in dealing with the government of a particular country. In addition to being territorially mobile, investment capital also has the capacity to expand and contract in response to investors' perceptions of the political-economic climate for business. Short of imposing punitive tax rates on savings, governments cannot force business and private investors to invest. Governments in all capitalist societies are concerned with levels of business confidence and are reluctant to take actions that carry a high risk of causing a cutback in investment. The consequences of such a cutback are felt politically by governments. Weak economic activity tends to translate into popular dissatisfaction and a loss of political support.[13]

The mobility of capital gives rise, in turn, to concern with *business confidence*. Politicians need to care about business confidence because of the very real possibility that they will not be re-elected if business's unwillingness to invest causes unemployment and falling incomes. But another factor that gives pause even to governments that can count on strong popular backing is the state's financial dependence on business. A decline in the levels of investment or profit will soon be felt as a drop in government revenues from the taxation of corporate and employment income and from the taxation of consumption. The problem of falling revenues is almost certain to be compounded by an increase in state expenditures on social programs whose costs are sensitive to changes in the level of economic activity. Borrowing on the public credit is only a temporary solution to this dilemma, which experience has shown to be both costly and subject to the limits of international investor confidence.

Neither Lindblom nor anyone else would argue that business interests 'win' all of the time, nor even that powerful business groups cannot experience major defeats. Instead, they maintain that there is a tendency to favour business interests over others because of systemic characteristics of capitalist societies. This is one of the few propositions about politics that manages to cut across the ideological spectrum, attracting support from the left and right alike (if rather more heavily from the left).[14] There are, however, dissenters.

Those who teach or write for a business school audience, for example, are likely to view business interests as being simply one set of interests in a sea of competing interest group claims on government.[15] Business historian Michael Bliss argues that whatever privileged access business people may have enjoyed in the corridors of political power, and whatever superiority business interests may have had in relation to rival claims on government, had largely disappeared by the 1980s. 'Groups with powerful vested interests,' he writes, 'including trade unions, civil servants, tenured academics, and courtesanal cultural producers, perpetuated a hostility toward business enterprise rooted in their own fear of competition on open markets.'[16]

In what is perhaps the most compelling rebuttal to the 'privileged position' thesis, David Vogel argues that, on balance, 'business is more affected by broad political and economic trends than it is able to affect them.'[17] Although Vogel focuses on the United States, he develops a more general argument about the political power of business interests in capitalist democracies. Popular opinion and the sophistication of interest group organization are, he maintains, the key to understanding the political successes and failures of business and other interest groups. Vogel argues that business's ability to influence public policy is greatest when the public is worried about the long-term strength of the economy and weakest when the economy's ability to produce jobs and to increase incomes is taken for granted.

The political organization of business interests is the second key to understanding the ebb and flow of business influence. Vogel maintains that the victories of environmental, consumer, and other public interest groups in the 1960s and 1970s were largely due to their ability to read the Washington map and work the levers of congressional and media politics. Business interests, by comparison, were poorly organized and amateurish. Since then, however, the political mobilization of business has been without equal. But despite its organizational prowess, divisions within the business community have generally served to check its influence on public policy.

Another factor that prevents business interests from dominating politics is what James Q. Wilson has called 'entrepreneurial politics'.[18] This involves the ability of politicians and interest groups to identify issues around which popular support can be mobilized. As a practical matter, Vogel maintains, business generally loses from this sort of support-mongering.

So who is right? Are business interests perched securely atop the heap of the interest group system in capitalist societies, or do business groups have to slug it out in the political trenches just like other groups and with no more likelihood of victory? Perhaps neither position is right. This is the conclusion suggested by much of the recent work on Canadian interest groups, what Paul Pross calls *post-pluralism* and others have called a *neo-institutionalist* approach.

This approach is based on a simple observable fact: policy-making generally involves the participation of a relatively limited set of state and societal actors, a *policy community* that is centred around a sub-government, i.e., that set of state institutions and interest groups usually involved in making and implementing policy in some field. We will have more to say about the approach later in the chapter. For now, the point is simply that groups representing business interests may or may not be members of a sub-government policy community. Whether they are and how influential they are depend on the policy field in question and on the particular configuration of interests active in the policy community. Moreover, neo-institutionalists tend to emphasize the capacity of state actors to act independently of the pressures and demands placed on them by societal interests. This capacity will vary across policy sectors, but the bottom line of the neo-institutionalist approach is that state actors in some policy communities may be quite capable of resisting pressures coming from highly organized, well-heeled business interests—or from any societal interests, for that matter.

Perspectives on Interest Groups

Pluralism

Pluralism or group theory may be defined as an explanation of politics that sees organized interests as the central fact of political life and explains politics chiefly in terms of the activities of groups. It is a societal explanation of politics in that it locates the main causes of government action in the efforts and activities of voluntary associations—trade associations, labour unions, churches, PTAs, etc.—outside the state. When it turns its attention to considering the role and character of the state in democratic societies, pluralist theory draws two main conclusions. First, the state itself is viewed as a sort of group interest or, more precisely, as an assortment of different interests associated with various components of the state. Second, despite the possibility that the state may have interests of its own, its chief political function is to ratify the balance of group interests in society and to enforce the policies that embody this balance of power. As Earl Latham graphically put it: 'The legislature referees the group struggle, ratifies the victories of the successful coalition, and records the terms of the surrenders, compromises, and conquests in the form of statutes.'[19]

The purest embodiment of group theory is found in the work of Arthur Bentley. Society, Bentley argues, can only be understood in terms of the groups that comprise it. He views government as simply a process of 'groups pressing one another, forming one another, and pushing out new groups and group representatives (the organs or agencies of government) to mediate the adjustments.'[20] This is an extremely reductionist approach. Pluralists after Bentley, including David Truman, Robert Dahl, and John Kenneth Galbraith,[21] have certainly been aware of the danger of trying to squeeze too much explanation out of a single cause. But they have remained faithful to a couple of basic elements of pluralist theory, one empirical and the other normative. The empirical element is the claim that politics is a competitive process where power is widely distributed, there is no single ruling élite or dominant class, and the interaction of organized interests outside the state is the chief force behind the actions of government. The normative element suggests that the outcome of this competitive struggle among groups represents the public interest and, indeed, that this is the only reasonable way of understanding the public interest in democracy.

Pluralism begat *neo-pluralism*. The neo-pluralist assault took issue with both the empirical and normative claims of group theory. Writers such as E.E. Schattschneider, Theodore Lowi,[22] and Charles Lindblom had little difficulty in showing that the interest group system was much less open and competitive than the earlier pluralists had argued. Regarding pluralism's normative features, Lowi took aim at its equation of the public interest with the outcome of struggles between special interests. He argued that the special interest state—what Lowi called interest group liberalism—actually trivializes the public interest and ends up undermining it by pretending that it is no more than the latest set of deals struck between the powerful through the intermediary offices of government. 'Interest group liberalism', he argued, 'seeks pluralistic government, in which there is no formal specification of means or of ends. In pluralistic government there is therefore no substance. Neither is there procedure. There is only process.'[23]

As if these indictments were not enough, pluralism also stands accused of misunderstanding the true character of political power. In focusing on the competitive struggle, pluralists, their critics argue, are inclined to see political life as relatively open and competitive because they focus on the observable struggles between groups and the decisions of governments. But as Bachrach and Baratz suggest, 'power may be, and often is, exercised by confining the scope of decision-making to relatively safe issues.'[24] Non-decision-making, the ability to keep issues unformulated and off the public agenda, is a form of power. Looked at from this angle, the interest group system appears much less competitive.

Class Analysis

Viewed through the prism of class analysis, interest groups do not disappear, but their edges become blurred and they take a back seat to the class interests they represent. Some of the major works of contemporary Marxist scholarship do not even mention such terms as 'interest group', 'pressure group', or 'social group'.[25] There is no heading for 'interest groups' in either the table of contents or the index to *The New Practical Guide to Canadian Political Economy*, a bibliographic reference book for class analysis writings in Canada.[26] Nor are interest groups considered in any of the chapters of a recent collection on Canadian class analysis.[27]

This is not to say that the reality of organized interests in politics is either denied or ignored by class analysis. 'Democratic and pluralist theory', observes Ralph Miliband,

> could not have achieved the degree of ascendancy which it enjoys in advanced capitalist society had it not at least been based on one plainly accurate observation about them, namely that they permit and even encourage a multitude of groups and associations to organize openly and freely and to compete with each other for the advancement of such purposes as their members may wish.[28]

Miliband's *The State in Capitalist Society* devotes an entire chapter to the role of organized interests in an attempt to refute the pluralist model that we discussed earlier. Some Canadian examples of how class analysis can include a careful analysis of interest groups include Wallace Clement's *The Challenge of Class Analysis*[29] and Rianne Mahon's study of Canada's textile industry.[30] Clement examines the complex network of unions, co-operatives, and associations in Canada's coastal fisheries to 'lend understanding to the material basis of class struggle'.[31] In *The Politics of Industrial Restructuring*, Mahon develops a sophisticated analysis of trade associations and labour unions in the textile sector in terms of the fundamental class interests they represent, the organizational capacity of these interests, and their ideological characteristics.

But interest groups, from the perspective of class analysis, are not the basic units of society and political life. Classes are. And so organized groups are seen as the bearers of more fundamental interests and ideologies, namely those of classes and their factions. This enables one to acknowledge the uniqueness of individual groups and associations while focusing on larger collective interests represented by individual groups. An association like the Business Council on National Issues, which represents 150 of the largest private sector corporations in Canada, would be seen as a representative of 'monopoly capital'. The Canadian Manufacturers' Association, although it represents over 3,000 corporations spanning virtually all manufacturing industries and ranging in size from thousands of employees to a mere handful,[32] is viewed as an organizational voice for the manufacturing faction of the capitalist class. In fact, some class analyses characterize the CMA as an instrument of the oligopolistic, American-oriented faction of the capitalist class. Labour unions are, of course, viewed from this perspective as representative of subordinate class interests and ideologies, as are groups representing women, Natives, and ethnic and racial minorities.

Corporatism

Corporatism is a political structure characterized by the direct participation of organizations representing business and labour in public policy-making. 'In its core', states Jurg Steiner, 'corporatism in a modern democracy deals with the interactions among organized business, organized labor, and the state bureaucracy. These three actors cooperate at the national level in the pursuit of the public good.'[33] Such structures are found in some of the smaller capitalist democracies of Western Europe, including Sweden, Austria, and the Netherlands, and, less solidly, in Germany and Switzerland.

The distinctiveness of corporatism as an interest group system is based on three characteristics. One is the existence of *peak associations* for business and labour. These are organizations that can credibly claim to represent all significant interests within the business and labour communities, respectively, and that have the ability to negotiate on behalf of the interests they represent. A second characteristic of a corporatist interest group system is the formal integration of business and labour into structures of state authority. Under corporatism, these interests do not simply have privileged access to state policy-makers, they have *institutionalized access*. A third characteristic of corporatism is its ideology of social partnership. As William Coleman says of corporatist ideology in Austria, 'There is a commitment to allow class conflict to grow only so far before it is internalized and addressed in ways judged a "fair" compromise.'[34] Compared to pluralism, which is characterized by an intensely competitive interest group system that stands outside the state, a corporatist system is more consensus-oriented and obliterates the barriers between the state and the societal interests represented through corporatist decision-making structures.

What possible relevance can the corporatist model have to an understanding of interest groups in Canada? The peak associations of business and labour necessary to make corporatism work do not exist in Canada. The most representative of Canadian business associations, the Canadian Chamber of Commerce, is on closer inspection just a loose federation of provincial and local chambers, individual corporations, and trade associations. The national organization exercises no control over its members, and the sheer range of interests represented within the CCC obliges it to focus mainly on general issues—lowering corporate taxation, cutting the level of government spending, reducing the amount of government regulation of business—where there is broad consensus among business people.[35] On labour's side, the ability of an association to claim to represent Canadian workers is weakened by the fact that less than four out of ten members of the labour force belong to a union. The Canadian Labour Congress is the largest of Canada's labour associations, with close to 100 affiliated unions that represent about 2 million workers. This is only about 15 per cent of the total labour force. Unions representing mainly Francophone workers have preferred to affiliate with the Confédération des syndicats nationaux.

The two other requirements for corporatism—tripartite decision-making structures bringing together the state, business, and labour and an ideology of social partnership between business and labour—are also absent from the Canadian scene. Indeed, Gerhard Lehmbruch, one of the leading students of corporatism, places Canada in the group of countries having the fewest characteristics of corporatism.[36] Canadian political scientist William Coleman agrees with this assessment, although he notes that corporatist policy-making networks are found in the agricultural sector of the Canadian economy.[37]

Some observers have claimed to detect elements of corporatism in various tripartite consensus-building efforts launched by governments in Canada and in the practice of labour and business organizations being invited to appoint representatives to various public boards and tribunals. Examples include the now defunct Economic Council of Canada, the sectoral task forces on industrial restructuring orchestrated by Ottawa between 1975–8, the Canadian Labour Market and Productivity Centre, various provincial bodies that bring together representatives of business and labour, and periodic 'economic summits' held by Ottawa and some provincial governments.[38] None of these produced any fundamental change in the process of economic policy-making. The obstacles to corporatism in Canada are enormous, including such factors as British parliamentary structures that cannot easily accommodate group representation, a political culture that is not favourable to the interventionist planning associated with corporatism, the decentralization of authority that exists in both the business and labour communities, and the division of economic powers between Ottawa and the provinces. Whether or not corporatist-style interest mediation is desirable or not is a different question.[39]

Neo-Institutionalism

Neo-institutionalism is a perspective on policy-making that emphasizes the impact of formal and informal structures and rules on political outcomes. '[T]he preferences and rules of policy actors', argue Coleman and Skogstad, 'are shaped fundamentally by their structural position. Institutions are conceived as structuring political reality and as defining the terms and nature of political discourse.'[40] What does this mean and how does it help us understand the behaviour and influence of interest groups?

First, what has been called neo-institutionalism or the new institutionalism is not so much a model of politics and policy-making as a theoretical premise shared by an otherwise diverse group of perspectives. The premise is, quite simply, that institutions—their structural characteristics, formal rules, and informal norms—play a central role in shaping the actions both of individuals and of the organizations to which they belong. This 'insight' is neither very new nor very surprising. The founders of modern sociology knew very well the importance of institutions in determining behaviour, a relationship that is most pithily expressed in Robert Michels's aphorism, 'He who says organization, says oligarchy.'[41] Moreover, few of us would blink at the rather bland assertion that 'where you stand depends on where you sit'. So where is the 'neo' in neo-institutionalism, and what special contribution can it make to understanding interest groups? Let us begin by examining the diverse roots of the neo-institutionalist approach.

Economics
Rational choice theory forms the bedrock of modern economics. Beginning in the 1950s and 1960s, economists began to apply systematically the concepts of individual (limited) rationality and market behaviour to the study of elections, political parties, interest groups, bureaucracy, and other political phenomena.[42] The economic theory of politics that has developed from this work emphasizes the role played by formal and informal rules in shaping individual choices and policy outcomes. Viewed from this perspective, 'institutions are bundles of rules that make collective action possible'.[43]

Organization Theory
Appropriately enough, organization theory has been an important source of inspiration and ideas for the neo-institutionalist approach. One of the first political scientists to apply the behavioural insights of organization theory to Canadian politics was Alan Cairns. His 1977 presidential address to the Canadian Political Science Association relied heavily on organization theory in arguing that Canadian federalism is influenced mainly by state actors, the 'needs' of the organizations to which they belong, and the constitutional rules within which they operate.[44] James March, Herbert Simon, and Johan Olsen are among the organization

theorists frequently cited by neo-institutionalists.[45] The spirit of the organizational perspective is captured in Charles Perrow's declaration that 'The formal structure of the organization is the single most important key to its functioning....'[46]

Society-Centred Analysis

The rising popularity of neo-institutional analysis can be attributed in part to a reaction against explanations of politics and policy-making that emphasize the role of such societal factors as interest groups, voters, and social classes. This reaction has produced an enormous outpouring of work on the autonomy of the state (i.e., the ability of state actors to act on their own preferences and to shape societal demands and interest configurations rather than simply responding to and mediating societal interests). Neo-institutionalism, which focuses on the structural characteristics of and relationships between political actors, has been inspired by this same reaction. This is not to say that neo-institutionalism is a state-centred explanation of politics. But in ascribing a key role to institutions—structures and rules—it inevitably takes seriously the structural characteristics of the state.

Neo-institutionalism deals intensively with what might be called the interior lives of interest groups: the factors responsible for their creation, maintenance, and capacity for concerted political action. James Q. Wilson identifies four categories of incentives that underlie the interior dynamics of interest groups.[47] They include:

- *material incentives* (tangible rewards that include money and other material benefits that clearly have a monetary value);
- *specific solidarity incentives* (intangible rewards such as honours, official deference, and recognition that are scarce, i.e., they have value precisely because some people are excluded from their enjoyment);
- *collective solidarity incentives* (intangible rewards created by the act of associating together in an organized group that are enjoyed by all members of the group, such as a collective sense of group esteem or affirmation);
- *purposive incentives* (Wilson describes these as being 'intangible rewards that derive from the sense of satisfaction of having contributed to the attainment of a worthwhile cause').

Economists have also attempted to explain what Mancur Olson first called the logic of collective action, including how the interior character of a group affects its capacity for political influence.

Neo-institutionalism tends to agnosticism when it comes to the old debate on whether societal or state forces are more important determinants of political outcomes. Such concepts as *policy communities*—the constellation of actors in a particular policy field—and *policy networks*[48]—the nature of the relationships between the key actors in a policy community—are the building blocks of the neo-institutional approach. Embedded in them is the irrefutable claim that 'the state' is in fact a fragmented structure when it comes to actual policy-making. So, too, is society. The interests that are active and influential on the issue of abortion, for example, are very different from those that are part of the official-language policy community. What Coleman and Skogstad describe as the 'diversity in arrangements between civil society and the state'[49] inspires agnosticism on the state versus society debate.

The observable reality is that the relative strength of state and societal actors and the characteristics of policy networks vary between policy communities in the same society.

A group's capacity for influence within a policy community will depend on both its internal characteristics and its external relationships to the larger political system and the state. Philippe Schmitter and Wolfgang Streeck call these the logics of membership and influence, respectively.[50] We have already mentioned some of the factors that may be relevant to understanding a group's interior life. On the logic of influence, Coleman and Skogstad argue that the key determinant of a group's influence is 'the structure of the state itself at the sectoral level',[51] i.e., within a particular policy community. Perhaps. But macropolitical factors like political culture, the dominant ideology, and the state system's more general characteristics are also important to understanding the political influence of organized interests. Policy communities are perhaps best viewed as solar systems that themselves are influenced by the gravitational tug of cultural and institutional forces emanating from the centre of the larger galaxy in which they move. In this way the diversity of state-society relations between policy communities can be reconciled with larger generalizations about the interest group system, such as Lindblom's claim that business interests occupy a privileged position within this system.

The Ingredients of Interest Group Success

There is no magic recipe for group influence. Successful strategies and appropriate targets will depend on the issue, the resources and actions of other groups, the state of public opinion, and characteristics of the political system. But although there is no single formula for influence, it is nevertheless possible to generalize about the factors associated with powerful interest groups. As we will see, these factors are more likely to characterize business groups and their dealings with government than any other set of societal interests.

Organization

It may seem a trite observation, but organized interests are usually more influential than unorganized ones and are always better equipped to apply sustained pressure on policy-makers. A mob of angry people outraged over an increase in the official (heavily subsidized) price of bread in Cairo may spontaneously gather and protest in the streets and in front of government buildings. This unorganized demonstration may prompt policy-makers to change their policy,[52] thus demonstrating influence without organization. But influence without organization is exceptional. 'To have a say', advises the *Financial Post*, 'you need a voice.'[53]

Paul Pross, Canada's foremost student of interest groups, points to the character of government and the policy-making process in explaining why organization is crucial. Modern government, he observes, is a sprawling, highly bureaucratized affair in which the power to influence policy is widely diffused. When government was smaller, the number of policies and programs affecting societal interests were fewer, and power was concentrated in the hands of a small group of senior bureaucratic officials and cabinet, groups did not require sophisticated organizational structures to manage their dealings with government. This was

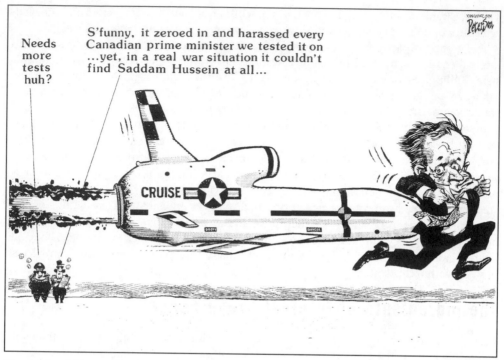

The public criticisms of interest groups can make life uncomfortable for governments and their leaders. (Roy Peterson, *Vancouver Sun*)

the era of the 'mandarins', the tightly knit group of deputy ministers who dominated the policy process.[54] Pathways to influence were relatively uncomplicated. A conversation with the minister or deputy minister in the restaurant of the Château Laurier or at the Five Lakes Fishing Club was the preferred method of communicating a group's views. Access at this rarefied level was, however, restricted largely to members of the corporate élite and those representing their interests.

This era began to pass into history during the 1960s. The more complex interventionist state that emerged was not as amenable to the informal, discrete style of influence that powerful economic interests had grown used to during the 1940s and 1950s. As the scope of state intervention widened and its regulation of economic and social matters deepened, it became increasingly imperative that groups have the ongoing capacity to monitor government and deal with it at those levels where power resided. Inevitably, a large intrusive state means that power is more widely diffused throughout the administrative apparatus of government, in the hands of officials who draw up regulatory guidelines, interpret and administer technical matters that are delegated to them under the authority of vaguely worded statutes, and provide advice on programs and policies that influences the options considered by those nominally in charge, i.e., the members of cabinet.

To deal with the reality of the modern administrative state, groups require organization. And organize they have. William Coleman shows that close to half of the associations representing business interests have been created since 1960.[55] A veritable explosion of associations representing environmental concerns, consumer interests, women, ethnic groups, official-language minorities, and other interests has taken place over the last few decades. Interest groups acquired prominence later in Canada than in the United States, and when they did it was largely due to a defensive reaction against a state that, like Kafka's castle, was fast becoming more impenetrable and mysterious—not to mention hostile from the standpoint of those in the business community.

The increasing size and complexity of the public sector spawned organized interests in another way as well. The active role of government in promoting the creation of associations that would in turn represent and articulate the interests of their members is well documented. It is a phenomenon that appears to have begun in World War One, when the federal Department of Trade and Commerce encouraged the creation of trade associations to represent corporations in the same industry.[56] During the 1960s and 1970s, the Department of Secretary of State was instrumental in the creation and proliferation of a large number of organizations representing women, ethnic groups, and official-language minorities, particularly through the provision of core funding to finance the activities of these groups.[57] In many cases it appears that the motivation of the state agencies that encouraged the creation of interest groups was at least partly self-serving. They were helping to organize the interests dependent on their programs and budgets and thereby created constituencies whose support could be useful to the bureaucracy in protecting its policy and budgetary turf.[58]

Sophisticated organization has become a *sine qua non* for sustained group influence. Paul Pross uses the term *institutional groups* to describe those interests that possess the highest level of organization. These groups have the following characteristics:

- they possess organizational continuity and cohesion;
- they have extensive knowledge of those sectors of government that affect their clients, and enjoy easy communications with those sectors;
- they have stable memberships;
- they have concrete and immediate objectives;
- the overall goals of the organization are more important than any particular objective.[59]

While many different types of groups can lay claim to having these characteristics, business associations certainly are more likely to conform to Pross's criterion for institutionalized groups than are those representing other interests. Indeed, associations such as the Business Council on National Issues, the Canadian Manufacturers' Association, the Canadian Chamber of Commerce, the Conseil du Patronat du Québec, the Business Council of British Columbia, and many of the major trade associations in Canada are among the organizationally most sophisticated of interest groups in this country (see Box 8.1).[60]

Resources

Lots of money is no guarantee of interest group success—but it usually doesn't hurt. The most sophisticated groups in terms of organization enjoy easy access to policy-makers and have the best track records of success in protecting and promoting the interests they represent, and these groups tend also to be well heeled. Money is necessary to pay for the services

---

Box 8.1 Portrait of a Lobbyist

The man who is among the most powerful lobbyists in Canada doesn't live in Ottawa, wear expensive suits, play golf at The Royal Ottawa, lunch with cabinet ministers or charge exorbitant fees for his services. Instead, Jacques Proulx [president* of the Union des Producteurs Agricoles du Québec] operates a farm with his cousin 50 kilometres east of Sherbrooke in Quebec's Eastern Townships. He doesn't even come to Ottawa very often, because the people he represents are back home in Quebec, and it is from there, from the towns and villages of rural Quebec, that the pressure comes to make federal politicians of whatever stripe tremble.

Quebec's dairy farmers, and their counterparts elsewhere in Canada, are to Canada what rice growers are to Japan and wheat farmers to the European Community: a tightly knit, well-funded, politically astute interest group capable of paralyzing any government contemplating an attack on their subsidies. The Quebec dairy farmers, in particular, have parlayed financial muscle, political savvy and nationalist sentiments into a force no Quebec politician can ignore.

Jeffrey Simpson, 'Milking the System', *Report on Business* Magazine, November 1990, 110.
*Mr Proulx left this position in 1995.

---

vital to interest group success. A permanent staff costs money—a good deal of money if it includes lawyers, economists, accountants, researchers, public relations specialists, and others whose services are needed to monitor the government scene and communicate with both the group's membership and policy-makers. The services of public relations firms, polling companies, and professional lobbyists are costly and certainly out of the reach of many interest groups.

It hardly requires demonstration that interest groups representing business tend to have more affluent and stable financial footings than other groups. Their closest rivals are major labour associations, some occupational groups such as physicians, dentists, lawyers, university professors, and teachers, and some agricultural producer groups (see Figure 8.1). The budgets of some non-economic groups may also appear to be considerable. For example, in 1994 Pollution Probe had a budget of over $1.6 million. The National Action Committee on the Status of Women had a budget of over $1.1 million for the same year. But there are three important differences between the monetary resources of the major business interest groups and those of other organized interests.

First, the members of business interest groups typically do not rely on their collective associations for political influence to the extent that the members of other interest groups do. Large corporations usually have their own public affairs departments, which, among other functions, manage their relations with government.[61] Moreover, corporations will often act on their own in employing the services of a professional lobbying firm or other service that is expected to help them influence policy-makers. Indeed, the clientele lists of such firms as Hill and Knowlton (formerly Public Affairs International), Government Consultants International, and Executive Consultants Ltd. read like a 'Who's Who' of the Canadian corporate élite (with many non-Canadian corporate clients in the bargain). Corporations are also major contributors to the Liberal and Progressive Conservative parties—business asso-

Figure 8.1 Annual Expenditures of Selected Associations, 1994

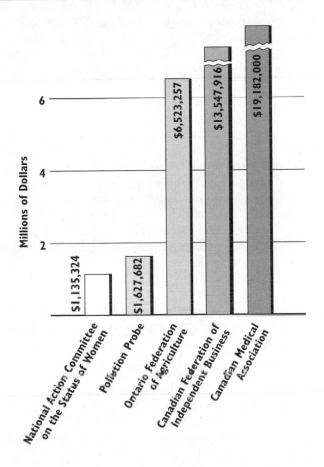

Sources: Annual audited financial statements.

ciations seldom donate at all—and annual contributions in the $50,000–$100,000 range are not unusual.[62] This is another channel of influence—purchasing access is a better way of describing it—that can be afforded by the individual members of business associations but seldom by the members of other types of interest groups.

The second important difference in the monetary resources of business and non-business associations relates to stability. Simply put, business groups rest on more secure financial footings. They are less subject to the vicissitudes of economic recession, and because they do not depend on government funding they are not exposed to the vagaries of cutbacks and budgetary shuffles. Many other groups cannot make this claim. For example, the recession of 1990–2 cut deeply into the revenues of environmental groups. 'We live and die on people in the street supporting wildlife conservation', said the president of the World

Wildlife Fund in 1992. 'If Canadians don't have discretionary income', he added, 'it shows [in our revenues].'[63] Several environmental groups laid off employees and axed projects as a result of a sharp dip in public contributions to them during 1991.[64] Women's groups face a somewhat different problem. Their dependence on government funding became a liability during years of fiscal restraint and under a Conservative government that probably was tired of being attacked by women's groups. Core funding for these groups was slashed in the late 1980s and continued to fall in the early nineties.

A third difference involves the ability of business and non-business groups to raise money to deal with a 'crisis' issue. Free trade and the federal election campaign of 1988 represent a case in point. Although no hard numbers exist, no one seriously denies that business associations in favour of the Canada–US Free Trade Agreement outspent their opponents by a wide margin in an attempt to influence public opinion on the deal and thereby ensure the election of the Conservatives, the only party that supported the FTA. Much of the pro-FTA money was spent through the Canadian Alliance for Trade and Job Opportunities, an *ad hoc* association financed by 112 Canadian-based corporations. Most of the major contributors to the Alliance were members of the élite Business Council on National Issues. The Alliance spent a good deal of money, probably at least a couple of million dollars, purchasing television and newspaper ads in the year before the election.[65] When a Conservative victory seemed in doubt, the Alliance financed a media blitz during the last three weeks of the 1988 campaign.

Money is not the only resource that is useful in promoting an interest group's objectives. John Kingdon identifies several other resources that enable a group to influence what gets on (or stays off) the policy agenda and the alternatives considered by policy-makers.[66]

Electoral Influence

The perceived ability to swing a significant bloc of votes is an important group resource. While all interest group leaders claim to speak on behalf of the group's membership, politicians know that the claim is more credible in some cases than in others. The sheer size of a group's membership can be an important resource, as can the status or wealth of its members and their geographic distribution. The distributional factor can cut in two ways. In political systems like Canada's, characterized by the election of a single-member from each constituency, the concentration of a group's members in a particular region will, other things being equal, increase the political influence of that group. Candidates and parties are likely to see the advantage of proposing policies that are attractive to such a regionally concentrated group, whose votes are crucial to win the seats in that region. On the other hand, geographic dispersion of a group's membership may also be advantageous, even under an electoral system like Canada's. A group's claim to speak on behalf of members who are found across the country, and who can be mobilized to vote in a particular way, can be an impressive electoral resource. It is, for example, an argument regularly used by the Canadian Federation of Independent Business, which has approximately 85,000 members across Canada.

Capacity to Inflict Damage on the Economy

The ability to 'down tools', close businesses, scale down investment plans, refuse to purchase government bonds, or in some other way inflict harm on the economy or public finances (or

both!) can be a powerful group resource. It is a resource that is possessed mainly by business groups. Unions and other occupational groups, such as physicians and agricultural producers, have a more difficult time using 'economic blackmail' to influence policy-makers. There are two reasons for this. First, when nurses, teachers, dockworkers, postal workers, truckers, or doctors attempt to tie up the economy or some important public service by withholding their labour, the linkage between the behaviour of such a group and the social or economic consequences of their actions is extremely visible. Regardless of the factors that led to their action, the general public is likely to perceive the situation as one where the *special* interest of such a group stands in sharp contrast to the *public* interest. A union or other occupational group that attempts to use the threat of economic or social chaos to back up its demands should not count on favourable public opinion. On the contrary, public support for or indifference toward a group's demands is likely to change to hostility in such circumstances. In the case of unions, they suffer from the additional disadvantage of being held in very low esteem by Canadians. Surveys regularly show that public confidence in labour unions is lower than for most other major social institutions (see Table 7.1).

A second reason why business interests are better able than other economic interest groups to use the threat of economic damage in pursuing their objectives has to do with culture. In a capitalist society like ours, the fundamental values that underpin the strength of business interests—the belief in private property, the importance of profits, and the market—lend legitimacy to the general interests of business. Particular industries or corporations may be perceived as being greedy or socially irresponsible, but the general values associated with a capitalist economy enjoy widespread support. When workers down tools to apply pressure in support of their demands there is a good chance that their action will be interpreted as being irresponsible. But if business 'downs tools' by refusing to invest in new plant and machinery, laying off workers, or relocating, the reactions of policy-makers and the public are likely to be quite different. After all, most of us accept that business is about making a profit. The damage that a failure of business confidence may do to an economy may be regrettable, but business people are less likely to be accused of being irresponsible because they are just acting in accordance with the rules of a system that most of us accept.

Group Cohesion

'United we stand, divided we fall' has always been a pretty sound rule of interest group influence. Other things being equal, an association's hand will be strengthened if it is able to convince policy-makers that it speaks with a single voice and genuinely represents the views of its membership. This is not always easy. We have already noted that both labour and business interests are highly fragmented in Canada, represented by a large number of associations, not one of which can credibly claim to speak on behalf of all labour or business interests. The same is true for many other collective interests in Canadian society. There are hundreds of organizations representing different groups of agricultural producers. Native Canadians are represented by many associations, the largest of which is the Assembly of First Nations. Its ability to speak on behalf of all Native groups is limited, however, by the fact that it does not speak for Métis and non-status Indians (who are represented by the Native Council of Canada) or for the Inuit (represented by the Inuit Tapirisat of Canada). Cohesion may appear to be greatest in the women's movement. The National Action Committee on the Status of Women is the umbrella association that represents about 600 smaller women's

organizations. The fact that it represents such a large number of smaller groups has not prevented the NAC from taking strong positions and making very specific recommendations for policy change, nor has NAC's credibility as the voice of the women's movement been seriously challenged by either governments or the media.

Group cohesion typically becomes less problematic as the number of members represented by an organization grows fewer and the similarity between members increases. But what is gained in cohesion may, of course, be lost as a result of the perception that an association represents a very narrow special interest. As well, it is easier to present a united front when an association is speaking on behalf of just one group. Alliances with associations representing other groups, however, may be politically useful. The downside is, again, the problem of submerging group differences in such a common front.

A rather different problem of cohesion involves the relationship between a group's leaders and its membership. Evidence of a gap between the goals of leaders and those they purport to represent will undermine an association's credibility in the eyes of policy-makers. A variation of this problem exists when an interest group claims to speak on behalf of a collectivity that is largely unorganized, or where there are good reasons for doubting that the group actually expresses the views of those they claim to represent. For example, women's groups like the NAC have sometimes been accused of not expressing the views of a large part of Canada's female population. Labour unions' claims to speak on behalf of Canadian workers are weakened, in the eyes of some, by the fact that they only represent about four out of ten workers.

The dynamics of group cohesion tend to favour certain types of interests more than others. As is also true of the other group resources we have examined, the winners are mainly business interest groups. To understand why this is the case, consider two widely accepted propositions about interest group cohesion.[67] First, as the number of members in an organization increases, the likelihood that some individuals will believe that they can reap the benefits of the organization's actions without having to contribute to it also increases. This is called the *free-rider* problem. Other things being equal, smaller groups are more cohesive than larger ones. Second, groups that are able to offer exclusive benefits to their members, i.e., benefits that are only available to members of the organization, will be more cohesive and more capable of concerted political pressure than those that rely on collective benefits, i.e., benefits that will accrue to society as a whole. A corollary of this second proposition is that organizations that rely on material incentives to attract and retain members, and that can motivate members with the prospect of shared material benefits, will be more cohesive than groups that rely on non-material incentives.[68]

If we turn now to the actual interest group system, we find that business groups tend to be smaller than other interest associations. Indeed, some are quite small, particularly those that represent companies in oligopolistic industries. For example, the Motor Vehicle Manufacturers' Association has only eight members, the Pharmaceutical Manufacturers' Association of Canada has only seventy members, and the Canadian Petroleum Association has fifty-four member companies. Some business associations, such as Chambers of Commerce, the Canadian Federation of Independent Business, and the Canadian Manufacturers' Association, have large memberships. But it is also true that these organizations represent more general interests of the business community, while the more specific

interests of corporations are represented through trade associations that have smaller memberships.

In regard to the incentives that groups use to attract, maintain, and motivate members, business groups are not the only ones to rely on exclusive benefits and material incentives. Labour unions, agricultural producer groups, and occupational associations do as well. But one needs to remember that cohesion is only one group resource. Farmers' groups or labour unions may be as cohesive as business associations but still inferior to business in terms of the other resources at their disposal.

Safety in the Shadows

Placard-waving animal rights activists, a blue-suited spokesperson for some organization presenting a brief to a parliamentary committee, or a full-page newspaper ad promoting a particular policy are all highly visible manifestations of interest groups in action. They are not, however, necessarily the most effective pathways of group influence. Often, what does not happen—the absence of visible signs of groups exerting themselves to influence policy—tells us most about the strength of organized interests. In the jungle that is the interest group system, there is often safety in the shadows.

The fact that the status, privileges, or interests of some group are not matters of public debate tells us something about the power of this group. As E.E. Schattschneider writes, 'The very expression "pressure politics" invites us to misconceive the role of special-interest groups in politics.'[69] 'Private conflicts', he argues, 'are taken into the public arena precisely because someone wants to make certain that the power ratio among the private interests most immediately involved shall not prevail.'[70] The point is obvious and yet profoundly important. Society's most powerful interests would prefer to avoid the public arena, where they have to justify themselves and respond to those who advocate changes that would affect their interests. They are safe in the shadows. But when the light of public debate is shone on them, they become prey to attacks from other groups and they lose their security. Conflict, Schattschneider notes, always includes an element of unpredictability. Consequently, even private interests with impressive group resources may suffer losses in their status and privileges, depending on what alliances form against them, the shape of public opinion, and the behaviour of political parties. Indeed, when previously unquestioned interests have reached the public agenda and are recognized as group interests, this indicates a loss of influence on the part of such a group.

When the security of the shadows is lost, the relative safety of a fairly closed policy community is a decent substitute. In the United States, the concept of an *iron triangle* has been used to describe the closed system of relations between an interest group and the administrative agencies and congressional committee with which it routinely deals. Most commentators agree that the 'iron triangles' that may have characterized policy-making in the United States have become less rigid over the last few decades. Moreover, because these triangular relationships were largely facilitated by the fragmented system of public authority in American politics, the 'iron triangle' concept never travelled very well beyond the United States. The terms sub-governments, policy communities, and policy networks are now more commonly used in both the United States and elsewhere to describe the reality of relatively exclusive constellations of state and societal actors who dominate routine policy-making in a particular field. Indeed, the ability to maintain the routine nature of policy-making is vital to preserving the privileged status of the dominant actors in a policy community.[71]

Federalism's Impact on Interest Groups

Hardly a corner of Canadian political life is not somehow affected by federalism, the interest group system included. Because the constitution divides political authority between two levels of government, one of the first challenges facing an interest group is to determine where jurisdiction lies or, as is often the case, how it is divided between the national and provincial governments. An extensive literature has developed on federalism and interest groups in Canada.[72] We will examine three of the more general propositions that emerge from this work.

The first has been labelled the *multiple crack hypothesis*.[73] According to this interpretation, the existence of two levels of government, each of which is equipped with a range of taxing, spending, and regulatory powers, provides interest groups with an opportunity to seek from one government what they cannot get from the other. Business groups have been the ones most likely to exploit the constitutional division of powers, and there are many well-documented cases where they have done so successfully.[74]

A second interpretation of federalism's impact on interest groups argues that a federal constitution tends to weaken group influence by reducing the internal cohesion of organized interests. According to this argument, divided authority to make policy on matters that affect a group's interests will encourage it to adopt a federal form of organization.[75] Although this may seem a politically prudent response to the realities of divided legislative authority, it may reduce the ability of groups to speak with a single voice and to persuade governments that they have the capacity for collective action to back up their demands. A group's influence may be weakened even further when the two levels of government are in serious conflict, a situation that may spill over to create division within the group itself (for example, on regional lines) and between its representative associations.[76]

A third proposition about federalism and interest groups involves what might be called the statist interpretation of federalism's impact. According to this view, governments and their sprawling bureaucracies increasingly dominate the policy-making scene, particularly when jurisdictional issues are involved. Societal groups, even those with considerable resources, may be largely frozen out of the process of intergovernmental relations. Alan Cairns implies as much in arguing that modern Canadian federalism is mainly about conflicts between governments and their competing political and organizational goals.[77] Leslie Pal draws similar conclusions—although he is careful not to overgeneralize his findings— from his study of the historical development of Canada's unemployment insurance program. Pal finds that the impact of societal groups on the original form of UI and on subsequent changes to the program was minor compared to the role played by bureaucratic and intergovernmental factors.[78] Unlike the 'federalism as opportunity' view, this interpretation sees federalism—at least the modern federalism of large, bureaucratic state structures at both the national and regional levels—as a constraint on the influence of business and other societal interests.

The 'federalism as opportunity' and 'federalism as constraint' views are best thought of as representing the two ends of a continuum along which actual cases fall. Examples can be found to support either of these interpretations. Between them are other instances (probably the majority) where the federal division of powers and the intergovernmental rivalry that it sets up provide opportunities for interest groups (the 'multiple cracks' referred to earlier) but also place limits on their influence. Opportunity or constraint, federalism does have some influence on the way in which interests organize for political action, the strategies they adopt when trying to influence policy, and the likelihood of their success.

Strategies for Influence

There are three basic strategies open to interest groups. One is to target policy-makers directly, through personal meetings with officials, briefs, and exchanges of information. This is the *lobbying option*. Another strategy is to target public opinion in the expectation that policy-makers will respond to indications that there is considerable popular support for a group's position. The media play a crucial role here because they are the channel by which a group's message will be communicated to the wider public. A variation of the *public opinion option* involves alliance-building. By building visible bridges with other groups on some issue, a group may hope to persuade policy-makers that its position has broad support. A third strategy involves *judicial action*. This is by its very nature a confrontational strategy because it involves a very public challenge and an outcome that is likely to leave one side a winner and the other a loser. For some groups it tends to be an option of last resort, used after other strategies have failed. But for other groups, such as the Women's Legal Education and Action Fund (LEAF) and the Canadian Civil Liberties Association, litigation is a basic weapon in their arsenal of pressure tactics.

These strategies are not mutually exclusive. A group may use more than one of them at once, or switch from one strategy to another. Nor can one draw firm conclusions about the relative effectiveness of different influence strategies. Much depends on the nature of the issue and the character of the policy community within which a group's actions reverberate. Despite the contingent quality of group influence, a few generalizations are possible. They include the following:

- Everyone recognizes that one of the keys to influence is being involved early in the policy-making process, when ideas are just being considered and legislation has not yet been drafted. Lobbying is the generally preferred strategy at this stage of the policy process. Confrontation and visibility are relatively low, and the importance of thorough preparation and credible technical information is high.
- Groups that are well-established members of a policy community, routinely consulted by government officials, will tend to prefer a lobbying strategy. More public and confrontational strategies involve the risk of bringing unpredictable elements into the policy-making process and will be used only as measures of last resort.
- Groups that are not well established within a policy community are more likely to rely on confrontation, media campaigns, and other public strategies to get policy-makers to pay attention and respond to the interests they represent.

- Where a group's interests are significantly affected by regulation, lobbying strategies that rely on research and technical information supplied to the bureaucratic officials doing the regulating will be most successful.
- The era of vested interests relying on lobbying strategies has passed. Lobbying remains a very important influence strategy, but even groups enjoying regular high-level access to policy-makers now often find that lobbying is not enough.
- A successful influence strategy is usually quite expensive. This is true whether one is talking about lobbying (which often involves hiring a professional government relations firm), aiming at public opinion (which may involve the use of paid advertisements and the services of public relations and polling experts), or going to court. Business groups tend to be better able to pay for these expensive strategies than other groups.

Just what is the price of influence? The business-financed National Citizens' Coalition paid the bills for a community college teacher's legal challenge to the practice of requiring all workers at unionized establishments to pay union dues even if they choose not to belong to the union. By time the Supreme Court of Canada handed down its decision, the NCC had paid in the ballpark of $1 million in legal bills. This price tag is not unusual for a case that reaches Canada's highest court. Expenses like these are obviously beyond the means of many groups.

A campaign directed at influencing public opinion can also be costly. We have already mentioned the multimillion-dollar campaign waged by the pro-FTA Canadian Alliance for Trade and Job Opportunities—probably over $2 million spent even before the final blitz during the 1988 federal election campaign. But business groups are not the only ones to spend lavishly in an effort to shape public opinion. Quebec's Cree Indians spent an estimated $500,000 on paid advertisements and the services of a New York public relations firm in an effort to stop the construction of the Great Whale hydroelectric project in Quebec. The public opinion they were targeting was in New York, the people who would be the consumers of power generated by Great Whale and exported to the United States.

The purchase of newspaper/magazine space or broadcast time to convey a political message is called *advocacy advertising*.[79] As the Great Whale case shows, business interest groups are not the only ones to buy advertising in an effort to influence public opinion on some issue. During the 1988 federal election campaign, for example, labour unions, nationalist coalitions like the Council of Canadians, and some agricultural groups were among those who used paid advertising to get their message across to voters. But among societal groups, business uses advocacy advertising most extensively. The crucial question raised by any form of advertising that carries a political message is whether the ability to pay for media time/space should determine what views get expressed. The critics of advocacy advertising were quick to denounce the blitz of pro-free trade advertising by business during the 1988 election campaign. They argued that the deep pockets of the corporate interests ranged behind free trade made a sham of the democratic political process and totally undermined the intention of the statutory limits on election spending by political parties. The Royal Commission on Elections agreed. Its 1992 report recommended that spending by organizations other than registered political parties be limited during elections (something that Parliament tried to accomplish through a law passed a decade earlier, but which the courts struck down as unconstitutional).

The defenders of advocacy advertising claim that it is a way for business to overcome the anti-business bias of the media and to bridge the 'credibility gap' that has developed between business and the public. Mobil Oil, one of the pioneers of this advertising technique, has called it a 'new form of public disclosure',[80] thereby associating it with freedom of information. Business and economic issues are complex, and advocacy advertising—most of which is done through the print media—provides an opportunity for business to explain its actions and to counter public misconceptions. And in any case, argue corporate spokespersons, the biggest spender on advocacy advertising is government, whose justification for this spending is essentially the same as that of business![81]

There is no doubt that strategies aimed at influencing public opinion have become increasingly important to interest groups. In fact, in discussing advocacy advertising we have only scratched the surface of these strategies.[82] Important as they are, however, strategies that target public opinion usually take a back seat to those that target policy-makers directly. These are lobbying strategies.

Lobbying may be defined as any form of direct or indirect communication with government that is designed to influence public policy. Although the term conjures up images of smoke-filled rooms, 'old boy networks', and sleazy deal-making, this is a somewhat unfair caricature of lobbying on two counts. First, lobbying is a basic democratic right. When a group of citizens organizes to demand a traffic light at a dangerous neighbourhood corner and meets with their local city councillor to express their concerns, this is lobbying. When the president of a powerful business association arranges a lunch rendezvous with an official in the Prime Minister's Office with whom he went to law school, this, too, is lobbying. The fact that lobbying is often associated in the minds of the public and journalists with unfair privilege and even corruption should not obscure the fact that it is not limited to organizations representing the powerful and, second, that in principle there is nothing undemocratic about lobbying.

Box 8.2 What Does a Government Relations Firm Sell?

Our Experience is Your Advantage

Our team of government relations specialists understands the political culture of Canada at every level, from the boardrooms of cabinet ministers to the offices of the public service. And all our services are available in both of Canada's official languages.

We can help you see legislation passed; win regulatory approval; sell a product or service to government; or simply stay abreast of government policies as they affect your interests. Hill & Knowlton will design and implement government relations strategies to meet your goals and your timetable.

The world of government is changing. And the effectiveness of your government relations depends on achieving a unique combination of seasoned experience with fresh, creative strategic thinking.

That's our Hill and Knowlton tradition—and your Hill and Knowlton advantage.

From a company brochure for the government relations division of Hill and Knowlton Canada, 1992

Box 8.3 What Do the Clients of a Government Relations Firm Buy?

Allan R. Gregg, Chairman

Well known in Canadian political and academic circles, Mr. Gregg founded Decima Research in 1979 and built it into the largest full-service public affairs research company in Canada. He has served in senior roles with the Progressive Conservative Party of Canada, and is the author of many published works. His latest book is entitled "The Big Picture: What Canadians Think About Almost Everything."

David MacNaughton, President

Mr. MacNaughton is one of the key public affairs consultants in North America. His extensive experience advising leading national and international businesses, combined with a keen awareness of how governments will have to tackle key issues in the future, makes him well suited to design and guide strategic partnerships between government and industry. He served as chairman of the Hon. Donald Johnston's federal Liberal leadership campaign (1984) and was Co-Chair of David Peterson's 1987 Ontario election campaign.

Peter Burn, Senior Consultant

Mr. Burn specializes in international trade and taxation matters. Mr. Burn has served on the staffs of two Canadian finance ministers and as a policy advisor to Prime Minister Brian Mulroney prior to the 1984 election. He has also advised the government on Canada/U.S. trade, financial services reform, and the privatizations of several crown corporations.

Gerald Caplan, Senior Associate

Mr. Caplan is a long-time New Democratic Party strategy and policy advisor. He has Co-Chaired the Federal Government Task Force on Broadcasting Policy and acted as Federal Secretary of the national NDP. Mr. Caplan has taught at a number of universities, is a political columnist and media commentator. He holds a Ph.D. from the University of London.

Brian L. Mersereau, Senior Vice President

Mr. Mersereau specializes in government procurement and industrial development. He brings to the company more than 15 years of direct experience with the Department of Supply and Services and is considered one of Canada's leading procurement professionals. He has been with the company since 1983 and has provided active counsel to many firms whose initiatives require some form of public sector participation.

Company brochure for Hill and Knowlton Canada, 1992

A second way in which the 'sleaze' caricature of lobbying conveys a wrong impression is by associating it with practices that, in fact, constitute only a small part of what lobbyists actually do. Direct meetings with influential public officials are certainly an aspect of lobbying. Likewise, there is no shortage of evidence that ethically dubious and sometimes downright illegal relations occasionally exist between lobbyists and policy-makers. But lobbying involves a much wider set of activities than simply buttonholing cabinet ministers or their senior officials.[83] Most professional lobbyists, whether they work for a company or interest group, or for a government relations firm that sells its lobbying expertise to clients, spend the better part of their time collecting and communicating information on behalf of the interests they represent. They monitor the political scene as it affects their client's interests. An effective lobbyist does not simply react but is like an early warning system, providing information about policy when it is still in its formative stages and tracking public opinion on the issues that are vital to a client's interests. Lobbyists provide information about how and where to access the policy-making system and strategies for influencing policies or winning contracts. They may also provide advice and professional assistance in putting together briefs, press releases, speeches and other communications, as well as public relations services such as identifying and targeting those segments of public opinion that influence policy-makers on some issue. Helping to build strategic coalitions with other groups is another function that lobbyists may perform.

Most interest groups lobby government on their own. But for those who can afford it, the services of a professional lobbying firm may also be purchased. The 1995 Ottawa telephone directory lists sixty-three firms under the 'Government relations' heading of the Yellow Pages. They range from large firms like Hill and Knowlton Canada, which employ dozens of staff and have annual billings in the tens of millions of dollars, to small one-person operations. In addition, several law firms also do lobbying work. Strategico Inc., one of the 'big boys' of the Canadian lobbying establishment, was in fact created as a result of the enormous growth in the government relations work of the law firm Lang Michener Lash & Johnson. At the end of the 1994–5 fiscal year there were 7,006 active Tier I lobbyists registered under Canada's Lobbyists Registration Act and 1,744 Tier II lobbyists.[84] Tier I lobbyists are those who, for a fee, hire themselves out to various clients. About three-quarters of their clients are corporations. Tier II lobbyists are those who work for a single association or company, and who lobby only on behalf of their employer. Most of these lobbyists work for corporate clients: business associations and individual corporations. In fact, as Box 8.4 suggests, the clientele lists of Canada's leading government relations firms read like a 'Who's Who' of the Canadian corporate world (with a strong leavening of international clients as well).

Box 8.4 Who Do Government Relations Firms Represent?

Lobbyist	Company	Clients
Gil Barrows	Hill and Knowlton Canada	H.J. Heinz Company Procter & Gamble Hoffman-LaRoche Canada
Brian Mersereau	Hill and Knowlton Canada	British Aerospace Stelco Babcock & Wilcox Inco
William Fox	The Earnscliffe Strategy Group	CP Rail Fletcher Challenge Bristol Myers Squibb Pharmaceutical Group

Box 8.4 Who Do Government Relations Firms Represent? (cont.)

Lobbyist	Company	Clients
		John Labatt
		Canadian Airlines International
		Canadian Pulp and Paper Association
Richard Bertrand	Executive Consultants Limited	Hershey Canada
		Newfoundland Offshore Development Constructors
		Canadian Petroleum Association
		Motor Vehicle Manufacturers' Association
		Canadian Construction Association
		Canadian Trucking Association

Consumer and Corporate Affairs, Canada, Lobbyists Registration Branch, *Report*, Tier I Lobbyists, as of 18 January 1994.

The media do not merely report political news, they are influential players in shaping the public agenda. (Greg Vickers)

Media impact on modern political life is profound. In this chapter the following aspects of media influence on politics are examined.

- ❖ Shaping the political agenda.
- ❖ What do the media produce?
- ❖ What determines the mass media product?
- ❖ The economic filter.
- ❖ The legal/regulatory filter.
- ❖ The technological filter.
- ❖ The organizational filter.
- ❖ The ideological filter.
- ❖ The media and democracy.

CHAPTER NINE

■ The Media

Before the dust had settled after the 1988 national election, indeed even before the returns were in, serious questions were being asked about what the two-month campaign indicated about Canadian democracy. These questions involved the role of the media in Canadian politics. What the critics found particularly disturbing were the blitz of pro-free trade publicity paid for by Canadian business during the last few weeks before voting day and, second, the media preoccupation with reporting and interpreting the results of dozens of polls taken by various organizations throughout the campaign. The millions of dollars spent by business to assuage Canadians' fears about a free trade agreement with the United States seemed to demonstrate the old saw that 'Elections are free, for those who can pay for them.' Money bought superior media access for certain points of view and, according to some observers, helped 'buy' a Conservative victory. Poll-mongering by journalists raised a rather different issue: to what extent was the media's fixation on the latest poll result a factor affecting voter behaviour? Are some voters influenced by polls predicting that their favoured party is heading for defeat? Do the parties attempt to manipulate voters through their release of poll results to the media?

These questions are not new. Media reporting of public opinion polls has been an issue for as long as the practice has existed. Indeed, the 'father' of the industry, George Gallup, wrote a lengthy defence of polls and their public uses back in 1940.[1] In jurisdictions as diverse as British Columbia and France the publication or broadcasting of poll results is regulated during the latter portions of election campaigns. The ability of moneyed interests to buy media exposure for their points of view is an even older issue, going back to the emergence of the first mass circulation newspapers in the late nineteenth century. Like the media's use—or abuse—of polls, this issue raises the question of whether democracy is promoted or impaired by media behaviour.

All of this assumes that the media can influence politics. Obviously they do. But how much does this matter? When? How is their influence felt? And finally, what is the relationship between media activities and power in society? These are basic questions that must be addressed in any attempt to understand the media's role in politics. We begin by examining these general issues, after which we will consider some particularly (though not uniquely) Canadian controversies.

'The Pictures in Our Heads'

The media are purveyors of images and information. As such, they play a role in social learning, i.e., the process of acquiring knowledge, values, and beliefs about the world and ourselves. This is a role the media share with other agents of social learning: the family, schools, peer groups, and organizations that one belongs to. Studies of social learning, including those that focus on the acquisition of politically relevant attitudes and personality characteristics, have long concluded that the family is the most important agent of social learning. It has a crucial influence on the development of an individual's sense of self-esteem, trust, and disposition toward authority, all of which have been linked to political attitudes and behaviour. As well, the family typically has a major impact on one's acquisition of communication skills, class identification, and social attitudes (e.g., gender roles). Although none of this learning is about politics *per se*, it has important consequences for politics.

While the family and other agents of social learning all contribute to what Walter Lippmann called 'the pictures in our heads', none of them rivals the media in its impact on the political agenda. Lippmann wrote, 'The only feeling that anyone can have about an event that he does not experience is the feeling aroused by his mental image of that event.'[2] The contours of modern political discourse are largely determined by the mass media as they process and report on 'reality'. Moreover, when it comes to matters that are remote from one's personal experience and daily life—political turmoil in the countries of the former Soviet Union, global pollution, conflict in the Middle East, or the latest Canadian federal budget—the media provide the only source of images and information about the events, issues, and personalities involved. Politicians and generals realize the media's importance, which is why one of the first steps taken in any serious *coup d'état* is to seize control of broadcasting and either shut down or muzzle any newspapers not sympathetic to the new regime.

It has often been remarked that the media do not determine *what we think* so much as *what we think about*. This is, of course, a formidable power. It is the power to shape the public consciousness by conveying certain images and interpretations and excluding others. The responsibility that accompanies such power is enormous. A 'free press' has been viewed as a necessary ingredient of democratic politics since the American Revolution. The reasoning behind this view is that all other groups and individuals—political parties, candidates for public office, corporations, labour unions, government officials, and so on—are self-interested. They cannot be counted on to give an objective assessment of their goals and actions. Too often their interests will be best served through concealment, deception, and manipulation—by *propaganda*. Only the media, so the argument goes, have an interest in presenting the facts. They may perform this function imperfectly, and particular media organs may have political biases that reflect the views of their owners, the values of their editors, producers, and journalists, or the prejudices of their readership/viewership (would one expect the Christian Broadcasting Network to give positive coverage to pro-choice abortion groups, or equal time to atheists?). But competition ensures that all significant points of view reach the public.

Is this an accurate picture of the media's role in political democracies? How well do the media cover all 'significant' points of view? Who determines the facts, or are they self-evident? Regardless of what the intentions of those in the media might be, what are the actual consequences of their behaviour for politics? Let us start by considering the 'products' of the mass media.

What Do the Media Produce?

Only a small portion of television and radio time is devoted to public affairs. Most programming, including during the prime-time periods when people are most likely to be watching or listening, aims to entertain rather than inform. Despite the existence of a hardcore minority who tune in mainly or exclusively for news and public affairs, television and radio are essentially entertainment media. According to a survey carried out for the Task Force on Broadcasting Policy, roughly 60 per cent of viewing time among Anglophone and Francophone Canadians is spent watching drama, comedy, and other entertainment programming. As Figure 9.1 shows, the vast majority of this viewing time in English Canada is

Figure 9.1 Percentage of Television Viewing Time Spent Watching Canadian Content Programs, Anglophones and Francophones, 1993

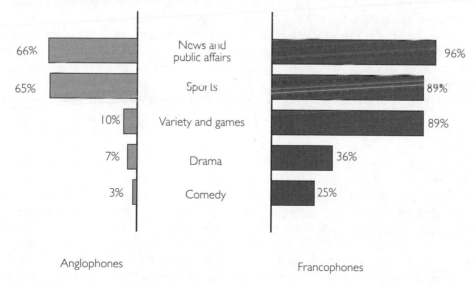

	Anglophones		Francophones
News and public affairs	66%		96%
Sports	65%		89%
Variety and games	10%		89%
Drama	7%		36%
Comedy	3%		25%

Anglophones   Francophones

Source: Statistics Canada, Cat. 87-208.

devoted to foreign programs. In fact, nearly two-thirds of all television watched by Canadians in 1991 was foreign, mostly American.[3]

The pattern is similar for radio. Private broadcasters account for about 90 per cent of the market, and most of what they offer is music. Although the Canadian Radio-television and Telecommunications Commission (CRTC), the industry's regulatory watchdog, requires all radio stations to carry news, only the largest privately owned stations generate any significant amount of news themselves. Most rely on information supplied by wire services, newspapers, and local sports and weather to meet their news quota.[4] Only stations affiliated with the state-owned Canadian Broadcasting Corporation and the odd campus station broadcast a significant amount of public affairs programming.

Like most radio stations—the CBC is the main exception—newspapers are geared primarily to the local market. Although all dailies carry national and international news, much of their space is devoted to community affairs. A survey carried out for the Royal Commission on Newspapers found that newspapers were considered to be better than either radio or television for information about 'what happens in your area' (59 per cent selected newspapers) and for 'things you're personally interested in' (49 per cent chose newspapers).[5] When asked which medium was most essential to the community, twice as many people mentioned newspapers as mentioned either radio or television.[6] Television, on the other hand, was considered to be the best source of information for international, national, and even provincial news. It was also judged to be most up-to-date, fair and unbiased, believable, influential, and essential to the country.[7]

Newspapers are relied on by most readers chiefly as a source of local information. Only the Toronto-based *Globe and Mail* does not conform to this community model. Of all Canadian dailies, it is the only one that has a significant national circulation. Although the mix of news, entertainment, sports, classified advertising, and commercial advertising is not much different from that in other large dailies, the emphasis on national and international news is greater in the *Globe and Mail*. Its daily 'Report on Business' section is another feature that distinguishes it from community-oriented papers and places it in competition with national business papers like the *Financial Post* and the *Financial Times*. Finally, the *Globe's* reputation as Canada's 'national' newspaper—English Canada's, at least—a reputation that has been acquired in part because of high-calibre journalism, has enabled it to continue attracting some of Canada's foremost journalists. Its political columnists and editorial writers are major players in defining the country's political agenda. Montreal-based *Le Devoir* plays a similar role in Quebec.

Generalization is more difficult in the case of magazines. The best-selling ones include scandal sheets like the *National Enquirer*, current affairs weeklies like *Newsweek*, *Time*, and *Maclean's*, *National Geographic*, *Reader's Digest*, *TV Guide*, and magazines like *Ladies' Home Journal* and *Chatelaine* that are directed mainly at a female readership. All of these sell hundreds of thousands of copies monthly, and in some cases weekly. In fact, a mere handful of magazines representing a limited number of genres account for the majority of total magazine sales in Canada.[8] Most of them are not oriented toward coverage of politics and public affairs, unless one considers matters like the O.J. Simpson saga or Elvis-sightings to fall into these categories. Those that focus on 'hard news' occupy the conventional middle ground of Canadian and American politics—*Time* and *Newsweek* are American magazines—as reflected in their pretensions to be non-ideological and politically independent. As we explained in

Chapter 2, the conventional wisdom in politics is commonly described as being 'pragmatic' or 'non-ideological'. We will examine the reasons for their orthodoxy later in this chapter.

Compared to the media we have discussed so far, film may appear relatively insignificant. The average Canadian goes to the cinema only about four times per year (more often among those who live in major cities), but some of the time he or she spends in front of the television is spent watching films. Cable television, pay-TV, and the video-cassette recorder have all increased the market penetration of films, freeing the film industry from the movie theatre and bringing its product directly into the home of the consumer. In a sense, this new technology has produced a new 'golden age' for the film industry, enabling it to recapture some of the prominence it held between the 1930s and the 1950s, before the television set became a standard feature of most households.

Film is at the centre of the modern imagination. If a person has not read the book, he or she probably has seen its film adaptation. Indeed, recent years have seen the emergence of the ultimate tribute to the power of the visual medium, the book based on the motion picture. Blockbusters like the *Star Wars* trilogy, the adventures of *Indiana Jones*, *Rambo*, *Batman*, *Robin Hood: Prince of Thieves*, the *Godfather* films, and *Beverly Hills Cop* are familiar to most of us. The stories they tell, the characters they contain, and the stereotypes they convey both shape and reflect our popular culture. At the extreme, life imitates art, as when gangs of British youths copied the random violence seen in Stanley Kubrick's adaptation of *A Clockwork Orange*, or when former US President Ronald Reagan borrowed from *Star Wars* to label the Soviet Union the 'evil empire' and to call for a 'star wars' defence system (formally referred to as the Strategic Defence Initiative). The archetypes and icons of popular culture are more likely to be associated with movies than with any other mass medium.

What does the film industry offer the viewing public? With hundreds of new releases every year from the studios of Hollywood and elsewhere, one might assume that the industry produces a richly varied product. It does. But only a narrow band of the entire range of film production is made easily available to movie viewers. This band represents the commercial feature film. The genre may vary, but what distinguishes such a film is the fact that it must appeal to a large mass audience to recoup the millions of dollars—often running to the tens and even hundreds of millions of dollars (*Waterworld* reputedly cost about US $260 million to make)—spent on its production and marketing. Documentary and artistic films generally cost much less to make, but also earn smaller profits. They usually are made by small independent film companies or by state-owned filmmakers, such as Canada's National Film Board. Little is spent on marketing them and public access to non-commercial films is limited because distributors do not want to show them and most video rental stores do not want to stock them (or at least not too many of them).

The images and stories purveyed by the commercial film industry are often disturbing and occasionally critical of 'the system'. Indeed, one of the most popular motifs of popular film has long been the lone good man versus the bad system. The careers of Clint Eastwood, Sylvester Stallone, Harrison Ford, and Charles Bronson have been built around this simple theme. *It's a Wonderful Life* is a classic example, as are the archetypal westerns *Shane* and *High Noon*. More recent examples include *To Kill a Mockingbird*, *Places in the Heart*, *Silkwood*, and *Grand Canyon*. But on balance, commercial film does much more to reinforce dominant values and institutions than it does to challenge them. The economics of the industry make this inevitable, as we will explain later in this chapter.

Advertisements are another important part of the media product. It has been estimated that Canadians are exposed to an average of over 1,500 advertisements per day.[9] Television and radio are heavily laced with them. Newspapers and magazines are fairly bursting with them. Even films have become vehicles for advertising, with companies willing to pay thousands of dollars for fleeting glimpses of their product in a favourable context. Billboards, storefront signs, pamphlets, flyers ... there is no escape. Close to US $100 billion was spent on mass media advertising in North America in 1991, and about three times that amount world-wide.[10] The advertising assault is so massive and unremitting that the vast majority of it fails to pierce our consciousness. Advertisers have long been aware of this and search continually for ways to capture the attention of the viewers, listeners, or readers to whom they want to sell something. Whether we pay attention or tune out, advertising constitutes a continuous 'buzz' in the background of our daily lives.

In the case of most advertising, the intended message is 'buy this.' We say 'most' because some advertising aims to persuade people to vote or think in particular ways, or simply provides them with useful information (much public service advertising by governments would fall into this last category). The vast majority of advertising, however, aims to affect our behaviour as consumers.

But there is much more to commercial advertising than the intended message, 'buy product x.' We are urged to buy, period. The high-consumption economy is sustained by the frenetic materialism that pervades our culture. This materialism, in turn, is reinforced by the mass media through advertising and entertainment programming. When the message 'buy this' is hurled at us hundreds of times a day from our tender youth, the cumulative impact is to instil and sustain a high-consumption mindset.

This is only one of the incidental messages communicated through commercial advertising. Gender stereotyping and the use of sexual imagery and innuendo are rampant. The youthful, the slender, the muscular, the large-breasted, the extroverted, and the materially successful are far more likely to appear in television, magazine, and billboard ads than are those who appear to be deficient in these qualities. Who and what are excluded from visual advertising—and the same holds true for all visual media—are as important as who and what are included. The silences and blindspots of advertising and of all mass media include the poor, visible minorities, men and women who do not conform to fairly traditional stereotypes (female executives in ads still tend to show a good deal of leg and to be 'sexy'; males in the kitchen or pushing a stroller tend to be portrayed in a humorous or ironic light), the physically unattractive, and the socially non-conforming. There are, of course, exceptions. But in general, advertisers find it more profitable to appeal to conventional beliefs and prejudices and to very basic emotional needs and insecurities (see Box 9.1).

What Determines the Mass Media Product?

The facts of modern life do not spontaneously take a shape in which they can be known. They must be given a shape by somebody.[11]

No one except the naive and those with a professional interest in self-deception believes that the mass media simply mirror reality. Confronted with more information than can possibly

Box 9.1 The Arts of Selling

The principles underlying this [commercial advertising] are extremely simple. Find some common desire, some widespread unconscious fear or anxiety; think out some way to relate this wish or fear to the product you have to sell; then build a bridge of verbal or pictorial symbols over which your customer can pass from fact to compensatory dream, and from the dream to the illusion that your product, when purchased, will make the dream come true. 'We no longer buy oranges, we buy vitality. We do not buy just an auto, we buy prestige.' And so with all the rest. In toothpaste, for example, we buy, not a mere cleanser and antiseptic, but release from the fear of being sexually repulsive....In every case the motivation analyst has found some deepseated wish or fear, whose energy can be used to move the consumer to part with cash and so, indirectly, to turn the wheels of industry. Stored in the minds and bodies of countless individuals, this potential energy is released by, and transmitted along, a line of symbols carefully laid out so as to bypass rationality and obscure the real issue.

Aldous Huxley, *Brave New World Revisited* (New York: Harper Brothers, 1958), 63–4.

be conveyed to their readerships/audiences, those who produce the media product must choose what stories, images, and 'facts' to communicate. What ultimately is offered to the media consumer is a selective pastiche, an abridged and inevitably somewhat distorted version of a 'reality' that is constructed in the process of being communicated.

The choices made by reporters, editors, producers, and others who contribute to the media product are not random. Several factors influence how reality is processed and how news is reported by the media. These factors may be understood as a series of filters that are more likely to let through certain information and images than others. To oversimplify a great deal, information and images that threaten the privileges of dominant social and economic groups are less likely to make it through these media filters than those that are fairly orthodox and non-menacing. This will strike many readers as being an absurd claim, conditioned as most of us are to believe that the media are independent and frequently critical of the powerful. On balance, however, the media do much more to support the status quo, including the distribution of power in society and the economy, than they do to erode it. In other words, their role in politics is essentially conservative.

The Economic Filter

Most media organs are privately owned, and as such they are subject to the iron law of the marketplace. That law is very simple: they must be able to sell a product that will attract enough subscribers, advertisers, buyers, or patrons—the exact source of revenue depends on the media product—to cover production costs and, usually, earn a competitive return on invested capital. Given the high costs involved in producing a daily newspaper, a slick magazine, a television series, or a feature film, profitability requires a mass market. No media organ needs to appeal to everyone to survive, and none tries. But particularly when a marketplace is competitive, there will be a tendency to avoid programming or content that seems likely to have limited appeal in favour of that which will hold on to, or even increase, sales.

State ownership alters, but does not eliminate, the economic pressures to which the mass media are exposed. Publicly owned broadcasters must be sensitive to charges of élitism. This is particularly true of television broadcasting, where the costs of producing high-quality entertainment programming are great. Few politicians will be willing to risk the loss of votes in order to subsidize broadcasting that attracts a tiny audience. Market influences become even greater when a publicly owned broadcaster is required to raise some part of its revenues from advertising or viewer/corporate support.

Economic pressures have an important impact on what the mass media produce. They cannot, however, explain all of media behaviour. What is finally offered to viewers, readers, and listeners is also affected by regulatory requirements, the legal system, and the cultural norms of society.

The economic filter operates mainly through the influence that advertising and industry structure have on the media product. Without advertising dollars, privately owned and even (to a lesser degree) publicly owned media companies are not economically viable. These media companies are in competition for the advertising patronage of business. It follows, then, that they will be sensitive to their patrons' needs and will tend to avoid reporting or programming that reduces their attractiveness in the eyes of advertisers. In the words of an American network executive, '[Television] is an advertising-supported medium, and to the extent that support falls out, programming will change.'[12] The advertising base of a newspaper or radio broadcaster is typically more local than that of a television network, but the maxim still holds: advertisers' preferences cannot be ignored by an ad-dependent media system.

How is this relevant to politics? First of all, dependence on advertising may reduce the likelihood that powerful economic interests will be portrayed in a negative light. This is not to imply that advertisers hold a power of economic blackmail over the heads of media organs. There have, however, been occasions when particular programs were boycotted by corporate sponsors or where their broadcast was followed by advertiser reprisals. In some instances, the anticipated reaction of corporate advertisers is enough to either kill a story or moderate its tone. But the influence of advertising is much more subtle and pervasive than these occasional incidents might suggest. When a thirty-second commercial spot during prime time on a major American network can cost US $300,000–$400,000, the economic costs of broadcasting material that offends powerful corporate advertisers obviously are great. Those who make programming decisions certainly are aware of this.

There is little evidence, however, to support the occasionally expressed view that news reporting is 'censored' or slanted as a result of advertiser interference. In *News from Nowhere*,[13] Edward Jay Epstein declares that none of the hundreds of correspondents and production personnel he interviewed for his study could recall an incident of sponsor interference in a network news broadcast. On the contrary, Epstein observes that stories directly conflicting with the interests of major sponsors were not uncommon.[14] The fear that advertisers may withhold their business has, he argues, little impact on the content of national news programming, although it may occasionally affect news documentaries and other public affairs programs.

The influence of advertising operates in a second, more powerful way. Most television broadcasting and most viewing time are, we have seen, devoted to entertainment programming. Naturally, the most lucrative advertising slots are associated with this sort of programming. There is, therefore, an economic pressure on ad-dependent broadcasters to maximize the amount of high audience-appeal programming during prime-time hours. Most public affairs programming does not have the draw of a popular sitcom or drama, and consequently is subject to pressures that it be marginalized (relegated to off-peak viewing times or left up to state-owned or viewer-supported broadcasters) or that it adopt an entertainment format. The emergence of what has been called 'infotainment' or 'soft news'—news that is packaged using an entertainment, celebrity journalist format—has become prevalent in the United States. Infotainment is clearly linked to the high price fetched by advertising spots during popular viewing hours. The Canadian industry has not gone as far in breaking down the traditional barriers between entertainment and public affairs programming. But the economics of broadcasting in Canada also work against the viability of programming that does not attract a mass audience.

State-owned media organs like the CBC, TV Ontario, and Radio-Québec in Canada, and the viewer-supported Public Broadcasting Stations (PBS) network in the United States, are not immune from the influence of advertising. Both the CBC and Radio-Québec rely on advertising for part of their revenue. In the case of the CBC, advertising income accounts for about a fifth of its annual budget. Viewer-supported broadcasters like the American PBS system rely on state subsidies (directly and through the tax system) and corporate sponsorship of programs for part of their revenue needs. Some critics have argued that corporate sponsorship, like advertising, tends to filter out socially divisive and controversial programming, including criticism of powerful economic interests and the capitalist system.

Dependence on state subsidies does not necessarily remove all constraints on media content. Public broadcasters must constantly be sensitive to charges of bias and ideological favouritism. Over the years CBC television programs like *This Hour Has Seven Days*, *the fifth estate*, and *Marketplace* and CBC Radio's *Sunday Morning* have been accused of having a leftist political bias and of being anti-business. The in-house monitoring of CBC broadcasting for 'fairness' has reached unprecedented levels of sophistication. Much of this, as during election campaigns, is intended to ensure that the Corporation is even-handed in its treatment of the major political parties and their leaders. But monitoring also focuses on the treatment of social and economic groups, including business. In the world of public broadcasting, culturecrats' and politicians' aversion to controversy may substitute for the check that dependence on advertising imposes on private broadcasters.

Industry structure is the second component of the economic filter. As the costs associated with producing a newspaper have increased, competition has suffered. The daily newspaper industry in Canada (as in the United States) is characterized by local monopoly. In only six Canadian cities (Toronto, Edmonton, Calgary, St John's, Montreal, and Quebec) is there competition between same-language, mass-circulation dailies that have different owners. Chain ownership is a feature of both the English and French-language markets. About 60 per cent of daily circulation in the English market is controlled by the Southam and Thomson chains, and about 90 per cent of the French market by the Québecor, Power Corporation, and Unimédia groups.

Broadcasting markets are more competitive. However, levels of corporate concentration have been increasing rapidly in recent years. A handful of owners, including Rogers

Communication, Vidéotron, Power Corporation, Baton Broadcasting, CHUM, CanWest Global Communications, and Télémédia, in addition to the publicly owned CBC, dominate Canada's television and radio markets. Ever more concentrated levels of ownership and vertical integration in mass media industries do not signify, however, a reduction in the number of 'voices' providing information and images to Canadians. On the contrary, the proliferation of domestic and global broadcasting sources as a result of cable systems, satellites, and computer networks have actually increased the number of sources available to consumers, at the same time as these industries have become dominated by fewer and fewer giant corporations.[15]

Media firms are sometimes part of a larger corporate conglomerate that includes non-media businesses. Thomson Newspapers, for example, owns Thomson Newsprint and controls Augusta Newsprint, while it is a holding within the Woodbridge conglomerate whose other assets span retailing, information services, tourism travel services, and publishing. Power Corporation, which owns Montreal's most popular daily newspaper, *La Presse*, has important holdings in the pulp and paper, insurance, book retailing, broadcasting, and financial services industries.

But the most remarkable Canadian instance of a conglomerate that combines media and non-media interests is the corporate empire of New Brunswick's Irving family. In addition to owning all five of that province's English-language daily newspapers, as well as television and radio stations in Saint John, the Irving family has wide-ranging interests in shipyards, all phases of the petroleum industry, forest products, transportation, construction, and retailing. The Royal Commission on Newspapers expressed the view that the Irvings' hammerlock on English newspapers in New Brunswick, combined with their extensive industrial holdings, was contrary to the public interest: 'Irving papers are noteworthy for their obeisance to every industrial interest. They are not known for probing investigations into pollution, occupational health dangers, industrial wastes or any of the other darker consequences of industrial power.'[16] On the other hand, the Commission provided no evidence to prove that Irving papers are any less critical of these matters than most other newspapers.

Critics of Canada's mass media have focused on a number of specific concerns relating to industry structure. They include the following:

- Concentrated ownership in the newspaper industry, and to a lesser extent in broadcasting, has been argued to limit the range of ideas and information that reaches the public. However, weak competition has less of an impact on the range of media information than the need to make profits and the organizational structure of news gathering and reporting. The organizational filter through which the media product must pass is discussed in a subsequent section.
- Media companies that are part of larger corporate networks that include non-media interests may be reluctant to cover stories and interpret events in ways that put their owners' other interests in a bad light. Again, however, the empirical proof for this claim is weak. Incidents of owner interference or, more often, self-censorship that appear clearly to be based on media people's sensitivity to their owner's interests do occasionally happen.[17] But as Edward Herman and Noam Chomsky argue, it is too simplistic to look for direct correlations between ownership and the way particular issues or stories are handled by

the media. Instead, they maintain, owners exercise their influence more diffusely through 'establishing the general aims of the company and choosing its top management.'[18]

- Chain ownership will produce a certain uniformity in the partisan orientations of newspapers within the chain. This claim, while superficially plausible, is not supported by the evidence. Studies carried out by researchers at the University of Windsor have found no proof that chain ownership is associated with either the patterns of news reporting or editorial policy.[19] The differences one finds between newspapers are determined far more by their readership characteristics than by who owns them. Moreover, their market shares do not appear to coincide with political divisions, unlike the situation in France, Belgium, and Italy, where particular papers have distinct partisan or ideological readerships.

Weak competition, media ownership by large industrial conglomerates, and the dominance of chains in the newspaper industry can all be traced to the conditions necessary for profitability in a privately owned mass media system. Indeed, profit orientation, more than industry structure, exerts a general influence on media behaviour. Profitability in the newspaper and television industries depends on large markets. This is due to a combination of enormous production costs and the fact that even a slight shift in market share vis-à-vis that of competitors is likely to result in serious losses of advertising revenue. Chain ownership in the newspaper industry and the domination of television production by a handful of networks can both be traced to the economics of the market. Anything that reduces the reach of a media company necessarily reduces its appeal to advertisers, and therefore weakens profitability. The question then becomes, 'What sort of media product succeeds in reaching the markets that advertisers want to attract?'

There is no simple or single answer to this question. Sellers of BMW automobiles or of Rolex watches will seek a different sort of media vehicle than those who want to sell headache pills or domestic beer. But in the case of both newspapers (where people expect to pay a low price that in fact covers only a fraction of production costs) and broadcasting (where the media product is provided 'free', or at a relatively small charge in the case of cable television), profitability depends on the ability to deliver to advertisers a large circulation/audience. Newspapers and magazines that have tried to rely on subscriber revenues to cover their costs have typically faced bleak prospects.

The Legal/Regulatory Filter

Print media in Canada and in most other democracies are basically free from direct regulation by government. Unlike radio and television broadcasters and cable system companies, they do not require a special licence to do business. Newspapers and magazines essentially regulate themselves through press councils created and operated by the industry. These councils receive and investigate complaints; they do not systematically monitor performance. Calls for greater state regulation of their behaviour invariably provoke cries of censorship from those in the newspaper and magazine business.

A number of indirect forms of regulation, however, may affect content in the print media. Most of these involve measures whose ostensible aim is to promote Canadian values through newspapers and magazines. The federal Income Tax Act permits advertisers to deduct from their taxable income only the cost of ads placed in newspapers or magazines that are at least 75 per cent Canadian-owned. This explains why foreign ownership of Canadian newspapers has never been an issue, despite the fact that the industry has been extremely profitable over the years and might therefore have been expected to attract foreign capital.

It is doubtful, however, whether the provisions of the Income Tax Act favouring Canadian-owned publications have much of an impact on newspaper content. With the exception of the *Globe and Mail* and, within Quebec, *Le Devoir*, newspapers are geared to local markets. Community news and classified ads account for a large share of these papers. Their profitability depends on a large local readership they can 'sell' to local advertisers. This, and not the nationality of their owners, will influence newspaper content.

One might argue, however, that the owner's nationality could influence the way a newspaper covers national and international news, as well as sports and comics—two of a paper's most widely read sections—but even Canadian-owned papers depend heavily on news purchased from foreign news agencies such as the Associated Press wire service, particularly for international news and sports. Most comic strips—and we should not dismiss comics and cartoons as purveyors of values—are produced by American cartoonists. The economics of news gathering, not the nationality of the owners, is responsible for this dependence on foreign sources of news.

In the end, the Income Tax Act almost certainly does more to promote Canadian ownership than Canadian culture. The same cannot be said of the magazine industry. Despite the fact that the Canadian ownership provisions of the Income Tax Act also apply to magazines, the English-Canadian market is dominated by American magazines and 'Canadian editions' (a category that includes *Reader's Digest*, *Time*, *Newsweek*, *TV Guide*, and *Sports Illustrated*). They account for close to two-thirds of all magazine sales in Canada.

Unlike newspapers, magazines tend to be targeted at a national and even international readership. As is also true of television and film, the much larger American market enables magazine publishers to turn out a glossy product and pay better rates for articles than their Canadian counterparts. Moreover, the revenue base of Canadian magazines is undermined by the fact that most advertisers can reach the Canadian market through ads placed in American magazines.

Given the economics of magazine publishing, the wonder is that Canadian magazines account for as large a share of the market as they do. It probably is fair to say that a significant Canadian presence in the English-language market is due to the cost advantage Canadian-owned magazines receive under the Income Tax Act. But even this is not enough to secure the financial viability of the smaller magazines that, even more than *Maclean's*, *Chatelaine,* and *Canadian Living*, are vehicles for distinctly Canadian viewpoints and cultural values.

Protection for Canadian magazines and newspapers was the stated aim of two other federal measures that existed until the early 1990s. These were the exemption from federal sales tax enjoyed by all magazines and newspapers, whether produced in Canada or imported, and the postal rate subsidy for mailed periodicals and newspapers. The irony was that the main beneficiaries of the sales tax exemption have always been foreign magazines, exactly the opposite effect of the nationalist goal expressed in the Income Tax Act. A federally appointed task force estimated that about two-thirds of the benefits from this exemption flowed to foreign magazine publishers.[20] In any case, this subsidy was wiped out in January, 1991, with the introduction of the GST.

At the same time as Ottawa eliminated this long-standing tax exemption to the publishing industry, it also moved to slash the postal rate subsidy for newspapers and magazines printed and mailed in Canada. This subsidy reduced mailing costs to about one-fifth of what they would otherwise have been and provided an estimated benefit to the industry of about $220 million in 1989. Like the sales tax exemption, the official justification for the special postal rate was the promotion of Canada's publishing industry. Ironically, though, two of the magazines that benefited most from the postal rate subsidy were *Time* and *Reader's Digest*, both of which printed their Canadian market edition in Canada in order to qualify for cheaper mailing costs.

For small magazines that typically lead a hand-to-mouth existence during the best of times, the decision to phase out the postal rate subsidy came as a particularly crushing blow. But the Conservative government did not retreat altogether from financial support for the Canadian magazine industry. Some of the savings from the gradual elimination of the postal rate subsidy were earmarked to 'support publications of social and cultural value that really can never make it in the marketplace'. As cultural journalist Bronwyn Drainie observed, 'The strategy is clear. The government can dole out dribs and drabs of money to small literary and arts quarterlies with tiny subscription lists, thereby flashily saving "Canadian culture" for very few dollars. But the medium-to-large publications, the ones that might have some hope of genuinely competing with popular US magazines, will be left to flounder on their own.'[21] This charge was not entirely fair. The 1992 announcement that about $150 million would be channelled to Canadian publishers provided some relief for the industry. But it came too late to save those who had already succumbed to the market and the dismantling of the subsidies that had enabled them to survive.

Regulation is much more intrusive in the case of the electronic media. The original reason for treating broadcasting differently from print media was the need to prevent chaos on overcrowded airwaves. Controlling entry in a market through the licensing of broadcasters seemed the only practical solution to this potential problem. At the same time, however, broadcasting policy has always been based on the assumption that only extensive state intervention can prevent complete American domination of the Canadian market.[22]

The American 'threat' is a matter of simple economics, and content regulations for both radio and television constitute one of the pillars of Canadian broadcasting policy. The CRTC establishes and enforces a complicated set of content guidelines that all licensed broadcasters must observe. The idea behind the guidelines is to ensure that more Canadian content reaches the airwaves than would be available without regulation (see Box 9.2).

Whether or not the system works depends on what one means by 'Canadian content'. If this signifies that some of the major people involved in the production of a television program or piece of music are Canadian, then the policy has been a success. But if Canadian content is taken to mean the subjects, values, and ideas conveyed through these media, then the verdict is rather different. In fact, the *Report* of the Task Force on Broadcasting characterized the content system applied to television broadcasters as 'regulatory tokenism'. Many of the programs that qualify as Canadian content, it observed, 'could be mistaken for

---

Box 9.2　What Is Canadian Content?

Radio:

According to the Canadian Radio-television and Telecommunications Commission (CRTC), a musical selection qualifies as Canadian content if it meets any two of the following criteria:

· The music was composed by a Canadian.
· The lyrics were written by a Canadian.
· The instrumentation or lyrics were principally performed by a Canadian.
· The live performance was wholly performed in Canada and broadcast live in Canada or wholly recorded in Canada.

For AM radio, at least 30 per cent of all music aired must meet this definition of Canadian content. Moreover, a Canadian must have composed the music or written the lyrics to a minimum of 5 per cent of the number of selections broadcast. In recognition of FM radio's diversity of formats (and the corresponding supply of appropriate Canadian content recordings), the CRTC allows different levels of required Canadian content. The quota ranges from 10 to 30 per cent for different groups of FM radio stations. AM and FM stations must also play at least 25 per cent Canadian content between 6:00 a.m. and 7:00 p.m., Monday through Friday.

Television:

To be considered Canadian, a television program must have a Canadian producer and must earn a minimum six of a possible ten points based on key creative positions. The CRTC awards points when the duties of these positions are performed by Canadians. There are additional criteria regarding financial and creative control for programs involving foreign production partners. The CRTC requires that Canadian programs be used to fill at least 60 per cent of the overall schedules of both public and private television broadcasters.

Canadian Social Trends, vol. 2 (Toronto: Thompson Educational Publishing, 1994), 298.

American productions and seem to have been made on the assumption that references to their Canadian origin would hurt their appeal to audiences outside Canada, particularly in the United States.'[23] The same may be said of content regulations for radio. The economics of the recording industry encourage products that are marketable outside of Canada. Radio stations typically deal with Canadian content requirements by relying heavily on recordings by such performers as Bryan Adams, Cory Hart, Alanis Morissette, Anne Murray, and k.d. lang, whose music seems as at home in Boston as Toronto, and by marginalizing much of their Canadian content to off-peak hours.

　　Governments also affect the content of the electronic mass media through subsidies paid to Canadian film and television producers and through their direct participation in the industry as broadcasters and filmmakers. The Canadian content quotas established by the CRTC are, in the case of television, met largely through sports and public affairs programming. But most viewing time is spent watching entertainment programs. Very few of these programs are Canadian, again, simply because it makes economic sense to purchase an American-made product for a fraction of its production costs—a product that, moreover, benefits from the inevitable spillover into Canada of advertising that American networks use to promote audience interest. In English-speaking Canada only the CBC broadcasts a significant amount of Canadian-made entertainment programming. Indeed, as of autumn, 1996, the CBC will not broadcast American programs during prime time.

To compensate for the unfavourable economics of domestic production, Ottawa offers subsidies. This is done through Telefilm Canada, which finances an average of between 30 and 40 per cent of the production costs of Canadian-made television programs and feature films. Since the fund's inception in 1983, the major users of this money have been the non-commercial public broadcasters—chiefly CBC/Radio Canada, TV Ontario, and Radio-Québec. Private television and film producers have also drawn on the fund, but fears have been expressed that they have used public money to produce 'American clone programming'. The problem is, quite simply, that even with the maximum level of Broadcast Fund support, the typically low license fees paid by Canadian broadcasters still leave a producer with a significant share of production costs uncovered. There are, therefore, economic pressures to turn out an exportable product to recoup costs through foreign (this will usually mean American) sales.

Despite the unfavourable economics of producing recognizably Canadian programs, a situation that subsidies appear not to correct, such programs do get produced. In the end, the CBC/Radio Canada and the National Film Board do most to show Canadians what is distinctive about their society and culture. Indeed, this is what these organizations were intended to do. Under the Broadcasting Act the CBC is required to be 'a balanced service of information, enlightenment and entertainment for people of different ages, interests and tastes covering the whole range of programming in fair proportion'. As mentioned earlier, the CBC has borne most of the burden of Canadianizing television programming, particularly in the case of drama and during prime viewing hours. Its ability to do so, however, is threatened by budget cuts that began in the late 1970s. The most recent, a cut of about 20 per cent over two years, was announced in 1995. The CBC has responded by increasing its dependence on advertising. If this trend continues it seems likely that the CBC will come under growing pressure to produce programs that are more similar to those shown by its private-sector competitors.

The NFB's mandate is to 'interpret Canada to Canadians and the rest of the world' (Film Act). For over fifty years the NFB has done this to critical and international acclaim, turning out documentaries and serious drama that the private sector has been unwilling to produce. There is, of course, a very simple reason why private companies have not invested in these sorts of productions: theatres do not want to show them and ad-dependent television stations do not want to broadcast them. As in the case of the CBC, the burden of showing Canadians images of themselves falls to a publicly owned corporation.

Another form of indirect regulation of media content involves obscenity, pornography, and what is called hate literature. None of these terms is defined very precisely in Canadian law, but the federal Criminal Code and Customs Act, as well as provincial statutes dealing with hate literature, restrict the sorts of printed matter and films that may enter Canada or be distributed here. The censorship they impose on the mass media, virtually by definition, caters to the conventional mainstream of Canadian society. Unorthodox material and marginal groups, particularly homosexuals, are the main targets of this censorship.

The Technological Filter

Few things date more quickly than news. The technology of broadcasting is instantaneous and that of newspapers involves a matter of hours. The mass media are thus capable of providing their audiences with the latest developments, and our general expectations are that they will communicate what is happening now. What is happening now, of course, can be reported in the context of the larger background against which events unfold. The practical problem is that 'stories' must be edited down to a length suitable for inclusion in a thirty-minute news program or the pages of a newspaper.

Television, we have already noted, is the medium relied on by most people for their knowledge of national and international events. The visual character of this medium lends itself to the personalization of reality—an emphasis on individuals and personalities at the expense of broad social forces that are not captured by the eye of a camera. Consequently, the media, and in particular the technology of television, are disposed toward the personal, the immediate, and the concrete. Reality becomes a constantly shifting pastiche of images, as though those who produce the news assume that the average viewer has an attention span that lasts a minute or two at best. Entertainment programming tends to assume the same faster-than-life character. According to Morris Wolfe, this is because of what he calls the First Law of Commercial Television: 'Thou shalt give them enough jolts per minute (jpm's) or thou shalt lose them.'[24] Too few jpm's and viewers will lose interest, change channels, and ratings will suffer. And if ratings suffer, advertising revenue will fall and profits will drop. But are the networks simply giving the viewers what they want? And what difference does it make for politics if, in Wolfe's words, 'all television increasingly aspires to the condition of the TV commercial'?[25]

Industry people are doubtless correct when they claim that many viewers are easily bored and that a rapid pace and frequent jolts are necessary to capture and hold their attention. But it may also be true that viewers have come to expect the sort of high jpm product at which commercial television and film excel. Morris Wolfe explains: '[A] steady diet of nothing but high jpm television tends to condition viewers' nervous systems to respond only to certain kinds of stimulation. Their boredom thresholds are frequently so low that TV viewers find it difficult to enjoy anything that isn't fast-paced.'[26] Whatever the cause, it can hardly be denied that most television and commercial film have the staccato rhythm and jumped-up energy level that Wolfe and countless other media watchers have commented on.

Wolfe's First Law of Commercial Television captures only part of the explanation for what he calls the 'TV wasteland'. The technology of television and film is also responsible. It is often said that one picture is worth a thousand words. This is doubtless true—sometimes. But it is often the case that the moving images on the screen capture only the surface of events, and this substitutes for an explanation that is more complicated and *non-visual* than the medium can deal with. Of course, people can turn to newspapers, magazines, and books to fill in those parts of the picture that are not covered well by television. But there are good reasons for believing that most do not. We mentioned earlier that a clear majority of Canadians rely on television for their knowledge of national and international affairs and, furthermore, believe this medium to be the most unbiased and believable. In other words, they count on what they see before their eyes.

Politicians and others who regularly come under the eye of the camera have long understood the biases of the visual medium. Photo opportunities and highly structured, controllable events are among their ways of using television's need for the immediate, the personal, and above all the visual to their own advantage. Television has had an enormous impact on how elections are fought, how special interests attempt to influence public policy, and how public officials communicate with the people. One of the masters of the medium, the American politician Jesse Jackson, remarked on the importance of speaking in short memorable sentences—'sound bites', as they are called today—over three decades ago. They conform to the needs of television technology; long, rambling, or complex statements do not (see Box 9.3).

Those who produce television programs, including the news, operate on the assumption that action and motion are far more likely to hold viewer attention than 'talking heads'. There is, therefore, an exaggerated emphasis on action, and particularly on two-sided conflict. As Edward Jay Epstein explains,

> ... the high value placed on action footage by executives leads to a three-step distillation of news happenings by correspondents, cameramen and editors, all of whom seek the moment of highest action. Through this process, the action in a news event, which in fact may account for only a fraction of the time, is concentrated together and becomes the central feature of the happening. This helps explain why news on television tends willy-nilly to focus on activity.[27]

The visual character of television introduces other biases as well, including dependence on stereotypes and emphasis on confrontation.

Box 9.3 The Philosophy Behind the Thirty-Second TV News Story

Because the television commercial is the single most voluminous form of public communication in our society, it was inevitable that Americans would accommodate themselves to the philosophy of television commercials. By 'accommodate', I mean that we accept them as a normal and plausible form of discourse. By 'philosophy', I mean that the television commercial has embedded in it certain assumptions about the nature of communication that run counter to those of other media, especially the printed word. For one thing, the commercial insists on an unprecedented brevity of expression. One may even say, instancy. A sixty-second commercial is prolix; thirty seconds is longer than most; fifteen to twenty seconds is about average. This is a brash and startling structure for communication since, as I remarked earlier, the commercial always addresses itself to the psychological needs of the viewer. Thus it is not merely therapy. It is instant therapy. Indeed, it puts forward a psychological theory of unique axioms: The commercial asks us to believe that all problems are solvable, that they are solvable fast, and that they are solvable fast through the interventions of technology, techniques and chemistry. This is, of course, a preposterous theory about the roots of discontent, and would appear so to anyone hearing or reading it. But the commercial disdains exposition, for that takes time and invites argument.

Neil Postman, *Amusing Ourselves to Death: Public Discourse in the Age of Show Business* (New York: Penguin, 1985), 130–1.

Dependence on a repertory of stereotypes. Writing early in this century, Walter Lippmann argued that newspaper reporting consisted largely of fitting current news to a 'repertory of stereotypes'. There are cultural reasons for this, but in the case of a visual medium there are also technological reasons for this dependence. '[V]iewers' interest', observes Epstein, 'is most likely to be maintained through easily recognizable and palpable images, and conversely, most likely to be distracted by unfamiliar or confusing images.'[28]

Emphasis on confrontation. From the standpoint of a visual medium confrontation has two virtues. First, it involves action, which is one of the requirements of most television news and public affairs coverage. Second, conflict helps to present a story in a way that viewers can easily grasp. Epstein notes that 'Situations are thus sought out in network news in which there is a high potential for violence, but a low potential for audience confusion.'[29] When the events themselves do not include the necessary visual drama, this can always be provided through the use of file films—action in the can and ready to go!

The Organizational Filter

News gathering and reporting are carried out by organizations. The needs and routine procedures of these organizations influence the content of the news: both what is reported and how it is covered. The organization's dilemma is that news developments are not entirely predictable, yet it does not have the resources to be everywhere news might break or to cover all stories equally well. News organizations rely on various strategies to deal with this dilemma.

In the case of television, several criteria help impose predictability on the news. Those who have a reputation for being influential or who occupy an official position of some power are more likely to make the news than those whose public profile is lower or whose position does not, in the eyes of news gatherers, automatically confer on them a mantle of credibility. Prime ministers, premiers, and the leaders of opposition parties are automatically assumed to be newsworthy, as are mayors and leading councillors when the news item is local. Spokespersons for what are considered to be important organizations—the Canadian Manufacturers' Association, the Canadian Labour Congress, the National Action Committee on the Status of Women, the Catholic Church, and so on—are also considered to be newsworthy and can count on being sought out when an issue falls into their sphere of concern.

Government officials and powerful private interests understand that news organizations operate within a system of routines and requirements, for example, the need to have the evening news film footage in the can by a certain hour to allow time for editing. Accommodating the media's needs through well-timed press conferences, photo opportunities, news releases, and staged events—what Daniel Boorstin has called 'pseudo-events'—is simple prudence from the standpoint of groups that want to affect public opinion. This practice has been called *news management.* Obviously, governments and the public affairs/media relations bureaucracies of the powerful are not able to control the news agenda. But they are able to influence news reporting.

Publicly acknowledged experts will also be sought out by the media. What makes one a 'publicly acknowledged expert'? Affiliation with a respectable institution is one of the key determinants of this status. Specialists who are associated with an established institution such as the C.D. Howe Institute, the Conference Board of Canada, the National Research Council, or a university—particularly a university located in a city where a network has production facilities—are those most likely to be considered newsworthy. The point here is not that only 'establishment' voices will be heard on an issue, but that spokespersons for mainstream views are almost certain to receive a hearing because their institutional affiliation confers on them the status of 'acknowledged expert', while spokespersons for marginal groups and unconventional views are much less certain to be deemed newsworthy.

The mass media's demand for the ideas and information generated by experts is based on a combination of factors. One of these is the media's self-image as dispenser of the news, reporter of the facts. Fulfilment of this role requires access to sources of information whose credibility is sound and whose claim to objectivity is generally accepted. Related to this is a second factor: the media's need for low-cost information and instant analysis. To conduct their own analysis would be expensive and time-consuming, and most journalists are in any case not trained as professional economists, sociologists, political scientists, or whatever other field of expertise a 'story' may call for. It therefore makes economic sense to tap the knowledge of those whose training, reputation, and/or institutional affiliation confer on them the social standing of 'expert'. Third, in order to protect themselves against charges of bias and lawsuits, media organizations and reporters need information 'that can be portrayed as presumptively accurate'.[30] Expert knowledge meets this requirement, and that provided by those with socially respected professional or institutional credentials is particularly useful. In fact, the media's need for expert opinion and information helps to confer this social respectability on individuals and institutions, and in many instances probably serves to reinforce the political status quo.

Predictability is important in determining what becomes 'news'. Any news organization operates within the framework of a budget and the limited resources—camera crews, journalists, researchers, and so on—that this implies. Other things being equal, it makes sense to concentrate organizational resources where news is most likely to happen: Parliament Hill, the provincial capitals, Toronto and Montreal, and internationally as resources permit. Of course, this becomes a bit of a self-fulfilling prophecy. The unplanned, especially unexpected happenings that occur too quickly or too far away to send a journalist and film crew are less likely to be covered than scheduled events that take place near where a news crew is stationed. As Epstein puts it, 'The more predictable the event, the more likely it will be covered.'[31]

Visual appeal is also important. Television obviously needs pictures. But some subjects are more telegenic than others. Epstein writes:

> ... priority is naturally given to the story in a given category that promises to yield the most dramatic or visual film footage, other things being equal. This means, in effect, that political institutions with rules that restrict television cameras from filming the more dramatic parts of their proceedings are not routinely assigned coverage.[32]

Canadians see much more of what is happening in House of Commons debates, where cameras are allowed, than they do of the Supreme Court, where cameras may not intrude, yet the Court's decisions have an enormous impact on public policy, more of an impact, some would argue, than the fairly predictable antics of parliamentarians. Likewise, closed meetings of first ministers, the proceedings of regulatory commissions, and the institutions of the bureaucracy generally are either inaccessible to cameras or lack the sort of visual spice that is usually considered a crucial ingredient of televised news. The result, therefore, is to over-emphasize the importance of those actors and individuals who can be filmed in action—action that is often stage-managed by the actors themselves—and to under-emphasize the significance of those who are more reclusive or who do not lend themselves to confrontational or sensational visual bites.

A news organization's need for stories that are newsworthy, predictable, and visually appealing produces a situation where 'the news selected is the news expected'.[33] Along with the other filters we have discussed, the organizational one creates biases that affect media content. Simple dramatized confrontation, familiar players and issues, and a relatively narrow range of locales where most news happens are among these biases.

The Ideological Filter

Those who report the news are often accused by conservatives and business people of having liberal-left and anti-business biases. They are more likely, it is argued, to favour stories and groups that challenge established authority. The CBC in general and some of its programs in particular have occasionally been accused of ideological bias against the Reform Party, conservatism, and big business (especially American business). Similar charges have been heard in the United States, where Republicans, conservatives, fundamentalist Christians, and business interests have often accused the major networks, and journalists generally, with harbouring liberal biases.

Studies seem to confirm these claims. An American study that looked at the social backgrounds, personality traits, ideologies, and world views of business and media élites found that media respondents typically gave more liberal responses to such statements as 'Government should substantially reduce the income gap between rich and poor.'[34] The researchers concluded that 'leading journalists seem to inhabit a symbolic universe which is quite different from that of businessmen, with implications for the manner in which they report the news to the general public.'[35] Several American studies have confirmed that those in the media, particularly the electronic media, tend to be more liberal than members of the general population. A study of CBC Radio, directed by Barry Cooper, concluded that 'on the whole, [the CBC] adopted a left-wing, rather than right-wing critical stance.'[36] Cooper's recent study of CBC television news coverage arrives at a similar conclusion, although he expresses it rather differently. 'The CBC,' he argues, 'like all modern media, has directed its energies towards the production of a specific configuration of opinion—namely progressive opinion—and not toward the provision of reliable information about the world.'[37]

But even if one accepts the plausible claim that journalists are more likely to have leftist political leanings than are some other groups, including business people, these differences need to be understood in the context of what 'left' and 'right' mean in Canadian society. 'Left' does not mean serious reservations about the basic institutions of the capitalist economy. To be on the left in the predominantly liberal societies of Canada and the United States has always meant to be ambivalent about business: to distrust excessive concentrations of economic power and to believe that business must be regulated, while accepting the superiority (in most circumstances) of private property and the market system of allocation. But this is the ambivalence of family members who do not see eye to eye on all matters at all times.

News and public affairs reporting focuses on conflict and controversy, often involving government officials and powerful private interests, so this naturally gives the impression that those in the media are anti-establishment critics. The impression is somewhat misleading. Ralph Miliband is almost certainly correct when he observes that only a minority of those in the mass media have strong left-wing or right-wing commitments. The majority occupy various locations toward the middle of the ideological spectrum and generally experience little difficulty in accommodating themselves to the needs of the organization within which they work. 'They mostly "say what they like,"' says Miliband, 'but this is mainly because their employers mostly like what they say, or at least find little in what they say which is objectionable.'[38]

It bears repeating that most of what the mass media produce does not fall into the categories of news and public affairs. It should not be assumed, however, that the entertainment and information products of the media industry carry no political messages or ideological biases. They do, both through the images, themes, and interpretations they communicate and through their silences. If the mass media are 'more important in confirming or reinforcing existing opinions than they are in changing opinions',[39] as studies generally suggest, this is partly due to the ideological orthodoxy of most writers, producers, editors, and others who have an influence on the media product.

This is not to suggest that there is no place in the mass media for people whose political views lie outside the safer familiar mainstream. The point is, rather, that those in media industries cluster mainly in the uncontroversial centre of the political spectrum. For these cultural workers the other four filters affecting media content are largely beside the point. The conformity of their value systems with that of society's dominant ideology ensures that they seldom, if ever, test the limits of what the system will allow.

The Media and Democracy

In regard to propaganda the early advocates of universal literacy and a free press envisaged only two possibilities: the propaganda might be true, or it might be false. They did not foresee what in fact has happened, above all in our Western capitalist democracies—the development of a vast mass communications industry, concerned in the main neither with the true nor the false, but with the unreal, the more or less totally irrelevant. In a word, they failed to take into account man's almost infinite appetite for distractions.[40]

The media, it often appears, have few friends except themselves. Politicians, business people, and those on the right of the political spectrum regularly accuse the media of having liberal-left biases, of irresponsible scandal-mongering, and of being inherently and unfairly opposed to established authority. Those on the political left, however, are no less critical of the media. They are apt to view the media as the servile handmaidens of powerful interests,

Despite the availability of political reporting and advertisements conveyed through the mass media, particularly during election campaigns, it is not clear that voters are better informed as a result. (Roy Peterson, *Vancouver Sun*)

particularly economic ones. Both ideological camps, right and left, accuse the media of having strongly anti-democratic tendencies. Conservatives argue that those in the media tend to be more liberal-left than society as a whole, but that they foist their interests and perspectives on the public behind a smokescreen of journalistic detachment and objectivity. Left-wing critics of the media claim that the media help to 'manufacture consent'[41] for a social system—including political and economic structures—that operates mainly in the interests of a privileged minority. Leftist critics charge that the mass media foist on the public not so much their own ideological biases as the false consciousness of the dominant ideology.

In this chapter we have argued that the behaviour of the mass media is shaped by a number of filters. These filters cumulatively determine the sort of 'product' likely to reach the consuming public. Our general conclusion is that the products of the mass media are supportive of established values and institutions. Thus, the media tend to reinforce the power of those groups whose interests are best served by the status quo. In order to play this role it is not necessary that the media avoid all criticism of powerful interests. This would be a ludicrous claim. All that is necessary is that an overwhelming preponderance of what appears on the page, screen, and over the airwaves conforms to mainstream values. This test is amply met.

On the other hand, it must be admitted that the gains made in recent years by socially marginal, politically weak interests such as Aboriginal Canadians, women, and environmental activists have been in large measure due to media coverage of their demands and spokespersons. This, in turn, has raised public consciousness of the issues and discourse—'equal pay for work of equal value', 'Aboriginal self-government', 'sustainable development'—associated with their demands. Moreover, it can hardly be denied that the media usually do a better job of scrutinizing and criticizing government actions, to say nothing of those of powerful societal groups, than do the opposition parties. Indeed, it is precisely the critical and even irreverent tenor of much public affairs journalism that contributes to the widespread belief in the mass media's independent and anti-establishment character.

Most of what the mass media offer does not have this character. Frank Lloyd Wright's description of television as 'chewing gum for the eyes' is in fact a fairly apt characterization of much of the mass media, electronic and print. Wright's judgement was basically an aesthetic one. But Aldous Huxley's argument that the 'mass communications industry [is] concerned in the main neither with the true nor the false, but with the unreal, the more or less totally irrelevant', expresses a political judgement about the mass media. Huxley is suggesting that the media—particularly their entertainment and advertising components—help foster a false consciousness among the public, the sort of pacified somnolence that characterizes the masses in his *Brave New World*. This may seem rather harsh, but Huxley is certainly right in suggesting that one should not assume that only news and public affairs reporting has political consequences.

On balance, democracy is not served very well by Canada's mass media. The biases of the mass media are toward familiar images and stories—what Lippmann called a 'repertory of stereotypes'—oversimplified conflict, the personalization of events, drama and action, and 'respectable' opinion. These biases are much more supportive than threatening of the status quo. Moreover, as we saw in Chapter 7, the media can be an important channel for the manipulation of public opinion by political parties and well-heeled societal interests, particularly business. Given their enormous importance as mediators of reality for Canadians, one might wish for something better than this.

PART FIVE

Contemporary Issues in Canadian Political Life

Since the Charter of Rights and Freedoms was entrenched in the constitution, the Supreme Court of Canada has assumed a much more prominent role in our political system. (Greg Vickers)

In modern democracies political demands are often expressed in the language of rights and freedoms. This chapter examines some of the controversies associated with rights and freedoms, and discusses the impact of the Canadian Charter of Rights and Freedoms on Canadian politics. Topics include the following:

- ❖ What do rights and freedoms mean?
- ❖ The origins and meanings of rights.
- ❖ The pre-Charter era: 1867–1981.
- ❖ The Charter and constitutional supremacy.
- ❖ The notwithstanding clause.
- ❖ Applying the Charter.
- ❖ Individual rights and freedoms.
- ❖ Equality and the Charter.

■ Rights and Freedoms

L ike the Ten Commandments, rights and freedoms are usually expressed in uncompromising language. Those who argue the case for a woman's right to control her body, a fetus's right to life, a person's freedom of conscience, or an individual's right not to be discriminated against on the basis of race, gender, or some other personal attribute that is beyond one's control typically advance their claims as moral absolutes. Moral absolutes, like biblical injunctions, are non-negotiable. Either a right or freedom exists or it does not. And if it exists, it must be respected in all cases and not simply when governments or the majority find it convenient to do so.

In reality, however, no right or freedom is absolute. There are two reasons for this. One is that rights and freedoms may collide, necessitating some compromise. Does freedom of expression, for example, protect the right of an individual to shout 'Fire!' in a crowded theatre? This hypothetical case was used by American Supreme Court Justice Oliver Wendell Holmes to explain when and why limits on free speech are justified. Holmes established the 'clear and present danger' test,[1] according to which freedom of expression could legitimately be curtailed when it posed an unmistakable and immediate danger to others. Falsely shouting 'Fire!' in a crowded theatre obviously endangers the safety of those in the room. To guarantee an individual's freedom of expression in such circumstances could jeopardize the right of other individuals to be protected from unreasonable danger.

In fact, the trade-offs between competing values are seldom this simple. Should freedom of expression protect people who publicly communicate statements that 'willfully promote hatred'[2] against some group distinguished by race, ethnicity, language, or religion? When do national security considerations or society's interest in preventing trafficking in drugs warrant wiretaps and other violations of the individual's right to privacy? How far should the public's interest in minimizing fraudulent claims on the public purse be allowed to justify intrusions into the homes and lives of welfare recipients? Is affirmative action a legitimate means for promoting social equality, or is it reverse discrimination against those who are not members of the groups targeted for special consideration? When does one right or freedom 'trump' another? Who should determine these issues, the courts or the people's elected representatives?

A second reason why no right or freedom can be treated as an absolute is because this is often impractical. If, for example, a constitution guarantees the right of official-language minorities to public education or services in their mother tongue, does that mean that all government services, everywhere in the country, should be available in each of the official languages? Does it mean that minority-language education should be provided in a community where there is a bare handful of families demanding their own school? Common sense suggests that there are limits to how far, and in what circumstances, the principles of linguistic equality and minority rights should apply.

What about administrative procedures that are determined by budget and personnel restrictions, but which impose hardship on individuals? For example, in 1990 an Ontario Superior Court judge decided that the time spent by many accused persons in jail or on bail while waiting for their trial dates violated section 11(b) of the Charter, i.e., the right 'to be tried within a reasonable time'. Given the existing number of judges and the limits on court resources, enormous backlogs had developed. He proceeded to dismiss hundreds of cases that had been in the dock for months. Can the bureaucratic procedures and budget constraints that lead to these delays and inflict real hardship on individuals be justified as 'practical limitations' on rights? Or are they matters of mere administrative convenience or policy that should not take precedence over individual rights?

Dilemmas like these await us at every turn. Despite this, and despite the passions usually unleashed by such controversies, rights and freedoms have had a low profile in Canadian politics for most of this country's history. The courts were reluctant to question the authority of elected legislatures to pass laws, whatever their content and effects, except to decide whether the matter in question constitutionally belonged to Ottawa or the provinces. As a result, civil liberties issues were transformed—deformed, some would say—into squabbles over the federal-provincial division of powers.

This changed with the passage of the Charter of Rights and Freedoms in 1982. As we noted in Chapter 5, the Charter entrenched various rights and freedoms in the constitution. Moreover, by establishing the principle of constitutional supremacy (sections 32 and 52(1) of the Constitution Act, 1982), the 1982 constitutional reforms placed these rights more or less beyond the interference of governments—'less', because section 1 of the Charter states that these rights and freedoms are 'subject only to such reasonable limits prescribed by law as can be demonstrably justified in a free and democratic society', and section 33(1) enables either Parliament or a provincial legislature to declare that a particular law or provision of a law shall operate even if it violates rights or freedoms guaranteed in sections 2 or 7 to 15 of the Charter. Together, sections 1 and 33 operate to maintain some measure of parliamentary supremacy over the courts and the Charter.

There is little doubt, however, that the Charter has decisively changed the face of Canadian politics. The authority of elected legislatures has receded before the authority of the constitution and the courts. A transformation has taken place in the venues and language of Canadian politics. The discourse of 'rights', always a part of the political scene, has assumed much greater prominence since passage of the Charter. Individuals, organized interests, and even governments have turned increasingly to litigation as a means of influencing public policy. An average of roughly 1,000 Charter cases a year are decided by Canadian courts,[3] reflecting the increased importance of the courts as a forum for political conflict. As Michael Mandel puts it, 'the Charter has legalized our politics'.[4]

With what consequences? Which groups (leaving aside lawyers) have won as a result of Charter politics, and which have lost ground? Has Canadian society become more democratic as a result of the unprecedented prominence accorded to rights and freedoms since the Charter's passage? These are crucial questions for which there are no easy answers. Let us begin by examining the concepts of rights and freedoms. We will then examine the history of rights and freedoms in Canada, pre- and post-Charter.

Coming to Terms: What Do Rights and Freedoms Mean?

Although there is a long tradition in Western constitutional law of distinguishing between rights and freedoms, often the distinction is not so straightforward in practice. An individual's freedom to believe something or to behave in a particular way is often expressed in terms of a right. 'I have a right to picket this employer' (freedom of assembly), or 'I have a right to distribute pamphlets explaining that the [you fill in the blank] are responsible for most of the evils that beset the world' (freedom of expression). Likewise, the right to fair and equal treatment by the law is often framed in terms of the conditions necessary to ensure an individual's freedom. For example, an accused person's right to be tried within a reasonable time—a right guaranteed by section 11(b) of the Charter—is probably violated if he or she has to spend a year in prison or 'free' but under onerous bail restrictions. Obviously, this individual's personal freedom is seriously compromised in such circumstances. Or consider the case of abortion. Those who argue against legal restrictions on a woman's access to abortion claim that such laws violate a woman's right to control her body. In this case the right being claimed is nothing less than freedom from interference by the state, or what Alan Borovoy calls the 'right to be left alone'.

Rights and freedoms are not, therefore, watertight compartments in reality. Nevertheless, constitutional experts usually reserve the term 'rights' for those individual and group entitlements that 'are considered so fundamental to human dignity that they receive special protection under the law and usually under the constitution of a country'.[5] Freedoms involve an individual's liberty to do or believe certain things without restraint by government. Whereas the defence of rights often requires some government action, the protection of freedoms requires that government refrain from interfering in certain matters. Rights suggest an active role for government, freedoms a limited one.

Civil liberties or *civil rights* are terms that are sometimes used to refer to all the basic rights and freedoms of citizens. Under the influence of the United Nations Universal Declaration of Human Rights (1948), the term *human rights* has become the more commonly used designation for this bundle of rights and freedoms. Included among them are the following:

- *Political rights/fundamental freedoms*. These include freedom of association, assembly, expression, the media, conscience, and religion.
- *Democratic rights*. Among these are the rights of all adult persons to vote and stand for public office. Requirements that elections periodically be held and that the law apply equally to those who govern and those who are governed are also important democratic rights.
- *Legal rights*. These are essentially procedural rights intended to ensure the fair and equal treatment of individuals under the law. They include, *inter alia*, the right to due process of law, freedom from arbitrary arrest, the right to a fair hearing, and the right not to be subjected to cruel or unusual punishment.
- *Economic rights*. Although they usually are not listed as a separate category of entrenched rights, economic rights occupy an important place in all capitalist democracies. They include the right to own property and not to be deprived of it without fair compensation, the right to withhold one's labour, and freedom of contract.
- *Equality rights*. This is the most recent and probably the most controversial category of rights. The American constitution, the first modern constitution to include an entrenched guarantee of equality rights, refers only to every person's right to 'equal protection of the laws'.[6] The more recent tendency, however, has been to enumerate the proscribed bases of legal discrimination, such as race, religion, ethnicity, gender, and age. Canada's Charter also includes mental or physical disability. Some argue that sexual preference should be added to the list.

These four categories by no means exhaust the rights that may be protected by law. *Language rights* represent an important category of group rights in many societies, Canada included. Other group rights, such as for religious minorities or Native peoples, may also be protected by law. Some argue that *social rights*, or what are sometimes called *entitlements*, including the right to a job, economic security, decent housing, and adequate health care, should also have the status of entrenched constitutional rights. *Environmental rights* have also been advocated by some groups, including the Canadian Bar Association.

In Canada, all of these main categories of human rights are entrenched in the Charter. Table 10.1 identifies the sections of the Charter that correspond to each of them. A word of warning: this classification should be read as a general guide to the location of specific rights in the Charter. Due to the imagination of lawyers, the complex circumstances of particular cases, and the inevitable overlap that exists between different rights claims, the basis for a particular right may be found under what appears to be an unrelated heading.

For example, unions have argued that collective bargaining is a right that belongs to working people. They have claimed (unsuccessfully) that it should be implied by and protected under section 2(d) of the Charter, which guarantees 'freedom of association'. Business interests have argued (successfully) that section 8 of the Charter, which guarantees 'the right to be secure against unreasonable search and seizure', limits the search powers that were being exercised by a government agency with responsibility for investigating collusive business practices.[7] Protection for economic rights was found under a legal rights guarantee. In *Irwin Toy* (1986),[8] a company successfully challenged a Quebec law banning commercial television advertising targeted at children by relying on the Charter's protection of freedom

Table 10.1 Human Rights and the Charter

Rights Category	Pre-Charter Protections	Charter Protections
1. Political rights/ fundamental freedoms	Common-law protections implied in the preamble of the Constitution Act, 1867	s. 2
2. Democratic rights	Constitution Act, 1867, ss. 41, 50, 84, 85	ss. 3 5
3. Legal rights	Common law	ss. 7–14
4. Economic rights	Common-law rights re: contract, property, etc.	s. 6 (and implied under some other sections)
5. Equality rights	Common law; s. 93 of Constitution Act, 1867, guaranteeing educational rights of religious denominations	ss. 15, 28
6. Language rights	Constitution Act, 1867 s. 133	ss. 16–23
7. Aboriginal rights	Treaties	s. 25; s. 35 of Constitution Act, 1982
8. Social rights	None	None

of expression (s. 2(6)). An economic right was disguised as a fundamental freedom. But perhaps the most striking case of one sort of right—again, an economic one—being claimed under a different category of rights involved business's successful challenge to the federal Lord's Day Act.[9] Hardly anyone seriously believed that the case had anything much to do with the Charter's guarantee of freedom of religion (s. 2(a)). It had a lot to do, however, with the right to make money on Sundays.

It is no accident that cases involving what obviously are economic claims are packaged in the language of other rights. Except for the Charter's reference to mobility rights, a right intended to guarantee the free movement of Canadian citizens between provinces, it is silent as regards economic rights. Moreover, the Supreme Court of Canada has declared on a number of occasions that the Charter does not include economic and property rights. '[T]he overwhelming preoccupation of the Charter', declared the majority in a 1987 decision denying the right to strike, 'is with individual, political, and democratic rights with conspicuous inattention to economic and property rights.'[10] This interpretation of the Charter has also worked against business interests on occasion. In particular, business's efforts to find some protection for property rights in the Charter's guarantee of security of the person (s. 7) have been expressly rejected by the Court.[11]

Denied explicit constitutional recognition of their rights, economic interests have urged their claims under what appear to be non-economic provisions of the Charter. This has produced some curious distortions, as the protagonists to a political conflict attempt to fit their claims into the categories available under the Charter and the interpretative tendencies of judges. Michael Mandel refers to this process as the 'legalization of politics'. Legalized politics, he argues, inevitably favours established interests and serves to reinforce the status quo because of the biases built into the law and the legal/judicial profession (see Chapter 6). We would agree. But, the legalization of politics does not express strongly enough the deformation of politics that the Charter has encouraged. This deformation is not limited to economic conflicts. Moreover, it is not clear, despite Mandel's claims, that established interests have been the chief beneficiaries of Charter politics. Ted Morton argues that groups located primarily on the left of the political spectrum, groups that he labels 'the Court Party', have been far more successful than so-called establishment interests in using the Charter to win political victories.[12]

On the Origins and Meanings of Rights

There is no inevitability either to the precise rights recognized by the constitution or to the meanings that come to be associated with them. Rights, like a society's notions of justice, are constructed out of concrete historical circumstances. The rights that are claimed in present-day Canada and the rights discourses that emerge around these claims and counterclaims are very different from those of even twenty-five or thirty years ago. And much of Canadian rights discourse would be unrecognizable in a society like Iran, where very different religious, cultural, and economic forces have contributed to the recognition of and meaning ascribed to rights. There are, therefore, no absolute rights that may be adduced from human history. What may appear to be the most obvious and uncontroversial rights claims—for example, the right to vote or the right to express one's personal beliefs—are denied in many societies.

Rights come from political struggles. A claim made by an individual or a group will be expressed as a right only when it is denied or placed in jeopardy by the words or actions of some other party. For example, the claim that a woman has a right to abort her pregnancy arises because of legal and practical restrictions on access to abortion. The experience of limitations on freedom of speech, religion/conscience, or association produced calls for their constitutional protection. Likewise, when a linguistic group claims the protection or promotion of its language as a right, this is an indication that conflict exists between linguistic groups in that society.

Political struggle is a necessary condition for rights claims. It is not, however, a sufficient condition. Only some political conflicts acquire the character of rights issues. To be recognized as legitimate, a rights claim must be successfully linked to one or more of a society's fundamental values. These fundamental values operate as limits on rights discourse.

Consider the familiar issue of abortion. Those who argue for a woman's right to abort her pregnancy when she chooses have often linked this claim to individual freedom of choice, a fundamental value in liberal-democratic society. Those who oppose abortion, or who favour serious restrictions on access to it, often argue that the human fetus has a right to life, the most fundamental of rights in any civilized society. Those who favour access to abortion would, of course, object to the imputation that they do not value human life, just as those who oppose abortion would deny that they undervalue individual freedom. Behind these rights, as behind all of the rights that are widely recognized in democratic political systems, are one or more fundamental values, such as the equality of human beings, the autonomy of the individual, and, most importantly, the nature of the good society.

The abortion issue illustrates well the way in which rights claims tend to be squeezed into existing ideological and legal categories, and how unconventional political discourses are discouraged by legalized politics. When individual women, women's organizations, and abortionists like Henry Morgentaler have been successful in challenging legal restrictions on access to abortion, this has been because their case has been framed in legal arguments and moral claims that fall within the dominant ideology. Beginning in the 1970s, Morgentaler was involved in a number of court cases where he was charged with violating section 251 of Canada's Criminal Code, which placed limits on a woman's access to abortion. He was acquitted by juries on a number of separate occasions, each time successfully invoking the 'defense of necessity'. This is a common-law principle that, applied to medical procedures, provides immunity from criminal prosecution if the procedure is necessary to save the life of the patient. Pregnancy was treated, in these cases, as an illness and abortion as a medical procedure necessary to deal with it.

The passage of the Charter opened up new legal avenues to abortion advocates. In a 1983 Ontario trial, Morgentaler's lawyer argued that Canada's existing abortion law violated a long list of rights and freedoms that the Charter had entrenched in Canada's constitution. These included freedom of conscience and expression, the rights to life, liberty, and security of the person, and the right not to be subjected to cruel and unusual treatment. Anti-abortion activist Joe Borowski was busy invoking some of the same rights, i.e., the Charter's section 7 guarantee of life, liberty, and security of the person, arguing that the unborn fetus should be considered a legal person entitled to these rights.[13] Canada's abortion law was eventually ruled unconstitutional by a 1987 Supreme Court decision in which the majority ruled that it violated security of the person. But the same majority agreed that the state has an interest in protecting the fetus, although at what stage of fetal development and in what circumstances the Court did not say. This acknowledgement of fetal rights provided some encouragement to the anti-abortion coalition, whose political strategy focused increasingly on claiming the personhood of the unborn.

When appealing to public opinion and in arguing their case before the courts, both pro- and anti-abortion forces have resorted to symbols and values that are well-established parts of the dominant ideology. The political temptation to do so is overwhelming. But the consequences of fitting a group's objectives into the available framework of rights discourse, including the concepts and interpretations that the legal system provides, tend to be conservative in two main ways.

First, the issue may be misdefined or, what amounts to the same thing, defined in terms that conform to prevailing notions of what rights are legitimate and what strategies are appropriate for pursuing them. This delegitimizes alternative ways of conceptualizing the issue—and even what is really at issue—and the discourses associated with these alternatives. For example, is the abortion issue primarily about 'security of the person' and about procedural fairness in the application of the law, the rights that have provided the basis for successful legal challenges to Canada's abortion law? Or is the struggle over abortion really just an element in a larger political struggle involving male domination of women and/or competing notions of the good society? Most feminists would take the latter position, arguing that legal restrictions on access to abortion and the tendency in law to treat abortion as a health problem are manifestations of the social dominance of males, in this instance, of males defining female experiences. Frontal attacks like this tend, however, to be labelled— and largely dismissed—as radical and unrepresentative of majority opinion. Moreover, the sweep and general character of such critiques pose a strategic dilemma. 'Patriarchy' is not a concept recognized by the law. The law does, however, recognize various individual rights. Strategically, then, it makes sense for women's groups to use the legal tools that are available in order to make a difference in the short term. But in succumbing to what Carol Smart calls the 'siren call of law',[14] the sweep and character of feminist demands may be changed.

The second way in which recourse to rights discourse and the law may result in conservative consequences involves the idea that legal solutions to a problem are possible and desirable. '[I]n engaging with law to produce law reforms,' argues Smart, 'the women's movement is tacitly accepting the significance of law in regulating social order. In this process the idea that law is the means to resolve social problems gains strength and the idea that the lawyers … are the technocrats of an unfolding Utopia becomes taken for granted … while some law reforms may benefit women, *it is certain that all law reforms empower law*.'[15] But the law and the legal/judicial profession, as argued in Chapter 6, have some inherent biases toward the status quo.

Enforcing Rights

During the 1980–1 debate on constitutional reform, critics of an entrenched charter of rights warned that entrenchment would lead to the Americanization of Canadian politics. Since then, they have lamented that their prediction has come true. The 'Americanization' that they warned of, and that many still regret, has two main aspects. One involves a more prominent policy role for unelected judges and a related decline in the status of elected legislatures. The other is an increase in recourse to the courts to solve political disputes.

Some of those who opposed entrenched rights, including former Manitoba Premier Sterling Lyon, argued that rights and freedoms are better protected by elected legislatures, accountable to the electorate for their actions, than by unelected judges. By 'better', they meant that the decisions of elected politicians are more likely to correspond with the sentiments of citizens—or at least that if they do not there exists a democratic mechanism, i.e., elections, to hold politicians accountable for their choices. Rights, the opponents of entrenchment argued, should not be interpreted independently of popular opinion. Nor should important political controversies be determined by unelected officials.

What the critics denounced as the undemocratic flaws of entrenchment, advocates of the Charter acclaimed as its virtues. Rights, they argued, should not be subject to the vicissitudes of public opinion as registered in the legislature. The fact that judges are not elected and are virtually unremovable before the age of seventy-five serves to protect, not undermine, democracy. What sort of democracy, entrenchment advocates ask, would permit rights and freedoms to depend on shifting popular sentiments and politicians' calculations of political expediency?

The difference between the opponents and advocates of entrenchment is not over the importance of rights. It is not even primarily about the appropriate balance between the rights of individuals and minorities versus those of the majority. As unflinching a civil libertarian as Alan Borovoy, general counsel of the Canadian Civil Liberties Association, argues against the entrenchment of rights.[16] The difference between these two positions is over how best to *protect rights*. Those who advocate the American model of entrenched rights prefer to put their faith in the constitution and the judges who interpret it. Those who prefer the British model of parliamentary supremacy are more dubious about judge-made law and more inclined to place their trust in the prudence and democratic responsiveness of elected governments.

Does the record of rights enforcement in different countries permit us to draw conclusions about whether the American or British model is 'best'? Has the Charter made a difference in how well rights are protected in Canada? There are no easy answers to these questions. Rights activists are themselves divided in their assessment of the impact of entrenchment. But if definitive answers are elusive, we can at least attempt to understand how rights have been argued and enforced in Canadian politics. The Charter, we will see, represents an important watershed.

The Pre-Charter Era: 1867–1981

There is not a single reference to the subject of rights in R. MacGregor Dawson's *Constitutional Issues in Canada, 1900–1931*, published in 1933.[17] In Dawson's *The Government of Canada* (1947), the first textbook on Canadian government, one finds a mere handful of references to fundamental rights and liberties.[18] J.A. Corry and J.E. Hodgetts's *Democratic Government and Politics*[19] pays greater attention to rights, devoting an entire chapter to a comparison of civil liberties in Britain, the United States, and Canada. Generally, however, rights issues occupied a distinctly marginal place in Canadian political science and even in legal circles until the middle of this century.

A couple of factors were responsible for blunting the profile of rights questions. The most important was undoubtedly federalism. The Constitution Act, 1867, contains very few references to the rights and freedoms of Canadians. It does, however, include a very detailed catalogue of the 'rights' of governments, i.e., the legislative and fiscal powers of Ottawa and the provinces. Faithful to the principle of parliamentary supremacy, the courts were unwilling to overrule the authority of elected legislatures. As a result, throughout most of Canada's history, issues that clearly involved the protection of rights and freedoms were dealt with by the courts as federalism questions. To have a chance at success, therefore, rights claims had to be packaged in the constitutional categories of federalism. The resulting jurisprudence was bizarre, to say the least. Consider the following cases:

- *Reference re Alberta Statutes* (Alberta Press case, 1938).[20] The law in question was The Accurate News and Information Act, passed by the Alberta legislature in 1937. It imposed censorship restrictions on the province's newspapers, based on the Social Credit government's belief that the press was unfairly critical of its policies. Ottawa referred this and two other pieces of Social Credit legislation to the Supreme Court for a ruling on their constitutionality. The Court was unanimous in striking down the press censorship law. Two of the judgements in this case referred to the 'right of free public discussion of public affairs' as being a right fundamental to parliamentary democracy and implied under the preamble to the Constitution Act, 1867, which states that Canada is adopting 'a constitution similar in principle to that of the United Kingdom'. But both of these judgements, although using somewhat different reasoning, suggested that the federal government possessed the authority to impose restrictions on freedom of the press. The Alberta law was, therefore, struck down essentially on federalism grounds.

- *Saumur v. City of Quebec* (1953).[21] Quebec City had passed a by-law forbidding the distribution in the streets of any printed material without the prior consent of the chief of police. Without explicitly singling out any group, this by-law was intended to curb proselytizing activities by the Jehovah's Witness sect, whose activities and teachings strongly offended Catholic Church authorities. In a five-to-four decision, the Court struck down the by-law. An analysis of the judges' reasoning reveals just how disinclined they were to place the protection of fundamental freedoms over the authority of government. On the majority side, four of the five justices decided that the by-law was *ultra vires*. The fifth was willing to concede that the regulation fell within provincial jurisdiction, but felt that the right to disseminate religious material was protected by Quebec's Freedom of Worship Act. On the dissenting side, two of the judges argued that the by-law fell within the province's jurisdiction over civil rights. No one suggested that freedom of religious expression ought to be protected from interference by any level of government.

- *Switzman v. Elbling* (Padlock Case) (1957).[22] In 1937 the Quebec government had passed a law declaring illegal the use of a house for the propagation of communism, authorizing the Quebec police to put a padlock on premises where such activities were suspected. The Supreme Court of Canada ruled that the impugned Act had the effect of making the propagation of communism a crime. But criminal law is under the exclusive jurisdiction of Ottawa, and so the 'Padlock Law' was struck down as being *ultra vires* (i.e., beyond the legal authority of the government in question). The issue of political censorship was raised by a couple of justices, but this was not the basis for the Court's ruling.

- *Attorney-General of Canada and Dupond v. Montreal* (1978).[23] This case involved a Montreal by-law that restricted freedom of assembly in public places. The by-law was used in the 1960s to prevent public demonstrations during a period of political turmoil and occasional terrorist incidents. By a five-to-three vote the Supreme Court upheld the constitutionality of this restriction. The majority argued that the impugned by-law regulated matters of a local or private nature and therefore came under the authority of the province. Interestingly, the dissenting judges did not focus on the issue of freedom of assembly. Instead, they argued that the Montreal by-law was *ultra vires* because it represented a sort of 'mini-Criminal Code' and thus intruded on Ottawa's exclusive authority to make criminal law. As a final note, the judgement in this case was unequivocal in dismissing the relevance of the Canadian Bill of Rights (1960). 'None of the freedoms referred to', wrote Justice Beetz, 'is so enshrined in the constitution as to be above the reach of competent legislation.'[24]

Federalism was not the only factor responsible for the relatively low profile of rights issues until well into this century. Public opinion was generally sanguine about the treatment of rights and freedoms in Canada. The feeling of most informed Canadians was probably that rights were best protected by legislatures, the common law, and a vigilant public: the system that Canada had inherited from the United Kingdom. But increasing doubts about the adequacy of these guarantees were being expressed during the 1940s and 1950s. These doubts were sown by such apparent rights violations as Quebec's infamous 'Padlock Law' (1937), the Alberta government's attempt to censor the press (1937), the threatened deportation of Japanese Canadians in 1945–6, and the arbitrary measures taken during the Gouzenko spy affair of 1946. These constituted, according to political scientist Norman Ward, 'disturbing signs of a weakening concern by Dominion and provincial governments for personal rights and liberties'.[25] Corry and Hodgetts agreed, arguing that the protections provided under British parliamentary government were not sufficient in a young country facing the challenge of absorbing large numbers of persons of diverse ethnic origins and cultural backgrounds.[26]

This growing concern over civil liberties was shared by influential groups like the Canadian Bar Association. The solution, they argued, was a bill of rights that would be entrenched in the constitution. Canada's participation in the United Nations, and the human rights commitments entered into through the UN, reinforced the voices of those calling for constitutionally entrenched rights. When the Conservative Party came to power in 1957 under the leadership of John Diefenbaker, who had long been an outspoken advocate of entrenched rights, the timing for a bill of rights seemed propitious.

But there was a major snag. A constitutional bill of rights would affect the powers of both Ottawa and the provinces and, it was believed, would therefore require provincial consent. It was clear that some of the provinces would oppose entrenchment, consequently the Conservative government chose to introduce the Bill of Rights as a statute, requiring only the approval of the House of Commons and the Senate. The Canadian Bill of Rights became law on 10 August 1960.

The Bill of Rights proved to be a major disappointment for civil libertarians. The first Supreme Court decisions on its application were very conservative. In a case involving a challenge to the federal Lord's Day Act, the Court took the position that the Bill of Rights only reaffirmed the rights and freedoms status quo that existed at the time it became law. Speaking for the majority, Justice Ritchie declared that '[The Canadian Bill of Rights] is not concerned with "human rights and fundamental freedoms" in any abstract sense, but rather with such "rights and freedoms" as they existed in Canada immediately before the statute was enacted.'[27]

After nearly a decade of judgements that, to paraphrase Saskatchewan former Chief Justice Emmett Hall, whittled away at the Bill of Rights,[28] the Supreme Court suddenly gave evidence of abandoning its cautious approach. The case involved an Indian, Joseph Drybones, who was convicted under section 94(b) of the Indian Act, which made it an offence for an Indian to be intoxicated off a reserve. In challenging this provision, Drybones's lawyer argued that it conflicted with the Canadian Bill of Rights guarantee of 'equality before the law', subjecting Indians to criminal sanctions that other people were not exposed to. This was obviously true. But if the Court remained faithful to its earlier interpretation, this would not be sufficient to render the discrimination unconstitutional.

By a five-to-three vote the Supreme Court used the Bill of Rights to strike down section 94 of the Indian Act.[29] This proved, however, to be an aberration. Perhaps realizing the Pandora's box they were opening through this more activist interpretation of the Bill of Rights, a majority of the judges retreated from this position after *Drybones*. This became crystal clear a few years later in the *Lavell* case,[30] where the majority upheld the constitutionality of another provision of the Indian Act against a challenge that it denied equality before the law.

Another nail was hammered into the Bill of Rights coffin by the Court's decision in *Hogan v. The Queen* (1975).[31] In *Hogan*, a person suspected of driving while intoxicated refused to take a breathalyzer test before seeing his lawyer. He ultimately took the test and this evidence was key to his conviction. The question before the Supreme Court was whether evidence should be excluded if it has been obtained in an improper manner. Under the common law, Canadian judges had followed the rule that such evidence would be admitted so long as it was relevant to the case at hand. But the Canadian Bill of Rights included a number of legal rights, including the right of an accused or detained person 'to retain and instruct counsel without delay' (s. 2(c)(ii)).

The Supreme Court was unwilling to apply the Bill of Rights in this case. It appeared, therefore, that not only could the Bill of Rights not be used to strike down conflicting federal legislation—at least laws on the books before 1960—it did not take precedence over established rules of the common law. Chief Justice Laskin's dissenting argument that the Bill of Rights should be interpreted as a 'quasi-constitutional instrument' was never supported by a majority of his colleagues. The glimmer of hope that the *Drybones* decision had sparked was extinguished during the 1970s, producing renewed calls for constitutionally entrenched rights.

Before passage of the Charter, the only rights entrenched in Canada's constitution were associated with religion and language. Section 93 of the Constitution Act, 1867, declares that the educational rights of denominational minorities may not be diminished from what they were when a province entered Confederation. Section 133 establishes the equal standing of French and English in Parliament and in federal courts, and in the Quebec legislature and in the courts of that province. Neither of these sections proved to be very effective in protecting minority rights.

The major test of section 93 involved the Manitoba Public Schools Act. This law eliminated the Catholic and Protestant schools that had existed in the province and replaced them with a single public school system. In *Barrett*,[32] the Judicial Committee of the Privy Council decided that this law did not violate the educational rights of the Roman Catholic minority because Catholics, like the members of any religious denomination, were free to set up their own private schools. Of course, they would have to pay for them out of their own pockets, in addition to having to pay the local and provincial taxes that financed the public schools. This, in the JCPC's view, did not diminish the rights they had enjoyed when both Protestant and Catholic schools were financed out of public revenues.

In two other cases involving section 93, the courts refused to accept the argument that this section also protected the educational rights of language minorities. The argument had at least a ring of plausibility because of the fact that, historically, the Roman Catholic schools in Manitoba and Ontario were predominantly Francophone, while Quebec's Protestant schools were Anglophone. Thus, when in 1913 the Ontario government issued regulations banning the use of French as a language of instruction in both public and separate (Catholic) schools, this had a negligible impact on public schools but dealt a major blow to the predominantly Francophone Catholic schools of eastern Ontario. The issue arose again in the 1970s when the Quebec government passed Bill 22, restricting access to the province's English-language schools, most of which were under the control of Protestant school boards. In both instances the courts rejected outright the claim that section 93 should be read as a protection for linguistic rights in addition to denominational ones.[33]

From the standpoint of promoting bilingualism outside of Quebec, the courts' unwillingness to read language rights into section 93 represented a real setback. On the other hand, the 'victories' for language rights in a pair of Supreme Court decisions handed down in 1978 and 1979 produced little in the way of practical consequences. Both of these decisions involved the limited guarantee of bilingualism established by section 133 of the Constitution Act, 1867. In both cases the Court declared that this guarantee was beyond the interference of governments, thus repudiating the idea that no action lay outside the competence of Parliament or a provincial legislature so long as it did not encroach on the constitutional powers of the other level of government.

In *Attorney-General of Quebec v. Blaikie*,[34] the Court upheld a Quebec Superior Court decision that had ruled unconstitutional those sections of Quebec's Bill 101 that attempted to make French the sole official language in that province. While Bill 101 did not ban the use of English from the legislature and the province's courts, and the Quebec government continued to print and publish laws and legislative documents in both languages, the law's clear intent was to make French the only official language for all government activities and the dominant language in the province's courts. This, the courts decided, violated the spirit—if not the strict letter—of section 133.

The issue in *Attorney-General of Manitoba v. Forest* (1979)[35] was essentially the same, although the circumstances were quite different. In 1890, the Manitoba legislature had passed a law making English the sole official language of the province's government and courts, and went the further step of actually banning the use of French in the legislature and the courts. This flatly contradicted the Manitoba Act, 1870 (an Act of the British Parliament creating the province of Manitoba), which imposed on Manitoba the same language requirements that section 133 of the Constitution Act, 1867, imposed on Quebec. Ironically, Manitoba's Official Language Act, 1890, had been ruled unconstitutional by a lower court judge in 1892 and then again in 1909. These rulings were apparently ignored by the provincial government. The successful challenge in the *Forest* case was a hollow victory, to say the least. In the words of René Lévesque, Québec's Premier at the time, the decision came ninety years too late to make a difference for Manitoba Francophones.

The Charter Era: 1982–Present

Life in what Peter Russell has called 'Charterland'[36] is different from the pre-Charter era in two main ways. On a quantitative level, the Charter has been the direct stimulus for explosive growth in the number of rights cases that come before the courts. On average, about

1,000 Charter cases are decided each year, and about two dozen of these are rulings by the Supreme Court or one of the provincial superior courts.

In terms of 'quality', the change produced by the Charter has been no less pronounced. The previous pattern of deciding rights issues as federalism cases, asking only whether a government was transgressing the jurisdictional turf of the other level of government, has been abandoned. Rights issues are now dealt with head on, argued by litigants and decided by judges on the basis of the Charter. Moreover, the courts have shed some of their traditional reluctance to question the substance of duly enacted laws and regulations. Emboldened by the Charter's unambiguous declarations that the 'Constitution is the supreme law of Canada' and that the courts have exclusive authority to interpret and enforce the Charter's guarantees, judges have struck down provisions in dozens of federal and provincial statutes. As we will see, although judges are quite aware of the expanded role they play in the political process, they continue to exercise a measure of self-restraint when it comes to second-guessing elected governments.

Reasonable Limits and the Charter

The courts are 'invited' to exercise self-restraint by the opening words of the Charter. Section 1 declares that the guarantees set forth in the Charter shall be 'subject only to such reasonable limits prescribed by law as can be demonstrably justified in a free and democratic society'. What are these 'reasonable limits'? The Supreme Court established a test in the case of *The Queen v. Oakes* (1986).[37] The first part of this test asks whether a government's objective in limiting a right is of sufficient importance to warrant such an encroachment. The second part of the test asks whether the extent of the limitation is proportionate to the importance of the government's objective. To satisfy this second criterion, a limitation must meet three conditions: (1) it must be rationally connected to the government's objective; (2) it should impair the right in question as little as is necessary to meet the government's objective; and (3) the harm done to rights by a limitation must not exceed the good that it accomplishes.

In *Oakes*, the Court was called upon to determine whether a 'reverse onus' provision in the Narcotic Control Act violated the presumption of innocence set forth in section 11(d) of the Charter. Under that Act, a person found guilty of possessing drugs was automatically considered guilty of trafficking unless he could prove his innocence on this more serious charge. The Court did not question the importance of the objective associated with this provision of the Act, i.e., to prevent drug trafficking. But in applying the second part of the test that they developed in *Oakes*, the justices decided that the means were disproportionate to the end.

The separation of legislative ends, part one of the *Oakes* test, from an assessment of the means used to accomplish them may appear to be a way around the thorny problem of judges second-guessing the decisions of duly elected governments. In fact, however, it is not possible to answer such questions as whether a right is impaired as little as possible in the circumstances or whether the means are proportionate to the ends without trespassing into the realm of political value judgements. Since *Oakes*, the courts have been reluctant to question the ends associated with laws and regulations limiting rights. But they have not been shy about using the second part of the *Oakes* test to dismiss governments' section 1 justifications.

This was apparent in the Supreme Court's decision in *Ford v. Atto.* (1988).[38] The case involved a challenge to those sections of Quebec's b. ited commercial advertising in languages other than French. The Que. argued that this limitation was necessary to preserve the economic value of u. guage and the predominantly French character of the province. The Court accep. was a perfectly legitimate policy goal (it passed part one of the *Oakes* test), but an..... at the Quebec government had not shown that 'the requirement of the use of French only is either necessary for the achievement of the legislative objective or proportionate to it'.[39] Not content to let matters rest here, the Court suggested what the Quebec government perhaps should have done to accomplish its legislative purpose in a way acceptable under section 1 of the Charter. 'French could be required', it suggested, 'in addition to any other language or it could be required to have greater visibility than that accorded to other languages.'[40]

In fairness to judges, why shouldn't they give legislators an idea of how the law needs to be changed to bring it into line with their interpretation of the constitution? The point is, however, that means and ends are not neatly separable in the real world of politics. Moreover, tests like means being proportional to the ends just beg the question: who should determine how much or little of what is enough? Is proportionality an appropriate matter for unelected judges to decide, or should this be determined by elected legislatures?

These questions resurfaced with a vengeance when the Supreme Court ruled on 21 September 1995 that the federal ban on tobacco advertising violated the Charter's guarantee of freedom of expression. The total ban did not, in the eyes of the majority of the Court, satisfy the second part of the *Oakes* test. 'The government had before it a variety of less intrusive measures when it enacted the total ban on advertising', observed Madam Justice Beverly McLachlin. Commenting on the government's refusal to allow the Court to see documents pertaining to advertising and tobacco consumption, including one on the alternatives to a total ban on advertising, she added, 'In the face of this behaviour, one is hard-pressed not to infer that the results of the studies must undercut the government's claim that a less invasive ban would not have produced an equally salutary result.'[41] Anti-smoking groups responded to the decision by calling on Ottawa to use the 'notwithstanding clause' to override Charter protection for tobacco advertising. Many staunch Charter boosters became sceptics overnight. They were awakened by the tobacco advertising decision to a basic truth of constitutionally entrenched rights: the price of entrenchment is that judges assume a more important role in political life.

The Notwithstanding Clause: Section 33

'What the Charter giveth, the legislature may taketh away.' This appears to be the meaning of section 33 of the Charter, the 'notwithstanding clause'. It states that either Parliament or a provincial legislature may expressly declare that a law shall operate even if it offends against sections 2, 7-14, or 15 of the Charter. This provision was not part of Ottawa's original Charter proposal but was inserted at the insistence of several provinces. Indeed, it appears that federal-provincial agreement on the constitutional deal that produced the Charter would have died without this concession.[42]

Although the notwithstanding clause appears to provide governments with a constitutional escape hatch from much of the Charter, it is not clear that it actually has this effect. It has been resorted to on only a handful of occasions. Why have governments generally been reluctant to use section 33 to avoid or reverse court decisions declaring their laws to be in violation of the Charter? In the words of civil libertarian Alan Borovoy, 'The mere introduction of a bill to oust the application of the Charter would likely spark an enormous controversy....Without solid support in the legislature and the community, a government would be very reluctant to take the heat that such action would invariably generate.'[43]

Borovoy's confidence that public support for the Charter and vigilant media provide adequate protection against section 33 is not shared by everyone. Civil liberties groups and the legal profession have generally been outspokenly critical of the notwithstanding clause, to the point that a court challenge was launched against it immediately after the Charter was proclaimed.[44] The basis of this challenge was that if the constitution is the supreme law of the land, as the Constitution Act declares, then no part of it should be placed beyond the powers of judicial review. By this reasoning, a legislature's decision to invoke section 33 should itself be reviewable, and therefore able to be overturned, by the courts. In a 1985 ruling, the Quebec Court of Appeal agreed. This decision was, however, overruled by the Supreme Court of Canada in *Ford v. Attorney-General of Quebec*. The Court pronounced in favour of a literal interpretation of section 33—which also happens to correspond with the intentions of those provincial governments who insisted on the notwithstanding clause—requiring only that a legislature expressly declare its intention to override the Charter.

It appears, therefore, that there are no serious legal roadblocks in the way of a government using section 33 to circumvent the Charter. But in fact, it has been invoked on only a handful of occasions. (If, that is, one does not take into account the PQ policy, between 1982 and 1985, of inserting the notwithstanding clause into all laws passed by the Quebec legislature and retroactively into all existing provincial statutes. These actions were part of that government's symbolic and legal strategy against the constitutional reforms of 1982, to which the PQ government had not agreed.) This suggests that there are significant political barriers to its use. Quite simply, governments do not want to give the appearance of denying rights to their citizens. There are, however, circumstances where the denial of rights inflicts little political damage on government and may even produce political dividends.

This was certainly true of the Quebec Liberal government's decision to use the notwithstanding clause to re-pass, with some modifications, the provisions of Bill 101 that had been ruled unconstitutional by the Supreme Court (see Chapter 11). Public opinion, the province's Francophone media, and the opposition PQ were all strongly supportive of legislative restrictions on the use of languages other than French. While the government's move precipitated the resignation of three Anglophone cabinet ministers and drove many English-speaking voters into the arms of the newly formed Equality Party in the next provincial election, there is no doubt that the political costs of not overriding the Charter would have been far greater.

The political costs were also negligible when Saskatchewan's Conservative government inserted section 33 in a 1986 law passed to force striking public servants back to work. The government feared that, without the notwithstanding clause, the courts might rule that back-to-work legislation infringed the freedom of association guaranteed by section 2 of the Charter. Rather than run this risk, it chose to act pre-emptively to override this right. (As it turned out, the Supreme Court later decided that collective bargaining and strike action are not protected by the Charter.) Denying government employees the right to strike is popular with the public. Some analysts suggest that the Saskatchewan Conservatives' use of section 33 against public servants may even have produced a net gain in votes for the party in the election that followed about a year later.[45]

So do public opinion and vigilant media provide adequate protection against legislative abuses of the notwithstanding clause? Ultimately, the answer depends on our expectations for democracy. For some, the mere fact that public opinion may be overwhelmingly supportive of a law that denies rights to some persons is not a legitimate basis for invoking section 33. They would argue that if the Charter does not protect rights when they are vulnerable, guarding them from the 'tyranny of the majority', then it fails what should be the real test of its worth. Rights are either entrenched against popular passions and legislative assault, they would insist, or they are not. But for others, the notwithstanding clause is a mechanism for asserting the popular will in exceptional circumstances. The only other way of overcoming an unpopular court decision on the Charter would be to amend the constitution, a difficult and time-consuming process. The controversy over section 33 is, in the final analysis, nothing less than the familiar debate over parliamentary versus constitutional supremacy.

Applying the Charter

News stories of yet another attempt to use the Charter to challenge some law or administrative procedure have become routine. These attempts range from matters whose social importance is obvious to challenges that appear trivial, even by charitable standards. Only a small fraction of the hundreds of trial court rulings on the Charter ultimately reach the provincial superior courts, and fewer still are appealed to the Supreme Court. Even so, a large share of the workload of these courts is now consumed by cases requiring them to apply the Charter. After more than a decade in 'Charterland' it is possible to identify the main tendencies in judicial interpretation of the rights and freedoms it purports to guarantee.

To understand these tendencies, three issues are of special significance. First, how have the courts interpreted the Charter's scope and authority? Second, what difference has the Charter had on the relationship between the state and individuals? Third, what have been the Charter's effects on equality in Canada? The last two issues are, of course, fundamental to our assessment of Canadian democracy.

Scope and Authority

In one of its first Charter decisions, *Law Society of Upper Canada v. Skapinker* (1984), the Supreme Court made clear its position on judicial review of the Charter. Consciously modelling its position along the lines of *Marbury v. Madison* (1803), the landmark American Supreme Court ruling that established that Court's supervisory role over the US constitution, the Supreme Court of Canada declared its intention to assume a similar role in applying the Charter. 'With the Constitution Act, 1982,' wrote Justice Willard Estey, 'comes a new dimension, a new yardstick of reconciliation between the individual and the community and their respective rights, a dimension which, like the balance of the Constitution, remains to be interpreted and applied by the Court.'[46]

How far would the Court be willing to go in using the Charter to strike down laws passed by elected legislatures? Here, too, the ruling in *Skapinker* borrowed from *Marbury v. Madison*. Although the constitution must be considered the supreme law of the land, judges should interpret it in ways that 'enable [the legislature] to perform the high duties assigned to it, in the manner most beneficial to the people.'[47] In other words, judges should not be too quick to second-guess elected law-makers.

Skapinker was more a broad statement of intent than a clear signpost. But a year later the Court was given the opportunity to show how activist it was prepared to be in applying the Charter. The *Singh* case involved a challenge to procedures under Canada's Immigration Act, whereby applicants for political refugee status were not given an automatic right to a hearing. By a 6–0 vote, the Supreme Court decided that this violated fundamental principles of justice. However, three of the justices based their ruling on a section of the Bill of Rights that guarantees the 'right to a fair hearing', while the other three went further in arguing that the right to a hearing is implied under section 7 of the Charter, guaranteeing 'the right to life, liberty and security of the person and the right not to be deprived thereof except in accordance with the principles of fundamental justice'. Justice Bertha Wilson took the most aggressive approach to the Charter, arguing that 'the guarantees of the Charter would be illusory if they could be ignored because it was administratively convenient to do so'.[48] At least some of the judges, then, demonstrated their willingness to take a hard-line approach to the Charter, whatever the administrative and political effects on government policy might be. As it transpired, the *Singh* decision resulted in thousands of additional cases being added to what was already a huge backlog of refugee claims and precipitated the introduction of a new law whose intent was to limit refugees' access to Canada.

Singh was followed by a string of 1985 rulings that defined in sharper hues the Supreme Court's approach to the Charter. In *The Queen v. Big M Drug Mart* (1985), the Court struck down the federal Lord's Day Act on the grounds that it violated the Charter's guarantee of freedom of religion. From the standpoint of the interpretive rules being developed by judges in applying the Charter, the most significant feature of the *Big M* case was the willingness of all of the justices to inquire into the purposes associated with the rights and freedoms set forth in the Charter. The Court signalled its readiness to go beyond the simple words of the Charter and the stated intentions of those who drafted it to interpret the historical meaning and social purposes of a concept like, in this particular case, freedom of religion. This is the very hallmark of judicial activism.

The issue of what the Charter's drafters actually intended was raised again in *Reference re B.C. Motor Vehicle Act* (1985). In this case, British Columbia's Attorney-General argued that section 7 protection for the 'principles of fundamental justice' was meant by the governments who agreed to the Charter to be a guarantee of procedural fairness (the issue raised in *Singh*). It was not, he argued, intended to enable the courts to assess the fairness of the 'substance' of laws. In rejecting the government's argument, the Court quite correctly reasoned that it is not always possible to separate substance and procedure. For example, a law whose substance is the denial of a procedural right associated with the principles of fundamental justice is both procedurally and substantively unfair. The majority was quick to add, however, that judicial review under section 7 should be limited to the criminal law and legal rights, and should not extend to general public policy. This declaration was intended to prevent section 7 from being used by any group or individual who believed that a law treated them unfairly.

On the question of what the Charter's drafters had intended for section 7, the Court ruled that arguments about intentions could not be binding for two reasons. First, it is not possible to state categorically what legislative bodies intended for the Charter as a whole or for particular provisions of it. Second, if the original intentions were treated as binding on the courts, then 'the rights, freedoms and values embodied in the Charter in effect becomes [sic] frozen in time to the moment of adoption with little or no possibility of growth, development and adjustment to changing societal needs'.[49] This implies, of course, that judges will determine what constitute 'changing societal needs'.

As reasonable as these arguments about legislative 'intentions' sound, it should be pointed out that the Court has sometimes taken these intentions very seriously. This was true in the *Quebec Protestant School Board* (1984)[50] ruling, where the Court relied on the drafters' intentions for section 23 of the Charter in striking down the education provisions of Quebec's Bill 101. It has also been evident in other decisions, including *Re Public Service Employee Relations Act* (1987).[51] In denying that the right to strike is protected by the Charter, the Court argued that the drafters of the Charter were deliberately silent on economic rights. It appears, then, that legislative intentions do matter when judges find them convenient.

The issue of the Charter's scope was the focus of another of the Court's 1985 decisions, *Operation Dismantle v. the Queen*.[52] A coalition of groups opposed to testing of the cruise missile in Canada argued that these tests violated the Charter's guarantee of the right to life and security of the person by making nuclear war more probable. The Court rejected this argument on the grounds that the alleged facts in the plaintiff's claim were unprovable speculations. But the other question before the Court was whether cabinet decisions—the decision to allow cruise missile tests was taken by cabinet—and foreign policy defence issues are reviewable by the Courts. The federal government argued that cabinet decisions are 'Crown prerogatives' and therefore off-limits to the courts. The Supreme Court disagreed. It argued that section 32 of the Charter should be interpreted to apply to all government actions. On the precise question of whether foreign policy and defence issues are inherently political and beyond the reach of judicial review, the Court did not express an opinion.

There is an additional feature of the Court's approach to the Charter's scope that deserves mention. This involves its insistence that the Charter applies only to relationships between the state and citizens, not to private-sector relationships. Thus, the Charter cannot be used by someone who believes that he has been denied a job or an apartment because of his race, or by a person whose private-sector employer requires that she retire at the age of sixty-five. Forms of discrimination like these are pervasive throughout society, but they are not inequalities that can be overcome using the Charter. The Supreme Court has on several occasions articulated this distinction between public (covered by the Charter) and private, as in *Dolphin Delivery* (1986)[53]: '[The Charter] was set up to regulate the relationship between the individual and the government. It was intended to restrain government action and to protect the individual.'[54] This position is, in fact, faithful to the intentions of those who framed and agreed to the Charter.

The Court's refusal to recognize economic rights is related to this public/private distinction. As noted earlier, the Charter is deliberately silent on economic and property rights, except for the qualified protection it extends to the right to live, work, and be eligible for social benefits in any province. Claims that certain economic rights are implied by provisions of the Charter have generally received a cold reception. For example, the courts have expressly rejected business's arguments that corporations should fall within the ambit of section 7 of the Charter, which guarantees the 'right to life, liberty and security of the person'. The economic rights claims of workers have fared no better at the hands of judges. In a 1987 ruling on whether a right to strike exists, the Supreme Court declared that 'The constitutional guarantee of freedom of association ... does not include, in the case of a trade union, a guarantee of the right to bargain collectively and the right to strike.'[55] The right to bargain collectively and to strike are not, the Court ruled, fundamental rights or freedoms that deserve the constitutional protection of freedom of association under the Charter. 'They are', the majority declared, 'the creation of legislation, involving a balance of competing interests',[56] and their scope and limitations are appropriately determined by legislatures. To put it very simply, economic rights were viewed as subordinate to political ones.

It may seem, then, that the courts are at least even-handed in rejecting the economic rights arguments of both business and labour. In fact, this appearance of neutrality is deceiving for two reasons. First, business interests have been able to use some of the 'political' rights in the Charter to protect property rights, in some cases arguably at the expense of workers, consumers, or other community interests. Second, much of the inequality that exists in society is generated by private economic relations—relations between employers and employees, men and women in the workplace, landlords and tenants, buyers and sellers. To declare that the Charter recognizes only 'political' and 'democratic' rights but not 'economic' ones, as the courts have done, has the effect of freezing the inequalities that currently exist in society and in the economy. Dominant groups tend to win from this public/private distinction, which places important sources of inequality beyond the authority of the Charter, while subordinate groups lose.

It is true, of course, that every major Supreme Court ruling on the Charter serves to clarify the scope and authority of judicial review. We have focused on several early Charter decisions to demonstrate that the Court very quickly assumed the mantle of judicial activism. How far judges go in using the Charter to strike down laws and administrative practices is, to a large extent, up to them. There are, however, two provisions of the Charter that were intended to rein in the courts' authority. One is the 'reasonable limits' clause (s. 1), the other is the notwithstanding clause (s. 33).

Individual Rights and Freedoms

Some individual rights and freedoms are better protected today as a result of the Charter. Court decisions have expanded the rights of, among others, those accused of crimes, immigrants, women seeking abortions, and business people wanting to advertise in English in Quebec. On the other hand, Supreme Court decisions have declared that the Charter's freedom of association does not provide unionized workers with the right to strike; upheld the constitutionality of terribly vague provincial anti-hate laws against claims that they violate freedom of expression; and ruled that secularly worded Sunday closing laws have the effect of being an 'indirect and unintentional' violation of freedom of religion, but that they qualify as 'reasonable limits' under section 1 of the Charter. The Court came down on the side of freedom of expression over anti-hate restrictions in the *Zundel* decision (1992) and over the federal ban on tobacco advertising (1995). Although the courts have not unleashed a torrent of individualism on Canadian society, it is fair to say that individual rights claims tend to do better, and certainly do no worse, under the Charter than previously.

This was certainly true in the *Big M* case, when the Supreme Court was asked to decide whether the federal Lord's Day Act violated the freedom of religion guarantee set down in section 2 of the Charter. The Court had little trouble in deciding that it did. What could not be achieved using the Canadian Bill of Rights became possible under the Charter.

The courts' rulings on legal rights challenges to Canada's criminal law provides another clear illustration of the more liberal treatment of individual rights in the Charter era. Charter decisions have produced many important changes in law enforcement practices, including the following:

- 'Reverse onus' provisions, requiring a defendant to prove his innocence of a charge, have been ruled unconstitutional.
- Evidence obtained by inappropriate means, such as confession obtained without informing an accused person of his right to legal counsel, cannot be used to help convict that person.
- Writs of assistance, under which the police were able to enter premises at any time without a search warrant, were ruled unconstitutional.
- Search and seizure powers have been restricted.
- Thousands of persons accused of criminal offences have had the charges against them dismissed because of an Ontario Superior Court ruling that lengthy delays in getting them to trial contravened their s. 11(b) right 'to be tried within a reasonable time'.

In probably the most publicized Charter decision to date, the Supreme court struck down Canada's twenty-year-old abortion law. Under section 251 of the Criminal Code a woman wanting an abortion required the approval of a hospital's therapeutic abortion committee. In most communities, however, the local hospital(s) did not have such a committee and did not perform abortions. Even in communities where hospitals did perform abortions (about 20 per cent of all hospitals at the time), there was considerable difference between them in the likelihood that an abortion would be permitted. The majority in *Morgentaler* (1988)[57] ruled that the obvious practical inequalities in the application of the law violated section 7 of the Charter, guaranteeing the principles of fundamental justice.

Is there an identifiable pattern in the Court's interpretation of the individual rights guaranteed by the Charter? Aside from what most commentators characterize as a moderately activist approach, the Court has shown few sharply pronounced tendencies. In the *Morgentaler* case, for example, the Court's decision was supported by three distinct sets of reasons. This is not uncommon, nor is it rare for the Court to be sharply divided in its interpretation of important provisions of the Charter. Even where the Court has adopted what appears to be a clear interpretation rule, it is difficult to predict how it will be applied in particular circumstances. Finally, it needs to be kept in mind that the court is sometimes sharply divided in its approach to individual rights, as was seen in its 1995 ruling on Ottawa's tobacco advertising ban (see Box 10.1).

Equality and the Charter

Some Charter decisions have contributed to greater equality in Canadian society, but others clearly have not. Any attempt to assess the Charter's overall impact on equality is fraught with difficulties. But given that its supporters have always claimed that the Charter represents a major victory for democracy in Canada and given the undeniable importance of many Charter rulings for public policy, the issue needs to be addressed.

Section 15 of the Charter deals explicitly with equality rights. Those who drafted this section, the precise wording of which provoked as much controversy as anything in the Charter, expected that it would have significant consequences for the laws and administrative practices of governments. For this reason the equality section did not become operative until three years after the Charter was proclaimed. In fact, however, section 15 has had less of an impact on equality in Canada than some other sections of the Charter.

Box 10.1   A Court Divided

The Decision
In September 1995 the Supreme Court rules in a 5–4 decision that the 1988 Tobacco Products Control Act is unconstitutional because Ottawa's near-total advertising ban violates the industry's right to free speech.

What It Means
Tobacco companies are free to resume all forms of advertising, including the television and radio ads that they voluntarily pulled in 1972.

Bold unattributed health warnings, such as 'Smoking can kill you', are unconstitutional and may disappear.

Companies can put their logos and trademarks back on promotional items such as T-shirts and cigarette lighters. The federal government must pass a new law if it wants to continue to restrict tobacco advertising.

What Was Said
'... there was no direct evidence of a scientific nature showing a causal link between advertising bans and decrease in tobacco consumption.'

Madam Justice Beverly McLachlin

'The harm engendered by tobacco and the profit motive underlying its promotion, place this form of expression as far from the core of freedom of expression values as prostitution, hate mongering, or pornography and thus entitle it to a very low degree of protection under [section 1 of the Charter].'

Mr Justice Gérard La Forest,
one of the four dissenters on the court

Many court decisions on the Charter have been highly controversial. (Roy Peterson, *Vancouver Sun*)

First and most importantly, it does not extend to discrimination in private-sector relationships. We have already discussed the practical consequences of limiting the Charter to abuses of governmental power. As constitutional expert Peter Hogg puts it,

> The real threat to civil liberties in Canada comes not from legislative and official action, but from discrimination by private persons—employers, trade unions, landlords, realtors, restaurateurs and other suppliers of goods or services. The economic liberties of freedom of property and contract, which imply a power to deal with whomever one pleases, come into direct conflict with egalitarian values.[58]

Although section 15 cannot be used to fight these private forms of discrimination, provincial human rights codes enforced by commissions do cover private-sector relations.

The potential impact of section 15 is also limited by the courts' unwillingness to treat equality rights as superior to other rights in the Charter or to other parts of the constitution. Not only must the courts balance equality rights against the 'reasonable limits' provision of the Charter—this is a tightrope they must walk with all of the rights set forth in the Charter—they must also weigh section 15 rights against other rights and freedoms. How to strike this balance was the issue before the Supreme Court in *Re Education Act* (1987),[59] dealing with the constitutionality of an Ontario law extending full public funding to that province's Roman Catholic schools.[60] The Supreme Court ruled that the equality of religion guaranteed by section 15 did not override provincial governments' authority to grant special educational rights to Catholics and Protestants under section 93 of the Constitution Act, 1867.

In the final analysis the Charter and the courts send out mixed and sometimes confusing signals about equality. The same can be said, of course, about governments. Despite the courts' willingness to go beyond formal legal equality to see whether the effects of a law meet the requirements of the Charter (as the Supreme Court did in *Morgentaler*), the usefulness of the Charter as an instrument for overcoming the most prevalent and deeply rooted forms of social and economic inequality is limited. The predominant message is that equality involves the equal treatment of individuals by the state.

It is not that the courts are oblivious to the social and economic context of the inequalities that appear before them as Charter claims. On the contrary, several of the major Charter rulings read like sociological or historical treatises.[61] This is precisely what alarms many of the Charter's critics, who recoil at what they see as judicial usurpation of the legislature's function (see Box 10.2). Moreover, experience under the Charter has shown that society's 'haves', as well as the 'have nots', are able to use the Charter to advance their interests. Whatever its drafters intended, it is not clear that the Charter has done much to promote social and economic equality in Canada. On the other hand, some would argue that the pursuit of such goals—how and to what extent they should be achieved—ought to be the business of elected politicians, not judges.

Box 10.2 The Charter Revolution

Just as the 1960s are remembered by Canadian historians as the decade of the Quiet Revolution, so the 1980s will be remembered as the decade of the Charter Revolution. The adoption of the Charter of Rights and Freedoms in 1982 has transformed both the practice and theory of Canadian politics. It has replaced a century-old tradition of parliamentary supremacy with a new regime of constitutional supremacy that verges on judicial supremacy. Judges have abandoned the deference and self-restraint that characterized their pre-Charter jurisprudence and become active players in the political process. Encouraged by the judiciary's about-face, interest groups—many funded by the very governments whose laws they are challenging—have increasingly turned to the courts to advance their policy objectives. The Charter has made the courtroom a new arena for the pursuit of politics. Charter litigation— or its threat—also casts its shadow over the more traditional arenas of electoral, legislative, and administrative politics.

F.L. Morton, 'The Charter Revolution and the Court Party',
Osgoode Hall Law Journal, 30, 30 (1992), 627–8.

On 30 October 1995, Quebecers rejected separation by the narrowest of margins. (Greg Vickers)

Conflict over language has always been a central feature of Canadian politics. This chapter explains why language and the status of Quebec are such prominent issues in Canada. It also examines the chief aspects of federal and Quebec language policies. Topics include the following:

- ❖ The demographics of language politics.
- ❖ The trajectory of nationalism.
- ❖ The Quiet Revolution and its legacy.
- ❖ Language policy in Quebec.
- ❖ Federal language policy.
- ❖ Is Quebec a distinct society?

CHAPTER ELEVEN

■ Language Politics

L ike the theme of unrequited love in an Italian opera, the status of Quebec is an issue that surfaces repeatedly when Canadians and their governments turn their thoughts to constitutional reform. And like Italian opera, elements of tragedy and comedy mingle freely when the related issues of Quebec's constitutional status and language rights are on the table. But unlike an Italian opera, the 'Quebec question'—which might just as fairly be called the 'Canada question' (or at least one of the fundamental Canada questions, the other one being Canada's relationship to the United States)—has no neat finale. Even the scenario of a separate Quebec would not bring down the curtain on the 'Canada/Quebec' question. No one doubts that an enormous number of practical matters would still have to be dealt with, including such thorny issues as the nature of economic relations between the remnants of *l'ancien Canada* and the status of the French language in a Canada without Quebec.

Why are Quebec and language so central to Canadian politics? Why is the issue of language rights so closely tied to that of Quebec's constitutional status? Why do Lord Durham's words about 'two nations warring in the bosom of a single state', words written over 150 years ago, sound so apt today? What does Quebec want from the rest of Canada, and the rest of Canada from Quebec? Why has nationalism always been the key to unlocking the mysteries of Quebec politics?

Questions do not always have answers. These are big questions, and despite all the attention paid them throughout this country's history they are far from being settled. Let us at least try to understand why these particular questions have so often been asked and why answers have been so elusive.

The Demographics of Language Politics

When New France was formally placed under British control in 1763, Francophones out-numbered Anglophones by about eight to one in the territory that would become Canada. Forty years later, the two groups were of roughly equal size. During the mid-1800s the English language gained ground on the French because of the wave of immigrants from the British Isles, so that by the 1871 census—Canada's first—Canadians of French origin comprised about one-third of the population.[1] The extraordinarily high birth rate among French-Canadian women enabled Francophones to hold their own until the end of the 1950s against an English-speaking population that was buoyed by immigration—immigrants of whatever language group overwhelmingly adopted English as their new language. Since then birth rates have dropped precipitously in Quebec, where the vast majority of Francophones reside, and the Francophone share of Canada's population has nudged down to its present all-time low of about 24 per cent (see Figure 11.1).

The end of *la revanche des berceaux*—the high birth rate that for close to a century enabled French Canada to maintain its numerical strength against English Canada—coupled with the fact that the vast majority of immigrants have chosen English as their adopted language, finally led to a decline in the Francophone share of the Canadian population by the early 1960s. More worrisome from the standpoint of Quebec governments was the fact that demographers began to predict a fall in the Francophone share of that province's population, particularly in Montreal where most new immigrants chose to establish themselves. Montreal, which proudly called itself the second largest French-speaking city in the world

Figure 11.1 Mother Tongues of the Canadian Population, 1931-91

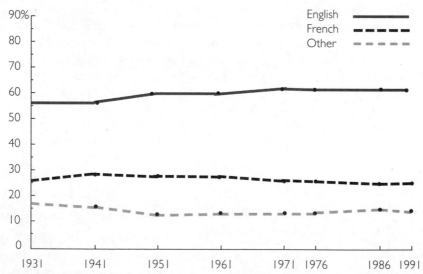

Sources: Leacy, ed., *Historical Statistics of Canada*, Series A185-237; *Canada Year Book 1990*, 2–25; *Canada Year Book 1994*, 122.

(after Paris), would, according to demographer Jacques Henripin, be about equally divided between Anglophones and Francophones by the early twenty-first century.[2] The possibility that Francophones would become a minority in Quebec was often raised by Quebec nationalists, although serious demographers like Henripin argued that this possibility was quite remote.[3] Nevertheless, this decline provided the impetus for provincial language laws intended to stem this tide.

The key factor in shifting the linguistic balance of Quebec, it should be emphasized, was immigration. Given that the province's Anglophones were no more fecund than Francophones, the language choices of allophones—Canadian demographers' unlovely term for those whose native language is neither English nor French—would be crucial in shaping Quebec's future linguistic contours. Immigration became the sole reason for provincial population growth by the 1960s, given that the provincial fertility rate had fallen below the replacement level (i.e., the average number of births per female needed to offset the mortality rate).

With the exception of the relatively few immigrants whose native tongue was French, all other groups overwhelmingly adopted English for themselves and their children. As of the 1961 census, 46 per cent of foreign-born residents of Quebec spoke only English, another 25 per cent spoke English and French, and only 17 per cent spoke only French.[4] Despite provincial language laws that require immigrants to send their children to French schools, make French the sole official language for provincial public services, and promote the use of French in the Quebec economy, evidence points to the fact that many allophones still opt for English. Figure 11.2 shows that the percentage of Quebecers claiming French as their mother tongue is identical to the percentage who speak mainly French in the home. But the percentage speaking English in the home is greater than those who claim English as their mother tongue. The gains made by the English-speaking community can only be explained by the linguistic choices of those whose mother tongue is neither French nor English. New Quebecers have continued to find English an attractive choice, although less often than before the existing provincial language laws were put into place.

Inside Quebec, the current demographic picture includes the following characteristics.

- French is spoken at home by about 82 per cent of the population (1991 census).
- Contrary to projections made in the 1960s and early 1970s, Quebec has become increasingly Francophone. The 82 per cent of the population speaking French at home compares to 80 per cent in 1901 and 81 per cent in 1961.[5]
- Most of the province's population increase is due to immigration. Recent studies suggest that almost as many immigrants choose English as their adopted language as choose French, despite the provincial *francisation* measures targeted at them.[6]
- Quebec's share of Canada's total population has fallen over the last two decades, from 28 per cent in 1971 to about 24 per cent in 1995.

Outside Quebec the language picture looks very different. With the exceptions of New Brunswick and Ontario, the Francophone populations of the other provinces are tiny. In fact, in certain provinces some of the non-official language communities are considerably larger than the French-speaking minority. For example, in British Columbia native speakers of

Figure 11.2 Mother Tongue and Language Spoken at Home, 1991

A. Canada

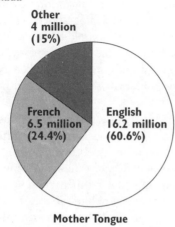

Other
4 million
(15%)

French
6.5 million
(24.4%)

English
16.2 million
(60.6%)

Mother Tongue

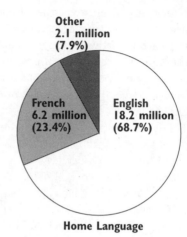

Other
2.1 million
(7.9%)

French
6.2 million
(23.4%)

English
18.2 million
(68.7%)

Home Language

B. Quebec

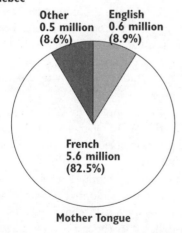

Other
0.5 million
(8.6%)

English
0.6 million
(8.9%)

French
5.6 million
(82.5%)

Mother Tongue

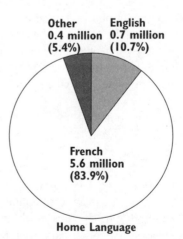

Other
0.4 million
(5.4%)

English
0.7 million
(10.7%)

French
5.6 million
(83.9%)

Home Language

Source: Census of Canada, 1991.

Chinese outnumber those whose mother tongue is French by more than three to one, and there are 50 per cent more people who claim Punjabi as their mother tongue as claim French.[7]

In all provinces except Quebec, the French language community loses some of its members to the English majority. This may be seen from the difference between the number of people for whom French is their mother tongue compared to the number for whom it is their home language. The difference represents the rate of language transfer to the dominant language group (see Table 11.1). Only in Quebec and, to a lesser degree, New Brunswick is the rate of French language retention high. By contrast, the rate of language retention among native English-speakers is high everywhere in Canada.

This is not a recent development. In *Languages in Conflict*, Richard Joy carefully documented the trend toward the assimilation of Francophones outside Quebec. Joy was the first to make what today seems an obvious point, namely, that the rate of language transfer is greatest among the younger generations. For example, using data from the 1961 census he found that the transfer rate from French to English in the four western provinces was 25 per cent among those aged 45–54 but 60 per cent for those aged 5–14 and 67 per cent among infants aged 0–4.[8] Only in what Joy called 'the bilingual belt', the narrow region running from Moncton, New Brunswick, in the east to Sault Ste Marie, Ontario, in the west, was the rate of assimilation among all generations significantly lower. The reason, of course, was the ability to shop, work, go to church, and do the other things that keep a language alive. Outside the bilingual belt, this supportive milieu was seldom encountered. Nor is it today,

Table 11.1 Language Transfer from French to English, by Province (1991)

	French Mother Tongue	French Home Language	English Home Language	Transfer Rate
Canada	6,502,865	6,038,705	389,880	6%
Nfld	2,770	1,125	1,520	55%
PEI	5,590	2,850	2,615	47%
NS	36,635	20,605	15,280	42%
NB	241,565	215,015	23,350	10%
Que.	5,556,105	5,455,720	58,040	1%
Ont.	485,395	286,240	178,975	37%
Man.	49,130	22,780	24,605	50%
Sask.	20,885	5,975	14,100	68%
Alta	53,710	16,680	34,630	64%
BC	48,835	10,820	35,545	73%
Yukon	865	345	465	54%
NWT	1,380	560	740	54%

Note: French home language and English home language do not add up to the total in the first column because of transfers to groups other than English. Those who report both English and French as home languages have not been counted as transfers from the French-language community.

Source: Statistics Canada, *Census of 1991, Language Retention and Transfer*, 93–153.

At this point some readers may protest that the gloomy picture Joy drew three decades ago is no longer accurate. They will point to statistics suggesting that bilingualism outside of Quebec has been increasing in recent years. Indeed, it is today highest among the young (see Figure 11.3), the very group that Joy argued was most likely to transfer to the dominant language group. The rapid expansion of French immersion schools during the 1980s, particularly in Ontario, which accounts for over half of all immersion students in Canada, is responsible for most of this increase. The future of French outside Quebec, they argue, is assured.

What is one to conclude from the fact that while the Francophone share of Canada's population outside of Quebec has been declining, the proportion of the population claiming to be bilingual has been increasing? Does this represent a reprieve for French-language minorities? Or are they, as René Lévesque once said, 'dead ducks', or as Quebec writer Yves Beauchemin has characterized them, 'des morts vivantes' ('warm corpses' would be a reasonable translation)?

The pressures of assimilation continue unabated throughout most of the predominantly English-speaking provinces. A recent study by Roger Bernard of the University of Ottawa

Figure 11.3 Bilingualism in Canada, 1931–91

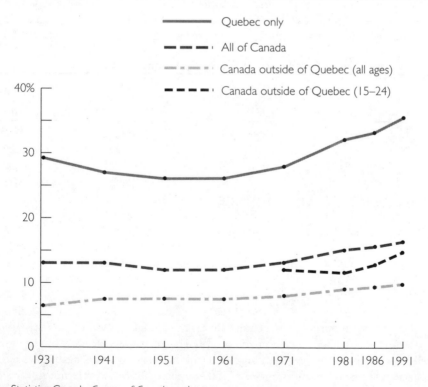

Source: Statistics Canada, *Census of Canada,* various years.

concludes that a combination of aging populations, low birth rates, marriage to non-Francophones, and the general lack of a supportive social and economic milieu for French speakers will lead to the collapse of many Francophone communities outside Quebec within a generation or two.[9] It appears, however, that the fate of larger Francophone communities in northern and eastern Ontario and in New Brunswick may be less bleak. Jacques Henripin cautiously suggests that official bilingualism in New Brunswick and the extension of French language services and education in Ontario may have slowed the assimilationist tide in those provinces.[10]

As for the increasing level of bilingualism in Canada, we would not draw from this the conclusion that the prospects for living in French outside of Quebec have improved. The census question that measures bilingualism ('Can you carry on a conversation in the other official language?') does not provide a measure of languages in use. The fact that increasing numbers of those whose mother tongue is English are 'functionally fluent' in French does not mean that French will be used more often in the home, the workplace, on the tennis court, and wherever else communication takes place. Indeed, there is a good deal of evidence suggesting that three decades of French immersion education[11] have produced a wave of *receptive bilinguals*—people who are capable of responding to French communications but do not themselves initiate conversations in French, consume French-language media, or seek out opportunities to live in their acquired second language. We will discuss the phenomenon of immersion education in greater detail later in this chapter.

Finally, the fact that functional bilingualism appears to be on the rise does not mean that the social and economic milieux outside Quebec have become more supportive for Francophones. It is true that provincial government services for the Francophone communities of Ontario have improved since the mid-1980s, and those in New Brunswick are quite good. But it is also true that few people outside the 'bilingual belt' can manage in French to shop, work, and do the other daily social activities that help keep a language alive. Even Francophone schools in predominantly English-speaking communities experience the pressures of language erosion. René Lévesque's characterization of Francophones outside Quebec as 'dead ducks' is somewhat overstated. Lame ducks might be closer to the truth.

The Trajectory of Nationalism

French-Canadian nationalism, Pierre Trudeau writes, was originally a system of self-defence. This was certainly true. Conquered by arms, the French-speaking population of New France found itself subordinated to an Anglophone minority about one-eighth its size. English was the language of the new political and commercial élites. The Conquest left French a second-class language within Quebec and Francophones largely excluded from the colony's structures of power.

Why did Francophones not succumb to assimilationist pressures, as they did in Louisiana after it, too, passed from French control? The answer is complex, but three chief factors can be identified. One involved the policies of the British colonial authorities in New France. By the terms of the Quebec Act, 1774, they granted formal protection to the status of the Roman Catholic religion and the *code civil*, the basis of civil law in New France.[12] The British faced rebellion in the Thirteen Colonies, which two years later successfully declared their independence from Britain, and this recognition for the rights of the French-Canadian population may have been motivated chiefly by the desire to ensure the allegiance of the clerical and civil leaders of that population. Regardless, it involved official recognition of the rights of the Francophone Catholic majority and reinforced the leadership role of that community's clerical élite.

A second factor that explains the different fates of the French language and culture in Louisiana compared to Quebec is demography. French-speakers in the south of the United States were very quickly swamped by a rapidly growing Anglophone population. But as we observed earlier in this chapter, although immigration of Loyalists from the United States and English-speakers from the British Isles tipped the linguistic balance in Canada toward English by the early nineteenth century, the high fertility rate among French Canadians enabled them to hold their ground at about one-third of Canada's population between Confederation and the 1950s.

The defensive posture that Trudeau argues was characteristic of French-Canadian nationalism is the third factor that explains the ability of French Canada to resist the pressures of assimilation. Under the guidance of a clerical élite whose leading social role was strengthened when Anglophones occupied the political and commercial élites of the colony, French Canada met the challenge of Anglophone domination by remaining loyal to traditional values and institutions. The nationalist ideology that developed in French Canada after the Conquest is summed up in a famous passage from *Maria Chapdelaine*, the classic novel of traditional French Canada:

> Round about us strangers have come, whom we are wont to call barbarians; they have seized almost all the power; they have acquired almost all the money, but in the country of Quebec nothing has changed.... [W]e have held our own, so that, it may be, after several centuries more, the world will turn to us and say: these people are of a race that knows not how to perish....
>
> ... In the country of Quebec, nothing shall die, and nothing shall be changed....[13]

Traditional French-Canadian nationalism was guided by the idea of *la survivance*—survival, against the pressures of a dominant culture that was Anglicizing, Protestant, materialistic, liberal-democratic, and business-oriented. In other words, a dominant culture that was all the things that French Canada, according to the spokespersons for this ideology, was not and should not become. The main ideas expressed in the writings and public pronouncements of the exponents of the traditional nationalism can be summarized fairly briefly:

- French Canada comprised a distinct nation, whose chief characteristics were the Catholic religion and the French language. Preservation of the French language and the Catholic religion were inseparable, as the title of Henri Bourassa's book *La langue, guardienne de la foi*[14] explicitly declared. 'The preservation of language', Bourassa wrote, 'is absolutely necessary for the preservation of a race, its spirit, character and temperament.'[15]
- French Canada had a mission, a special vocation as a people. The mission was to remain faithful to its roots and to resist the lure of materialistic English Protestant pressures. The democratic belief in the separation of church and state was ludicrous. It was a lamentable heresy spawned by the French Revolution and the American constitution.

- The character of the French-Canadian people was most secure in the province of Quebec, but French Canada was not restricted to the boundaries of that province. In other words, French Canada was defined by socio-cultural characteristics, not by the territory of Quebec.

While these were the chief characteristics of the nationalist ideology that became dominant in French Canada during the nineteenth century, a dominance it maintained until the middle of this century, there were voices of dissent. In fact, sociologist Marcel Rioux argues that the idea of the French-Canadian nation was first developed by the secular élites of Quebec who espoused liberal and often aggressively anti-clerical views.[16] Political scientist Denis Monière concurs, noting that the authority of the Church was much weaker before and in the decades immediately following the Conquest than is usually believed (especially by English-Canadian historians).[17] He maintains that the 'victory' of the conservative traditional nationalism only became assured after the defeat of Louis Papineau's liberal forces in the Lower Canada Rebellion of 1837. But even during the 'high noon of ultramontanism', as Monière calls the century of ideological dominance by the exponents of the traditional nationalism, liberal voices of dissent were occasionally heard.[18]

The traditional nationalism came under mounting pressure during the middle of the twentieth century. Its chief tenets were increasingly at odds with the economic and social reality of Quebec. The emigration of hundreds of thousands of French-speaking Quebecers to the northeastern United States during the nineteenth century demonstrated more clearly than anything the empty idealism of the traditional nationalism's hymn to the pastoral vocation of French Canadians. There simply was not enough arable land to support the rural parish lifestyle that the ideologues of the traditional nationalism clung to so tenaciously. The urban population of Quebec surpassed the rural population in the 1921 census (56 per cent to 44 per cent). Between 1926 and 1950 the number of people employed in Quebec's manufacturing sector increased by about 220 per cent, slightly higher than the rate of increase for Canada as a whole (210 per cent) but significantly higher than the rate for the rest of the country if Ontario—where most new investment in manufacturing was located—is omitted from the picture.[19] By mid-century manufacturing workers outnumbered farm workers in Quebec by a large margin.[20] In short, by the early twentieth century the 'typical' Québécois lived in a city or town, worked in a factory, store, or office, and had family members who had left the province in search of employment opportunities.

Quebec was following the path of modernization. But the urbanization and industrialization this involved also produced a political side effect of enormous importance. This was the increasing realization that Francophones, despite accounting for about four-fifths of the Quebec population, were largely shut out of the centres of economic decision-making and controlled relatively little of the province's wealth. 'Is there any inherent or unavoidable reason why', asked Abbé Groulx in 1934, 'with 2,500,000 French Canadians in Quebec, all big business, all high finance, all the public utilities, all our water rights, forests and mines, should belong to a minority of 300,000?'[21] Although the question was not new—Edouard Montpetit, Errol Bouchette, Étienne Parent, and others had raised basically the same issue in arguing that educated Francophones needed to rid themselves of their apparent distaste for careers in industry and finance—it was being asked with increasing frequency between the 1930s and the 1950s.[22]

These decades saw the emergence of the first serious challenge to the conservative ideology since the crushed rebellion of 1837. It brought together a diverse group of university professors and students, journalists, union activists, liberal politicians, and even some elements within the Catholic Church (particularly Action catholique). They were united by their opposition to the so-called 'unholy alliance' of the Church, Anglophone capital, and the Union Nationale party of Maurice Duplessis, and, of course, to the conservative nationalism that sought to justify French-Canadians' marginal economic status. Marcel Rioux calls this anti-establishment challenge the ideology of contestation and recoupment.[23] It contested the traditional élites' monopoly over power in the province and what was argued to be their backward characterization of French Canadian society and culture. Its goal was to recoup lost ground, to bring Quebec's society, economy, and government up to date, a goal that became known in Quebec as *rattrapage* (catching up).

The nerve centre of this challenge to the conservative establishment and ideology included the Faculty of Social Sciences at Laval University, the intellectual revue *Cité libre*, founded by such figures as Pierre Trudeau and Gérard Pelletier, and the provincial Liberal Party. As the political party attempting to depose Duplessis, it was natural that the Quebec Liberal Party would attract the energies of those who saw the Union Nationale under *le chef* as one of the chief obstacles to reform.

Like the dinosaurs, the traditional ideology and the interests it defended were doomed by their failure to adapt to a changing environment. As Marcel Rioux observes, 'the ideology and old power structure in Quebec were becoming anachronistic in the face of the demographic, economic, and social changes that Quebec was experiencing.'[24] They managed to hold on until the 1960s largely because of the tight web of patronage politics that Maurice Duplessis used to keep the ideologically conservative Union Nationale in power between 1945 and his death in 1959. The death of Duplessis was followed by disorder within the governing Union Nationale. Paul Sauvé, who succeeded Duplessis as Premier, died suddenly within a year. The Union Nationale went into the 1960 provincial election under a leader, Antonio Barrette, who was opposed by many powerful members of the party. The Liberal Party's election victory probably owed as much or more to disorder within the Union Nationale as to popular support for change. Regardless, the opportunity for reform had come.

The Quiet Revolution and Its Legacy

The first several years of the 1960s are justly considered a turning point in the history of Quebec.[25] Duplessis's death in 1959 and the election of the provincial Liberals under Jean Lesage in 1960 opened the way for the political reforms and social changes that generally are referred to as the Quiet Revolution. At the heart of these reforms lay an increased role for the Quebec state. It replaced the authority of the Catholic Church in the areas of social services and education, and also acquired a vastly broader range of economic functions. The provincial state was seen as the *moteur principal* of Quebec's attempt to modernize social and political institutions that were ill-suited to the urbanized, industrialized society that Quebec had become. The state, traditionally viewed as a second-class institution in a province where most social services were controlled by the Church and where government was associated with crass patronage, became the focus of nationalist energies.

The nationalism that emerged in the crucible of the Quiet Revolution marked a sharp break with the past. The traditional nationalism had emphasized preservation of the *patrimoine*—the language, the faith, the mores of a community whose roots went back to New France. Although some of its chief spokespersons, including Abbé Lionel Groulx, associated this community with the region of the St Lawrence River and even with the vision of a Laurentian state whose territory would include what is today the southern region of the province, the essential elements of the traditional nationalism were not defined by either the territory or the powers of the Quebec state.

Marcel Rioux has characterized the traditional nationalism as an ideology of conservation. Its goals were the preservation of the traditional values and social structures of French Canada, including the leading role played by the Church in articulating these values and controlling these structures (i.e., the schools, hospitals, labour unions, etc.). The modern welfare state necessarily threatens the dominant social role of the Church and was generally rejected by spokespersons for the traditional nationalism. Although they insisted on constitutional protections for the province's exclusive right to make education policy and put limits on Ottawa's ability to interfere with social affairs in the province, they did not expect that the Quebec state would actively occupy these fields. The traditional nationalism attached no particular value to the Quebec state, except insofar as its powers could be used to ward off federal intrusions that challenged the status of conservative values and the power of the traditional élites—the clergy, Anglophone business leaders, and provincial politicians.

Nationalism is always based on some concept of the nation: who belongs to it and who does not. The traditional nationalism did not identify *la nation canadienne-française* with *la société française du Québec*. The boundaries of *la nation* extended beyond Quebec to embrace French Canadians throughout Canada. There were two reasons for this. First, Catholicism and the role of the Church were important elements of the traditional nationalism. Obviously, neither of these stopped at the Quebec border. Second, the anti-statist quality of the traditional nationalism prevented it from associating the French-Canadian nation with the Quebec state.

History had shown that assimilationist pressures and unsympathetic governments faced Francophones outside of Quebec. Nevertheless, to identify the nation with the Quebec state would have challenged the dominant social role of the Church. The survival of the nation did not depend, according to the traditional nationalism, on the activities of the Quebec state. Instead, it depended primarily on those institutions that were crucial to the continuation from generation to generation of the French language and the Catholic religion—family, school, and parish. Family and parish obviously fell outside the state's authority. And although the schools were under the constitutional jurisdiction of the provincial state, their control was mainly left in the hands of the Church. This did not change until the early 1960s.

The central elements of the traditional nationalism were located outside of the state. This would not be true of the new nationalism that both spurred and was influenced by the Quiet Revolution. Instead of defining *la nation* in terms of language and religion, the ascendant nationalism of the 1960s developed an understanding of Quebec's history, its economy, and its social structure that was based on language and dependency. The dependency perspective portrayed Quebec as a society whose evolution had been shaped and distorted by the economic and political domination of English Canadians.

This secularized version of French-Canadian history, and more particularly of Francophone Quebec, cast an entirely different light on the future of the Quebec nation and its relationship to English Canada. If the problem was that Québécois were dominated economically and politically, then the solution required that they take control of their economic and political destiny. To do so, they would have to use the Quebec state. All of the major reforms of the Quiet Revolution—the establishment of a provincial Ministry of Education, the nationalization of privately owned hydroelectric companies, the creation of such Crown corporations as la Caisse de dépôt et placement and la Société générale de financement, and passage of the Quebec Pension Plan—involved using the Quebec state in a newly assertive way.

The replacement of the traditional nationalism by the state-centred one of the Quiet Revolution was not as abrupt as history might suggest, nor was this new nationalism unchallenged. The traditional social order and its values had been crumbling at the edges for at least a couple of decades before the death of Duplessis and then of Sauvé finally provided the opportunity for opposition groups to gain power. Once the doors were opened to reform, it quickly became apparent that the anti-Duplessis forces shared little more than a common antipathy toward the old order. They were divided on at least three main levels.

First, there was a split between the federalists and those who advocated either special status or independence for Quebec. The federalists included such prominent figures as Pierre Elliott Trudeau, Jean Marchand, and Gérard Pelletier, all of whom entered federal politics through the Liberal Party in 1965. Leadership of the Quebec autonomy side would fall on René Lévesque, who became the first leader of the Parti Québécois in 1968. The second division concerned the size and functions of the Quebec state. Even within the reformist Liberal government of Jean Lesage, there were sharp differences over such major policies as the nationalization of the hydroelectricity industry and the role of the province's investment agency, la Caisse de dépôt et placement. Agreement that the provincial state should play a larger role in Quebec society was not matched by consensus on what that role should be. Finally, Quebec separatists were divided on ideological lines. Those who came to form the leadership of the *indépendantiste* Parti Québécois, such figures as René Lévesque, Jacques Parizeau, and Claude Morin, were ideologically liberal. But there were others, within the PQ and in other pro-independence organizations, for whom Quebec independence was inseparably linked to the overthrow of what they argued to be a bourgeois state. PQ members Pierre Bourgault and Robert Burns, for example, wanted the end of *la domination anglaise* of the Quebec economy. Although the electoral strength of these left-wing groups never amounted to much, they managed to have a significant impact on political discourse in Quebec, particularly through the province's universities, labour unions, and in the extraparliamentary wing of the PQ.

In view of these divisions, two developments justify the claim that a state-centred nationalism emerged out of the Quiet Revolution. First, the identification of French Canada with the territory of Quebec was a view shared by most nationalists. Indeed, the entry of Trudeau and his fellow federalists into national politics was chiefly a reaction to this Quebec-oriented nationalism. The provincial Liberals' 1962 campaign slogan, '*Maîtres chez nous*', captured a nationalist consensus that ever since has been an accepted tenet of Quebec politics. Second, key institutional reforms of the Quiet Revolution, including la Caisse de dépôt et placement, Hydro-Québec, and the jurisdictional terrain that the Quebec government wrested from Ottawa in the areas of social policy, immigration, and taxation, have left an important mark on Quebec nationalism. They constitute the hard core of the provincial state upon which the aspirations summed up in the phrase 'Maîtres chez nous' depend.

The Unilingual Approach of Quebec

The origins of present-day language policy in Canada lie in developments in Quebec during the 1960s. With the election of the Quebec Liberal Party in 1960, the political obstacles to change were largely removed and the outdated character of Quebec's conservative ideology was exposed. It was replaced by an emphasis on catching up with the level of social and economic development elsewhere. As many commentators have observed, the construction of the Manicouagan dam in northern Quebec—engineered and built by Québécois—became a popular symbol for the new confidence in the ability of French-speaking Quebecers to cope with a modern world and to compete economically. The state, traditionally viewed as a second-class institution in a province in which most social services were controlled by the Church and government was associated with crass patronage, became the focus of nationalist energies. The fact that the new nationalism of the Quiet Revolution turned to the provincial state, in which French-speaking Quebecers were unquestionably in the majority, reinforced the identification of French Canada with the territory of Quebec.

The ideology of *rattrapage* and the identification of French Canada with Quebec had important consequences for language policy in that province. As the instrument for economic and social development, the Quebec state assumed functions previously administered by the Church authorities and also expanded the scope of its economic activities. In doing so it provided career opportunities for the growing number of educated Francophones graduating from the province's universities. Access to high-paying managerial and technical jobs in the private sector, however, remained blocked by Anglophone domination of the Quebec economy. The relative exclusion of Francophones from positions of authority above that of foreman and the concentration of Francophone businesses in the *petites et moyennes entreprises* sector of the economy had long been known.[26] This situation ran directly counter to the expectations of the Quiet Revolution and became an important political issue when the capacity of the public sector to absorb the increasing ranks of highly educated Francophones became strained.

Demographic trends comprised an additional factor that shaped provincial language policy in Quebec. Immigrants to the province overwhelmingly adopted the English language. This fact, combined with the dramatic reduction in the birth rate among Francophones, lent credibility to a scenario where Francophones might eventually become a minority even within Quebec. Along with evidence of the exclusion of Francophones from much of the province's economic structure, these trends formed the basis for the policy recommendations of the Quebec Royal Commission of Inquiry on the Position of the French Language and on Language Rights in Quebec (the Gendron Commission, 1972). That Commission's recommendation that the provincial government take legislative action to promote the use of French in business and in the schools was translated into law under the Quebec Liberal government, which introduced the Official Language Act,[27] and in the Charte de la langue française[28]—or Bill 101 as it is more commonly known outside

Quebec—passed under the subsequent Parti Québécois government. Without going into the detailed provisions of this legislation, three principal features of Quebec language policy since the passage of Bill 101 can be identified.

(1) French is established as the sole official language in Quebec and therefore the exclusive official language for proceedings of the provincial legislature and the courts and the main language for public administration in the province. In a 1979 decision the Supreme Court of Canada ruled that this section of Bill 101 violated section 133 of the BNA Act, which guarantees the co-equal status of the French and English languages at the federal level and in the province of Quebec.[29] Nevertheless, the principal language of provincial government services in Quebec is French, and many provincial and local services are not available in English.

(2) Through the requirement that businesses with fifty or more employees receive a *francisation* certificate as a condition of doing business in the province, the Quebec government seeks to increase the use of French as a working language of business in the province. The language charter does not establish linguistic quotas for corporations. Instead, it leaves the conditions of certification a matter for individual negotiations between a firm and the Office de la langue française. Despite some initial resistance from the Anglophone business community, symbolized by the immediate move of Sun Life's head office from Montreal to Toronto, this section of Bill 101 has generally been accepted by employers. More controversial have been the provisions requiring that public signs and advertisements be in French only. This blanket prohibition was relaxed in 1983 to make exception for bilingual advertising by 'ethnic' businesses, and in a 1988 decision the Supreme Court ruled that it violated the freedom of expression guaranteed in the Charter of Rights and Freedoms.[30]

(3) The provisions of Bill 101 that initially excited the most controversy were those restricting access to English-language schools in Quebec. Under this law, children could enrol in an English school if one of the following conditions was met: their parents had been educated in English in Quebec; they had a sibling already going to an English school; their parents were educated in English outside of Quebec but were living in the province when the law was passed (1977); they were already enrolled in an English school when the law came into effect. The intent was obviously to reverse the overwhelming preference of immigrants for the English language, a preference that demographers predicted would eventually change the linguistic balance in the province, and even more dramatically in Montreal, which attracted the vast majority of immigrants. In one of the first Supreme Court decisions on the Charter of Rights and Freedoms, the Court held that the requirement that at least one of a child's parents must have been educated in English in Quebec violated section 23 of the Charter, a section that clearly had been drafted with Bill 101 in mind. The practical importance of this ruling is small, given the low level of migration to Quebec from other Canadian provinces. More significant is the fact that the Supreme Court was unwilling to accept the Quebec government's argument that the demographic threat to the position of the French language justified this restriction on language rights under the 'reasonable limits' section of the Charter.

Despite some setbacks in the courts, Quebec's language policy has remained substantially unchanged since the passage of Bill 101. The only significant reform occurred after the Supreme Court's 1988 ruling that the prohibition on languages other than French for commercial signs in Quebec violated the Charter's guarantee of freedom of expression. Within weeks the Quebec legislature passed Bill 178, which invoked the notwithstanding clause of the Charter to reaffirm the ban on languages other than French for commercial signs outside a business. Bill 178 allowed, however, the use of other languages on signs inside a business, but French signs had to be predominant. Legal restrictions on commercial signs were removed in 1993. Judged according to its two main objectives—increasing the use of the French language in the Quebec economy and stemming the decline in the Francophone share of the provincial population—Bill 101 must be judged a success.[31]

Language policy in Quebec has been shaped by the idea that French Canada is co-extensive with the boundaries of that province. The Office de la langue française and the law it administers build on an approach to language promotion that can be traced back to the early 1960s. The Liberal government of Jean Lesage set out to increase Francophone participation in the economy through such provincial institutions as la Société générale du financement, la Caisse de dépôt et placement, Sidérurgie québécoise, and an expanded Hydro-Québec.[32] The common denominator since then has been the use of the provincial state as an instrument for the socio-economic advancement of Francophones.

The Bilingual Approach of Ottawa

A very different approach to language policy—one based on a conception of French and English Canada that cuts across provincial borders—has been pursued by successive federal governments since the 1960s. Responding to the new assertive nationalism of the Quiet Revolution, the signs of which ranged from Quebec's demands for greater taxation powers and less interference by Ottawa in areas of provincial constitutional responsibility to bombs placed in mailboxes and at public monuments, the Liberal government of Lester Pearson established the Royal Commission on Bilingualism and Biculturalism. As Eric Waddell writes, 'The federal government was facing a legitimacy crisis in the 1960s and 1970s and had the immediate task of proposing a Canadian alternative to Quebec nationalism.'[33] The B&B Commission was a first step toward the adoption by Ottawa of a policy of official bilingualism. This policy was to some degree intended to defuse the indépendantiste sentiment building in Quebec, especially among young Francophones, by opening Ottawa as a field of career opportunities to rival the Quebec public service.

The alternative Ottawa offered, which was expressed in the federalist philosophy of Pierre Trudeau, was of a Canada in which language rights would be guaranteed to the individual and protected by national institutions. In practical terms this meant changing the overwhelmingly Anglophone character of the federal state so that Francophones would not have grounds to view it as an 'alien' level of government from which they were largely excluded. These changes have been carried out on two main fronts. First, what Raymond Breton refers to as the 'Canadian symbolic order' has been transformed since the 1960s.[34] Through a new flag, the proclamation of 'O Canada' as the official national anthem, new designs for stamps and currency, and the language neutering of some federal institutions, documents, and celebrations (for example, Trans-Canada Airlines became Air Canada, the BNA Act is now officially titled the Constitution Act, and Dominion Day is now called Canada Day), a deliberate attempt has been made to create symbols with which French Canadians can better identify. Second, the passage of the Official Languages Act (1969) gave statutory expression to the policy of bilingualism that had been set in motion under Lester Pearson. This Act established the Office of the Commissioner of Official Languages as a 'watchdog' agency to monitor the three main components of language equality set forth in the Act: (1) the public's right to be served by the federal government in the official language of their choice; (2) the equitable representation of Francophones and Anglophones in the federal public service; and (3) the ability of public servants of both language groups to work in the language of their choice. The situation that the Official Languages Act was intended to redress was one where Francophone representation in the federal state was less than their share of the national population. Francophone underrepresentation was greatest in managerial, scientific, and technical job categories (see Figure 11.4). Moreover, the language of the public service—the language that officials worked in and, in most parts of the country, the language that citizens could realistically be expected to be served in—was English. In view of these circumstances, Ottawa's claim to 'represent' the interests of Francophones lacked credibility.

Among the main actions taken to increase the bilingual character of the federal bureaucracy have been language training for public servants, the designation of an increasing share of positions as bilingual, and the creation of the National Capital Region as the office blocks of the federal state spread into Hull during the 1970s. Language training for public servants has been the most controversial of these measures. In his annual report for 1984 the Commissioner of Official Languages, D'Iberville Fortier, noted that a relatively small proportion of public servants in positions designated bilingual appeared to have acquired their second-language skills as a result of taxpayer-funded language training. This led Fortier to question the extent to which language training was capable of making public servants, particularly Anglophones who are the main consumers of federal language courses, effectively bilingual.

In view of the fact that two of the objectives of the Official Languages Act have been to increase the number of Francophones recruited into the public service and to improve Francophones' opportunities for upward mobility within it, the designation of positions according to their linguistic requirements has been probably the most significant feature of Ottawa's language policy. At the present time about 35 per cent of positions in the public service are designated either bilingual or French (28.8 per cent bilingual; 6.5 per cent French).

Evidence on recruitment to the federal public service and upward mobility within it demonstrate that the linguistic designation of positions has worked to the advantage of Francophones. A clear majority of appointments to bilingual positions are filled by Francophones. This is true both for new appointments to the public service (71 per cent of these went to Francophones in 1992) and for reappointments within the federal bureaucracy (73 per cent to Francophones). But as the Commissioner of Official Languages regularly observes, increased representation of Francophones should not be taken as an indication that the French and English are approaching greater equality as languages of work in the federal state. Outside of federal departments and agencies located in Quebec, the language of work remains predominantly English. As the 1985 annual report of the Commissioner of Languages put it:

Figure 11.4 Anglophone and Francophone Representation in the Federal Public Service as a Whole, in the Management Category of the Public Service, and in the Canadian Population, Selected Years

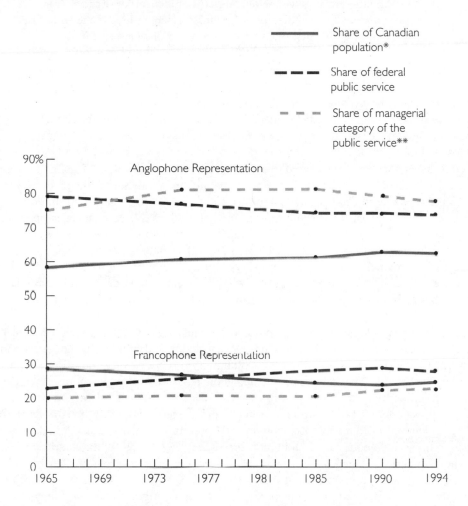

*Data for the representation of French and English language groups in the Canadian population are taken from the censuses for 1961, 1976, 1986, and 1991. The question refers to mother tongue, and therefore the figures do not add up to 100 per cent.

**The 1965 survey used to determine the language of those in the management category asked respondents to indicate their mother tongue; 5.2 per cent indicated a language other than English or French.

Sources: Figures provided in various annual reports of the Commissioner of Official Languages, the *Canada Year Book,* and the *Report of the Royal Commission on Bilingualism and Biculturalism,* volume 3A (Ottawa: Queen's Printer, 1969), 215, table 50.

> The fact of the matter is that, in the bilingual regions, French is not used in communications between public servants to anything like the extent or anything like the freedom or regularity that the numerical presence of Francophone public servants would lead one to expect. If one were to judge the official status of French, for instance, from its use in inter-departmental committees or at meetings of deputy heads, one would be hard pressed not to conclude that it has no status to speak of whatsoever.[35]

The domination of English as the *lingua franca* of the bureaucracy persists even in the National Capital Region. This led a previous Commissioner of Official Languages to conclude that French has become a valuable attribute from the standpoint of career advancement without becoming a working language on a par with English.[36] Recent annual reports of the Commissioner confirm this picture of English dominance as a working language, particularly at the top of the public service ladder.

Ottawa's language policy acquired two additional thrusts in the 1970s. The first of these has involved financial assistance to organizations and individuals seeking to defend or expand the rights of official-language minorities and to local Francophone cultural organizations outside of Quebec. Most significant in terms of results has been financial support for court challenges to provincial laws respecting language rights. These challenges have included Supreme Court decisions in 1979 and 1985 that established the official status of French in the province of Manitoba[37] and successful challenges to the restrictions on education and public signs and advertising contained in Quebec's Bill 101.[38] Until 1985, language rights cases were the only ones supported by Ottawa under its Court Challenges Program.[39]

A second thrust of federal policy to promote bilingualism in Canadian society has been through financial assistance for second-language instruction and minority-language schools controlled by the provinces, including French immersion schools and support for summer immersion programs. The immersion phenomenon has seen the proliferation of French immersion schools in cities throughout English Canada. The number of elementary and secondary schools offering French immersion programs increased from 237 in 1977–8, with 37,881 students enrolled, to 2,063 schools and 301,668 students in 1993–4. More than half of these schools and about half of all immersion students in Canada are in Ontario.[40]

The popularity of French immersion education continues to grow, fuelled by non-Francophone parents' perception that bilingualism will give their children an edge in the future competition for good jobs. This perception of greater opportunities for bilinguals, at least in the private sector, remains to be substantiated. Indeed, a 1985 study of bilingual job opportunities by the Commissioner of Languages answered the question, 'Do immersion graduates make good use of their French after high school?' with 'Yes, they do—in Ottawa.'[41] Despite the rapid growth of immersion education, one should not assume that Canada is on the fast track to becoming a nation of polyglots in the manner of some of the small Western European democracies. The 1991 census showed that about 20 per cent of Canadians between the ages of fifteen and twenty-four claimed to be able to carry on a conversation in both French and English. The percentage for young Canadians living outside of Quebec was only 14.7, compared to 44.6 per cent in Quebec.[42] Moreover, studies of immersion graduates demonstrate that the experience tends to produce 'receptive' bilinguals—people who neither initiate conversations in French nor consume French-language newspapers, radio, or television after leaving immersion. Bilingualism becomes in some sense a badge of social distinction rather than a part of their lifestyle. This has led many to comment on the incidental effects of immersion on social class distinctions. Eric Waddell writes:

> There is much to suggest that the current fascination for French language education is more an expression of class (and indirectly of ethnic class) interests than of a concern to forge a new national identity. French immersion schools give the impression of con-stituting an élite system of education functioning within the public system. The state, through federal intervention, is in the process of elaborating a dual system, one for tomorrow's leaders and one for the followers. For this 'new' class, the bilingualism that mastery of the French language confers constitutes something profoundly Canadian in the sense of being sophisticated and more 'European'. Hence it serves increasingly to demarcate this class from other social classes and, strikingly, from our southern neighbours.[43]

A Distinct Society?

Does Quebec comprise a distinct society? Is Quebec more distinct from the other nine provinces than any one of those other provinces is from the rest? What is the basis for

Some political analysts have argued that many Francophone Quebecers vote for nationalist parties in order to extract greater concessions from Ottawa and the other provinces. (Roy Peterson, *Vancouver Sun*)

Quebec's claim to be distinct? Even if Quebecers' claim to distinctiveness is valid, should distinct society status be entrenched in the constitution? Is this necessary? Is it desirable?

It is a fair bet that few Canadians had heard of 'distinct society' before the late 1980s, when the Meech Lake Accord came to grief over the proposal to recognize Quebec as a distinct society within Canada (see Chapter 5). It is also reasonable to assume that most Canadians are today no wiser about what 'distinct society' means. This, it should be added, is after tens of millions of dollars were spent by a phalanx of federal and provincial task forces, commissions, and committees on the constitution that sprung into existence in the two years after the failure of the Meech Lake Accord. Average Canadians perhaps may be forgiven whatever confusion they have over the distinct society issue. Constitutional experts, political scientists, journalists, and politicians cannot agree on what it means!

About all that is clear is that the demand for constitutional recognition of Quebec as a distinct society has been a non-negotiable item on the agenda of Quebec's political élite since the late 1980s. It is also clear that the issue excites a popular emotional response both inside Quebec and in the rest of Canada that other constitutional proposals—reforming the Senate, tinkering with the Supreme Court, changing the amendment process, and so on—do not. Let us try to understand the controversy over a distinct society clause by addressing the questions posed at the beginning of this section.

Whether or not Quebec is a distinct society depends on what criteria we use in comparing Quebec to the other provinces. In terms of how people in Quebec make their living, the films they watch, the popular novels they read, how and where they spend their vacations, and in most other aspects of their lifestyle they are not remarkably different from Canadians in other regions of the country. In fact, if material and lifestyle criteria are used then there is a good case for arguing that Quebec and Ontario are more similar than, say, Ontario and Newfoundland.

Not everyone agrees. And it is true that one can point to several important social characteristics of the Quebec population that distinguish it from those of the other provinces. Québécois marry less often and later than other Canadians; they have fewer children;[44] they are heavier smokers; they eat more poutine and drink more wine than their compatriots. But to base an argument for constitutional recognition of Quebec as a distinct society on such social characteristics trivializes the meaning of distinct society. Many of these phenomena have no political relevance. Moreover, in some cases the differences between Quebec and the rest of Canada are too slight to warrant reading much significance into them.

Another possibility is that the beliefs and values of the Québécois set them apart from other Canadians. Here the evidence is mixed. Several early studies on regional variations in political culture concluded that Canada is, in fact, comprised of several distinctive regional political cultures. Richard Simeon and David Elkins found that levels of political trust, efficacy, interest in politics, and participation varied significantly between provinces and that this variation persisted even after eliminating the impact of socio-economic factors (i.e., levels of education and income) known to influence these attitudes/behaviours. The implication is, of course, that while Quebec may be a 'special case' in terms of its politically relevant values, it is not the only regional special case.

Conversely, other studies of regionalism conclude that there are no significant attitudinal differences between citizens in different parts of the country. Based on their analysis of data from the 1977 national Quality of Life survey, Bernard Blishen and Tom Atkinson conclude that personal values do not differ significantly between provincial populations.[45] But either way, whether Quebec's political culture is argued to be broadly similar to that in the rest of Canada or if one takes the position that there are several distinct regional cultures in Canada, this weakens the argument for constitutional entrenchment of distinct society status for Quebec.

Nonetheless, one's conclusions may depend on what questions are asked and what values they tap. Surveys that ask Canadians whether they think of themselves as Canadians first or as citizens of their province reveal that those in Quebec are most likely to see their primary attachment as provincial. But Newfoundlanders are just about as provincialist and Prince Edward Islanders are not terribly far behind. A recent study of Canadians' attitudes toward civil liberties suggests much more similarity than difference between French-speaking Québécois and other Canadians.[46] On the other hand, one of the most rigorous empirical investigations of regional variations in political ideology concludes that 'the extent of ideological differentiation in English Canada is very small' and that 'the ideological difference between Quebec and English Canada is greater than the internal variation within English Canada'.[47] Michael Ornstein shows that ideological values in Quebec are considerably to the left of those in the other provinces.[48]

In view of these apparently contradictory findings, we probably cannot conclude that Quebec comprises a distinct society in terms of the values and beliefs of its citizens. Differences between Quebec and the rest of Canada are sharpest on attitudes relating to language. A 1991 Gallup poll (Figure 11.5) found that 78 per cent of Montrealers, compared to 23 per cent of Torontonians, thought that English-language rights were well protected in Quebec. Asked about the protection of French-language rights outside Quebec, 82 per cent of Torontonians thought they were well protected, compared to only 27 per cent of Montrealers. The two solitudes were perfect in their mutual mistrust! But on other political issues, differences are often slight or non-existent. Even if we concur with those, like Ornstein, who argue that Quebec is more different attitudinally from the rest of Canada than the predominantly English-speaking provinces are from one another, it does not follow that this difference warrants constitutional recognition of special status. Values and beliefs are not set in stone, as any student of changes in French-Canadian nationalism over the last half century knows.

A third possible argument for Quebec's distinctiveness relies on history. The basic outline of such an argument goes as follows. French-Canadian society goes back to the seventeenth century when the first immigrants came over from France. Most French Canadians are, in fact, descended from those who were already settled in New France at the time of the Conquest. Current generations of French Canadians are heirs to three centuries of tradition and resistance against assimilating pressures. This continuity can be seen in the distinctive French that is spoken in Quebec (and, for that matter, in the dialects spoken in the French-speaking communities outside of Quebec); in Quebec folksongs, popular music, films, and literature; in institutions like Quebec's distinctive system of civil law (based on the French civil code rather than English common law); and in the history that Québécois children learn in school—a history that has always told a rather different story from that learned by students in English schools across Canada. This shared history as one of Canada's two 'founding peoples' justifies distinct society status for Quebec. Moreover, history has demonstrated that only in Quebec, where Francophones have always formed the majority and have

Figure 11.5 Two Solitudes: Anglophone and Francophone Perceptions of Protection for Minority Language Rights

A. Percentage agreeing that the rights of English-speakers are well protected in Quebec

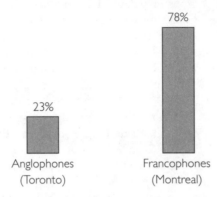

B. Percentage agreeing that the rights of French-speakers are well protected outside Quebec

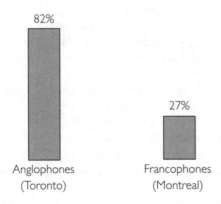

Source: CIPO, *Gallup Report,* 5 December 1991.

been able to control the levers of provincial government, are the distinctive language and traditions of French Canadians secure against Anglicizing pressures and discrimination.

Variations on this basic argument are standard features of Quebec government documents on the constitution and in the literature of both the Quebec Liberal Party and the Parti Québécois. It is a view widely shared by Francophones in Quebec. Not only does this form the basis of demands for constitutional recognition of Quebec as a distinct society, but historical arguments also are used to make the case for a Quebec veto over constitutional amendments, as indicated by the 1991 *Report* of the Commission on the Political and Constitutional Future of Quebec:

> At its origin, Canada's federal system was founded, from Quebec's point of view, on Canadian duality [French/English] and the autonomy of the provinces. Canadian duality, which rests on the relationship between the French-Canadian and English-Canadian peoples, is seen as the founding principle of the federal system. The federal union is thus conceived of as a pact between these two peoples, that may only be changed with the consent of each of these parties.[49]

The problem with the historical case for constitutional recognition of Quebec as a distinct society is not that it is based on incorrect or flimsy evidence. Indeed, the historical record speaks for itself. The problem is, rather, that the governments and people of some of the other provinces appear to be convinced that their regional histories are equally distinct. Western Canadians and their governments tend to be unimpressed by arguments that Quebec's history is somehow more distinctive than their own. Newfoundlanders are also unlikely to be convinced. The unsympathetic reception that spokespersons for the predominantly English-speaking provinces give to the historical argument for Quebec as a distinct society has recently been joined by that of Native Canadians. They argue that if any community has an historical right to distinct society status it is theirs. After all, their languages and traditions had been established for centuries before the arrival of Canada's European 'founders'. No discussion of 'founding peoples' or 'distinct societies' is complete, they argue, without recognition of the historical status and rights of Aboriginal Canadians.

The final and most persuasive grounds for arguing Quebec's right to distinct society status is the province's linguistic character. As noted earlier, 82 per cent of the Quebec population claims French as its mother tongue and an equal percentage reports speaking French at home. No other province comes close to this level of French-language dominance; indeed, in no other province do Francophones comprise a majority of the population. Close to 90 per cent of all Canadian Francophones reside in Quebec. It was no accident that the Commission on the Political and Constitutional Future of Quebec, established by the Bourassa government after the failure of the Meech Lake Accord, emphasized the distinctive linguistic character of Quebec as the first point in the section of its *Report* on Quebec's *identité propre* (special or unique identity).[50] Moreover, both the distinct society clause proposed by the Meech Lake Accord and that in the Charlottetown Accord were explicit in declaring that what is distinct about Quebec society is primarily its linguistic character (see Appendix 1 to this chapter).

This argument cannot be refuted. Of course, each province has its own distinctive linguistic character. But it requires either a very dull wit or very impressive powers of denial to not appreciate the remarkably unique linguistic character of Quebec within Canada and, for that matter, in all of North America. In no other jurisdiction, provincial or state, is English not the language regularly spoken by a clear majority of the population.

But if the distinct society clauses of the Meech Lake and Charlottetown accords are merely statements of demographic reality, why the fuss? There are a couple of reasons. One is that some people will readily acknowledge Quebec's distinctive linguistic character, but deny that this warrants constitutional recognition of Quebec as a distinct society any more than, say, Saskatchewan deserves to be recognized as a distinct society because of its special economy, history, and demographic character.[51] Why, they ask, should language be elevated above other social characteristics in determining which provincial societies are distinct and which are not?

A second and probably more important reason why some provincial governments, the Reform Party, and many English-speaking Canadians resist what might appear to be a compelling linguistic argument for a distinct society clause involves the consequences that would follow from entrenching this in the constitution. Many English Canadians believe that this would give to Quebec legislative powers not possessed by other provinces. Some worry that minority rights—those of non-Francophones in Quebec and those of Francophones outside the province—would suffer from constitutional recognition of Quebec as a predominantly French-speaking society and of the rest of Canada as predominantly English-speaking. Fears have been expressed that a distinct society clause could undermine Charter guarantees of rights and freedoms in Quebec.

But above all, what probably bothers English-speaking Canadians outside of Quebec more than anything else is their gut sense that distinct society status for Quebec undermines their idea of Canada. 'Two nations' theories of Canada, while enjoying some popularity in certain political parties and among Anglophone political scientists, have never been very popular with the English-Canadian public. In an unarticulated way they sense that distinct society recognition for Quebec is a sort of Trojan horse for a two-nations conception of Canada. This offends against a particular understanding of equality that—again, while usually inarticulate—objects to the idea that there are categories of Canadians instead of Canadians, period. Former Conservative Prime Minister John Diefenbaker probably expressed this best when he inveighed against what he called 'the anglo-phonies, the franco-phonies, and all the other phonies' whose insistence on defining Canada in linguistic and ethnic terms, he believed, undermined national unity.

Although spokespersons for the three major national political parties have for years denied that the 'one Canada' aspirations of most English Canadians conflict with the recognition of Quebec as a distinct society, Québécois political leaders suffer from no illusions on this count. The *Report* of the Commission on the Political and Constitutional Future of Quebec makes this very clear, arguing that the 'one Canada' and 'dual societies' conceptions have become increasingly irreconcilable since the passage of the Charter and the other constitutional reforms of 1982. This is because, the *Report* claims, the Constitution Act of 1982 is based on three principles that, while popular outside of Quebec, are fundamentally opposed to the recognition of Quebec as a distinct society (see Appendix 2 to this chapter). These principles are:

- The equality of all Canadian citizens and the unity of the society in which they live.
- The equality of all cultures and cultural origins in Canada.
- The equality of the ten provinces of Canada.

Whatever a distinct society clause in the constitution might mean in practice—and, notwithstanding the confident blusterings of many politicians and constitutional experts, we should have learned from the experience with the Charter that it is often impossible to predict how Canadian judges will interpret important sections of the constitution—there can be no doubt that the Quebec élites who have insisted on it expect it to make a difference.

They reject the 'one Canada' vision that they argue is represented in the Charter and in the procedure for amending the constitution adopted in 1982, which did not give Quebec a veto. Distinct society is, in their eyes, a corrective against the centralizing implications of the Charter and, moreover, represents a return to the founding spirit of Canada.

Bur distinct society status and a veto over constitutional change may no longer be enough. Several weeks after the 1995 Quebec referendum, the Liberal government passed a motion recognizing Quebec as a distinct society and giving the province (as well as British Columbia, the prairie provinces, Ontario, and the Atlantic provinces) a veto over constitutional reform. Neither the PQ government in Quebec, the Bloc Québécois in Ottawa, nor Quebec's French-language media were particularly impressed by Ottawa's action. Even the Quebec Liberal Party argued that Ottawa's proposals—whose constitutional status was uncertain, to say the least —did not go far enough. Ottawa's hope, of course, was to satisfy the demands of enough 'soft nationalists' to undercut the separatists in the next referendum. For their part, the PQ and BQ have been determined to shift the debate away from distinct society and constitutional vetoes, terms that imply a federalism framework, and onto a different plane. That plane involves political independence and economic association.

Appendix 1: The Distinct Society

Version I: Meech Lake Accord (1987)

1. The Constitution Act, 1867, is amended by adding thereto, immediately after Section 1 thereof, the following section:
2. (1) The Constitution of Canada shall be interpreted in a manner consistent with: (a) The recognition that the existence of French-speaking Canadians, centred in Quebec but also present elsewhere in Canada, and English-speaking Canadians, concentrated outside Quebec but also present in Quebec, constitutes a fundamental characteristic of Canada; and, (b) The recognition that Quebec constitutes within Canada a distinct society;
   (2) The role of the Parliament of Canada and the provincial legislatures to preserve the fundamental characteristic of Canada referred to in paragraph (1) (a) is affirmed;
   (3) The role of the Legislature and Government of Quebec to preserve and promote the distinct identity of Quebec referred to in paragraph (1) (b) is affirmed;
   (4) Nothing in this section derogates from the powers, rights or privileges of Parliament or the Government of Canada, or of the legislatures or governments of the provinces, including any powers, rights or privileges relating to language.

Version II: Charlottetown Accord (1992)

The Constitution Act, 1867, is amended by adding thereto, immediately after Section 1 thereof, the following section:
2. (1) The Constitution of Canada, including the Canadian Charter of Rights and Freedoms, shall be interpreted in a manner consistent with the following fundamental characteristics:

   ...

   (c) Quebec constitutes within Canada a distinct society, which includes a French-speaking majority, a unique culture and a civil law tradition;

   ...

   (2) The role of the legislature and Government of Quebec to preserve and promote the distinct society of Quebec is affirmed.

Version III: Notice of Motion announced by Prime Minister Chrétien on 27 November 1995

THAT
Whereas the people of Quebec have expressed the desire for recognition of Quebec's distinct society;
   (1) the House recognize that Quebec is a distinct society within Canada;
   (2) the House recognize that Quebec's distinct society includes its French-speaking majority, unique culture and civil law tradition;
   (3) the House undertake to be guided by this reality;
   (4) the House encourage all components of the legislative and executive branches of government to take note of this recognition and be guided in their conduct accordingly.

Appendix 2

(from *Rapport de la commission sur l'avenir politique et constitutionnel du Québec*, mars 1991, 38–40; author's translation)

The Constitution Act, 1982, and the principles that it enshrines have in fact given to Canada a centralizing direction unknown previously. This Act has contributed to the reinforcement of certain political ideas about the Canadian federation and to the perception of a Canadian national identity that is difficult to reconcile with the effective recognition and political expression of Quebec's distinct identity. These political ideas and this perception manifest themselves in the following dimensions [of the Act]:

> The equality of all Canadian citizens, from one ocean to the other, and the unity of the society in which they live.

By virtue of this political vision, which is based on the Charter of Rights and Freedoms contained in the Act of 1982, equality is a strictly individual notion and applies uniformly across Canada: it does not allow for the special constitutional recognition of the Quebec collectivity. The concept of Quebec as a distinct society is thus perceived as a source of inequality and as being incompatible with the principle of the equality of all Canadians.

> The equality of all cultures and cultural origins in Canada.

This vision proceeds from the principle of multiculturalism enshrined in the Canadian Charter, that promises to maintain and promote the multicultural heritage of Canadians. In the eyes of many, the French language and Francophone cultural origins are among the many mother tongues and cultures that form the multicultural heritage of Canada and are equal to them: the French language and Francophone cultural origins should not require special recognition or guarantees in the Canadian constitution. The notions of 'linguistic duality' and of 'two founding peoples' do not reflect the Canadian reality shared by a large number of Canadians and in which they see themselves reflected.

> The equality of the ten provinces.

This notion has become one of Canada's dominant political principles. It was consecrated in the constitutional amendment procedure adopted in 1982, more precisely in the unanimity rule for certain amendments and in the '7 provinces representing 50% of the Canadian population' rule that is the general amending formula....

By virtue of this principle of the equality of all provinces, any constitutional change, prerogative or competence obtained by Quebec must be obtained equally by the nine other provinces. The strict application of this principle thus has the effect of preventing Quebec from achieving a special status.

The equality of the provinces requires, consequently, a uniform decentralization toward all the provinces of any competence or prerogative assigned to Quebec. This decentralizing effect is not acceptable to those who see in it a weakening of the central government.

CANADIAN DEMOCRACY

Under the combined effect of the principle of provincial equality and of positions favouring the centralization of powers in the hands of a single 'national' government that dominates the country, it becomes difficult to respond to the needs of Quebec and accommodate, within the Canadian constitution, the political recognition of its distinctiveness within the federation.

On the left, Nellie McClung, leader of the Canadian women's movement in the early twentieth century; on the right, Judy Rebick, former president of the National Action Committee on the Status of Women and a leading Canadian feminist today. (Public Archives 30212; CBC Newsworld)

Gender issues, in the past twenty years, have occupied a prominent place in Canadian politics. In this chapter the roots of these issues and development of the feminist movement are examined. Topics include the following:

- ❖ The social construction of gender differences.
- ❖ The roots of underrepresentation.
- ❖ Women in politics.
- ❖ Early feminism.
- ❖ Contemporary feminism.
- ❖ Organization.
- ❖ Strategies.
- ❖ Achievements.

CHAPTER TWELVE

■ Gender and Politics

Today there are no formal barriers to the full participation of women in politics on the same basis as men. And yet many people argue that the political equality of men and women is still far from having been achieved. They claim that women continue to be discriminated against in public life and by public policy. Is this true? If men and women have the same democratic rights, how can one reasonably claim that women are politically subordinate to men and discriminated against by the state?

The answer offered by the feminist movement that emerged in the 1960s was summed up in its slogan, 'The personal is political.' The fact that women had the right to vote and stand for public office was not enough to overcome the reality of their subordination to men in virtually all social and economic structures. Equal in law—but not even in this, as we will see—men and women were very unequal in life. These inequalities undermined their ability to participate in public life on an equal footing with men.

'The personal is political' means more than this. It suggests that settings like the family, workplace, schools, churches, and clubs do not simply affect the ability of women to participate in politics, they are themselves venues where politics takes place. This is a position that abolishes the line dividing the public and private spheres. Sexual practices, pop music and films, billboards and television ads, and language are, according to this view, all suffused with political significance. Where there is power, there is also politics.

Social learning patterns that discourage females from participating fully in public life, thereby reproducing male dominance, undeniably have political consequences. But what about a phenomenon such as the tendency to think of child care as 'women's work' and to pay daycare workers considerably less than those in some male-dominated occupations where the skills required and the responsibilities are fewer? The lower value that the market places on some predominantly female jobs cannot be explained solely by the laws of supply and demand. To the extent that predominantly female jobs pay less because they are generally viewed as female occupations, this represents female subordination. The labour market is not always gender blind. Rather, it sometimes operates so as to maintain the social and economic superiority of males over females.

So is it not fair to say that the practice of paying those in female-dominated occupations less than those in male-dominated ones is political? Not necessarily. The 'laws' of the economic marketplace also discriminate against the poor and in favour of the rich. They also favour those whose geographic situation enables them to take advantage of opportunities to buy or sell on advantageous terms, or pay less taxes, and against others who are disadvantaged by geography. But until these inequalities and the power relations that generate them are argued to be public matters on which governments should act, they have not entered the realm of politics.

What is the point of this distinction between the exercise of power in the public versus the private realm? Subordination is, after all, subordination, even if it is accepted as 'God's will' or the natural course of things. But as was discussed in Chapter 1, political conflict is often about where the boundary between public and private should be drawn. How far should the scope of the state's authority extend, and what are appropriate matters for public deliberation and action? Political conflict is, in other words, often about what should count as political. If we start, however, from the premise that all forms of domination/subordination are political, we lose the ability to understand the state and political life as historically and culturally determined. One of the chief things that is different about Canadian politics today compared to a century ago is the much wider range of matters that are now on the public agenda. The private realm has retreated as the public realm has advanced. For the student of politics, two of the most basic and interesting questions about the subject are 'what is politics about?' and 'why?' These are questions about the boundaries of politics, how they are established and maintained, and why they change.

Let us bring this discussion down to earth by considering the contemporary issue of pay equity. The advocates of pay equity argue for laws requiring employers to pay those in predominantly female jobs as much as those in predominantly male jobs where skill levels, responsibilities, and qualifications are similar. To do this, employers must be legally obliged to re-evaluate pay levels for predominantly female jobs, according to whatever criteria are established by law. It is also necessary that mechanisms be established for monitoring compliance and dealing with appeals. The opponents of pay equity suggest that this would represent political interference with the laws of the marketplace and that wage levels should be determined solely on the basis of negotiations between those who buy and those who sell labour.

Who is right? The question is a normative one, and the answer depends on one's personal values. But the fact that the question is even asked means that this particular form of subordination, the undervaluation of certain jobs that traditionally have been done by women, has entered the realm of politics. The major accomplishment of the women's movement over the last couple of decades has been to get onto the public agenda various forms of subordination that previously were considered private and/or normal.

In the seventeenth century, French writer Poulain de la Barre claimed that 'All that has been written about women by men should be suspect, for men are at once judge and party to the lawsuit.'[1] There might have been pretty reasonable grounds for such an argument in the seventeenth century, but it is an unfair generalization today—even though it survives as a minority view within the women's movement. Should we dismiss what Anglophones have written about Francophones, or white Canadians about Aboriginal Canadians, or the affluent about the poor on the grounds that a person's point of view is bound to be influenced by one's linguistic, racial, or class background?

There is, however, a basis for arguments like Poulain de la Barre's in that mainstream history and social interpretation are, virtually by definition, written from the viewpoint of society's dominant interests. The intellectuals who create these histories and interpretations are often members of privileged social groups—white, male, affluent professionals—whose objectivity may often seem questionable. But history also shows that there is nothing inevitable about such bias. In the end we should judge the story, not the storyteller.

The Social Construction of Gender Differences

Men and women are biologically different. Although obvious, the social implications of this simple fact have been the subject of enormous controversy. Until a few decades ago, both popular opinion and scientific consensus agreed that the biological attributes of the sexes played a major role in the determination of their respective personality traits, intellectual aptitudes, general abilities, and social roles. Males were considered to be more aggressive, rational, analytical, adventurous, and active than females, and more fitted to leadership roles. Females were generally believed to be more nurturing, emotional, intuitive, cautious, and passive. Nature, not nurture, was considered to be the primary reason for the behavioural and attitudinal differences between males and females and for the social superiority of men over women.

This view was even shared by the first wave of the women's movement. Beginning in the late 1800s, the objectives of this movement focused on extending voting rights to women and on legal and social reforms that were geared toward the protection of the family and traditional values. The arguments used to support these demands fell into two main camps. One maintained that extending voting rights to women and eliminating some of the grosser forms of legal discrimination against them—such as the common law's ambiguity about whether a woman was a person in law and the law's failure to ensure a woman's right to property acquired during the course of married life—were matters of fundamental justice based on the equal humanity of the sexes. This argument did not, however, challenge the conventional wisdom on the biological determination of gender differences.

Suffragists often allied themselves with organizations promoting such causes as temperance, educational reform, child labour laws, and public service reform (to eliminate corruption). These causes were, in fact, central to the character of the early women's movement. Such groups as the Woman's Christian Temperance Union (WCTU), the National Council of Women of Canada (NCWC), and the Women's Institutes comprised the movement's organizational hub. These organizations supported female enfranchisement on the grounds that woman voters would inject a morally uplifting element into the grubby business of politics.

It was in a woman's nature, they argued, to care more about life and the conditions that nurtured it. Extending full democratic rights to women would immediately elevate the prominence of those issues that most concerned the women's movement, including mothers' pensions, minimum wage laws for women, better industrial health and safety standards, prison and family law reform, and more public spending on education. Women were the morally superior sex, and their participation in politics would make the world a better, more civilized place.

These arguments formed the basis of what has come to be called *social feminism* or *maternal feminism*. Far from challenging the notion that gender role differences are the inevitable product of biology, maternal feminists accepted this assumption wholeheartedly. But they turned it from an argument against political rights for women into the basis of their case for political equality. Some of the leaders of the feminist movement, such as Nellie McClung, in fact used both contemporary-sounding and maternal feminism arguments in demanding the vote and social reforms.[2] The mainstream of this first wave of the women's movement was, however, dominated by the more moderate arguments of social feminism and by traditional family and Christian values. Indeed, looking back on women's struggle to achieve political rights, the wonder is that female suffrage was resisted so vigorously and for so long. Although it challenged men's monopoly on public life, the early women's movement did not threaten the social and economic pillars of male dominance.

But the second wave of feminism does. Simone de Beauvoir's declaration that 'One is not born, but rather becomes, a woman'[3] suggests that gender role differences are not inherent. They are socially constructed—passed on and re-learned from generation to generation. This is the basic premise of the contemporary women's movement.

If the real roots of gender inequality lie in the institutionalized practices and cultural norms of society, then the solution must go beyond the formal political equality of the sexes. Anything that promotes stereotyped gender roles that are not based on inherent differences between males and females restricts individual freedom. If one learns that certain careers are not for the members of one's sex, or that childrearing and homemaking are primarily female responsibilities, this limits one's freedom to choose and to act. Moreover, because many of these stereotyped differences are linked to power relations between men and women, their existence undermines human equality.

This is not the place to attempt the perilous task of resolving the nature versus nurture controversy. It is clear, however, that the inherent differences between males and females are much less significant than used to be believed. In one of the most frequently cited studies on the subject, Maccoby and Jacklin claim that scientific research provides firm support for the existence of only four non-physiological differences between the sexes.[4] Three of these differences involve cognitive skills: verbal ability (females better), mathematical ability (males better), and visual-spatial ability (males better). The fourth involves personality: males are more aggressive than females. In the case of both verbal and mathematical ability, differences between the sexes only appear during adolescence, suggesting that social learning may play a role in the development of these skills. All of the four differences claimed by Maccoby and Jacklin are matters of tendency only: males tend to be more aggressive than females, females are more likely than males to excel in verbal ability, and so on. A good deal of recent research, however, points to the impact of hormonal changes on the development of male and female brains and suggests that the tendencies identified by Maccoby and Jacklin are more rooted in biology than social learning.[5]

The debate continues. One of its most controversial aspects involves the relationship of males and females to children. In virtually all societies throughout recorded history women have assumed primary responsibility for raising children. Are females more nurturing and child-oriented by nature? Or is this gender role difference a product of social learning?

The evidence is inconclusive. As prominent an anthropologist as Margaret Mead is cited by both sides of this debate. Based on her study of three primitive societies in New Guinea, the 'early' Mead argued that:

> Many, if not all, of the personality traits which we have called masculine or feminine are as lightly linked to sex as are the clothing, the manners, and the form of headdress that a society at a given period assigns to either sex ... the evidence is overwhelmingly in favor of the strength of social conditioning.[6]

But the 'later' Mead had this to say on the subject:

> The mother's nurturing tie to her child is apparently so deeply rooted in the actual bio-logical conditions of conception and gestation, birth and suckling, that only fairly com-plicated social arrangements can break it down entirely women may be said to be mothers unless they are taught to deny the child-bearing qualities. Society must distort their sense of themselves, pervert their inherent growth-patterns, perpetrate a series of learning-outrages upon them, before they will cease to want to provide, at least for a few years, for the child they have already nourished for nine months within the safe cir-cle of their own bodies.[7]

The different roles played by men and women in the family and the social learning that prepares them for these roles contribute to the underrepresentation of women in public life. The question is, are the duties and roles associated with motherhood and homemaking mainly the products of what Mead calls the 'inherent growth-patterns' of females, or are they chiefly determined by social learning?

This is an old question. Over 100 years ago John Stuart Mill commented on the hypocrisy of society's attitudes toward women. Stripped of its moral pretensions, Mill argued that this attitude could be summarized as follows: 'It is necessary to society that women should marry and produce children. They will not do so unless they are compelled. Therefore it is necessary to compel them.'[8] Mill was not suggesting that women did not have biological impulses or nurturing tendencies that perhaps in most cases would cause them to assume a disproportionate share of childrearing and household tasks. His argument was simply that the weight of the law and social convention left them with no choice.

Mill's explanation had two parts. He argued that the subservient condition of a married woman—her lack of rights, standing, and personhood in relation to a husband whom the law and society treated as her master—was not one that would be voluntarily chosen by many women, and certainly not by women capable of doing something else. But at the same time, this form of legalized 'slavery' or 'impressment'—the analogies are Mill's—provided men with a free source of domestic labour. Rather than pay women the 'honest value of their labour',[9] male-dominated society chose to institutionalize this sexual exploitation, at the same time claiming that woman's condition was naturally and even divinely ordained.

According to Mill, men wanted to deny women equal recognition and fair compensation for their domestic labour, quite simply, because most men preferred the status and privileges of master, even if their mastery was limited to the confines of their home. This was, argued Mill, an egotism that inflicted costs on society. By depriving women of opportunities outside of marriage and the home, male-dominated society deprived itself of the talents, intelligence, and contributions of half the population.

Mill's arguments on the social construction of gender differences and the subordination of women were in the tradition of liberal utilitarianism. A rather different angle on women, the family, and power was provided at about the same time by Karl Marx and Frederick Engels.[10]

Marx and Engels sought to show that the subservience of women to men within the family and, by extension, in society was based on economic foundations. They argued that the free domestic labour provided by women subsidized capitalist production by reducing the wages that employers had to pay to attract the services of male employees. The male breadwinner/female homemaker family served the interests of the capitalist class because it ensured the reproduction of the working class at low cost. Marxists ever since have pointed out that the values associated with the traditional family also perform an ideological function, helping to ensure the acceptance by subordinate classes and by women of a social system that ensures their subordination. The state actively promoted the sexual exploitation of women within the family through laws restricting the legal and property rights and opportunities of females.

Within the institution of marriage, Marx and Engels contended, the relationship between man and woman was analogous to that between the bourgeoisie and the proletariat in society. The property relations that provided the basis for inequalities in power between social classes were mirrored in the relations between husband and wife. It followed from this, they argued, that the emancipation of women required their full integration into society and the economy in order to eliminate their dependence on male wage-earners. Women cannot be dependent and equal at the same time, an argument that became an important part of second-wave feminism.

The Roots of Underrepresentation

Women constitute about 52 per cent of the Canadian population and a slightly larger percentage of the electorate. Despite their numerical superiority, only one female, Kim Campbell, has held the office of Prime Minister, and two, Rita Johnston of BC and Catherine Callbeck of PEI, have been provincial premiers. Of these three, only Callbeck led her party to election victory. Only a handful of women have ever been elected as leaders of political parties in Canada. There are, however, some signs of change. The percentage of female candidates nominated by the major political parties has never been as high as it is today. Women comprised almost one-quarter of all candidates for the five main parties in the 1993 federal election (Table 12.1). Over 40 per cent of these female candidates ran for the NDP. In 1989 the NDP became the first major political party to elect a woman as its leader.

Table 12.1 Female Candidates for the Five Main Parties† in the 1993 Federal Election

Province	No. of constituencies	Percentage of const. with at least one female candidate*		Females as percentage of all candidates**		Percentage of all female candidates who were NDP candidates***	
Ontario	99	69%	(68)	21%	(82)	43%	(35)
Quebec	75	71%	(53)	24%	(73)	41%	(30)
BC	32	63%	(20)	26%	(33)	33%	(11)
Alta	26	62%	(16)	21%	(22)	45%	(10)
Sask.	14	64%	(9)	21%	(12)	42%	(5)
Man.	14	64%	(9)	23%	(13)	54%	(7)
NS	11	73%	(8)	25%	(11)	36%	(4)
NB	10	60%	(6)	27%	(10)	50%	(5)
Nfld	7	43%	(3)	31%	(4)	50%	(2)
PEI	4	50%	(2)	15%	(2)	100%	(2)
Yuk. & NWT	3	100%	(3)	27%	(3)	33%	(1)
Canada	295	67%	(197)	23%	(265)	42%	(112)

†Liberal Party, Reform Party, Bloc Québécois, NDP, Progressive Conservative Party.

*The number of constituencies with at least one female candidate is indicated in brackets.

** The number of female candidates is indicated in brackets.

*** The number of female NDP candidates is indicated in brackets.

Source: Calculated from Chief Electoral Officer of Canada, *List of Official Candidates*, 35th General Election (Ottawa, 1993).

A similar pattern of underrepresentation is found in the case of non-elected positions within the state. Before the 1982 appointment of Justice Bertha Wilson, no woman had ever been a member of the Supreme Court of Canada. Since then Justice Claire L'Heureux-Dubé (1987) and Justice Beverly McLachlin (1989) have been appointed to the Supreme Court. Overall, however, only a small percentage of judges in Canada are women. Somewhat deeper inroads have been cut into the senior ranks of the bureaucracy. Women account for close to 20 per cent of senior management personnel in the federal public service.[11] While it is not uncommon for women to be appointed to the boards of directors of Crown corporations, no woman has ever been the CEO of a major commercially oriented Crown corporation at either the federal or provincial level. In this respect, such Crown corporations as Canadian National, the Canadian Wheat Board, Ontario Hydro, Hydro-Québec, and la Caisse de dépôt et placement du Québec simply mirror the pattern of female exclusion that characterizes Canada's corporate élite. Why are females underrepresented in political life? Does it matter that the levers of the state are overwhelmingly in the hands of men? These questions are not new. The reasons behind female underrepresentation are, however, more easily explained than are its consequences. Let us begin with the relatively uncontroversial part.

Why Aren't More Women Involved in Political Life?

At a superficial level, the riddle of women's underrepresentation in public life may appear to be simple: they have been less interested than men. Female participation levels have long been about the same as men's for political activities like voting and campaigning, but they have been much lower for more demanding activities, such as joining a political party and running for office. 'The higher, the fewer' is how Sylvia Bashevkin describes the political participation gap between males and females.[12] This gap has narrowed over time, but continues to exist.

If interest is one of the key determinants of participation, what explains different levels of interest? The answer lies in social learning. Traditionally, females learned from the world around them that politics was a predominantly male occupation. The signals were unmistakable. The Prime Minister/President was a man. So, too, were all but a handful of cabinet ministers and elected representatives. More subtle than the evident maleness of the political profession, but probably more important in discouraging most females from seeing themselves in political roles beyond those of voter and perhaps member of the women's auxiliary of Party X, was the sheer weight of social customs and expectations, communicated in the family, in school, in churches, and through the media. Leadership and an active involvement in the world beyond the family and neighbourhood were associated with masculinity. If females were not actively discouraged from developing an interest in politics, they generally were not encouraged to apply their energies and time to such matters.

The influence of social learning was reinforced by the sexual division of labour in society, particularly in the family but also in the workplace. The traditional male breadwinner/female homemaker family and the more contemporary two breadwinner/female homemaker household are universally acknowledged by feminists as important sources of female subordination to males, including their comparatively marginal status in politics. This subordination/marginalization operates on two main levels:

(1) *Psychological*. Childrearing and housework are useful and necessary activities. Society's attitude toward them, however, is ambivalent. Because they are forms of unpaid labour, at least when carried out by a household member, there exists no objective yardstick for determining their value. Hence, they tend to be undervalued, particularly in comparison to paid work outside of the home. A good deal of evidence suggests that society's general failure to recognize the value of domestic work, or to praise it while labelling it 'woman's work', generates frustration and low self-esteem among many women.[13] Moreover, the traditional roles of mother and homemaker have often operated to limit women *spatially* (tied to the physical demands of the domestic routine), *cognitively* (the relevant world and its activities are more likely to centre on the family and household than in the case of men), and *emotionally* (expressive, nurturing, caring functions are associated with the homemaker, while instrumental, active, and rational qualities are associated with the breadwinner). In brief, the consciousness produced by the traditional roles of mother and homemaker is not likely to generate the motivations, interests, and personal resources for political activism.

(2) *Status and professional achievements*. Traditionally, women have been underrepresented in precisely those occupations from which political office-holders tend to be drawn:

law, business, and the liberal professions. Their formal educational attainments have tended to be less than those of men and they have not been found in significant numbers in such fields as finance, economics, and engineering, which are important professional backgrounds for many senior positions in the public service. But even when women have made what were and (in some cases, such as engineering) still are viewed as non-traditional career choices, the likelihood has been great that they have had to take time out and/or not pursue opportunities that would make greater demands on their time or require them to uproot their families because of the expectation that the nurturing of children and household duties will fall primarily to women.

The sexual division of labour within the household has, therefore, worked to reduce women's opportunities to achieve the sorts of experience and professional status that often provide the basis for recruitment into parties and other political organizations. If, however, a woman has the motivation and the status achievements to break into public life, there is still a good chance that the competing pressures of household responsibilities will limit the scope of her aspirations. It is certainly true that males are less likely to feel the constraining tug of these responsibilities than females.

The traditional male breadwinner/female homemaker family is, of course, much less common than it used to be. About 58 per cent of Canadian women over the age of fifteen are in the work force. About the same percentage of women with children under the age of three are in the labour force, and about two-thirds of these women work full-time. Whereas 65 per cent of Canadian families were one earner/male breadwinner ones in 1961, only 17 per cent conform to this model today.[14] Although the average female income is still only about 72 per cent of a man's, the proportion of women in relatively high-status professions like law, accounting, and university teaching and in middle management positions in both the private and public sector has increased significantly during the last generation. Nonetheless, the traditional sexual division of household labour still limits women's psychological resources and opportunities for political participation.

Women in Politics

Women were active in politics before being entitled to vote and run for office. Much of this activity was aimed at achieving full citizenship rights for women. But this was far from being the sole concern of women's groups during the pre-suffrage era. They were also active in demanding a long list of social reforms ranging from pensions for widowed mothers to non-militaristic policies in international relations. By contemporary standards, however, the early women's movement was small and politically weak. Moreover, its demands and values—although radical in the context of the times—today appear to have been very moderate and in some cases even reactionary.

Although the women's movement of today looks and sounds very different from earlier versions, elements of continuity span the movement's history. In tracing the history of women's political involvement in Canada, we will focus on the social and ideological forces that have influenced the women's movement, as well as the issues, organizations, strategies, and accomplishments that have characterized the movement at different points in time.

Phase One: The Contradictions of Democracy and Industrialization

Feminist writings and occasional incidents of women mobilizing around particular events or issues before the 1800s were quite rare. The democratic impulses released by the overthrow of absolute monarchy in Britain (1688) and by the American (1776) and French revolutions (1789) generated some agitation for equality of political rights, but their consequences were negligible. Although married women did have the right to vote in some societies, it appears that they were expected to follow the lead of their husbands—particularly during an era before the secret ballot. In matters of law and property, women were subsumed under their fathers and, after marriage, their husbands.

The origins of the women's movement usually are located in the mid-nineteenth century. As Sheila Rowbotham writes, 'Feminism came, like socialism, out of the tangled, confused response of men and women to capitalism.'[15] The progress of capitalism produced both affluence and misery. As more and more people crowded into the cities, where growth was spawned by factory production, a new set of social problems arose. Working-class women, girls, and children were employed in many industries. In fact, their cheap labour provided the basis for the profitability, for example, in the textile, clothing, footwear, and cigarmaking industries. As historian Terry Copp observes:

> Large numbers of working class women were 'emancipated' from the bondage of unpaid labour at home long before their middle class counterparts won entry into male-dominated high income occupations. There was no need to struggle against an exclusionist policy, since employers were only too happy to provide opportunities for women in the factories, shops, and garment lofts of the city.[16]

Hard numbers on female participation in the work force do not exist before the twentieth century, when census-takers began to keep track of such things. It has been estimated, however, that women comprised about 20 per cent of the labour force in Montreal during the 1890s. There is no reason to think that the percentage was lower in other cities. The low wages they were invariably paid put downward pressure on the wages of all unskilled working people.

Working conditions in most manufacturing establishments were hard, to say the least. There were no laws regulating the hours of work, minimum wages, or safety and sanitation in the workplace. A disabling injury on the job usually meant personal financial disaster. While both men and women suffered under these conditions, the exposure of women—usually single—to the harsh environment of the factory and sweat shop was considered more serious because of the era's views on femininity. A woman's natural place was considered to be the home, and her participation in the wage economy was believed, by political reactionaries and social reformers alike, to be 'one of the sad novelties of the modern world ... a true social heresy'.[17]

Early industrialization took its toll on women in other ways as well. The brutal grind and crushing squalor that characterized the lives of many working people could be numbed through drink. And in an era before heavy 'sin taxes', beer and spirits were very cheap.

Alcohol abuse, although by no means restricted to the working class, was one of the side effects of the long hours of work, inadequate wages, and sordid workplace conditions that were characteristic of workers' lives. It not only contributed to the ruin of individuals, but to the suffering of their families. Poor sanitation, overcrowding in improperly ventilated housing, and improper diet combined to produce low life expectancy—tuberculosis was a major killer among the urban working class—and high infant mortality.

The harshness of early industrialization was experienced by both men and women. Its manifestations—child labour, poverty, alcohol abuse—became central issues in the early women's movement because of their perceived impact on the family and on prevailing standards of decency. The Woman's Christian Temperance Union, the Young Women's Christian Association, and the Women's Institutes that sprang up in cities across Canada starting in the late nineteenth century were keenly aware of the clash between the material conditions of working-class women and prevailing notions of femininity and family. The social reforms they urged on government were intended to protect women and the family from what they saw as the corrosive influences of industrial life.

Early feminism was not, however, merely a response to the contradictions that industrialization created for women. The achievement of democracy was also full of contradictions. If democracy was a system of government based on the will of the people that recognized the equal humanity and dignity of human beings, half of the population could not be denied the rights and status enjoyed by the other half.

As John Stuart Mill observed in his essay 'The Subjection of Women',[18] arguments against the political and legal equality of the sexes took several forms. The main ones, and Mill's refutations (in italic), included the following:

- Unlike the slavery of one race by another, or the subordination of a defeated nation by its military conqueror, the subjection of women to men is natural. *When hasn't the subordination of one category of the human race by another been labelled 'natural' by members of the dominant group? What is said to be natural turns out to be, on closer examination, merely customary.*

- Unlike other forms of domination, the rule of men over women is accepted voluntarily by the female population. *This is not true. Some women do not accept the subordinate lot of their sex. And if a majority appear to acquiesce in their second-class status, this should surprise no one. From their earliest years women are trained in the habits of submission and learn what male-dominated society expects of them.*

- Granting equal rights to women will not promote the interests of society. *What this means, in fact, is that equality will not promote the interests of male society. It is a mere argument of convenience and self-interest.*

- What good could possibly come from extending full political and legal rights to women? *Leaving aside the good that this would produce for women—for their character, dignity, and material conditions—all society would benefit from a situation where the competition for any particular vocation is determined by interest and capabilities. Society loses when any group is barred from contributing its talents to humanity. Finally, equality for women would improve the character of men, who would no longer enjoy the sense of being superior to one-half of the human race because of an accident of birth, rather than to any merit or earned distinction on their part.*

Despite the compelling quality of Mill's arguments for equality, men who would have been shocked at the imputation that they were anything but democratic continued to ignore and resist demands that women be treated as full citizens. The arguments used to deny political rights for women were intellectually flabby and often amounted to nothing more than 'nice women do not want the vote' or 'my wife doesn't want the vote'.[19] But the logic of democratic rights is universal, and the exclusion of the female half of the population from the enjoyment of these rights was one of the major contradictions of most democracies until well into this century (see Table 12.2).

Table 12.2 Women's Suffrage

Year	Number of countries where men and women could vote in national elections on equal terms
1900	1
1910	3
1920	15
1930	21
1940	30
1950	69
1960	92
1970	127
1975	129

Source: Kathleen Newland, Women in Politics: A Global Review (Washington: Worldwatch Institute, 1975), 8.

The early women's movement focused mainly on three sets of issues: political rights, legal rights, and social reform. Anti-militarism was a fourth, but less prominent, issue on the political agenda of feminists. The social feminism mainstream of the movement was concerned chiefly with what it perceived as threats to the security of women and the family and to the traditional values associated with them. The demands made by organizations like the WCTU and YWCA and by prominent feminists like Nellie McClung were based solidly on the middle-class morality of the times.

The dominant middle-class morality could, and eventually did, accommodate itself to political rights for women. 'Respectable' feminists were those who consented to play by the rules of the game as they found it. Political rights for women were expected to make the political parties and government more sensitive to issues of concern to women, such as working conditions for females, child labour, alcohol abuse, and pensions for widowed mothers. Legal rights enabling a married woman to own property in her own name and protecting her from disinheritance in the event of her husband's death were demanded in order to provide more economic security for women and their dependent children. Social reforms—the prohibition of alcohol sales, family allowances, more humane conditions in women's prisons, and labour legislation dealing with women and children—were expected to produce a more civilized, compassionate society. Finally, peace issues within the women's movement were tied directly to the image of woman as the giver and nurturer of life, to what were believed to be the maternal instincts of women.

The mainstream of the women's movement was represented by the Woman's Christian Temperance Union, the Young Women's Christian Association, the National Council of Women of Canada, and the Federated Women's Institutes. They were politically moderate organizations in terms of both their goals and their strategies for attaining them. Indeed, it would be fair to say that the goals of social feminism were fundamentally conservative, aimed at protecting women and the family from the corrosive influences of the industrial age. The political discourse of the movement drew on the middle-class morality of the times. Even Nellie McClung, who was considered a firebrand of the movement, did not in the least suggest that the social roles of man the provider and woman the nurturer be changed. Instead, McClung and most other leaders of the early women's movement wanted to put woman's role on a more secure material footing.

The political tactics employed by mainstream women' s groups hardly ever strayed beyond the familiar bounds of accepted practice. Unlike their sisters in Great Britain and the United States, Canadian suffragists did not resort to such confrontational methods as chaining themselves to the fences surrounding Parliament, physically resisting the police, or hunger strikes. Instead, they relied on petitions to government and efforts to persuade public opinion.

After about forty years of campaigning, the first success came in Manitoba in 1916. The other three western provinces and Ontario followed suit within about a year. In the Maritimes, where the suffrage movement was comparatively weak, the achievement of political rights for women was preceded by much less agitation than in the West. Nova Scotia (1918), New Brunswick (1919), PEI (1922), and Newfoundland (1925) extended political rights to woman, although in the case of New Brunswick women were granted only voting rights. They could not hold provincial public office until 1934. Quebec was the straggler among Canada's provinces. Opposition from the Catholic Church blocked political rights for women until 1940.

Nationally, women became citizens between 1917 and 1919. The Wartime Elections Act of 1917 extended voting rights to the relatively small number of women serving in the military and to the much larger pool of females whose male relatives were in military service. This was broadened in 1918 to include all women twenty-one and older. The right to hold office in the House of Commons followed a year later, although women appeared to be barred from entry into the non-elected Senate and from holding other appointive public offices, such as judgeships, by virtue of not qualifying as 'persons', as this term was understood in law.

Absurd though it may seem, the personhood of women was considered to be dubious in the years following their enfranchisement.[20] Two prime ministers rejected calls for the appointment of a woman to the Senate on the grounds that women, not being persons as understood in law, were not eligible. The right of females to sit as judges was challenged in the handful of cases where they were appointed to the bench. After a couple of provincial rulings in their favour, the question was placed before the Supreme Court of Canada in 1927. Feminists were shocked when the Court ruled that the legal meaning of 'persons' excluded females.

This decision was reversed on appeal by the Judicial Committee of the Privy Council. Its ruling was blunt: 'The exclusion of women from all public offices is a relic of days more barbarous than ours ... and to ask why the word [person] should include females, the obvious answer is, why should it not?'[21] While logic and justice won the day in this particular legal battle, they have lost a number of others. Indeed, some contemporary feminists express strong doubts about the courts and law as vehicles for achieving the movement's goals. Voting rights for women and formal access to the male world of politics and the professions did not change the fact that society still viewed a woman's place as being in the home. Social feminists never really challenged this belief.

Political rights for women might have provided the basis for the reforms envisaged by feminists if two conditions had existed: (1) a sufficient number of voters were prepared to cast their ballots for candidates and parties who supported the reforms advocated by the women's movement; and (2) a political vehicle existed to articulate the movement's agenda and provide a feminist alternative in electoral politics. Indeed, it appears to have been the belief of many in the women's suffrage movement that the major political parties either would crumble when a flood of independent candidates was elected or would tremble submissively before the demands of reform-minded female voters. In fact, however, the parties continued to set the agenda of electoral politics along the familiar lines that had long served them so well. That the parties felt no need to respond to the agenda of the women's movement or to recruit more women into their inner circles showed how slight was the impact of feminism on public consciousness.

The major parties' indifference to the demands of the women's movement was matched by the movement's distrust of the party system. Early feminists were reluctant to rely on the established political parties as vehicles for reform for two main reasons. One involved the attitude of the parties. It was not simply that the Liberal and Conservative parties showed little enthusiasm for the goals of the women's movement, including political rights for women; rather, they were often dismissive and even hostile toward women's concerns and those expressing them. So after achieving the same formal political rights as men, women found that little of substance had changed. They were marginalized within parties dominated by men who, in the words of Canada's first female MP, Agnes Macphail, 'Want to Hog Everything'.[22] This was not surprising. The parties reflected the dominant beliefs of the time, which made women in public life—or in any of what were traditionally male preserves—appear an oddity. Even the more egalitarian of Canada's male politicians were not immune to sexism when it came to women in politics. J.S. Woodsworth, at the time a Labour MP from Winnipeg, probably summed up male politicians' grudging acceptance of women in *their* game when he said, 'I still don't think a woman has any place in politics.' [23]

A second reason why early feminists were reluctant to work within the framework of the party system was that their movement, like the farmers' movement of the same era, was issue-based. The organizations that formed the core of the movement took hard, uncompromising positions on such issues as prohibition, political rights for women, and social reform. Political parties, the two major ones at least, were based on principles that rejected the issue-based approach. One of these principles was partisan loyalty, the chief manifestation of which was the sheep-like obedience of elected members to the positions established by their party's leaders. Feminists wanted to be able to take positions based on their perception of what was in the interests of women, without having to compromise the movement's goals. This concept of direct representation was shared by the farmers' movement of the time but was discouraged by the partisan rules of British parliamentary government.

The anti-party inclinations of feminists were reinforced by the parties' tendency to avoid, if possible, and fudge, if avoidance was not possible, issue stances that might alienate important groups of voters. This has been called 'brokerage politics' (see Chapter 7). It is an approach that had no appeal to single-issue groups like prohibitionists and suffragists, or to the reform-minded women's movement more generally.

But working outside the established party system and the legislature, in an era when the media were less effective channels for political influence than they are today, carried heavy costs. A legislator who sits as an independent is marginalized in British parliamentary government, not sharing in the opportunities for participation available to the members of political parties. Moreover, the organizational and financial resources of the parties are important advantages that their candidates have over independents. It very quickly became apparent that non-partyism could not be made to work in practice.

Phase Two: After the Vote, What?

'Is Women's Suffrage a Fizzle?' asked a 1928 article in *Maclean's*. The question reflected the disillusionment experienced by many in the women's movement only years after having won the vote. Little, it seemed, had changed. Men still dominated the political process. The issues that interested women's groups, with the exception of prohibition, were no more prominent than before women's suffrage. And despite having the same formal political rights as men, women were still viewed as a not-quite-appropriate oddity in public life, rather like a dog walking on its hind legs. The dog can do it, but it's unnatural and, anyway, what is the point?

Part of the disappointment felt by feminists was due to their unrealistic expectations. Those who spearheaded the fight for women's suffrage believed—wrongly, as it turned out—that the vote would be the tool that women would use to change the world. As Nellie McClung put it, 'Women have cleaned up things since time began; and if women ever get into politics there will be a cleaning out of pigeon-holes and forgotten corners, on which the dust of years has fallen, and the sound of the political carpet beater will be heard in the land.'[24] When the millennial expectations of social feminists were not met, worse than this, when hardly anything appeared to have changed after the victory that was supposed to change so much, frustration and gloom were natural reactions.

It is usual to treat the period from suffrage to the new feminism that gained momentum in the 1960s as one long hiatus in the women's movement.[25] A small number of women did run for public office, and an even smaller number won election. Of those elected or appointed to public office, some achieved national prominence. Among them were Ottawa mayor Charlotte Whitton, five-time MP and twice Ontario MPP Agnes Macphail, British Columbia judges Emily Murphy and Helen Gregory MacGill, and Conservative cabinet minister Ellen Louise Fairclough. But the distinction of being the first woman to enter what had been an exclusive preserve of men, or to achieve recognition for one's talents and capabilities, had little impact on the political and social status of women in general. The breakthroughs and accomplishments of a few stood in sharp contrast to the unchanged status of the many. A number of plausible reasons help to explain this lack of change, chief among them the nature of early feminism, the party system, and societal attitudes.

The nature of early feminism. The mainstream of the women's movement was essentially conservative. Far from wanting to break down traditional gender roles, social feminists wanted to protect the social values and family structure on which they rested. Early feminists tended to believe that the political subordination of women was based on their inferior political and legal rights. What they failed to see was that traditional gender roles in the family, the workplace, and other social settings prevented women from participating more fully and effectively in public life.

The party system. We have already explained how the anti-party stance of feminist reformers proved difficult to maintain once they became part of a parliamentary process based on partisanship. This was not, however, the only impact the party system had on women's political involvement. Within the two traditional parties, as well as the CCF-NDP, women's involvement was organized around support services. The women's auxiliary or club was the symbol of the complementary role that women were encouraged to play in parties dominated by men. These separate organizations for women actually predated women's suffrage by a few years.[26] By the 1960s, this segregation of active male roles from supportive female roles—essentially an extension of the gender relations that existed within the family and society—was increasingly seen as an impediment to the equal and effective participation of women in politics.

Societal attitudes. Feminism failed to make a greater mark on social attitudes in part because the social feminist mainstream of the women's movement did not challenge conventional ways of thinking about appropriate gender roles. Outside of the mainstream was a more radical feminist fringe, what William O'Neill calls 'hard-core feminists',[27] who were not satisfied with the political rights and the social reforms that constituted the agenda of social feminism. Hard-core feminists like Flora MacDonald Denison demanded the legal emancipation of women and sexual equality in education, employment, the family: in short, wherever women were systematically subordinated to men.[28] Their ideas were not, however, considered to be 'respectable'.

If mainstream feminism was a weak force in Canadian politics, which it was, hard-core feminism barely scratched the surface of public life and political discourse. Its more radical critique of female subordination was marginalized in left-wing political organizations that themselves were on the near-irrelevant periphery of Canadian politics. Even within the CCF, the only left-wing political organization that managed to occupy an important place in Canadian politics, hard-core feminism ran up against some intransigent barriers. As historian Joan Sangster writes:

> [E]vidence indicates that women were channelled into [the CCF's] social committees; that women's feminine character was often described as emotional and sensitive, implying a female inability to cope with the 'rational' world of politics; and that women were seen as more apathetic and politically backward than men. Perhaps most important of all, because women's primary responsibility for the family was never questioned, an essential barrier to women's whole-hearted participation in politics remained unchallenged and unchanged.[29]

But this raises the question of why social attitudes about gender roles were slow in changing. It is a complex issue that cannot be reduced to a single explanation. We would argue, however, that the ability of women to exert some greater degree of control over their reproductive role was a chief factor contributing to this change. Reliable contraceptive devices became widely available and used during the 1950s (mainly condoms and diaphragms) and the 1960s (the birth control pill). It was no coincidence that women began to have fewer children. Smaller families and the ability to be sexually active without fear of becoming pregnant provided the opportunity for women to stay in school longer or participate in the work force for more years of their reproductive lives. Choice in the realm of reproduction was a crucial material condition for women's liberation in other aspects of life.

The pill made it possible, but not inevitable. We still need to understand why the second wave of feminism that became a political force in the 1960s—it already was something of an intellectual force, influenced by writers like Margaret Mead and Simone de Beauvoir—was more critical and, as it turned out, more effective than the early women's movement. The explanation has three parts: sexuality, secularism, and economics.

Sexuality had been the deafening silence of the first wave of feminism. The entire topic of sexuality was shrouded in mystery and taboo before the 1960s. While there still is a good deal of half-baked thinking surrounding the subject, the period since the sixties has been marked by a much greater willingness to talk about sexuality and acknowledge its importance in social relationships. This was a necessary step that opened the way for public debate on such matters as reproductive rights and women's control of their bodies, pornography's possible impact on violence against women, and sexual stereotyping in education and the media.

Sexuality was not entirely in the closet before the 1960s. The subject had, in fact, received considerable attention from intellectuals since Sigmund Freud based the totality of human experience on males' and females' different struggles to resolve the conflict between their libidinal drives (sexual energy) and the demands of the super-ego (society's demands and taboos on behaviour). It is no accident that virtually every major intellectual leader of feminism's second wave took direct aim at Freud and what they argued was the patriarchal bias of twentieth-century psychology.[30] Essentially, they argued that Freudian psychology was phallocentric, and that concepts like the 'castration complex', 'penis envy', and 'masculinity complex' were pseudo-scientific justifications for male dominance, not biologically rooted facts of the human condition.

Once conventional beliefs about sexuality were challenged, this opened the door to a re-examination of traditional gender roles and stereotypes throughout society. The position taken by modern feminists was that these roles and their accompanying stereotypes were mainly social constructions rather than facts of nature. This was the reasoning behind the movement's slogan, 'The personal is political.' Conventional beliefs about female passivity, maternal instincts, and home-centredness were argued to be the ideological foundations, and the traditional division of labour in the home, workplace, church, and in other supposedly non-political settings the structural foundations, of women's political subordination. Differences that had been largely accepted and even promoted by maternal feminists earlier in the century were flatly rejected by the new feminism of the sixties.

Secularism was a second factor that contributed to the changed character of second-wave feminism. Many of the leading individuals in the first wave of feminism had been women of strong religious conviction and even fervour. As well, some of the key organizations in the suffrage and social feminism movements, including the WCTU, the YWCA, the Imperial Order of the Daughters of the Empire, and the National Council of Women of Canada, had either direct links or an affinity of views with some of the Protestant churches. Early feminism had strong ties to the social gospel movement of the period between the 1890s and the 1930s, a movement that 'attempt[ed] to apply Christianity to the collective ills of an industrializing society'.[31] Those in the social gospel movement, like the early feminist leaders, believed that a New Jerusalem could be created on earth through social reforms. Their Christianity was secular insofar as it focused on changing conditions in the here and now. But their vision of reform was inspired by traditional Christian ideals.[32]

The second wave of the women's movement was secular in both its goals and inspiration. Its worldly character was broadly in tune with the changed social climate of the post-fifties world, where the traditional moral authority of religion was weaker than previously. In fact, traditional religious values regarding the family, procreation, and appropriate behaviour for males and females, as well as the patriarchal authority structures of most churches, were targets of feminist criticism. While some of the movement's earlier leaders, for example, Nellie McClung,[33] had been outspokenly critical of certain church teachings and practices, they had generally embraced traditional moral values, not seeing them as impediments to equality for women.

Economic change was a third factor that influenced the second wave of the women's movement. Women had long constituted an important part of the labour force. Single women in particular provided a pool of cheap labour in some manufacturing and service industries. The unpaid domestic work of women helped to subsidize the private economy by reducing the price that employers would otherwise have had to pay to male employees. Moreover, women constituted what has been called a 'reserve army' of labour that could be mobilized in unusual circumstances, as during the two world wars. Their participation in the wage economy was limited, however, by two conventional beliefs: women should not take jobs that could be held by men, and outside employment was fine for single women but should stop after marriage.

These constraints began to weaken during the 1950s and 1960s. As Figure 12.1 shows, the labour force participation rate of women (i.e., the percentage of working-age women who hold jobs or are looking for jobs outside the home) increased dramatically between 1951 and 1971. Most of this increase was the result of an explosion in the number of married women working outside the home. Their participation rate increased 300 per cent over these twenty years. Women's share of the total labour force also increased sharply.

A number of explanations have been offered for this increased participation rate. Economists have favoured three main arguments:

- Falling real family incomes have compelled women to enter the work force to maintain the household's purchasing power.
- Labour-saving household appliances and higher female educational attainment have produced feelings of boredom and dissatisfaction in the home, leading more and more women to seek outside employment.
- As the real wages associated with some 'female' jobs increased, outside employment appeared increasingly attractive to women.

Figure 12.1 Labour Force Participation Rates, 1901–93

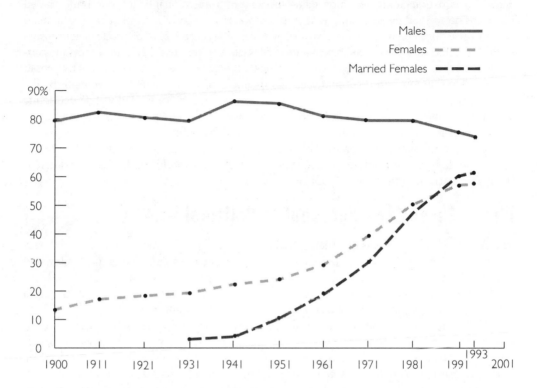

Sources: F.H. Leary, ed., *Historical Statistics of Canada*, 2nd edition (Ottawa: Supply and Services Canada, 1983), D107-122 and D431-448; Statistics Canada, *Labour Force Annual Averages*, Cat. 71-220 annual.

There is doubtless some truth in each of these explanations. But as is so often true of conventional economics, it misses the mark by ignoring the obvious. Women had become increasingly bored with their traditional role. Betty Friedan called this 'the problem that has no name'.[34] Although difficult to label and express in a culture that told women they should feel fulfilled in the home, the problem amounted to this: 'I want something more than my husband and my children and my home.'[35] A paying job was often seen to be that 'something more'.

Yet another factor, however, should not be ignored. Most of the new jobs created in advanced industrial economies since World War Two have been in service industries, and many of these jobs have been relatively low-paying ones traditionally viewed as female occupations. Expansion of the service economy thus produced an increase in the supply of the clerical, secretarial, retail sales, cashier/teller, and waitressing jobs that were predominantly held by females. Many economists have a difficult time dealing with this factor because their model of the economic world says that if the demand for something increases, in this case secretaries and so on, the price should also increase. This did not happen—underpaid 'female' occupations remained underpaid—because of conventional beliefs that undervalued the work performed by women, seeing it as temporary or merely a supplement to the main (male) breadwinner's income. The world of work is a central part of modern feminism's reform agenda. Of course, the exploitation of female workers had been an important concern of social feminists, but they never questioned the belief that a married woman's proper place was in the home and that marriage was the most desirable estate for a woman. By the 1960s, the material basis of these conventional views had become shaky. The economic forces that caused a growing number of married women to seek wage employment, combined with the psychological impetus for women to seek fulfilment beyond the homemaker role, changed the nature of women's involvement in the economy. The reality of their segregation into low-pay, low-prestige occupations[36] became less and less palatable to women as their participation in the wage economy increased.

Phase Three: The Personal Is Political

The decade of the fifties was like the quiet before the storm. Post-war economic growth and the 'baby boom' combined to reinforce traditional gender roles and stereotypes. Television sitcoms, films, and popular magazines almost unfailingly portrayed the male breadwinner/female homemaker family as the pinnacle of human happiness. Once women had achieved political rights, it seemed that equality was no longer an issue.

The syrupy bliss of the era was, it turned out, an illusion. By the early sixties voices of discontent were being increasingly heard. Women were challenging the deep-seated beliefs and social structures that limited their participation in the male-dominated world. The 'problem that has no name' was being named, and the name was sexism. This word is not found in dictionaries before the 1970s, a fact that reflected the unconscious acceptance by most people of gender role differences as natural and even desirable. 'Sexism' was coined in the 1960s as a label for behaviour that treated males and females unequally for no better reason than their sexuality. Sexism in its numerous forms and wherever it took place was the target of the women's movement that emerged during these years.

The revival of the women's movement was the result of several factors. Intellectually, Simone de Beauvoir in France, Germaine Greer in Britain, and Betty Friedan and Gloria Steinem in the United States were developing a powerful analysis of women's subordination to men. Their critique went far beyond matters of political and legal rights and social reform, the chief concerns of earlier feminists. Instead, they exposed the social, cultural, and economic roots of inequality. Friedan's approach was typical in its range. In *The Feminine Mystique* she traced the causes of female subordination to the family, the social sciences (particularly psychology, sociology, and anthropology), education, advertising and the media, mass consumption capitalism, and sexual mores.

Anti-establishment ideas always face an uphill struggle. They never triumph by their intellectual weight alone. What saved the feminist critiques of Beauvoir, Friedan, and company from the fate of many interesting but ultimately ineffectual intellectual movements were the supportive material conditions and social climate of the 1960s. With about one out of every three women of working age employed outside the home, including about one out of five married women (1961), and growing numbers of women enrolled in post-secondary education,[37] sexual double standards were increasingly apparent to more women than ever before. Articles on the dilemmas facing the 'new woman', telling her how to juggle family, romance, and job, became standard fare in women's magazines like *Chatelaine* and *Redbook*. Such terms as 'women's lib' and 'women's libbers' were more frequently said with a sneer than not, and most women (and men) probably would not have recognized the names of people like Betty Friedan and Germaine Greer. Nevertheless, modern feminism's argument that the personal is political, that the fight for gender equality had to be waged in the workplace, the media, the schools, and over women's bodies, struck a responsive chord with many.

What the lived experience of women confirmed, the social climate of the 1960s encouraged. This was the era of the civil rights movement in the United States, mounting opposition to American military involvement in Vietnam, and anti-establishment political causes generally. Attacks on the 'establishment' and its values were common. Student radicalism, protest marches, sit-ins, and occasional violence were the visible signs of a reaction against the status quo. While the feminist movement did not spearhead the protest movement of the 1960s, it profited from the movement's tendency to see all established power relations as unjust.

The protest politics of the 1960s affected the women's movement in a second, more enduring way as well. Civil rights advocates in the United States argued that affirmative action programs were necessary to provide real equality of opportunity for Blacks. Quotas and preferential hiring policies for targeted minorities were justified, they reasoned, because these groups were the victims of a systemic discrimination that ensured that few of them would acquire the formal qualifications—degrees, professional school admission scores, job-relevant experience—needed to compete with the members of more advantaged groups. The opponents of affirmative action—reverse discrimination, as they were more likely to call it—charged that such a policy just shifted the burden of injustice onto the shoulders of the qualified members of advantaged groups who were not personally responsible for the plight of the minority groups targeted for special treatment. But despite considerable opposition, affirmative action policies were widely adopted by governments and educational institutions in the United States.

The arguments and demands of the North American women's movement bear a strong resemblance to those that emerged during the struggle to advance the rights of American Blacks. Affirmative action does not have nearly the same prominence in several of the Western European democracies. Part of the explanation for this may have to do with lower barriers to the participation of women in politics and the professions in some European societies than in North America. Also, many European countries have more supportive structures, such as publicly financed crèches that accept children from the age of two or younger (e.g., eighteen months in Belgium), enabling women to continue their careers with minimal interruption. But an important part of the answer, we would argue, is the influence that the American civil rights movement has had on the demands of the women's movement and the response of policy-makers. Affirmative action for women borrows arguments and policy measures that were pioneered in the struggle to increase the economic and social status of Blacks in the United States.

Although Canada had no first-hand experience with racially based affirmative action policies before the 1960s, the concept and practice were not totally imported. Language policies adopted in Quebec during the 1970s aimed to increase the representation of Francophones in the managerial ranks of that province's economy through agreements negotiated between the government and private companies. At the federal level, the period from the early 1970s saw an increasing number of administrative positions designated officially bilingual. This policy had the practical effect of favouring Francophones who, more often than Anglophones, had bilingual skills. During the 1980s, Ottawa began the practice of setting 'targets'—the word 'quota' was and continues to be rejected—for the representation of particular groups in specified categories of the public service, and eventually the government linked the performance evaluation of senior bureaucrats to their success in hitting these targets.

The logic of affirmative action was not, therefore, foreign to Canada. Language policies in Quebec and nationally incorporated elements of such an approach by the mid-1970s. Not only was the discourse of group rights already familiar in Canada, largely because of the struggles over language policies and Quebec's constitutional status, but the logic and machinery of targeting groups for preferred treatment was already embedded in the Canadian state.

Contemporary feminism is different from the first wave of the women's movement in more than its analysis and aims. The organizational network of women's groups is much more developed than when female suffrage and social reform were the key issues. Moreover, the movement's strategies distinguish it from its predecessor. We turn now to an examination of the organizations, strategies, and achievements of modern feminism.

Organizing for Influence

Women have long been active in Canadian politics. As may be seen in Appendix 1 to this chapter, several important women's organizations date from the pre-suffrage era. Moreover, the political parties provided a channel—though not a very effective one—for women's participation in political life. Over the last three decades these organizations have been joined by hundreds more, as the organizational network of the women's movement has proliferated. This proliferation has generated, in response, new state structures to deal with 'women's issues' and the groups expressing them.

The organizations listed in Appendix 1 represent only some of the most visible structures through which women's political involvement takes place. Approximately 600 national and local women's groups are represented by the National Action Committee on the Status of Women (NAC), an umbrella lobbying organization for the women's movement. In addition, there are women's church groups, professional associations, labour associations, and service organizations that are not members of NAC, as well as *ad hoc* groups that spring up around short-term issues.

While the network of women's groups has become denser over the last few decades, some argue that a focus on formal organizations and the structures of women's political involvement are misleading. Historian Anne Firor Scott argues that there has been a long but 'invisible' history of women's struggles against practices and conditions they wanted changed.[38] Many Canadian feminists agree.[39] They maintain that a female political culture operates through contacts and consciousness at the community level—based on issues that affect women in their daily lives—and this culture does not rely on the formal political institutions and decision-making processes dominated by men. These grassroots activities tend to be overlooked and undervalued because the dominant political culture 'puts a premium on formal, institutionalized political processes, predictable and regulated levels and types of participation and both bureaucratic and hierarchical structures'.[40] Some argue that women's influence diminishes and their perspective on issues becomes blunted when they play by the rules of a political game established by men.

Strategies

'There are fifty-six whooping cranes in Canada and one female federal politician.'[41] So began a 1971 article by Barbara Frum in *Chatelaine*. Half a century after winning the same political rights as men, the inroads made by women in Canada's political parties were pitifully small. Their participation was still channelled mainly into the activities of women's auxiliaries/associations, whose role was to provide support services for the mainstream of the parties. Although vital to the parties, these activities—social, administrative, fund-raising, and campaigning—had low prestige and were remote from the policy and strategy structures of the parties. Separate women's associations were singled out by the Royal Commission on the Status of Women as a serious barrier to the full participation of women in party politics. The Commission recommended that they be abolished.

Support-oriented women's associations within the parties were redolent of the sexual division of labour that modern feminism condemned. They have been eliminated at the national and provincial levels in all of the major parties, although they still exist at the constituency level in some parts of the country. The trend since the late 1960s has been to replace the traditional women's associations with new women's groups that are dedicated to increasing women's representation and policy influence. As Sylvia Bashevkin notes, this transition has not been frictionless.[42] Nevertheless, if men still dominate within Canada's political parties, which they do, and if the feminist political agenda is still resisted, which it is in the two older parties, the internal structures of the parties are no longer to blame.

Attempting to increase the representation and influence of women in parties that aspire to govern is a rather blunt strategy for achieving feminist goals. Parties in power, or even within sight of being elected to govern, are disinclined to alienate those voters and organized interests who object to such elements of the feminist agenda as the elimination of legal restrictions on abortion, affirmative action in hiring, and a national program of publicly subsidized day care. Consequently, the women's movement has sought influence by other means.

One of these means has been the courts. Litigation in support of sexual equality claims has a long history in Canada, going back to the turn of the century when women challenged barriers to their entry into certain professions. But with the notable exception of the 1929 *Persons* case, which 'decided' that women were persons in law, most of the pre-Charter litigation on sexual equality resulted in defeats for women's claims.[43] Given this dismal track record in the courts, plus the high cost of litigation—several pre-Charter cases reached the

Supreme Court only because certain lawyers were willing to donate their time[44]—it comes as no surprise that this strategy was seldom chosen by women.

The Charter was expected to change all this. Indeed, women's groups fought hard and successfully for the inclusion of section 28 of the Charter, which states that 'the rights and freedoms referred to in [the Charter] are guaranteed equally to male and female persons.' Their efforts had already ensured that the equality section of the Charter (s. 15) proscribed discrimination based on sex. With sections 15 and 28 in hand, it appeared that women's groups would turn to the courts as never before.

They have, but with mixed results. In the first four years after the equality section came into effect (1985–9), forty-four cases of sexual discrimination under section 15 were decided by the courts. Most of these cases were instigated by or on behalf of men. In only nine cases were equality claims made by women. Despite victories in some of these cases feminist legal scholars quickly became dubious about the usefulness of section 15. Michael Mandel uses the term 'equality with a vengeance' to describe the tendency of courts, and of governments responding to court decisions, to interpret the Charter's equality provisions in ways that can backfire against women.[45]

Feminists have argued that the sexual equality guarantees of the Charter are undermined by two aspects of judicial interpretation. One is the courts' unwillingness to elevate equality rights over other rights and freedoms guaranteed in the Charter. For example, in *Casagrande v. Hinton Roman Catholic Separate School District* (1987),[46] a Catholic school board's decision to fire a pregnant teacher was upheld on the grounds that section 15 equality rights took a back seat to the rights of 'denominational, separate or dissentient schools' that are also guaranteed by the constitution. Second, and more serious according to feminists, is the tendency of judges to interpret equality in *formal* rather than *substantive* terms. What they mean by this is that judges will be satisfied that no discrimination has occurred if laws treat similarly persons who are similarly situated. This is an 'equality before the law' approach that, according to feminists, fails to understand the real mechanisms through which discrimination occurs. Systemic discrimination, the inequality that is created and maintained through social practices and beliefs, cannot be overcome by ensuring that the law is blind to the sex or other group characteristic of a section 15 claimant. Substantive equality, they argue, requires that judges determine whether a claimant belongs to a disadvantaged group and, second, 'whether the impugned law, policy or practice is operating to the detriment of [that disadvantaged group]'.[47]

In fact, however, this claim is not entirely fair. As early as 1984 the Supreme Court of Canada had declared its intention to look beyond the formal words of Charter sections to consider the interests they were meant to protect.[48] In *Edwards Books* (1986),[49] the majority expressed the view that 'the courts must be cautious to ensure that [the Charter] does not simply become an instrument of better situated individuals to roll back legislation which has as its object the improvement of the condition of less advantaged persons.'[50] A year later, Justices Dickson and Wilson argued that one of the important purposes of the Charter was to assist social and economic 'underdogs'.[51] These intimations of judicial activism were acted on in the *Morgentaler* abortion decision (1988), where the majority was willing to look at the actual effects of Canada's abortion law to determine whether it violated the 'liberty' and 'security of the person' guarantees in section 7 of the Charter.

Then, in *Andrews v. Law Society of British Columbia* (1989),[52] Canada's highest court showed that it was prepared to go beyond the wooden requirements of formal equality in interpreting section 15 of the Charter. The Supreme Court argued that the Charter's equality section prohibits laws that have had a discriminatory impact on the members of some group or groups. The decisions written by Justices Wilson and McIntyre both cited approvingly an American Supreme Court precedent that identified 'discrete and insular minorities' as groups requiring the protection of constitutional equality guarantees. In fact, the formal equality test so maligned by feminist legal scholars was explicitly rejected by all of the Supreme Court justices.[53] *Andrews* has been interpreted as a positive signal by Canadian feminists, but many of them remain wary of relying on the Charter and the courts.

Activist Penney Kome identifies several political strategies, including legal action, that are open to women's groups. They range across grassroots organizing to deal with emergencies (e.g., a rash of sexual assaults in a neighbourhood) or chronic local problems (e.g., inadequate public transportation or pollution), representations through official channels, lobbying campaigns directed at decision-makers and potential supporters, and use of the media.[54] Lacking the financial resources and the personal access that characterize many business and professional interest groups, the women's movement has made extensive use of all of these political action strategies.

Achievements

The achievements of modern feminists can be grouped into three types of change: legislative reform, changes in the process of decision-making, and the material/social conditions of women. Together they add up to a mixed record of success and failure.

Let us begin with changes to the law. Some of the most celebrated achievements of the women's movement have been on this front. Sex was not one of the proscribed grounds of discrimination in the draft Charter proposed by the Liberal government in 1981. It became part of the Charter after the vigorous representations made by women's groups before the Special Parliamentary Committee on the Constitution. Likewise, the section 28 guarantee of legal equality for men and women was a direct product of intense lobbying by women's groups.[55] And in perhaps the most publicized of court decisions on the Charter, the Supreme Court of Canada struck down the section of the Criminal Code dealing with abortion, a decision that was greeted as a major victory for the women's movement.

Other legislative breakthroughs include the maternity leave provisions written into the Canada Labour Code in 1970; the 1983 amendment to the Unemployment Insurance Act that eliminated discrimination against pregnant women; and the pay equity laws passed by Ottawa and the provinces. Human rights codes and commissions to enforce them exist nationally and in all of the provinces. They have provided opportunities to challenge discriminatory employment and commercial practices in the private sector, practices that the courts have deemed to fall outside the ambit of the Charter.

So have the main legal barriers to sexual equality been eliminated? Not nearly, claim women's groups. They point to inaction or what they believe to be government's inadequate response to issues like day care, affirmative action, female poverty, pay equity, and pornography. Sandra Burt's 1984 survey of women's groups found that less than one-quarter of

Affirmative action programs targeted at women and some other groups can generate a political backlash, as appeared to happen in the 1995 Ontario election. (Roy Peterson, *Vancouver Sun*)

those who responded believed they had been successful in their efforts to influence government.[56] Today, many feminists argue that a popular backlash has enabled governments to roll back some of the gains made in the past.

A second measure of feminism's achievements involves the decision-making structures of the state. Among the striking characteristics of the modern women's movement are its financial and organizational links to government. The 1970 Report of the Royal Commission on the Status of Women was followed by the creation of the Canadian Advisory Council on the Status of Women (CACSW) and the creation of a women's portfolio in the federal cabinet. Similar advisory councils have been created by all provinces, and special cabinet positions have been established by some. Within government departments and agencies it is now common to have special divisions devoted to 'women's issues' or affirmative action. For example, the Public Service Commission of Canada has a Program Development (Affirmative Action) branch that monitors the representation of women, indigenous Canadians, disabled persons, and visible minorities in the federal bureaucracy. The Treasury Board Secretariat has an Affirmative Action Group and an Employment Equity section within its Human Resources Division. As Penney Kome observes, the creation of status of women councils was followed by a 'deluge of equal-opportunity officers, women's directorates, grant officers, labour specialists, and other women's advocates attached to various branches of government'.[57]

Financially, the women's movement is heavily dependent on money provided by government. This dependence operates through two main channels. One is the budget of the

Secretary of State (SOS), which has responsibility for the CACSW. Leslie Pal has documented the pattern of women's group dependence on money channelled through the department's Women's Program.[58] For example, in 1988 SOS funding accounted for 93 per cent of the total revenue of the Canadian Day Care Advocacy Association (CDCAA). Even after cuts made to the budget of SOS's Women's Program at the end of the decade, 84 per cent of CDCAA's 1990 revenues came from this program. The Canadian Congress for Learning Opportunities for Women (CLOW) received 87 per cent of its 1988 revenues from the Women's Program. This figure was down only marginally to 83 per cent for 1990. Funding from SOS's Women's Program is the single largest source of revenue for the NAC, Canada's major feminist organization, accounting for close to 30 per cent of its revenues in 1995.

The second channel involves social spending, much of which takes the form of transfers from Ottawa to provincial governments. Much of the money that ultimately reaches the hands of rape crisis centres, women's counselling services, halfway houses for battered women, and the vast network of services geared to meeting women's needs, as well as women's research and information organizations, is buried in the budget of the Canada Health and Social Transfer to the provinces. Cutbacks in Ottawa's transfers to the provinces, and to social spending generally, squeeze the financial lifeline of grassroots women's groups that depend on public money.

Those on the left of the women's movement have often criticized the organizational and financial ties between women's groups and the state, arguing that such ties have the effect of co-opting feminists into the state. The demands of these groups will perforce be more moderate and their influence strategies less confrontational—and perhaps less effective—than if they resisted the siren call of money and a seat at the table. On the other hand, the independent resources available to voluntary associations are often meagre, and so the temptation to seek and accept state support is strong. Likewise, direct representation on a government body provides an opportunity to be part of the process and to express women's perspectives from inside the state.

In fact, despite the financial dependence of women's groups on government, there is little evidence that this has made them more 'polite' toward the hand that feeds. Based on his examination of the Secretary of State Department's support for voluntary groups since the 1960s, Leslie Pal concludes that there is no evidence that these groups have been co-opted into an agenda set by the bureaucrats and politicians. On the contrary, he argues, women's groups in particular have not hesitated to criticize and embarrass the governments that have provided them with the means to publicize the alleged failures of government policy.[59] Sylvia Bashevkin's study of the NAC's strong opposition to the Conservative government's free trade initiative confirms this view. Bashevkin argues that the depth of Ottawa's cuts in NAC funding was certainly influenced by the NAC's vigorous opposition to free trade, in alliance with other critics of the Conservative government.[60] Reading through the annual reports and other publications of the CACSW, one would be hard pressed to conclude that representation within the state has muted the voice of feminist criticism.

What about the social conditions of women? Has the women's movement managed to improve their material circumstances or change social attitudes toward men and women? Reforming the law and the state is fine, but has it delivered more equality in the daily lives of women?

Here, the record of achievement is mixed. There is no doubt that social attitudes regarding appropriate roles and behaviour for males and females have changed. Polling data suggest that Canadians' beliefs about gender have undergone considerable change over the last couple of decades (see Table 12.3). There still is some resistance to equality, however, particularly regarding family matters. For example, almost as many Canadians today as in the early 1970s believe that working mothers have had a harmful effect on family life. And a large minority of both women and men—31 per cent and 28 per cent, respectively—say that they would prefer to work for a man.[61] Equal percentages of men and women, 43 per cent, are opposed to women in combat roles in Canada's military.[62]

Nevertheless, the overall pattern is one of greater equality. Moreover, the attitudes of men and women are basically the same on most gender-related issues. For example, about 70 per cent of both men and women favour some legal restrictions or a complete ban on abortion.[63] On the question of child-care responsibility, 44 per cent of men and 38 per cent of women say it should fall exclusively to the mother or family.[64] Eighty-four per cent of men and 75 per cent of women say that the gender of a national party leader is irrelevant to their decision on how to vote.[65] And 84 per cent of men versus 92 per cent of women believe that a woman could run most businesses as well as a man.[66]

Alongside the evidence of changed attitudes are signs that considerable sexism persists. These include gender characterizations in commercial advertising and entertainment programming, the childrearing practices of many, indeed probably most, parents, the unequal division of domestic responsibilities between men and women, and the relative infrequency of women's career choices taking precedence over men's even in this age of two-earner households. The findings of pollsters need to be weighed against the empirical evidence of inequality.

When one turns to the material conditions of women, one is reminded of the French phrase, *plus ça change, plus c'est la même chose*. Despite the fact that there are today more women lawyers, professors, accountants, and even engineers than in the past, the breakthroughs that have been made by middle-class women have not been matched by their less privileged sisters. Consider the following facts:

- About 60 per cent of working women are employed in clerical, sales, and service jobs where the pay tends to be low. This is almost exactly the same percentage that was employed in these occupations five decades ago.
- The average female worker makes about 72 per cent of what the average male earns. This represents progress when one considers that the figure was about 49 per cent in 1971. Most of this difference is accounted for by three factors: the segregation of women into low-paying occupations; more women than men having part-time jobs (although the wage gap remains large, women earn almost three-quarters of men's incomes when only full-time workers are taken into account); and the greater seniority of male employers.
- Women are more likely to be poor than men. Approximately 60 per cent of those below the poverty line established by Statistics Canada are women. Over time, poverty has assumed an increasingly feminine aspect. For example, in 1961 only about 15 per cent of low-income families (i.e., families with incomes below the poverty line) were headed by women. Today the share is closer to 35 per cent, as higher levels of marital breakdown

Table 12.3 Canadian Attitudes Toward Gender

A. 'Do you think women could run most businesses as well as men or not?' (percentage answering 'as well as men')

1971	1989
58%	88%

B. 'If you were taking a new job and had your choice of a boss, would you prefer to work for a man or a woman?' (percentage answering 'prefer a man')

1964	1974	1989
64%	42%*	30%*

C. 'There are more married women—with families—in the working world than ever before. Do you think this has a harmful effect on family life or not?' (percentage answering 'yes, it's harmful')

1973	1989
59%	56%

D. 'If in a national leadership convention, a federal political party chose a qualified woman as their leader, would you be more inclined to support that party, less inclined, or would it not make any difference?'

1975**			1989**		
More inclined	Less inclined	No difference	More inclined	Less inclined	No difference
13%	11%	73%	15%	4%	80%

*Most respondents said it did not matter.

**The percentages do not equal 100 because the 'don't know' responses are not included.

Source: CIPO, *The Gallup Report*.

produce many more female single-parent households. Single-parent families headed by women constitute the most poverty-prone group in Canada, 60 per cent of them living below the poverty line in 1993.[67]

- The *Financial Post Magazine* publishes an annual special issue on Canada's corporate élite, profiling the CEOs of the leading 200 corporations. As of 1995, one of these 200 business leaders was female.

The continuing exclusion of women from Canada's corporate élite, at the same time as their participation in the political élite has been increasing, may thwart some of the gains achieved by the women's movement. This, at least, is the conclusion reached by a Norwegian think tank. It argues that as economies become internationalized, domestic politics matters less and business matters more. Increasingly, decisions with major social implications are taken by the corporate élite, an élite from which women are still excluded (see Box 12.1).

Materially, women are much less well off than men. This is a reality that has remained stubbornly unchanged, despite the legal reforms and changed social attitudes that have been produced by the women's movement. Poverty and economic dependence undermine the ability of individuals to control their lives and to grasp the opportunities promised by formal legal and political equality. So far as women are concerned, Canadian democracy remains flawed.

Box 12.1 Women Left, Right, and Centre

An age-old division of labour is resurfacing in Norway. The men are out foraging while the women keep house. But the modern version of an old pattern has a difference. It is the national housekeeping that is falling to the women—starting with the country's prime minister, Gro Harlem Brundtland, leader of the Labour Party, who is now heading her third administration.

Two other women are following her example. Anee Inger Lahnstein has taken over the small but influential Centre Party, a farmers' party that opposed the idea of Norway joining the European Community. And next month Kaci Kullmann Five (pronounced 'fever') will be elected leader of the Conservatives, the main opposition party.

All three are mothers. Dr. Brundtland has four children, Mrs. Lahnstein three and Kaci—as Mrs. Kullmann Five is popularly known—has two. Between them. the parties they lead will get the votes of about 70% of the electorate.

Although women are taking over in politics, there are no women at the head of large Norwegian companies, which is where the men forage. A far-sighted Norwegian think-tank report called 'Scenario 2000', published in Oslo in 1987, noted that when women move into a main domain—doctoring, the priesthood, education—the men move on to higher-paid jobs with a rising social status. It suggested that the same trend was at work in politics. Politics was mattering less as economies were internationalised and markets mattered more. 'Women', said the report, 'may be moving from a marginal minority to a marginal majority.'

Up to a point. Few people would describe the powerful Dr Brundtland as 'marginal'—least of all the ten men she has admitted to her 19-member cabinet.

The Economist, 23 March 1991.

Appendix 1: Selected Women's Organizations in Canada

Date Established	Name
1870	Young Women's Christian Association
1893	National Council of Women of Canada
1897	Federated Women's Institutes of Canada
1897	National Council of Jewish Women
1908	Canadian Nurses' Association
1918	Federation of Women Teachers Association of Canada
1919	Canadian Federation of University Women
1920	Canadian Teachers' Federation
1930	Canadian Federation of Business and Professional Women's Clubs
1939	Canadian Association of Elizabeth Fry Societies
1960	Voice of Women
1967	Fédération des Femmes du Québec
1971	Women for Political Action
1972	National Action Committee on the Status of Women
1972	Canadian Congress for Learning Opportunities for Women
1974	Canadian Abortion Rights Action League
1975	National Association of Women and the Law
1976	Canadian Research Institute for the Advancement of Women
1983	REAL Women (Realistic, Equal, and Active for Life)
1985	Women's Legal Education and Action Fund

Appendix 2: Dates in Women's Progress Toward Legal and Political Equality

1916	Alberta, Saskatchewan, Manitoba give vote to women.
1918	Women given franchise in federal elections.
1921	Agnes Macphail first woman elected to Parliament.
1928	Supreme Court rules women are not 'persons' and cannot be appointed to Senate.
1929	British Privy Council overturns Supreme Court decision.
1931	Cairine Wilson first woman appointed to the Senate.
1940	Quebec gives vote to women.
1947	Married women restricted from holding federal public service jobs.
1955	Restrictions on married women in federal public service removed.
1957	Ellen Fairclough sworn in as first woman federal cabinet minister.
1967	Royal Commission on Status of Women established.
1971	Canada Labour Code amended to allow women seventeen weeks' maternity leave.
1973	Supreme Court upholds section of Indian Act depriving Aboriginal women of their rights.
	Supreme Court denies Irene Murdoch right to share in family property.

1977	Canadian Human Rights Act passed, forbidding discrimination on basis of sex.
1980	Jeanne Sauvé first female Speaker of the House of Commons.
1981	Canada ratifies UN Convention on the Elimination of all Forms of Discrimination Against Women.
1982	Madam Justice Bertha Wilson first woman appointed to Supreme Court of Canada.
1983	Affirmative action programs mandatory in the federal public service.
1984	Twenty-seven women elected in Parliament, six appointed to cabinet.
	Jeanne Sauvé first woman to be appointed Governor General of Canada.
1985	Section 15 of Charter of Rights and Freedoms comes into effect.
	Employment Equity legislation passed.
1988	*Morgentaler* decision strikes down Canada's abortion law.
1989	Indian Act amended to remove discrimination against Aboriginal women.
	Andrews decision introduces the concept of 'substantive equality' in applying section 15 of the Charter.
	Audrey McLaughlin chosen to lead the national NDP.
1991	Ontario passes pay equity law that applies to the private sector (repealed in 1995).
1993	Kim Campbell becomes Canada's first female Prime Minister.
1995	Alexa McDonough chosen to lead the national NDP.

Source: CACSW, 'Progress toward Equality for Women in Canada' (February, 1987), 15, and author's additions.

■ Notes

Chapter 1

[1]Charles Merriam, *Public and Private Government* (New Haven: Yale University Press, 1944).
[2]Leo Panitch, 'State', in *The Canadian Encyclopedia*, 2nd ed. (Edmonton: Hurtig, 1988).
[3]Noam Chomsky and Edward S. Herman, *Manufacturing Consent: The Political Economy of the Mass Media* (New York: Pantheon Books, 1988).
[4]C.B. Macpherson, *The Real World of Democracy* (Toronto: CBC Enterprises, 1965).
[5]Gabriel A. Almond and Sidney Verba, *The Civic Culture* (Princeton, N.J.: Princeton University Press, 1963).
[6]*The Canadian Encyclopedia*, 1933.

Chapter 2

[1]Pierre Berton, *Why We Act Like Canadians* (Toronto: McClelland & Stewart, 1982).
[2]Gabriel Almond, 'Comparative Political Systems', *Journal of Politics*, XVIII (1956), 396.
[3]Russell Kirk, *The Conservative Mind* (London: Faber and Faber, 1953).
[4]Daniel Bell, *The End of Ideology* (New York: Free Press, 1962), 402–3.
[5]Thomas Flanagan, *Waiting for the Wave: The Reform Party and Preston Manning* (Toronto: Stoddart, 1995), 15.
[6]David Bell and Lorne Tepperman, *The Roots of Disunity* (Toronto: McClelland & Stewart, 1979), 23.
[7]Fernand Ouellet, *Histoire économique et sociale du Québec, 1760–1850* (Paris: Fides, 1966).

[8]Bell and Tepperman note that the estimated number of Anglophones in what are now the Maritimes, Quebec, and Ontario at the time of the American Revolution was about 15,000. Between 30,000 and 60,000 Loyalists immigrated to these British colonies in the years immediately after 1776, and a steady stream of 'late Loyalists', perhaps attracted by British offers of free land, immigrated northward to Upper Canada over the next few decades. See *The Roots of Disunity*, 45, 80–1.

[9]William Christian and Colin Campbell, *Political Parties and Ideologies in Canada*, 2nd ed. (Toronto: McGraw-Hill Ryerson, 1982), 23–5; Gad Horowitz, 'Conservatism, Liberalism and Socialism in Canada: An Interpretation', *Canadian Journal of Economics and Political Science* (1966).

[10]Kenneth McRae, 'The Structure of Canadian History', in Louis Hartz, ed., *The Founding of New Societies* (New York: Harcourt, Brace & World, 1964), 235.

[11]Bell and Tepperman, *The Roots of Disunity*, 76–7.

[12]Horowitz, 'Conservatism, Liberalism and Socialism'.

[13]Seymour Martin Lipset, *Continental Divide* (Montreal: C.D. Howe Institute, 1989), 1.

[14]Bell and Tepperman, *The Roots of Disunity*, 61–2.

[15]Reg Whitaker, 'Images of the State in Canada', in Leo Panitch, ed., *The Canadian State* (Toronto: University of Toronto Press, 1977), 30.

[16]Patricia Marchak, *Ideological Perspectives on Canada* (Toronto: McGraw-Hill Ryerson, 1975), 115.

[17]Pierre Trudeau, 'Some Obstacles to Democracy in Quebec', in Trudeau, *Federalism and the French Canadians* (Toronto: Macmillan, 1968).

[18]In 1951, 80 per cent of Quebec's work force was in secondary industries (manufacturing and construction) and the service sector, a percentage that was higher than for Canada as a whole (78 per cent).

[19]See Kenneth McRoberts, *Quebec: Social Change and Political Crisis*, 3rd ed. (Toronto: McClelland & Stewart, 1988), 90–100.

[20]Gordon T. Stewart, *The Origins of Canadian Politics* (Vancouver: University of British Columbia Press, 1986).

[21]The 'court' and 'country' orientations are discussed ibid., 11–20.

[22]W.L. Morton, 'The Dualism of Culture and the Federalism of Power', in Richard Abbott, ed., *A New Concept of Confederation* (Proceedings of the Seventh Seminar of the Canadian Union of Students, Ottawa, 1965), 121.

[23]Donald Smiley, *The Canadian Political Nationality* (Toronto: Methuen, 1967).

[24]See the analysis of Oka in Robert Campbell and Leslie Pal, 'Feather and Gun', *The Real Worlds of Canadian Politics*, 2nd ed. (Peterborough, Ont.: Broadview Press, 1991), 267–345.

[25]All of these statements are based on the rankings in Charles Lewis Taylor and David A. Jodice, *The World Handbook of Political and Social Indicators*, 3rd ed., vol. 2 'Political Protest and Government Change' (New Haven: Yale University Press, 1983); see also Judith Torrance, *Public Violence in Canada 1867–1982* (Toronto: University of Toronto Press, 1986), 57–66.

[26]'Violence, Political', *The Canadian Encyclopedia*, 2265.

[27]McRoberts, *Quebec*, 240.

[28]Ibid., 239.

[29]En collaboration, *Québec: un pays incertain, réflexions sur le Québec post-référendaire* (Montréal: Québec/Amérique, 1980), 170–2.

[30]See the excellent analysis in Campbell and Pal, 'Feather and Gun'.

[31]Status Indians are those registered under the Indian Act.

[32]*Globe and Mail*, 26 September 1990.

[33]Seymour Martin Lipset, *Continental Divide* (Toronto: C.D. Howe Institute, 1989), 136.

[34]Berton, *Why We Act Like Canadians*, 16.

[35]Maclean's-Decima Poll, 'Portrait of Two Nations', *Maclean's*, 3 July 1989, 50.

[36]Robert Kudile and Theodore Marmor, 'The Development of Welfare States in North America', in Peter Flora and Arnold J. Heidersheimer, eds, *The Development of Welfare States in Europe and America* (New Brunswick, NJ: Transaction Books, 1981), 110.

[37]See the summary of studies in Lipset, *Continental Divide*, 155–8.

[38]Ibid., 156.

[39]Constitution Act, 1982, s. 27.

[40]Constitution Act, 1982, s. 15(2).

[41]Quoted in Lipset, *Continental Divide*, 187.

[42]Tom Wayman, ed., *A Government Job at Last* (Vancouver: MacLeod Books, 1975).

[43]The issue was voted on by Parliament in 1967, 1973, 1976, and 1987.

Chapter 3

[1]Speech by Prime Minister Jean Chrétien to the American Society of Newspaper Editors, 6 April 1995, Dallas.

[2]OECD, *Historical Statistics 1960–1989* (Paris: OECD, 1991), 45, table 2.20.

[3]See, for example, Stephen Cohen and John Zysman, *Manufacturing Matters* (New York: Basic Books, 1987).

[4]John Porter, *The Vertical Mosaic* (Toronto: University of Toronto Press, 1965), 3–4.

[5]'Native People, Economic Conditions', *The Canadian Encyclopedia*, 2nd ed. (Edmonton: Hurtig, 1988), 1449.

[6]See National Council of Welfare, *Women and Poverty Revisited* (Ottawa: Supply and Services, Summer, 1990).

[7]Monica Boyd et al., *Ascription and Achievement: Studies in Mobility and Status Attainment in Canada* (Ottawa: Carleton University Press, 1985).

[8]Harry J. Glasbeek and R.A. Hasson, 'Some Reflections on Canadian Legal Education', *Modern Law Review*, 50 (1987), 783n.

[9]John Goyder, 'Comparisons over Time', in Boyd et al., *Ascription and Achievement*, 192.

[10]Porter, *The Vertical Mosaic*; Wallace Clement, *The Canadian Corporate Elite* (Toronto: McClelland & Stewart, 1975).

[11]Milan Korac, 'Corporate Concentration and the Canadian Corporate Elite: Change and Continuity,' M.A. thesis, University of Windsor, 1992.

[12]Statistics Canada, Canadian Centre for Justice Statistics, *Homicide in Canada 1976–1985: An Historical Perspective* (Ottawa: Supply and Services, 1987).

[13]*Canadian Social Trends*, 2 (Toronto: Thompson Educational Publishing, 1994), 419–22.

[14]Comparisons of the data produced by national agencies are extremely treacherous because of the enormous variation in reporting procedures. For data on Canada, see Statistics

Canada, Canadian Centre for Justice Statistics, *Canadian Crime Statistics* (Ottawa: Supply and Services), cat. 85–205, annual.

[15]Statistics Canada, Centre for Health Information, *Health Reports*, 22, 4 (1990).

[16]The Economist, *The World in 1991* (London, 1991), 135.

[17]Statistics Canada, *Causes of Death*, vol. IV, cat. 84–203.

[18]'Alcoholism', *The Canadian Encyclopedia*, 59.

[19]G. Daly, 'A comparative assessment of programs dealing with the homeless population in the United States, Canada and Britain' (Ottawa: Canada Mortgage and Housing Corporation, 1990), 10.

[20]*Canadian Social Trends*, 2 (1994), 398.

[21]Canada, *Juristat Service Bulletin*, 11, 6 (Ottawa: Supply and Services, 1990), 10.

[22]Statistics Canada, *Homicide in Canada 1988: A Statistical Perspective* (Ottawa: Supply and Services, 1989), 68.

[23]'Native People, Social Conditions', *The Canadian Encyclopedia*, 1460.

[24]Canada, House of Commons, *Report of the Task Force on Broadcasting* (Ottawa: Supply and Services, 1986).

[25]Canada, Royal Commission on Newspapers, *Newspapers and their Readers* (Ottawa: Supply and Services, 1981), 26, table 19.

Chapter 4

[1]Constitution Act, 1982, s. 16(1).

[2]Trudeau, *Federalism and the French Canadians*, 187.

[3]Constitution Act, 1867, preamble.

[4]Constitution Act, 1867, s. 121.

[5]Constitution Act, 1867, s. 145 (repealed in 1893).

[6]Constitution Act, 1982, s. 36.

[7]Constitution Act, 1982, s. 6(3)(b).

[8]Constitution Act, 1982, s. 6(4).

[9]Supreme Court of Canada, *Morgentaler, Smoling and Scott v. The Queen* (1988), 37 CCC (3rd) 449.

[10]Constitution Act, 1982, s. 15(1).

[11]United States Constitution, 14th Amendment (1868).

[12]Constitution Act, 1982, s. 15(2).

[13]Constitution Act, 1867, preamble.

[14]The instability of the United Canadas legislature was one of the factors that motivated the politicians of Ontario and Quebec to pursue a wider union with the other colonies of British North America.

[15]Constitution Act, 1867, ss. 96–100.

[16]*The Queen v. Beauregard* (1986), 2 SCR 56.

[17]This was the basis of a 1986 court action brought against the Quebec government by several Provincial Court judges and the Chief Justice of the Quebec Superior Court.

[18]This happened most recently in early 1996, when Liberal Prime Minister Jean Chrétien appointed as cabinet ministers two high-profile Quebecers, Stéphane Dion and Pierre

Pettigrew. A few months later they both won House of Commons seats in by-elections. In 1975, after a Liberal government appointed former bureaucrat Pierre Juneau as Minister of Communications, he lost two successive by-elections and then resigned from cabinet.

[19]Philip Resnick, *Parliament vs. People* (Vancouver: New Star Books, 1984).

[20]Ibid., 19.

[21]Ibid., 25.

[22]Ibid., 38.

[23]Charles Lewis Taylor and Michael Hudson, *World Handbook of Political and Social Indicators*, 2nd ed. (New Haven: Yale University Press, 1972), 26–7, table 2.1.

[24]Section 91(1). Repealed by the Constitution Act, 1982.

[25]Section 92(1). Repealed by the Constitution Act, 1982.

[26]Supreme Court of Canada, *Re Constitution of Canada* (1981), 125 DLR (3rd) 1.

[27]*Re Attorney-General of Quebec and Attorney-General of Canada* (1982), 140 DLR (3rd) 385.

[28]Cited in Paul Gerin-Lajoie, *Constitutional Amendment in Canada* (Toronto: University of Toronto Press, 1950), 241.

[29]Cited ibid., 234.

Chapter 5

[1]William S. Livingston, *Federalism and Constitutional Change* (Oxford: Clarendon Press, 1956), 2.

[2]Ibid., 4.

[3]Based on the ranking system used in Charles Lewis Taylor and Michael C. Hudson, *World Handbook of Social and Political Indicators*, 2nd ed. (New Haven: Yale University Press, 1972), 271–3, table 4.15.

[4]Trudeau, 'Federalism, Nationalism and Reason', in *Federalism and the French Canadians* (Toronto: Macmillan, 1977), 195.

[5]The term is a translation of 'rois-nègres', coined by André Laurendau, in 'A Search for Balance', *Canadian Forum* (April, 1963), 3–4.

[6]Donald Smiley, *The Canadian Political Identity* (Toronto: Methuen, 1967), 30–1.

[7]Michael Ornstein, 'Regionalism and Canadian Political Ideology', in Robert Brym, ed., *Regionalism in Canada* (Toronto: Irwin, 1986), 67, table 2.

[8]Canadian Institute for Public Opinion, *Gallup Poll*, 13 August 1991.

[9]Peter Waite, *The Life and Times of Confederation 1864–1867* (Toronto: University of Toronto Press, 1962), 96.

[10]The diversity of expectations was reflected in newspaper accounts of the Confederation agreement. See ibid., 111.

[11]There are exceptions. In *Citizens Insurance Co. v. Parsons; Queen Insurance Co. v. Parsons* (1881), the JCPC ruled that Ottawa's trade and commerce power did not take pre-eminence over enumerated provincial powers. In the words of Sir Montague Smith, '[The founders] could not have intended that the powers exclusively assigned to the provincial legislature should be absorbed in those given to the dominion parliament.' In Peter H. Russell, ed., *Leading Constitutional Decisions*, 4th ed. (Ottawa: Carleton University Press, 1987), 35.

[12]Ibid., 527.

[13]These Qubec concerns, it should be pointed out, were all addressed by the Charlottetown Accord of 1992.

[14]See the discussion in Keith G. Banting, *The Welfare State and Canadian Federalism*, 2nd ed. (Montreal: McGill-Queen's University Press, 1987), 52–4.

[15]*Attorney-General of Ontario v. Attorney-General of Canada (Local Prohibition Case)*, 1896, in Russell, ed., *Leading Constitutional Decisions*, 59.

[16]*Re Board of Commerce Act and Combines and Fair Prices Act*, 1919, 1922, ibid., 75.

[17]*Co-operative Committee on Japanese Canadians v. A.-G. Canada*, 1947, AC 87; *Reference re Validity of Wartime Leasehold Regulations*, 1950, SCR 124.

[18]*Attorney-General of Canada v. Attorney-General of Ontario (Employment and Social Insurance Act Reference)*, 1937.

[19]See Peter Russell, 'The Anti-Inflation Case: The Anatomy of a Constitutional Decision', *Canadian Public Administration*, 10, 4 (Winter, 1977).

[20]Constitution Act, 1867, s. 91(2).

[21]Constitution Act, 1867, s. 92(13).

[22]Russell, ed., *Leading Constitutional Decisions*, 39.

[23]*The King v. Eastern Terminal Elevator Co.* (1925), SCR 434; *A.-G. of British Columbia v. A.-G. of Canada (Natural Products Marketing Reference)* (1937), AC 377; *Canadian Federation of Agriculture v. A.-G. of Quebec (Margarine Reference)* (1951), AC 179.

[24]*Ontario Farm Products Marketing Reference* (1957), SCR 198; *R. v. Klassen* (1959), 20 DLR(2nd) 406 (Manitoba Court of Appeal); *Caloil v. A.-G. of Canada* (1971), SCR 543.

[25]*Caloil*, 551.

[26]Russell, ed., *Leading Constitutional Decisions*, 194.

[27]Ibid., 199.

[28]Peter W. Hogg, *Constitutional Law of Canada* (Toronto: Carswell, 1988).

[29]Trudeau, 'Federalism, Nationalism, and Reason', 198.

[30]Henri Bourassa, 'The French Language and the Future of Our Race', in Ramsay Cook, ed., *French Canadian Nationalism* (Toronto: Macmillan, 1969), 141.

[31]Kenneth McRoberts, *Quebec: Social Change and Political Crisis*, 3rd ed. (Toronto: McClelland & Stewart, 1988), 214.

[32]See Richard Simeon, *Federal-Provincial Diplomacy* (Toronto: University of Toronto Press, 1972), 115–22.

[33]McRoberts, *Quebec*, 293–7.

[34]Quoted in George Woodcock, *Confederation Betrayed!* (Vancouver: Harbour Publishing, 1981), 8.

[35]This argument is developed by Barry Cooper in his lively essay 'Western Political Consciousness', in Stephen Brooks, ed., *Political Thought in Canada* (Toronto: Irwin, 1984), 213–38.

[36]James Bickerton, *Nova Scotia, Ottawa, and the Politics of Regional Development* (Toronto: University of Toronto Press, 1990).

[37]G.V. LaForest, *Disallowance and Reservation of Provincial Legislation* (Ottawa, 1955).

[38]Ottawa ceded control to Manitoba in 1930.

[39]Alberta and Saskatchewan acquired these powers in 1930.

[40]Doug Owram, 'Reluctant Hinterland', in Larry Pratt and Garth Stevenson, eds, *Western Separatism* (Edmonton: Hurtig, 1981), 61.

41Alan Cairns, 'The Governments and Societies of Canadian Federalism', in Cairns, *Constitution, Government, and Society in Canada* (Toronto: McClelland & Stewart, 1988), 153–4.

42R.A. Young, Philippe Faucher, and Andre Blais, 'The Concept of Province-Building: A Critique', *Canadian Jouranl of Political Science*, XVII, 4 (December, 1984), 785.

43Two of the major works using this concept are John Richards and Larry Pratt, *Prairie Capitalism* (Toronto: McClelland & Stewart, 1979), and McRoberts, *Quebec*.

44Donald Smiley, 'An Outsider's Observations of Federal-Provincial Relations', in R.D. Olling and W.M. Westmacott, eds, *Perspectives on Canadian Federalism* (Scarborough: Prentice-Hall Canada, 1988).

45Constitution Act, 1867, s. 118.

46Constitution Act, 1867, s. 111.

47Department of Finance Canada, *Budget 1995: Key Actions and Impacts*, unpaginated.

48*Western Report*, 3 April 1995, 19.

49*Budget 1995*.

50Ibid., unpaginated.

Chapter 6

1'The Executive Government and Authority of and over Canada is hereby declared to continue and be vested in the Queen', Constitution Act, 1867, s. 9.

2In the provinces, the Crown's authority is exercised through the lieutenant-governors, who are appointed by the Governor General to serve five-year terms.

3James R. Mallory, *The Structure of Canadian Government*, revised ed. (Toronto: Gage, 1984), 42–3.

4Canada, Royal Commission on Newspapers, *Newspapers and Their Readers* (Ottawa: Supply and Services, 1981), 26–7.

5Constitution Act, 1867, s. 54.

6Colin Campbell and George Szablowski, *The Super-Bureaucrats: Structure and Behaviour in Central Agencies* (Toronto: Macmillan, 1979).

7See David A. Good, *The Politics of Anticipation: Making Canadian Federal Tax Policy* (Ottawa: School of Public Administration, 1980).

8Financial Administration Act, 1967.

9Campbell and Szablowski, *The Super-Bureaucrats*, 29.

10Gordon Robertson, 'The Changing Role of the Privy Council Office', *Canadian Public Administration*, 14 (Winter, 1971), 506.

11Colin Campbell, *Governments under Stress* (Toronto: University of Toronto Press, 1983), 90.

12Canada, Public Service 2000, *The Renewal of the Public Service of Canada* (Ottawa: Supply and Services, 1990), 6.

13Statistics Canada, *Canada Yearbook* (Ottawa: Supply and Services, 1992).

14The word 'mandarin' has often been used to describe that group of senior officials whose ability to influence policy is believed to be enormous. The word was originally applied to the bureaucratic class of Imperial China.

[15]Alexander Brady, *Democracy in the Dominions* (Toronto: University of Toronto Press, 1947), 82.

[16]Robert J. Jackson and Michael A. Atkinson, *The Canadian Legislative System*, 2nd ed. (Toronto: Gage, 1980), 22.

[17]See the Constitution Act, 1867, s. 99(1). This phrase, or reference to 'misbehaviour', is found in the federal and provincial statutes that govern the removal of judges.

[18]Ralph Miliband, *The State in Capitalist Society* (London: Quartet Books, 1973), 124.

[19]Judges of county courts and all higher courts are appointed by Ottawa. Provincial court judges are appointed by the provinces. See Figure 6.4 in the text.

[20]Canada, Department of Justice, *Canada's System of Justice* (Ottawa: Supply and Services, 1988), 7.

[21]*Reference re Public Service Employment Relations Act* (Alta) (1987), 38 DLR (4th) 161.

[22]Ibid., 200.

[23]Ibid., 232.

[24]Ibid., 200.

[25]Ted Morton and Leslie Pal, 'Bliss v. Attorney General of Canada: From Legal Defeat to Political Victory', *Osgoode Hall Law Journal*, 24, 1 (Spring, 1986), 159–60.

Chapter 7

[1]As has been argued by, among others, Giovanni Sartori, in *Parties and Party Systems* (Cambridge: Cambridge University Press, 1976), ix.

[2]Michael Parenti, *Democracy for the Few*, 5th ed. (New York: St Martin's Press, 1988), ch. 10.

[3]Leon Epstein, *Political Parties in Western Democracies* (New Brunswick, NJ: Transaction Books, 1980 [1967]), 9.

[4]S.M. Lipset, 'Introduction', in M. Ostrogorski, *Democracy and the Organization of Political Parties*, ed. S.M. Lipset (Chicago: Quadrangle Books, 1964), xix. See also Max Weber, *From Max Weber*, ed. H.H. Gerth and C. Wright Mills (New York: Oxford University Press, 1946), 102; Epstein, *Political Parties in Western Democracies*, ch. 2.

[5]George M. Hougham, 'The Background and Development of National Parties', in Hugh G. Thorburn, ed., *Party Politics in Canada* (Toronto: Prentice-Hall, 1963), 3.

[6]Ibid., 13.

[7]Escott Reid, 'The Rise of National Parties in Canada', in Hugh G. Thorburn, ed., *Party Politics in Canada*, 5th ed. (Scarborough, Ont.: Prentice-Hall, 1985), 12. See also Norman Ward, *The Canadian House of Commons* (Toronto: University of Toronto Press, 1950), 157–62.

[8]See, in particular, Martin Shefter, 'Party and Patronage: Germany, England, and Italy', *Politics and Society*, 7, 4 (1977), 403–51; Epstein, *Political Parties in Western Democracies*, ch. 5.

[9]André Siegfried, *The Race Question in Canada* (Toronto: McClelland & Stewart, Carleton Library Edition, 1966 [English translation first published 1907]), 114.

[10]J.A. Corry, *Democratic Government and Politics*, 2nd ed. (Toronto: University of Toronto Press, 1951), 22. Variations on this theme can be found in R.M. Dawson and Norman Ward, *The Government of Canada*, 5th ed. (Toronto: University of Toronto Press, 1987), 430–3; and

Hugh G. Thorburn, 'Interpretations of the Canadian Party System', in Thorburn, ed., *Party Politics in Canada*, 5th ed., 20–40. For a critique of the adequacy of brokerage theory, see Janine Brodie and Jane Jenson, *Crisis, Challenge and Change: Party and Class Revisited* (Ottawa: Carleton University Press, 1988), ch. 1.

[11]Robert Alford, *Party and Society* (Westport, Conn.: Greenwood Press, 1963), 250–1. Alford computed his index of class voting by subtracting the percentage of non-manual workers voting for left parties (in Canada, the Liberals, and the NDP, according to Alford) from the percentage of manual workers voting for the left parties, on the assumption that a party of the left should receive the bulk of its support from the traditional 'blue-collar' (manual) occupations. See the discussion ibid., chs 4 and 5. Obviously, Alford's index leaves a great deal to be desired and has been subjected to substantial criticism over the years. Many critics of his work are particularly exercised by his classification of the Liberal Party of Canada as a party of the 'left'.

[12]Ibid., 251.

[13]Brodie and Jenson, *Crisis, Challenge and Change*.

[14]Janine Brodie and Jane Jenson, 'Piercing the Smokescreen: Brokerage Parties and Class Politics', in Alain-G. Gagnon and A. Brian Tanguay, eds, *Canadian Parties in Transition: Discourse, Organization, and Representation* (Scarborough, Ont.: Nelson, 1989), 28.

[15]Ibid., 34.

[16]John Porter, *The Vertical Mosaic* (Toronto: University of Toronto Press, 1965), 369.

[17]Charles Taylor, *The Pattern of Politics* (Toronto: McClelland & Stewart, 1970), 15.

[18]Quoted in Graham Fraser, *Playing for Keeps* (Toronto: McClelland & Stewart, 1989), 224.

[19]Robert M. Campbell and Leslie A. Pal, *The Real Worlds of Canadian Politics* (Peterborough, Ont.: Broadview Press, 1989), 5.

[20]Walter Young, *The Anatomy of a Party: The National CCF 1932–61* (Toronto: University of Toronto Press, 1969), 298, 300.

[21]Canada, Royal Commission on Electoral Reform and Party Financing, *Reforming Electoral Democracy*, vol. 7 (Ottawa: Supply and Services Canada, 1991), 221.

[22]*The Economist*, 'Bleeding-Heart Conservatives', Canada survey, 8 October 1988, 4

[23]William P. Irvine, *Does Canada Need a New Electoral System?* (Kingston: Institute of Intergovernmental Relations, Queen's University, 1979), 16–7.

[24]Alan Cairns, 'The Electoral System and the Party System in Canada, 1921–1965', *Canadian Journal of Political Science*, 1, 1 (March, 1968), 55–80.

[25]Irvine, *Does Canada Need a New Electoral System?* 14.

[26]This title is inspired by an observation made by Alan Cairns: 'That the results of an election are easier to justify by the principles of a lottery than by any principle of equity is not … a trivial matter.' In Howard Penniman, ed., *Canada at the Polls, 1979 and 1980* (Washington: American Enterprise Institute, 1981), 23.

[27]This section draws heavily on Stephen Brooks and Andrew Stritch, *Business and Government in Canada* (Scarborough, Ont.: Prentice-Hall, 1991), ch. 9.

[28]See Khayyam Paltiel, *Political Party Financing in Canada* (Toronto: McGraw-Hill Ryerson, 1970), 19–75.

[29]These services are discussed by Reg Whitaker, *The Government Party: Organizing and Financing the Liberal Party of Canada, 1930–1958* (Toronto: University of Toronto Press, 1977), 204–6, 216–63.

[30]According to Khayyam Paltiel, 'For the 1972 [national] election half the funds raised in Ontario by the Liberal Party were collected personally by the chairman of the party's Treasury Committee from 90 large corporations.' 'Campaign Financing in Canada and its Reform', in Howard Penniman, ed., *Canada at the Polls: The General Election of 1974* (Washington: American Enterprise Institute, 1975), 182.

[31]See A.B. Stevenson, *Canadian Election Reform: Dialogue on Issues and Effects* (Toronto: Ontario Commission on Election Contributions and Expenses, 1982); Whitaker, *The Government Party*.

[32]The number of hours per network and the division of time between the parties is determined by the CRTC. In deciding how much time each party receives the CRTC is guided by a formula weighted according to each party's share of the seats and popular vote in the previous election.

[33]The Income Tax Act includes a graduated schedule of tax credits: 75 per cent for donations up to $100; 50 per cent for contributions between $100 and $550; and 33.3 per cent for amounts over $550, to a maximum tax credit of $500.

[34]Khayyam Paltiel, 'Political Marketing, Party Finance, and the Decline of Political Parties', in Gagnon and Tanguay, eds, *Canadian Parties in Transition*, 342.

[35]See Larry Sabato, *The Rise of Political Consultants* (New York: Basic Books, 1981), especially ch. 4.

[36]Dalton Camp, *Points of Departure* (Toronto: Deneau and Greenberg, 1979), 91.

[37]Ibid., 91.

[38]Sabato, *The Rise of Political Consultants*, 279.

[39]Jeffrey Simpson, *Spoils of Power* (Toronto: Collins, 1988), 372.

Chapter 8

[1]V.O. Key, *Politics, Parties, and Pressure Groups*, 4th ed. (New York, 1958), 23.

[2]James Madison, *The Federalist Papers*, no. 10 (New York: New American Library, 1961).

[3]This slogan is attributed to Thomas Sloan, chairman of GM during the 1920s.

[4]*Associations Canada 1994–95: An Encyclopedic Directory* (Mississauga, Ont.: Canadian Almanac & Directory Publishing Co., 1995).

[5]*Canadian Women's Directory* (Montreal: Editions Communiqué Elles, 1989).

[6]Estimates based on *Associations Canada 1991*.

[7]Canada, Royal Commission on the Economic Union and Development Prospects for Canada, *Report* (Ottawa: Supply and Services, 1985).

[8]Quebec, Commission sur l'avenir politique et constitutionnel du Québec, *Les préoccupations et les perceptions se dégageant de la consultation populaire*, Document de travail, numero 3 (Québec: Bureau d'information, 1991), 3.

[9]E.E. Schattschneider, *The Semi-Sovereign People* (New York: Holt, Rinehart and Winston, 1960), 35.

[10]Ibid.

[11]Ibid.

[12]Charles E. Lindblom, *Politics and Markets* (New York: Basic Books, 1977), especially chs 13–16.

[13]Bruno S. Frey, *Modern Political Economy* (New York: John Wiley & Sons, 1978), ch. 11.

[14]For example, Diane Francis, editor of the *Financial Post*, argued that '[The concentration of corporate power] has become so significant that the country is hurtling towards a new form of economic and political feudalism.' This is a position that Canadian socialists, not generally counted among the admirers of the *Financial Post*, would approve wholeheartedly. See Diane Francis, *Controlling Interest: Who Owns Canada?* (Toronto: Macmillan, 1986), 3.

[15]Business's ideological and academic spokespersons adopt an essentially pluralistic position on the matter of interest group influence. William Stanbury's remarks are typical: 'The relationship between business firms and governments in either positive or normative terms cannot be characterized in a single phrase. It is inevitably plural and diverse. Depending upon the industry, the time, the other issues on the public policy agenda, the individuals involved, and what each 'side' is seeking to do vis-à-vis the other, the relationship might be characterized as adversarial, cooperative, symbiotic, supportive, or protective.' Stanbury, *Business-Government Relations in Canada* (Toronto: Methuen, 1986), 9.

[16]Michael Bliss, *Northern Enterprise: Five Centuries of Canadian Business* (Toronto: McClelland & Stewart, 1987), 578.

[17]David Vogel, *Fluctuating Fortunes: The Political Power of Business in America* (New York: Basic Books, 1989), 193.

[18]James Q. Wilson, 'The Politics of Regulation', in James Q. Wilson, ed., *The Politics of Regulation* (New York: Basic Books, 1980), 370.

[19]Earl Latham, *The Group Basis of Politics* (New York: Octagon Books, 1965), 35.

[20]Arthur F. Bentley, *The Process of Government* (Evanston, Ill., 1935), 208.

[21]David B. Truman, *The Governmental Process* (New York: Alfred Knopf, 1951); Robert Dahl, *Who Governs?* (New Haven: Yale University Press, 1961); John Kenneth Galbraith, *Counter-Vailing Power* (Boston: Houghton-Mifflin, 1956).

[22]Theodore Lowi, *The End of Liberalism* (New York: W.W. Norton, 1969).

[23]Ibid., 97.

[24]P. Bachrach and M. Baratz, 'Two Faces of Power', *American Political Science Review*, 56, 4 (1962), 948.

[25]This is true of Nicos Poulantzas, *Political Power and Social Classes* (London: New Left Books, 1973); Fred Block, *Revising State Theory* (Philadelphia: Temple University Press, 1987); and Bob Jessop, *The Capitalist State* (New York: New York University Press, 1982). Interest groups are given some passing mention in James O'Connor, *The Fiscal Crisis of the State* (New York: St Martin's Press, 1973); and Claus Offe, *Contradictions of the Welfare State* (Cambridge, Mass.: MIT Press, 1984). Among the leading Marxist intellectuals, it is perhaps fair to say that only Ralph Miliband has very much to say on interest groups: see *The State in Capitalist Society* (London: Quartet Books, 1973).

[26]Daniel Drache and Wallace Clement, eds, *The New Practical Guide to Canadian Political Economy* (Toronto: Lorimer, 1985).

[27]Wallace Clement and Glen Williams, eds, *The New Canadian Political Economy* (Montreal: McGill-Queen's University Press, 1989).

[28]Miliband, *The State in Capitalist Society*, 131.

[29]Wallace Clement, *The Challenge of Class Analysis* (Ottawa: Carleton University Press, 1988), chs 7–8.

[30]Rianne Mahon, *The Politics of Industrial Restructuring: Canadian Textiles* (Toronto: University of Toronto Press, 1984).

[31]Clement, *Challenge of Class Analysis*, 132.

[32]To qualify for membership in the CMA, a firm must have at least five employees and be involved in manufacturing. The dues that a member is required to pay and its voting weight within the CMA are based on the firm's size.

[33]Jurg Steiner, *European Democracies* (New York: Longman, 1986), 221.

[34]William D. Coleman, *Business and Politics: A Study of Collective Action* (Montreal: McGill-Queen's University Press, 1988), 224.

[35]It occasionally happens, however, that the CCC is capable of taking a firm position on issues that are more divisive in the business community. Its support for the Canada-US Free Trade Agreement was an example of this.

[36]Gerhard Lehmbruch, 'Concertation and the Structure of Corporatist Networks', in John Goldthorpe, ed., *Order and Conflict in Contemporary Capitalism* (Oxford: Clarendon, 1984), 65–6.

[37]Coleman, *Business and Politics*, ch. 6.

[38]These tripartite initiatives are discussed in detail in Pierre Fournier, 'Consensus Building in Canada: Case Studies and Prospects', in Keith Banting, research coordinator, *The State and Economic Interests*, vol. 32 of the research studies for the Royal Commission on the Economic Union and Development Prospects for Canada (Ottawa: Supply and Services, 1986), 291–335.

[39]William Coleman is among those who argue that such structures would benefit Canada economically. See Coleman, *Business and Politics*, ch. 13.

[40]William D. Coleman and Grace Skogstad, 'Introduction', in Coleman and Skogstad, eds, *Policy Communities and Public Policy in Canada* (Toronto: Copp Clark Pitman, 1990), 2.

[41]Michels's argument was that the specialization of function that accompanies organization inevitably results in domination of the organization by a minority and, therefore, creates the likelihood that the goals pursued by the organization will more closely reflect those of its leadership than its membership. Robert Michels, *Political Parties* (London: Jarrold, 1915).

[42]Some of the classics of this literature include Anthony Downs, *An Economic Theory of Democracy* (New York: Harper and Row, 1957); Mancur Olson, *The Logic of Collective Action* (Boston: Harvard University Press, 1965); James M. Buchanan and Gordon Tullock, *The Calculus of Consent* (Ann Arbor: University of Michigan Press, 1965); Anthony Downs, *Inside Bureaucracy* (Boston: Little, Brown and Company, 1967).

[43]Michael Atkinson, 'How Do Institutions Constrain Policy?' paper delivered at the conference 'Governing Canada: Political Institutions and Public Policy', McMaster University, 25 October 1991, 8.

[44]Alan Cairns, 'The Governments and Societies of Canadian Federalism', *Canadian Journal of Political Science*, X, 4 (December, 1977), 695–725.

[45]These works include James G. March and Herbert Simon, *Organizations* (New York: John Wiley, 1958); James G. March, *Decisions and Organizations* (Oxford: Basil Blackwell, 1988); James G. March, and Johan P. Olsen, 'The New Institutionalism: Organizational Factors in Political Life', *American Political Science Review*, 78 (1984), 734–49; James G. March and Johan P. Olsen, *Rediscovering Institutions: The Organizational Basis of Politics* (New York: Free Press, 1989).

[46]Charles Perrow, *Complex Organizations: A Critical Essay*, 3rd ed. (New York: Random House, 1986), 260.

[47]James Q. Wilson, *Political Organizations* (New York: Basic Books, 1973), 3–4.

[48]These definitions are the ones used in Coleman and Skogstad, 'Introduction'. They are not, however, agreed upon by everyone who mines this vein.

[49]Ibid., 25.

[50]Ibid., 23.

[51]Ibid., 24.

[52]The example provided here is not fanciful. Violent protests in the streets of Cairo over this very issue in the late 1980s led the government to back down on its policy of price increases.

[53]Quoted in A. Paul Pross, *Group Politics and Public Policy* (Toronto: Oxford University Press, 1986), 64.

[54]J.L. Granatstein, *The Ottawa Men* (Toronto: Oxford University Press, 1982).

[55]William D. Coleman, 'Canadian Business and the State', in Banting, *The State and Economic Interests*, 260, fig. 5–2.

[56]O. Mary Hill, *Canada's Salesman to the World: The Department of Trade and Commerce, 1892–1939* (Montreal: McGill-Queen's University Press, 1977), 172.

[57]Leslie A. Pal, *Interests of State* (Montreal: McGill-Queen's University Press, 1992), ch. 6.

[58]Pross, *Group Politics*, 68–9.

[59]Ibid., 114–16.

[60]See the discussion of these associations in Stephen Brooks and Andrew Stritch, *Business and Government in Canada* (Scarborough, Ont.: Prentice-Hall, 1991), 211–25.

[61]Andrew B. Gollner, *Social Change and Corporate Strategy: The Expanding Role of Public Affairs* (Stamford, Conn.: Issue Action Publications, 1983), 105.

[62]See Brooks and Stritch, *Business and Government*, ch. 9.

[63]Quoted in Erik Heinrich, 'Recession chills out of green groups', *Financial Post*, 10 February 1992, 8.

[64]Ibid.

[65]G. Bruce Doern and Brian W. Tomlin, *Fear and Faith: the Free Trade Story* (Toronto: Stoddart, 1991), 219.

[66]John W. Kingdon, *Agendas, Alternatives, and Public Policies* (Boston: Little, Brown and Company, 1984), 54–7.

[67]Mancur Olson, *The Logic of Collective Action* (Cambridge, Mass.: Harvard University Press, 1965).

[68]Wilson, *Political Organizations*, 36–8.

[69]Schattschneider, *The Semi-Sovereign People*, 37.

[70]Ibid., 38.

[71]Good analyses of several Canadian policy communities are found in Coleman and Skogstad, eds, *Policy Communities and Public Policy in Canada*.

[72]This literature is brought together in Hugh G. Thorburn, *Interest Groups in the Canadian Federal System*, vol. 69 of the research studies for the Royal Commission on the Economic Union and Development Prospects for Canada (Ottawa: Supply and Services, 1985).

[73]Richard J. Schultz, *Federalism, Bureaucracy and Public Policy: The Politics of Highway Transport Regulation* (Montreal: McGill-Queen's University Press, 1980), 148.

[74]See, for example, M.W. Bucovetsky, 'The Mining Industry and the Great Tax Reform Debate', in A. Paul Pross, ed., *Pressure Group Behaviour in Canadian Politics* (Toronto: McGraw-Hill Ryerson, 1975), 89–114.

[75]The long-accepted claim that Canada's federal constitution has led most associations to adopt a federal form of organization is not supported by the facts—at least not in the case of business associations. A recent survey by William Coleman finds that about three-quarters of business associations have unitary structures. Coleman's conclusion is that Canada's industrial structure has a far greater impact on how business associations organize themselves than does the constitution. Coleman, *Business and Politics*, 260.

[76]See Schultz, *Federalism, Bureaucracy and Public Policy*, especially ch. 8.

[77]Alan Cairns, 'The Governments, and Societies of Canadian Federalism', in Cairns, *Constitution, Government and Society in Canada* (Toronto: McClelland & Stewart, 1989), 167.

[78]Leslie A. Pal, *State, Class, and Bureaucracy* (Montreal: McGill-Queen's University Press, 1988).

[79]A lengthier treatment of advocacy advertising is found in Brooks and Stritch, *Business and Government*, 260–4.

[80]Quoted in Duncan McDowall, ed., *Advocacy Advertising: Propaganda or Democratic Right?* (Ottawa: Conference Board of Canada, 1982), v.

[81]For example, a former federal Minister of Justice defended his government's advertising on proposed constitutional reforms by saying, 'Government is too complex nowadays to rely on policy by press release. Programmes must be explained—not by reporters but by people who created them.' Ibid., 7.

[82]Privately funded think tanks like the C.D. Howe Institute, the Fraser Institute, and the Conference Board are another way of promoting group interests, in this case the general interests of business, by producing studies and funding experts whose perspectives and options for public policy are favourable to business interests. Direct-mail campaigns, targeted at selected groups whose opinions and actions may, in turn, affect policy-makers are another technique employed mainly by business groups.

[83]A fascinating account of contemporary lobbying in Canada is John Sawatsky, *The Insiders: Government, Business, and the Lobbyists* (Toronto: McClelland & Stewart, 1987).

[84]Canada, Consumer and Corporate Affairs, *Lobbyists Registration Act Annual Report* (Ottawa: Supply and Services, 1995).

Chapter 9

[1]George Gallup, *The Pulse of Democracy: The Public Opinion Poll and How it Works* (New York: Simon and Schuster, 1940).

[2]Walter Lippmann, *Public Opinion* (New York: Harcourt, Brace and Company, 1922), 13.

[3]*Canadian Social Trends*, 2 (Toronto: Thompson Educational Publishing, 1994), 300.

[4]Canada, *Report of the Task Force on Broadcasting* (Ottawa: Supply and Sources, 1986), 126–7.

[5]Canada, Royal Commission on Newspapers, *Newspapers and their Readers* (Ottawa: Supply and Services, 1981), 26, table 19.

[6]Ibid., 27, table 20.

[7]Ibid., 26–7, tables 19 and 20.

[8]Audit Bureau of Circulation, *Fas-Fax: United States and Canadian Periodicals and Canadian Circulation of U.S. Magazines* (Toronto).

[9]R. Rotenberg, *Advertising: A Canadian Perspective* (Toronto: Allyn and Bacon, 1986), 2.

[10]The Economist, *The World in 1991* (London), 96.

[11]Lippmann, *Public Opinion*, 345.

[12]Quoted in Todd Gitlin, *Inside Prime Time* (New York: Pantheon, 1983), 253.

[13]Edward Jay Epstein, *News from Nowhere: Television and the News* (New York: Random House, 1973).

[14]Ibid., 112.

[15]See the analysis of media ownership in Walter Romanow and Walter Soderlund, *Media Canada: An Introductory Analysis*, 2nd ed. (Toronto: Copp Clark Pittman, 1996), ch. 13.

[16]Quoted in Diane Francis, *Controlling Interest: Who Owns Canada?* (Toronto: Collins, 1986), 17.

[17]The Royal Commission on Newspapers expressed this view, although only the Irving case was cited explicitly. See also the comments of former Premier of Saskskatchewan, Allan Blakeney, in Francis, *Controlling Interest*, 316.

[18]Edward Herman and Noam Chomsky, *Manufacturing Consent* (New York: Pantheon, 1988), 8.

[19]Walter I. Romanow *et al.*, 'Correlates of Newspaper Coverage of the 1979 Canadian Election: Chain Ownership, Competitiveness of Market, and Circulation', study done for the Royal Commission on Newspapers' (Ottawa: Supply and Services, 1981).

[20]Canada, Task Force on Program Review, *Economic Growth: Services and Subsidies to Business* (Ottawa: Supply and Services, 1985), 58.

[21]Bronwyn Drainie, 'Triple threat has Canadian magazines running for cover', *Globe and Mail*, 17 February 1990.

[22]See the discussions in Frank Peers, *The Politics of Broadcasting 1920–1951* (Toronto: University of Toronto Press, 1969); Marc Raboy, *Missed Opportunities: The Story of Canada's Broadcasting Policy* (Montreal: McGill-Queen's University Press, 1990).

[23]*Report of the Task Force on Broadcasting*, 433.

[24]Morris Wolfe, *Jolts: The TV Wasteland and the Canadian Oasis* (Toronto: James Lorimer & Company, 1985), 14.

[25]Ibid., 16.

[26]Ibid., 18.

[27]Epstein, *News from Nowhere*, 263.

[28]Ibid., 262.

[29]Ibid.

[30]Herman and Chomsky, *Manufacturing Consent*, 19.

[31]Epstein, *News from Nowhere*, 146.

[32]Ibid., 147.

[33]Ibid., 199.

[34]Stanley Rothman and S. Robert Lichter, 'Personality, Ideology and World View: A Comparison of Media and Business Elites', *British Journal of Political Science*, 15, 1 (1984), 36.

[35]Ibid., 46.

[36]Cited in Barry Cooper, *Sins of Omission: Shaping the News at CBC TV* (Toronto: University of Toronto Press, 1994), xi.

[37]Ibid., 227.

[38]Ralph Miliband, *The State in Capitalist Society* (London: Quartet Books, 1973), 211.

[39]Leon Epstein, *Political Parties in Western Democracies* (New York: Praeger, 1967), 237.

[40]Aldous Huxley, *Brave New World Revisited* (New York: Harper & Brothers, 1958), 44.

[41]The term is used by Herman and Chomsky in their analysis of the political role of the American media. They, in turn, borrow it from Walter Lippmann, who had in mind, however, government's use of propagandistic techniques to cultivate popular acceptance of their rule.

Chapter 10

[1]*Schenck v. United States*, 249 US 47 (1919).

[2]These are the words used in the 'anti-hate' section of Canada's Criminal Code.

[3]University of Calgary, *Charter Database*.

[4]Michael Mandel, *The Charter of Rights and the Legalization of Politics in Canada* (Toronto: Wall and Thompson, 1989), 4.

[5]'Human rights', *The Canadian Encyclopedia*, 2nd ed. (Edmonton: Hurtig, 1988), 1024–5.

[6]United States Constitution, 14th amendment, 1868.

[7]*Hunter et al. v. Southam Inc.* (1984), 11 DLR (4th) 641.

[8]*Irwin Toy Ltd. v. Attorney-General of Quebec* (1986), 32 DLR (4th) 641.

[9]*R. v. Big M Drug Mart* (1985), 18 DLR (4th) 321.

[10]*Public Service Alliance of Canada et al. v. The Queen in Right of Canada et al.* (1987), 38 DLR (4th) 249 (Supreme Court of Canada).

[11]Mandel, *The Charter of Rights*, 218.

[12]F.L. Morton, 'The Charter Revolution and the Court Party', *Osgoode Hall Law Journal*, 30, 3 (Fall, 1992), 634–5.

[13]*Borowski v. Attorney-General for Canada* (1987), 39 DLR (4th) 731; *R. v. Morgentaler, Smoling and Scott* (1985), 48 CR (3rd) 1 (Ontario Court of Appeal).

[14]Carol Smart, *Feminism and the Power of Law* (London: Routledge, 1989), 160.

[15]Ibid., 161.

[16]Alan Borovoy, *When Freedoms Collide: The Case for our Civil Liberties* (Toronto: Lester & Orpen Dennys, 1988), ch. 10.

[17]R. MacGregor Dawson, *Constitutional Issues in Canada, 1900–1931* (London: Oxford University Press, 1933).

[18]R. MacGregor Dawson, *The Government of Canada* (Toronto: University of Toronto Press, 1947).

[19]J.A. Corry and J.E. Hodgetts, *Democratic Government and Politics* (Toronto: University of Toronto Press, 1946).

[20]*Reference re Alberta Statutes* (1938), SCR 100 (Supreme Court of Canada).

[21]*Saumur v. Quebec and Attorney-General of Quebec* (1953), 2 SCR 299 (Supreme Court of Canada).

[22]*Switzman v. Elbing and Attorney-General of Quebec* (1957), SCR 285 (Supreme Court of Canada).

[23]*Attorney-General of Canada and Dupond v. Montreal* (1978), 2 SCR 770 (Supreme Court of Canada).

[24]Quoted in Peter H. Russell, *Leading Constitutional Decisions*, 4th ed. (Ottawa: Carleton University Press, 1987), 390.

[25]Norman Ward, *The Government of Canada* (Toronto: University of Toronto Press, 1987), 84.

[26]Corry and Hodgetts, *Democratic Government and Politics*, 462.

[27]*Robertson and Rosetanni v. The Queen* (1963), quoted in Russell, ed., *Leading Constitutional Decisions*, 4th ed., 399.

[28]Quoted in Walter Surma Tarnopolsky, *The Canadian Bill of Rights*, 2nd ed. (Toronto: McClelland & Stewart, 1975), 132.

[29]*R. v. Drybones* (1970), SCR 282.

[30]*Attorney General of Canada v. Lavell* (1974), SCR 1349.

[31]*Hogan v. The Queen* (1975), 2 SCR 574.

[32]*City of Winnipeg v. Barrett* (1892), AC 445.

[33]*Ottawa Roman Catholic Separate School Trustees v. Mackell* (1917), AC 62; *Protestant School Board of Greater Montreal v. Minister of Education of Quebec* (1978), 83 DLR (3d) 645.

[34]*Attorney General of Quebec v. Blaikie* (1979), 2 SCR 1016 (Supreme Court of Canada).

[35]*Attorney General of Manitoba v. Forest* (1979), 101 DLR (3d) 385 (Supreme Court of Canada).

[36]Peter H. Russell, 'The first three years in Charterland', *Canadian Public Administration*, 28, 3 (Fall, 1985), 367–96.

[37]*R. v. Oakes* (1986), 26 DLR (4th) 20 (Supreme Court of Canada).

[38]*Ford v. Attorney-General of Quebec* (1988).

[39]Quoted in F.L. Morton, Rainer Knopf, and Peter Russell, *Federalism and the Charter* (Ottawa: Carleton University Press, 1989), 578.

[40]Ibid., 579.

[41]Quoted in 'Tobacco ad ban struck down', *Globe and Mail*, 22 September 1995, A1, A11.

[42]Roy Romanow et al., *Canada ... Notwithstanding: The Making of the Constitution 1976–1982* (Toronto: Carswell, 1984), 211.

[43]Borovoy, *When Freedoms Collide*, 211–12.

[44]*Alliance des Professeurs de Montreal et al. v. Attorney-General of Quebec* (1983), 9 CCC (3d) 268.

[45]F.L. Morton, 'The Political Impact of the Canadian Charter of Rights and Freedoms', *Canadian Journal of Political Science*, 20, 1 (March, 1987), 47.

[46]Morton, Knopf, and Russell, *Federalism and the Charter*, 446.

[47]Ibid., 389.

[48]*Singh v. Minister of Employment and Immigration* (1985), 17 DLR (4th) 469.

[49]Morton, Knopf, and Russell, *Federalism and the Charter*, 446.

[50]*Attorney-General of Quebec v. Quebec Protestant School Boards* (1984), 10 DLR (4th) 321 (Supreme Court of Canada).

[51]*Reference Re Public Service Employee Relations Act, Labour Relations Act and Police Officers Collective Bargaining Act* (1987), 38 DLR (4th) 161.

[52]*Operation Dismantle Inc. et al. v. The Queen* (1985), 18 DLR (4th) 481 (Supreme Court of Canada).

[53]*Retail, Wholesale & Department Store Union, Local 580 et al. v. Dolphin Delivery Ltd.* (1986), 33 DLR (4th) 174.

[54]Quoted in Mandel, *Charter of Rights*, 204.

[55]*Reference Re Public Service Employee Relations Act* (Alberta), quoted in Morton, Knopf, and Russell, *Federalism and the Charter*, 496.

[56]Quoted in Mandel, *Charter of Rights*, 193.

[57]*Morgentaler, Smoling and Scott v. The Queen* (1988), 37 CCC (3d) 449 (Supreme Court of Canada).

[58]Peter Hogg, *Constitutional Law of Canada*, 2nd ed. (Toronto: Carswell, 1988), 786.

[59]*Reference Re An Act to Amend the Education Act* (Ontario) (1987), 40 DLR (4th) 18 (Supreme Court of Canada).

[60]Before the law was passed, provincial support to Roman Catholic schools ended after grade 10.

[61]See, for example, the majority and dissenting judgements in the right-to-strike case, *Re Public Service Employees Relations Act* (1987), and in the Ontario Roman Catholic high school funding case, *Reference Re An Act to Amend the Education Act* (1987).

Chapter 11

[1]Information on mother tongue was first collected with the census of 1931. Before then, the census only asked about ethnic origin. Demographer Jacques Henripin suggests that French ethnic origin was probably a good surrogate measure for language group at the time of Confederation.

[2]In fact, Henripin predicted that over 40 per cent of Montrealers would be Anglophone by 2001. This prediction was based on census data from 1971. See *L'Immigration et le déséquilibre linguistique* (Ottawa: Main d'oeuvre et immigration, 1974), 31, tableau 4.7.

[3]Henripin estimated that at the rate of decline experienced in the early 1970s, Quebec would still be 77 per cent French-speaking by 2001.

[4]Richard Joy, *Languages in Conflict* (Toronto: McClelland & Stewart, 1972), 58, table 25.

[5]Ibid., 86, table 4.

[6]Canada, Commissioner of Official Languages, *Annual Report 1990* (Ottawa: Supply and Services, 1991), 249.

[7]Statistics Canada, *Census 1991*.

[8]Joy, *Languages in Conflict*, 39, table 14.

[9]Roger Bernard, *Le choc des nombres* (Ottawa: Université d'Ottawa, 1990).

[10]Jacques Henripin, *Language and Society*, 24 (Fall, 1988), 8–9.

[11]The first experience with immersion education was in 1965 in St Lambert, Quebec.

[12]See Peter C. Waite, *Pre-Confederation* (Toronto: Prentice-Hall, 1965), 54–5.

[13]Louis Hemon, *Maria Chapdelaine*, trans. by Sir Andrew Macphail (Toronto: Oxford University Press, 1921), 212–13.

[14]Henri Bourassa, *La langue, guardienne de la foi* (Bibliothèque de l'action française, 1918).

[15]Henri Bourassa, 'The French Language and the Future of Our Race', in Ramsay Cook, ed., *French Canadian Nationalism* (Toronto: Macmillan, 1969), 133.

[16]Marcel Rioux, 'Sur l'évolution des idéologies au Québec', English translation in Richard Schultz *et al.*, eds, *The Canadian Political Process*, 3rd ed. (Toronto: Holt, Rinehart and Winston, 1979), 99–102.

[17]Denis Monière, *Ideologies in Quebec* (Toronto: University of Toronto Press, 1981), especially ch. two.

[18]These voices included such figures as Gonzalve Doutre, Errol Bouchette, and Olivar Asselin and the activities of the Institut Canadien.

[19]F.H. Leacy, ed., *Historical Statistics of Canada* (Ottawa: Supply and Services, 1983), R1–22 and R81–97.

[20]The numbers were about 390,000 in manufacturing compared to 249,000 in agriculture. The figure for the agricultural labour force counts only males.

[21]Quoted by Trudeau in 'Quebec on the Eve of the Asbestos Strike', in Cook, ed., *French Canadian Nationalism*, 35–6.

[22]Victor Barbeau, *Mesure de notre taille* (1936); Barbeau, *Avenir de notre bourgeoisie* (Montreal: Editions de l'action canadienne française, 1939); Jacques Melançon, 'Retard de croissance de l'entreprise canadienne-française', *L'actualité économique* (janvier-mars, 1956), 503–22.

[23]Rioux, 'Sur L'évolution', 105–8.

[24]Ibid., 105.

[25]This section draws heavily on Stephen Brooks and Alain-G. Gagnon, 'Managing the French-English Conflict in Canada', *Fédéralisme*, 4 (1990), 1–25.

[26]See Melançon, 'Retard de croissance'.

[27]Lois du Québec, 1974, c. 6.

[28]Lois du Québec, 1977, c. 5.

[29]See *Attorney-General of Quebec v. Blaikie et al.* (1979), 101 DLR (3d) 394 (Supreme Court of Canada).

[30]*Ford v. Attorney-General of Quebec* (1988), Supreme Court of Canada.

[31]Calvin Veltman, 'Assessing the Effects of Quebec's Language Legislation', *Canadian Public Policy*, 12, 2 (June, 1986), 314–19. Veltman observes that the effectiveness of Bill 101 in promoting the use of French among the children of immigrants varies considerably among ethnic groups.

[32]See the discussion of these economic initiatives in Kenneth McRoberts, *Quebec: Social Change and Political Crisis*, 3rd ed. (Toronto: McClelland & Stewart, 1988), 132–5.

[33]Eric Waddell, 'State, Language and Society: The Vicissitudes of French in Quebec and Canada', in Alan Cairns and Cynthia Williams, eds, *The Politics of Gender, Ethnicity and Language in Canada*, vol. 34 of the research studies for the Royal Commission on the Economic Union and Development Prospects for Canada (Ottawa: Supply and Services, 1985), 97.

[34]Raymond Breton, 'The Production and Allocation of Symbolic Resources: An Analysis of the Linguistic and Ethnocultural Fields in Canada', *Canadian Review of Sociology and Anthropology*, 21, 2 (May, 1984), 129.

[35]Commissioner of Official Languages, *Annual Report 1985* (Ottawa: Supply and Services, 1986), 50.

[36]'Francophones in the National Capital Region represent over 35 per cent of the Public Service population but, on average, they work more than 60 per cent of their time in English. In bilingual areas of Ontario the corresponding figures are 23 per cent and 66 per cent; roughly one-quarter of all employees are thus working two-thirds of their time in their second language.' Ibid., 54.

[37]*Attorney-General of Manitoba v. Forest* (1979), 101 DLR (3d) 385 (Supreme Court of Canada); *Reference re Language Rights under the Manitoba Act, 1870* (No. 1) (1985), 19 DLR (4th) 1.

[38]*Attorney-General of Quebec v. Quebec Protestant School Boards* (1984), 10 DLR (4th) 321 (Supreme Court of Canada); *Ford v. Attorney-General of Quebec* (1988), Supreme Court of Canada.

[39]In 1985 the Conservative government broadened the scope of this program to include more of the areas covered by the Charter of Rights and Freedoms, with an emphasis on the Equality Rights section.

[40]These figures are from the Commissioner of Official Languages, *Annual Report 1994*.

[41]Commissioner of Official Languages, *Annual Report 1985*, 172.

[42]*Census of Canada*, 1991.

[43]Waddell, 'State, Language and Society', 101.

[44]'Le Québécois, une espèce menacée?' an interview with demographer Jacques Henripin, *L'actualité* (janvier, 1990), 18–22.

[45]Bernard Blishen and Tom Atkinson, 'Regional and Status Differences in Canadian Values' (Toronto: Institute of Behavioural Research, York University, 1981).

[46]Peter Russell *et al.*, 'Liberty, Authority, and Community: Civil Liberties and the Canadian Political Culture', paper presented at the annual meetings of the Canadian Political Science Association, University of Windsor, 9 June 1988.

[47]Michael Ornstein, 'Regionalism and Canadian Political Ideology', in Robert Brym, ed., *Regionalism in Canada* (Toronto: Irwin, 1986), 78.

[48]Ibid., 66, table 2.

[49]Québec, Commission sur l'avenir politique et constitutionnel du Québec, *Rapport* (Québec, 1991), 17.

[50]Ibid., 17.

[51]Robert Sheppard, 'For a really distinct society, try Saskatchewan, not Quebec', *Globe and Mail*, 20 November 1989.

Chapter 12

[1]Quoted in Simone de Beauvoir, *The Second Sex*, trans. by H.M. Parshley (London: Jonathan Cape, 1970), 21.

[2]Nellie McClung, 'Hardy Perennials', in *In Times Like These* (Toronto: University of Toronto Press, 1972), 43–58.

[3]Beauvoir, *The Second Sex*, 273.

[4]E.E. Maccoby and C.N. Jacklin, *The Psychology of Sex Differences* (Stanford, Calif.: Stanford University Press, 1974).

[5]Anne Moir, *Brain Sex: The Real Difference Between Men and Women* (New York: Carol Publishing Group, 1991).

[6]Margaret Mead, *Sex and Temperament in Three Primitive Societies* (New York: Dell, 1969), 260.

[7]Margaret Mead, *Male and Female* (New York: William Morrow, 1950), 191–2.

[8]John Stuart Mill, *On the Subjection of Women* (London: Dent, 1970), 244. First published in 1869.

[9]Ibid., 244.

[10]Karl Marx and Frederick Engels, *Women and Communism* (Westport, Conn.: Greenwood Press, 1973).

[11]Canada, Public Service Commission, *Annual Report, 1994*.

[12]Sylvia Bashevkin, *Toeing the Lines* (Toronto: University of Toronto Press, 1985).

[13]See the literature review in Pat Armstrong and Hugh Armstrong, *The Double Ghetto* (Toronto: McClelland & Stewart, 1984), 158–67.

[14]Canadian Advisory Council on the Status of Women, *Women and Labour Market Poverty* (Ottawa: 1990), 14–15.

[15]Sheila Rowbotham, *Hidden from History* (London: Pluto Press, 1974), 47.

[16]Terry Copp, *Anatomy of Poverty* (Toronto: McClelland & Stewart, 1974), 43.

[17]The statement was made by Lavis Guyan, Montreal's Chief Inspector of Factories in the late 1800s. Quoted ibid., 49.

[18]Mill, *On the Subjection of Women*.

[19]McClung, 'Hardy Perennials', 56.

[20]See the discussion in Penney Kome, *Women of Influence* (Toronto: Doubleday Canada, 1985), ch. 2.

[21]Quoted ibid., 32.

[22]This was the title of a retrospective article that Macphail wrote in 1949, after having served six terms as an MP for Ontario's South Grey constituency.

[23]Quoted in Bashevkin, *Toeing the Lines*, 16.

[24]McClung, 'Hardy Perennials', 18.

[25]See, for example, Bashevkin, *Toeing the Lines*, 20–3.

[26]Catherine L. Cleverdon, *The Woman Suffrage Movement in Canada* (Toronto: University of Toronto Press, 1974), 98, 114, 204.

[27]The terms 'hard-core' and 'soft-core' feminism were first used by O'Neill in *Everyone was Brave: A History of Feminism in America* (New York: Quadrangle, 1971).

[28]Deborah Gorham, 'Flora MacDonald Denison: Canadian Feminist', in Linda Kealey, ed., *A Not Unreasonable Claim: Women and Reform in Canada* (Toronto: Women's Press, 1979), 47–70.

[29]Joan Sangster, 'The Role of Women in the Early CCF', in Linda Kealey and Joan Sangster, eds, *Beyond the Vote: Canadian Women and Politics* (Toronto: University of Toronto Press, 1989), 127.

[30]Beauvoir, *The Second Sex*, ch. 2; Germaine Greer, *The Female Eunuch* (Nylesbury, UK: Hazel Watson and Viney, 1970); Betty Friedan, *The Feminine Mystique* (New York: W.W. Norton, 1963), ch. 5; Kate Millet, *Sexual Politics* (Garden City, NY: Doubleday, 1970).

[31]'Social Gospel', *The Canadian Encyclopedia* (Edmonton: Hurtig, 1988), 2026.

[32]See Richard Allen, *The Social Passion* (Toronto: University of Toronto Press, 1971).

[33]Nellie McClung, 'Women and the Church', *In Times Like These*, 67–79.

[34]Friedan, *The Feminine Mystique*.

[35]Ibid., 32.

[36]Armstrong and Armstrong, *The Double Ghetto*, 42–3.

[37]The ratio of males to females in universities was 5:1 in 1920, 3.1:1 in 1960, and 1.8:1 in 1970. About an equal number of males and females are enrolled in undergraduate programs today.

[38]Anne Firor Scott, *Making the Invisible Woman Visible* (Urbana: University of Illinois Press, 1984).

[39]See Kealey and Sangster, eds, *Beyond the Vote*.

[40]Ibid.

[41]Barbara Frum, 'Why there are so few women in Ottawa', *Chatelaine*, 44 (1971), 33, 110.

[42]Bashevkin, *Toeing the Lines*, 110–19.

[43]See the summaries of landmark judgements in National Action Committee on the Status of Women, *Women and Legal Action* (October, 1984), 8–27.

[44]This was true in *Murdoch* (1973), *Canard* (1975), and *Bliss* (1979).

[45]Michael Mandel, *The Charter of Rights and the Legalization of Politics in Canada* (Toronto: Wall and Thompson, 1995), 389–99.

[46]*Re Casagrande and Hinton Roman Catholic Separate School District* (1987), 38 DLR (4th) 382.

[47]Canadian Advisory Council on the Status of Women, *Canadian Charter and Equality Rights for Women: One Step Forward or Two Steps Back?* (September, 1989), 19.

[48]*Hunter v. Southam* (1984); *R. v. Big M Drug Mart* (1985).

[49]*Edwards Books and Art Ltd et al v. The Queen* (1986), 30 CCC (3d) 385.

[50]Quoted in F.L. Morton, Rainer Knopff, and Peter Russell, *Federalism and the Charter* (Ottawa: Carleton University Press, 1989), 483.

[51]*Alberta Labour Reference* (1987).

[52]*Andrews v. Law Society of British Columbia* (1989).

[53]See the abridged text of the ruling in Morton *et al.*, *Federalism and the Charter*, 582–603.

[54]Canadian Advisory Council on the Status of Women, *Every Voice Counts: A Guide to Personal and Political Action* (1989), 39–58.

[55]Penney Kome, *The Taking of Twenty-Eight: Women Challenge the Constitution* (Toronto: The Women's Press, 1983).

[56]Sandra Burt, 'Variations on an Earlier Theme: the Second Wave of the Canadian Women's Movement', in N. Gagnon and James Bickerton, eds, *Canadian Politics* (Peterborough, Ont.: Broadview Press, 1990), 555.

[57]Kome, *Women of Influence*, 93.

[58]Leslie A. Pal, *Interests of State* (Montreal: McGill-Queen's University Press, 1993), ch. 10.

[59]Ibid., ch. 10. See particularly the profile of the NAC in this chapter.

[60]Sylvia Bashevkin, 'Free Trade and Canadian Feminism: The Case of the National Action Committee on the Status of Women', *Canadian Public Policy*, XV, 4 (December, 1989), 363–75.

[61]Canadian Institute of Public Opinion (CIPO), *The Gallup Report*, October, 1989.

[62]CIPO, *The Gallup Report*, May, 1989.

[63]CIPO, *The Gallup Report*, August, 1989.

[64]CIPO, *The Gallup Report*, January, 1989.

[65]CIPO, *The Gallup Report*, February, 1989.

[66]CIPO, *The Gallup Report*, October, 1989.

[67]Statistics Canada, National Council of Welfare, *Poverty Profile 1993* (Ottawa: Supply and Services, Spring, 1995).

Appendix A: Excerpts from the Constitution Act, 1867 (as amended)

In the Constitution Act, 1867, those sections and subsections marked here with an asterisk are given footnotes that may include: indication of when the section/subsection was amended to the Act and by what legislation; text of repealed subsections, and when repealed; cross-references to statute law. Students who wish to pursue the detail of constitutional law and its revision should consult the full document.

VI. Distribution of Legislative Powers

Powers of Parliament

91. It shall be lawful for the Queen, by and with the advice and consent of the Senate and House of Commons, to make laws for the peace, order, and good government of Canada, in relation to all matters not coming within the classes of subjects by this Act assigned exclusively to the Legislatures of the Provinces; and for greater certainty, but not so as to restrict the generality of the foregoing terms of this section, it is hereby declared that (notwithstanding anything in this Act) the exclusive Legislative Authority of the Parliament of Canada extends to all matters coming within the classes of subjects next hereinafter enumerated, that is to say:—
    (1)   Repealed.*
    (1A) The Public Debt and Property.*
    (2)   The regulation of Trade and Commerce.
    (2A) Unemployment insurance.*
    (3)   The raising of money by any mode or system of Taxation.

(4) The borrowing of money on the public credit.

(5) Postal service.

(6) The Census and Statistics.

(7) Militia, Military and Naval Service, and Defence.

(8) The fixing of and providing for the salaries and allowances of civil and other officers of the Government of Canada.

(9) Beacons, Buoys, Lighthouses, and Sable Island.

(10) Navigation and Shipping.

(11) Quarantine and the establishment and maintenance of Marine Hospitals.

(12) Sea Coast and Inland Fisheries.

(13) Ferries between a Province and any British or Foreign country or between two Provinces.

(14) Currency and Coinage.

(15) Banking, incorporation of banks, and the issue of paper money.

(16) Savings Banks.

(17) Weights and Measures.

(18) Bills of Exchange and Promissory Notes.

(19) Interest.

(20) Legal tender.

(21) Bankruptcy and Insolvency.

(22) Patents of Invention and Discovery.

(23) Copyrights.

(24) Indians and lands reserved for the Indians.

(25) Naturalization and Aliens.

(26) Marriage and Divorce.

(27) The Criminal Law, except the Constitution of Courts of Criminal Jurisdiction, but including the Procedure in Criminal Matters.

(28) The establishment, maintenance, and management of Penitentiaries.

(29) Such classes of subjects as are expressly excepted in the enumeration of the classes of subjects by this Act assigned exclusively to the Legislatures of the Provinces:

And any matter coming within any of the classes of subjects enumerated in this section shall not be deemed to come within the class of matters of a local or private nature comprised in the enumeration of the classes of subjects by this Act assigned exclusively to the Legislatures of the Provinces.*

Exclusive Powers of Provincial Legislatures

92. In each Province the Legislature may exclusively make laws in relation to matters coming within the classes of subjects next hereinafter enumerated, that is to say,

(1) Repealed.*

(2) Direct Taxation within the Province in order to the raising of a Revenue for Provincial purposes.

(3) The borrowing of money on the sole credit of the Province.

(4)   The establishment and tenure of Provincial offices and the appointment and payment of Provincial officers.

(5)   The management and sale of the Public Lands belonging to the Province, and of the timber and wood thereon.

(6)   The establishment, maintenance, and management of hospitals, asylums, charities, and eleemosynary institutions in and for the Province, other than marine hospitals.

(8)   Municipal institutions in the Province.

(9)   Shop, saloon, tavern, auctioneer, and other licences, in order to the raising of a revenue for Provincial, local, or municipal purposes.

(10) Local works and undertakings other than such as are of the following classes:—

(a)   Lines of steam or other ships, railways, canals, telegraphs, and other works and undertakings connecting the Province with any other or others of the Provinces, or extending beyond the limits of the Province;

(b)   Lines of steam ships between the Province and any British or Foreign country;

(c)   Such works as, although wholly situate within the Province, are before or after their execution declared by the Parliament of Canada to be for the general advantage of Canada or for the advantage of two or more of the Provinces.

(11) The incorporation of companies with Provincial objects.

(12) The solemnization of marriage in the Province.

(13) Property and civil rights in the Province.

(14) The administration of justice in the Province, including the constitution, maintenance, and organization of Provincial Courts, both of civil and of criminal jurisdiction, and including procedure in civil matters in those Courts.

(15) The imposition of punishment by fine, penalty, or imprisonment for enforcing any law of the Province made in relation to any matter coming within any of the classes of subjects enumerated in this section.

(16) Generally all matters of a merely local or private nature in the Province.

Non-Renewable Natural Resources, Forestry Resources and Electrical Energy

92A. (1)   In each province, the legislature may exclusively make laws in relation to

(a)   exploration for non-renewable natural resources in the province;

(b)   development, conservation and management of non-renewable natural resources and forestry resources in the province, including laws in relation to the rate of primary production therefrom; and

(c)   development, conservation and management of sites and facilities in the province for the generation and production of electrical energy.

(2)   In each province, the legislature may make laws in relation to the export from the province to another part of Canada of the primary production from non-renewable natural resources and forestry resources in the province and the production from facilities in the province for the generation of electrical energy, but such laws may not authorize or provide for discrimination in prices or in supplies exported to another part of Canada.

(3)   Nothing in subsection (2) derogates from the authority of Parliament to enact laws in relation to the matters referred to in that subsection and, where such a law of Parliament and a law of a province conflict, the law of Parliament prevails to the extent of the conflict.

(4)   In each province, the legislature may make laws in relation to the raising of money by any mode or system of taxation in respect of

(a)   non-renewable natural resources and forestry resources in the province and the primary production therefrom, and

(b)   sites and facilities in the province for the generation of electrical energy and the production therefrom, whether or not such production is exported in whole or in part from the province, but such laws may not authorize or provide for taxation that differentiates between production exported to another part of Canada and production not exported from the province.

(5)   The expression 'primary production' has the meaning assigned by the Sixth Schedule.

(6)   Nothing in subsections (1) to (5) derogates from any powers or rights that a legislature or government of a province had immediately before the coming into force of this section.

Education

93.   In and for each Province the Legislature may exclusively make laws in relation to education, subject and according to the following provisions:—

(1)   Nothing in any such law shall prejudicially affect any right or privilege with respect to denominational schools which any class of persons have by law in the Province at the Union.

(2)   All the powers, privileges, and duties at the Union by law conferred and imposed in Upper Canada on the separate schools and school trustees of the Queen's Roman Catholic subjects shall be and the same are hereby extended to the dissentient schools of the Queen's Protestant and Roman Catholic subjects in Quebec.

(3)   Where in any Province a system of separate or dissentient schools exists by law at the Union or is thereafter established by the Legislature of the Province, an appeal shall lie to the Governor General in Council from any Act or Decision of any Provincial authority affecting any right or privilege of the Protestant or Roman Catholic minority of the Queen's subjects in relation to education.

(4)   In case any such Provincial law as from time to time seems to the Governor General in Council requisite for the due execution of the provisions of this section is not made, or in case any decision of the Governor General in Council on any appeal under this section is not duly executed by the proper Provincial authority in that behalf, then and in every such case, and as far only as the circumstances of each case require, the Parliament of Canada may make remedial laws for the due execution of the provisions of this section and of any decision of the Governor General in Council under this section.*

Old Age Pensions

94A. The Parliament of Canada may make laws in relation to old age pensions and supplementary benefits, including survivors' and disability benefits irrespective of age, but no such law shall affect the operation of any law present or future of a provincial legislature in relation to any such matter.*

Agriculture and Immigration

95. In each Province the Legislature may make laws in relation to Agriculture in the Province, and to Immigration into the Province; and it is hereby declared that the Parliament of Canada may from time to time make laws in relation to Agriculture in all or any of the Provinces, and to Immigration into all or any of the Provinces; and any law of the Legislature of a Province relative to Agriculture or to Immigration shall have effect in and for the Province as long and as far only as it is not repugnant to any Act of the Parliament of Canada.

VII. Judicature

96. The Governor General shall appoint the Judges of the Superior, District, and County Courts in each Province, except those of the Courts of Probate in Nova Scotia and New Brunswick.

97. Until the laws relative to Property and Civil Rights in Ontario, Nova Scotia, and New Brunswick, and the Procedure of the Courts in those Provinces, are made uniform, the Judges of the Courts of those Provinces appointed by the Governor General shall be selected from the respective Bars of those Provinces.

98. The Judges of the Courts of Quebec shall be selected from the Bar of that Province.

99. (1) Subject to subsection two of this section, the judges of the Superior Courts shall hold office during good behaviour, but shall be removable by the Governor General on Address of the Senate and House of Commons

    (2) A Judge of a Superior Court, whether appointed before or after the coming into force of this section, shall cease to hold office upon attaining the age of seventy-five years, or upon the coming into force of this section if at that time he has already attained that age.*

100. The Salaries, Allowances, and Pensions of the Judges of the Superior, District, and County Courts (except the Courts of Probate in Nova Scotia and New Brunswick), and of the Admiralty Courts in Cases where the Judges thereof are for the time being paid by Salary, shall be fixed and provided by the Parliament of Canada.*

101. The Parliament of Canada may, notwithstanding anything in this Act, from time to time provide for the Constitution, Maintenance, and Organization of a General Court of Appeal for Canada, and for the Establishment of any additional Courts for the better Administration of the Laws of Canada.*

Appendix B: Excerpts from the Constitution Act, 1982

Part I
Canadian Charter of Rights and Freedoms

Whereas Canada is founded upon principles that recognize the supremacy of God and the rule of law:

Guarantee of Rights and Freedoms

1. The *Canadian Charter of Rights and Freedoms* guarantees the rights and freedoms set out in it subject only to such reasonable limits prescribed by law as can be demonstrably justified in a free and democratic society.

Fundamental Freedoms

2. Everyone has the following fundamental freedoms:
   - (a) freedom of conscience and religion;
   - (b) freedom of thought, belief, opinion and expression, including freedom of the press and other media of communication;
   - (c) freedom of peaceful assembly; and
   - (d) freedom of association.

Democratic Rights

3. Every citizen of Canada has the right to vote in an election of members of the House of Commons or of a legislative assembly and to be qualified for membership therein.

4. (1) No House of Commons and no legislative assembly shall continue for longer than five years from the date fixed for the return of the writs at a general election of its members.

    (2) In time of real or apprehended war, invasion or insurrection, a House of Commons may be continued by Parliament and a legislative assembly may be continued by the legislature beyond five years if such continuation is not opposed by the votes of more than one-third of the members of the House of Commons or the legislative assembly, as the case may be.

5. There shall be a sitting of Parliament and of each legislature at least once every twelve months.

Mobility Rights

6. (1) Every citizen of Canada has the right to enter, remain in and leave Canada.

    (2) Every citizen of Canada and every person who has the status of a permanent resident of Canada has the right

    (a) to move to and take up residence in any province; and

    (b) to pursue the gaining of a livelihood in any province.

    (3) The rights specified in subsection (2) are subject to

    (a) any laws or practices of general application in force in a province other than those that discriminate among persons primarily on the basis of province of present or previous residence; and

    (b) any laws providing for reasonable residency requirements as a qualification for the receipt of publicly provided social services.

    (4) Subsections (2) and (3) do not preclude any law, program or activity that has as its object the amelioration in a province of conditions of individuals in that province who are socially or economically disadvantaged if the rate of employment in that province is below the rate of employment in Canada.

Legal Rights

7. Everyone has the right to life, liberty and security of the person and the right not to be deprived thereof except in accordance with the principles of fundamental justice.

8. Everyone has the right to be secure against unreasonable search or seizure.

9. Everyone has the right not to be arbitrarily detained or imprisoned.

10. Everyone has the right on arrest or detention

    (a) to be informed promptly of the reasons therefor;

    (b) to retain and instruct counsel without delay and to be informed of that right; and

    (c) to have the validity of the detention determined by way of *habeas corpus* and to be released if the detention is not lawful.

11. Any person charged with an offence has the right

    (a) to be informed without unreasonable delay of the specific offence;

    (b) to be tried within a reasonable time;

    (c) not to be compelled to be a witness in proceedings against that person, in respect of the offence;

(d)   to be presumed innocent until proven guilty according to law in a fair and public hearing by an independent and impartial tribunal;

(e)   not to be denied reasonable bail without just cause;

(f)   except in the case of an offence under military law tried before a military tribunal, to the benefit of trial by jury where the maximum punishment for the offence is imprisonment for five years or a more severe punishment;

(g)   not to be found guilty on account of any act or omission unless, at the time of the act or omission, it constituted an offence under Canadian or international law or was criminal according to the general principles of law recognized by the community of nations;

(h)   if finally acquitted of the offence, not to be tried for it again and, if finally found guilty and punished for the offence, not to be tried or punished for it again; and

(i)   if found guilty of the offence and if the punishment for the offence has been varied between the time of commission and the time of sentencing, to the benefit of the lesser punishment.

12.   Everyone has the right not to be subjected to any cruel and unusual treatment or punishment.

13.   A witness who testifies in any proceedings has the right not to have any incriminating evidence so given used to incriminate that witness in any other proceedings, except in a prosecution for perjury or for the giving of contradictory evidence.

14.   A party or witness in any proceedings who does not understand or speak the language in which the proceedings are conducted or who is deaf has the right to the assistance of an interpreter.

Equality Rights

15.   (1)   Every individual is equal before and under the law and has the right to the equal protection and equal benefit of the law without discrimination and, in particular, without discrimination based on race, national or ethnic origin, colour, religion, sex, age or mental or physical disability.

(2)   Subsection (1) does not preclude any law, program or activity that has as its object the amelioration of conditions of disadvantaged individuals or groups including those that are disadvantaged because of race, national or ethnic origin, colour, religion, sex, age or mental or physical disability.

Official Languages of Canada

16.   (1)   English and French are the official languages of Canada and have equality of status and equal rights and privileges as to their use in all institutions of the Parliament and government of Canada.

(2)   English and French are the official languages of New Brunswick and have equality of status and equal rights and privileges as to their use in all institutions of the legislature and government of New Brunswick.

(3) Nothing in this Charter limits the authority of Parliament or a legislature to advance the equality of status or use of English or French.

17. (1) Everyone has the right to use English or French in any debate and other proceedings of Parliament.

(2) Everyone has the right to use English or French in any debates and other proceedings of the legislature of New Brunswick.

18. (1) The statutes, records and journals of Parliament shall be printed and published in English and French and both language versions are equally authoritative.

(2) The statutes, records and journals of the legislature of New Brunswick shall be printed and published in English and French and both language versions are equally authoritative.

19. (1) Either English or French may be used by any person in, or in any pleading in or process issuing from, any court established by Parliament.

(2) Either English or French may be used by any person in, or in any pleading in or process issuing from, any court of New Brunswick.

20. (1) Any member of the public in Canada has the right to communicate with, and to receive available services from, any head or central office of an institution of the Parliament of Canada or government of Canada in English or French, and has the same right with respect to any other office of any such institution where

(a) there is a significant demand for communications with and services from that office in such language; or

(b) due to the nature of the office, it is reasonable that communications with and services from that office be available in both English and French.

(2) Any member of the public in New Brunswick has the right to communicate with, and to receive available services from, any office of an institution of the legislature or government of New Brunswick in English or French.

21. Nothing in sections 16 to 20 abrogates or derogates from any right, privilege or obligation with respect to the English and French languages, or either of them, that exists or is continued by virtue of any other provision of the Constitution of Canada.

22. Nothing in sections 16 to 20 abrogates or derogates from any legal or customary right or privilege acquired or enjoyed either before or after the coming into force of this Charter with respect to any language that is not English or French.

Minority Language Educational Rights

23. (1) Citizens of Canada

(a) whose first language learned and still understood is that of the English or French linguistic minority population of the province in which they reside, or

(b) who have received their primary school instruction in Canada in English or French and reside in a province where the language in which they received that instruction is the language of the English or French linguistic minority population of the province, have the right to receive primary and secondary school instruction in that language in that province.

(2)   Citizens of Canada of whom any child has received or is receiving primary or secondary school instruction in English or French in Canada, have the right to have all their children receive primary and secondary school instruction in the same language.

(3)   The right of citizens of Canada under subsections (1) and (2) to have their children receive primary and secondary school instruction in the language of the English or French linguistic minority population of a province

(a)   applies wherever in the province the number of children of citizens who have such a right is sufficient to warrant the provision to them out of public funds of minority language instruction; and

(b)   includes, where the number of those children so warrants, the right to have them receive that instruction in minority language educational facilities provided out of public funds.

Enforcement

24.   (1)   Anyone whose rights or freedoms, as guaranteed by this Charter, have been infringed or denied may apply to a court of competent jurisdiction to obtain such remedy as the court considers appropriate and just in the circumstances.

      (2)   Where, in proceedings under subsection (1), a court concludes that evidence was obtained in a manner that infringed or denied any rights or freedoms guaranteed by this Charter, the evidence shall be excluded if it is established that, having regard to all circumstances, the admission of it in the proceedings would bring the administration of justice into disrepute.

General

25.   The guarantee in this Charter of certain rights and freedoms shall not be construed so as to abrogate or derogate from any aboriginal, treaty or other rights or freedoms that pertain to the aboriginal peoples of Canada including

      (a)   any rights or freedoms that have been recognized by the Royal Proclamation of October 7, 1763; and

      (b)   any rights or freedoms that now exist by way of land claims agreements or may be so acquired. [As amended by the Constitution Amendment Proclamation, 1983]

26.   The guarantee in this Charter of certain rights and freedoms shall not be construed as denying the existence of any other rights or freedoms that exist in Canada.

27.   This Charter shall be interpreted in a manner consistent with the preservation and enhancement of the multicultural heritage of Canadians.

28.   Notwithstanding anything in this Charter, the rights and freedoms referred to in it are guaranteed equally to male and female persons.

29.   Nothing in this Charter abrogates or derogates from any rights or privileges guaranteed by or under the constitution of Canada of denominational, separate or dissentient schools.

30. A reference in this Charter to a province or to the legislative assembly or legislature of a province shall be deemed to include a reference to the Yukon Territory and the Northwest Territories, or to the appropriate legislative authority thereof, as the case may be.

31. Nothing in this Charter extends the legislative powers of any body or authority.

Application of Charter

32. (1) This Charter applies
    (a) to the Parliament and government of Canada in respect of all matters within the authority of Parliament including all matters relating to the Yukon and Northwest Territories; and
    (b) to the legislature and government of each province in respect of all matters within the authority of the legislature of each province.
    (2) Notwithstanding subsection (1), section 15 shall not have effect until three years after this section comes into force.

33. (1) Parliament or the legislature of a province may expressly declare in an Act of Parliament or of the legislature, as the case may be, that the Act or a provision thereof shall operate notwithstanding a provision included in section 2 or sections 7 to 15 of this Charter.
    (2) An Act or a provision of an Act in respect of which a declaration made under this section is in effect shall have such operation as it would have but for the provision of this Charter referred to in the declaration.
    (3) A declaration made under subsection (1) shall cease to have effect five years after it comes into force or on such earlier dates as may be specified in the declaration.
    (4) Parliament or the legislature of a province may re-enact a declaration made under subsection (1).
    (5) Subsection (3) applies in respect of a re-enactment made under subsection (4).

Citation

34. This Part may be cited as the *Canadian Charter of Rights and Freedoms*.

Part II
Rights of the Aboriginal Peoples of Canada

35. (1) The existing aboriginal and treaty rights of the aboriginal peoples of Canada are hereby recognized and affirmed.
    (2) In this Act, 'aboriginal peoples of Canada' includes the Indian, Inuit and Métis people of Canada.

Part III
Equalization and Regional Disparities

36. (1) Without altering the legislative authority of Parliament or of the provincial legis-
        latures, or the rights of any of them with respect to the exercise of their legislative
        authority, Parliament and the legislatures, together with the government of
        Canada and the provincial governments, are committed to

    (a) promoting equal opportunities for the well being of Canadians;
    (b) furthering economic development to reduce disparity in opportunities; and
    (c) providing essential public services of reasonable quality to all Canadians.

    (2) Parliament and the government of Canada are committed to the principle of mak-
        ing equalization payments to ensure that provincial governments have sufficient
        revenues to provide reasonably comparable levels of public services at reasonably
        comparable levels of taxation.

[Part IV (s.37) stipulated that a first ministers' constitutional conference, to include aboriginal leaders, be held within a year, with an express agenda item to be aboriginal rights. Three
such conferences were held in the mid-1980s, though with little progress being made.

[Part V (ss.38–49) delineates the procedure for constitutional amendment, as discussed
on pp. 107–11 of this book. These sections replace the repealed section 91(1) of the
Constitution Act, 1867.

[Part VI (ss.50–1) is an amendment to the Constitutional Act, 1867: s.92A (see
Appendix A).

[Part VII (ss.52–60) covers general 'housekeeping' aspects of the constitution, including
that s.23(1)(a) of the Charter 'shall come into force in respect of Quebec' only after autho-
rization 'by the legislative assembly or government of Quebec'.]

Index